P9-DED-335

HILL GUIDES™ SERIES

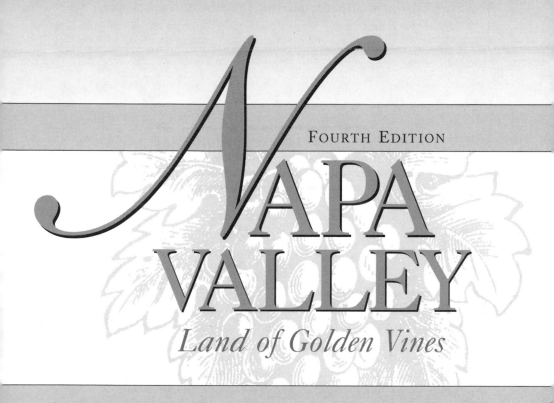

FOURTH EDITION

NAPA VALLEY

Land of Golden Vines

A FOOD AND WINE LOVER'S TRAVEL GUIDE

KATHLEEN THOMPSON HILL
AND GERALD N. HILL

INSIDERS' GUIDE®

GUILFORD, CONNECTICUT
AN IMPRINT OF THE GLOBE PEQUOT PRESS

The prices and rates listed in this book were confirmed at press time. We recommend, however, that you call establishments before traveling to obtain current information.

To buy books in quantity for corporate use or incentives, call **(800) 962–0973, ext. 4551,** or e-mail **premiums@GlobePequot.com.**

INSIDERS' GUIDE®

Copyright ©1999, 2001, 2003, 2005 by Kathleen Thompson Hill and Gerald N. Hill

All rights reserved. No part of this book may be reproduced or transmitted in any form by any means, electronic or mechanical, including photocopying and recording, or by any information storage and retrieval system, except as may be expressly permitted by the 1976 Copyright Act or in writing from the publisher. Requests for permission should be addressed to The Globe Pequot Press, P.O. Box 480, Guilford, Connecticut 06437.

Insiders' Guide is a registered trademark of The Globe Pequot Press.
Hill Guides is a trademark of Kathleen Thompson Hill and Gerald N. Hill.

Maps by Mary Ballachino © The Globe Pequot Press
Illustrations by Mauro Magellan
Historical illustrations by an anonymous newspaper illustrator, circa 1800s
Photos by Kathleen and Gerald Hill

ISSN 1544-0257
ISBN 0-7627-3443-4

Manufactured in the United States of America
Fourth Edition/First Printing

Contents

Acknowledgments

We thank the hundreds of winemakers, winery staff, chefs, restaurateurs, and shopkeepers for giving us their time, their stories, their soul, and their recipes. In particular we are indebted to Napans John and Janet Dunlap for their advice and information. Dear friends Susan Weeks and Sue Holman helped out by joining us in the arduous task of sampling restaurants. Our children, Erin and Mack, gave their tolerant support, as always.

Thanks to the people of Napa Valley for their encouragement and hospitality.

Preface

The Napa Valley continues to add new wineries and restaurants and somehow manages to become increasingly beautiful. The roadside community wildflower planting efforts make visitors smile almost at the instant they enter Napa County. We will introduce you to small, rustic, family-run wineries, as well as some of the largest corporate-owned wineries in the world. In this guide, we will take you to chefs who are cooking world-class food for world-class prices. But we also visit ethnic and home cooks who share their best cultural traditions with the public at extremely reasonable prices.

Movie directors and cartoon developers, video-game and computer-program inventors, traditional vintners, and pilots and doctors all nurse their vineyards and wineries in their own way, each offering their personal taste and expression to the public. The contrasts are astounding and wonderful.

Napa Valley has more restaurants, more people, more money, more wineries, more applauded wines, more visiting movie stars, and more attention than Sonoma Valley, its next-door neighbor. Things are often done with much greater flair and at greater expense in Napa. Napa wineries tend to have more expensive and dramatic designs; some wineries' art collections are brilliant and extensive, drawing more viewers than the local art galleries and museums.

A friendly rivalry exists between the Napa and Sonoma Valleys. Sonoma resident and comedian Tommy Smothers's line, "Sonoma makes wine, Napa makes auto parts," adorns T-shirts and posters and fuels the fires to keep this good-natured competition going. Still, vintners have grafted and traded vine cuttings, winemakers, and phylloxera back and forth between Napa and Sonoma for more than a century.

Each valley has its special charms. We encourage you to visit both Napa and Sonoma to maximize your pleasure!

Introduction

Napa Valley stretches about 30 miles from its northwestern end to its southeastern end, sprawling between the Mayacamas Mountains on the west and the Vaca Range (sometimes called the Silverado Range of hills) on the east. It is widest (5 miles) in the south around the city of Napa and narrowest (1 mile) in the north near Calistoga. The Napa River is widest around the city of Napa—where it used to flood annually—but the river is just a trickling stream where it begins in the north. Napa Valley ranges from windswept flats, to the Palisade Cliffs at the foot of Mount St. Helena, to the forests of the Mayacamas Mountains.

Napa Valley's mildest climate is in the south, which benefits from breezes off San Pablo Bay. The farther north you go, the rainier it gets, and the more extreme the temperatures. Microclimates are everywhere and contribute to some of the Valley's most unique wines. Napa Valley currently has 44,000 acres planted in grapes.

The Napa Valley has two principal north-south roads: Highway 29 (locals prefer to call it the St. Helena Highway as it gets closer to St. Helena) and the Silverado Trail. A number of smaller cross roads connect the two.

In this guide, we first take you on a route up one side of the Napa Valley, on Highway 29. After meandering up Highway 29, you'll cross the Valley at Tubbs Lane, north of Calistoga, through Calistoga, then head back south on the gorgeous Silverado Trail.

On each route, we recommend that you crisscross the highway as few times as possible, for your safety and that of others. These busy roads can be quite dangerous. (Remember, other drivers have been sipping wine, too.)

On the way you will find restaurants judiciously interspersed with wineries. Napa Valley is one place where you will never go thirsty for wine or hungry for good food. Or is it hungry for wine and thirsty for food?

Appellations

Several microclimates and soil characteristics have been identified in the Napa Valley, and more attention is now paid to the unique terrain and terroir, a French term that reflects the effect that a particular vineyard site, the earth, and its sociology have on its wine.

Within the original Napa Valley Appellation, several subappellations have become recognized and named. These include the Stag's Leap District, Atlas Peak, Howell Mountain, Los Carneros, Mt. Veeder, Oakville, Rutherford, St. Helena, Spring Mountain, the Diamond Mountain District, Chiles Valley, Yountville, the Oak Knoll District, and Wild Horse Valley.

Napa Valley is much more than world-famous wineries and wines. Each town has its own personality and is as attractive to visit as the wineries. The valley is in a constant state of change. Wineries have closed or sold to megacorporations like Constellation Brands of New York, while new smaller investors buy wineries with flair and hope. Restaurants close and reopen with even more new investors and hopeful chefs, all looking for "The land of golden vines." Since the year 2000 a flood control project has redirected the Napa River to prevent future flooding of the city of Napa; the new American Center for Wine, Food and Art (also known as COPIA) is a spectacular attraction working now to attract more local resident involvement; the restored Napa Mill complex at the foot of Main Street in Napa is the most lively location in downtown Napa; and the historic Napa Opera House has been painstakingly restored after more than a decade of community effort. New wineries, restaurants, hotels, and B&Bs open their doors at a breathtaking rate. We take you street by street, shop by shop, gallery by gallery through Napa, Yountville, Oakville, Rutherford, St. Helena, and Calistoga. We review every restaurant, from drive-up hamburger and taco stands to The French Laundry and the Culinary Institute of America, as we go along the route.

This guide also takes you mile by mile through the quasi-industrial auxiliary wine businesses south of the city of Napa—the part of the Valley you come to first if you travel from Oakland, Berkeley, the rest of the East Bay, or Sacramento.

In addition, you will explore the fascinating Los Carneros District, in the southern part of the Valley between the two main roads. (Carneros extends from Napa Valley into Sonoma Valley.)

In this guide we also offer the only concise and complete history of the Napa Valley. Read about the trials and travails of Robert Louis Stevenson, winemaking, wine lore, and wine fights.

And watch for new elegant recipes throughout the book, provided by generous winemakers and chefs from throughout the Napa Valley. These luscious gems will allow you to bring some of your Valley experience into your own home.

HOW TO GET HERE

Napa Valley is only about an hour from San Francisco or forty-five minutes from Berkeley and Oakland. But there's a catch: You can't reach the Valley via public transportation. You must have a car or private airplane to get here. (The only bus from the Bay Area airports is the Evans Airporter, a private bus service. It makes eight trips from Oakland International Airport and eleven trips from San Francisco International Airport to the Napa Valley daily. Fares on all runs are $20 each way per person.)

Getting Here by Car

From San Francisco: Take the Golden Gate Bridge north and continue on Highway 101 past San Rafael and through Marin County for about 30 miles. Turn east on Highway 37 toward Napa. Turn left (north) onto Highway 121 at Sears Point Raceway (Infineon), heading toward Napa and Sonoma. Here you enter the prized and highly esteemed Carneros Wine District, which traverses the county line between Sonoma and Napa.

At the Schellville Fire Station, Highway 12 goes north into Sonoma, while 121 from here is also Highway 12 and goes east to Napa. So, to get to Napa, continue eastward (straight) toward Napa from the intersection of Highways 12 and 121. This segment of road is known locally as Fremont Drive. It takes you to or past the Cherry Tree plant and store, Babe's Drive-In (great hamburgers), eventually Clover-Stornetta Dairy (where Laura Chenel makes wonderful chèvre cheeses), and on to Napa.

After you pass (or even visit) Carneros wineries, turn north (left) onto Highway 121, which also becomes Highway 29. Highway 121 will turn eastward on

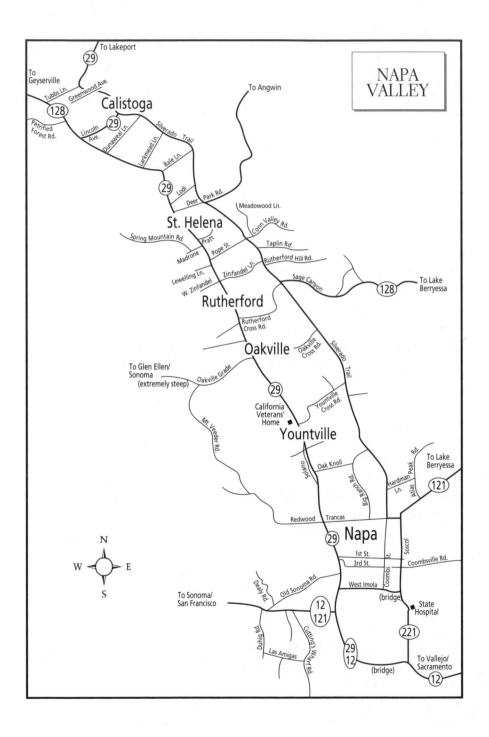

Imola Avenue in Napa and eventually becomes the Silverado Trail, running along the eastern side of the Napa Valley.

At this point, you have two Napa wine-touring choices: Follow Highway 29 northward along the western side of Napa Valley, or follow Highway 121 to the Silverado Trail and the eastern side of the Valley. We suggest that you explore both.

From Berkeley, Oakland, and the East Bay: From Berkeley and Oakland take Highway 80 east (it says east, but you are actually traveling north) through El Cerrito, Crockett, and across the Carquinez Bridge. Get in the left lanes of the bridge, because just after the toll gate you can turn leftish toward Napa and Highway 29, which will take you northward through Vallejo and American Canyon (no canyon in sight) to Napa.

Or you can follow Highway 80 to the Columbus Parkway exit and head toward Six Flags Marine World Africa U.S.A. From Marine World continue westward on Highway 37 to Highway 29 in Vallejo's outskirts. Turn right (north) on Highway 29 and follow it into Napa.

From Downtown Sonoma: From Sonoma Plaza in the middle of downtown Sonoma, go south on Broadway, then turn left (east) on Napa Road. Follow this road through two flashing red lights and on through the hills to the stoplight and intersection of Highway 12. Turn left onto Highway 12/121 toward Napa and take the road through the hills. Off to the wineries you go!

Getting Here by Air

Napa Valley Airport, "Skyport to the Wine Country," is located conveniently south of the city of Napa and west of Highway 29 across from its intersection with Highway 12. (While no commercial jets land at the airport, Japan Airlines maintains an enormous flight-training school here.)

From Other Airports via Private Aircraft: Twenty-nine nmi NW of Oakland International (OAK) airport, 30 nmi SE of Sonoma County (STS) airport, 17 nmi NW of Concord (CCR) airport, and 18 nmi SW of Nut Tree (045) airport, Napa Airport is 4 NM south of the city of Napa, 1 NMi(-) east of the Napa River, and 1 NM west of Highways 12 and 29 intersection. The control tower is south side of runway 06/24, with rotating beacon east side of airport and a golf course 2 NM east.

Communication Frequencies: Napa Tower 118.7, Napa Ground Control 121.7, Napa Atis 124.05, Scaggs VOR (SGD) 112.1, Napa ILS Localizer 111.3,

KVON (BDCST) 1440 KH 153, 4 NM to airport, Oakland Center 127.8, Oakland Radio 122.1T/112.1R.

Airport Information (APC): Field elevation 33 ft MSL; TPA: 1,033 ft MSL; Tower operates from 0700 to 2000 daily (may vary with season); VOR and localizer approaches available through Oakland Center (127.8); runway lights pilot activated. Key 118.7-3,5, or 7 times; San Francisco Sectional and L1-L2 Chart; Latitude 38-13; Longitude 122-17; Reil Runway 06; Papi Runway 18R.

Winds at Napa generally favor the use of either Runway 18 or 24. Landings and takeoffs are frequently conducted simultaneously from several runways, so pilots should be alert for other traffic.

At the airport, **Bridgeford Flying Service** (707–224–0887 or 707–644–1658) offers multitudinous goods and services, including Chevron fuel, flight instruction, ground school, pilot supplies, flying club, Cessna Pilot Center, maintenance, sales, and charter and scenic tours and rides. Office manager Adriann Harpst, a pilot herself, is most helpful and knowledgeable. Her office doubles as supply and gift shop, which includes pilot necessities, souvenirs, and an unusual collection of flying-related manuals and history books.

GETTING AROUND ONCE YOU'RE HERE

Once you arrive at the airport, you have to rent a car, which you can arrange at the airport or at your hotel, or take a taxi escorted tour.

Car Rental Agencies

Affordable Auto Rental, 473 Soscol Avenue, Napa; (707) 257–1911
Budget Rent-a-Car, 407 Soscol Avenue, Napa; (707) 224–7845
Enterprise Rent-a-Car, 230 Soscol Avenue, Napa; (707) 253–8000
Hertz, 1895 Salvador Avenue, Napa; (707) 226–2037
Rent-a-Wreck, 555 Main Street, St. Helena; (800) 300–3213
Sears Rent-a-Car, 407 Soscol Avenue, Napa; (707) 224–7847
Zumwalt Ford, 21 Main Street, St. Helena; (707) 963–2771

Taxi Companies

Napa Valley Cab ("The Red Ones"), (707) 257–6444
Taxi Cabernet, (707) 942–2226, (707) 963–2620, or (888) 333–TAXI (8294)

Public Transportation

Napa Downtown Trolley, (707) 255–7631, circulates constantly between the Napa Town Center shopping center, Napa Valley Opera House on Main Street, Premium Outlets, COPIA, and the Wine Train. Free.

Napa Valley Transit, also called the V.I.N.E. (Valley Intracity Neighborhood Express), (800) 696–6433 or (707) 255–7631, runs its route among ten towns along Highway 29 from Vallejo in Solano County to Calistoga at the northern end of Napa Valley, Monday–Saturday. Buses also stop at Oakville Grocery, Beaulieu Winery, Freemark Abbey, and Bothe Napa State Park. Costs approximately $1.00–$2.50, depending on destination.

Napa Valley Wine Shuttle, (707) 257–1950, picks up at hotels and gives all-day transport to ten wineries ($45; Visa, MasterCard, American Express, and Discover accepted). Web site: www.wineshuttle.com.

HOW TO BE A VISITOR AND NOT A TOURIST IN NAPA VALLEY

Don't worry about looking like a tourist in Napa Valley. The Valley is made for tourists! The wineries and restaurants thrive on your visit and are well aware of that fact, so you will be treated well. Just dress comfortably and bring your taste buds and money. There's no currency exchange—everyone's must be green or plastic.

It does help to know a few of the local rules, however. Smoking is not allowed in tasting rooms or restaurants, but it's occasionally okay outdoors. A few wineries even sell cigars. In addition, be sure to make dinner and accommodations reservations—this is a popular region.

1

Los Carneros District

L os Carneros, a world-famous wine region, runs from the southern part of Sonoma Valley across the hills to the southern end of Napa Valley. Less formally known as Carneros, it also has its own appellation.

The Carneros region is cooler than most other parts of the Napa and Sonoma Valleys due to the cool breezes and summer fog from the San Francisco Bay. These elements also provide for the slow maturation of the grapes—enhancing their flavor, color, and character—and are the ideal conditions for growing and producing Pinot Noir, Chardonnay, and Merlot.

In 1846 General Mariano Vallejo granted 18,000 acres of what is now known as Carneros to his brother-in-law, Jacob Leese. At that time, the land was called Rancho Huichica; a nearby, smaller grant of 2,500 acres known as Rincon de los Carneros gave its name to the region.

In the mid-1850s many farmers planted grapes on their parcels of land in Carneros. A stagecoach ran between the farms and Sonoma along what is now Highway 12/121, known locally as the Carneros Highway. In 1870 the first winery in the region opened (first known as Winter Winery and subsequently as Talcoa Vineyards).

In the late 1800s the first wave of phylloxera, a devastating disease of grape plants spread by the phylloxera louse, struck. Then Prohibition in the 1920s temporarily eliminated wine production in the Carneros. After the repeal of Prohibition in 1933, a winery named Garetto began making wine again. Louis Martini and Beaulieu both planted in the Carneros from the 1940s to the 1960s. In the 1970s Carneros Creek, Saintsbury, and Acacia all achieved recognition as a new breed of winery.

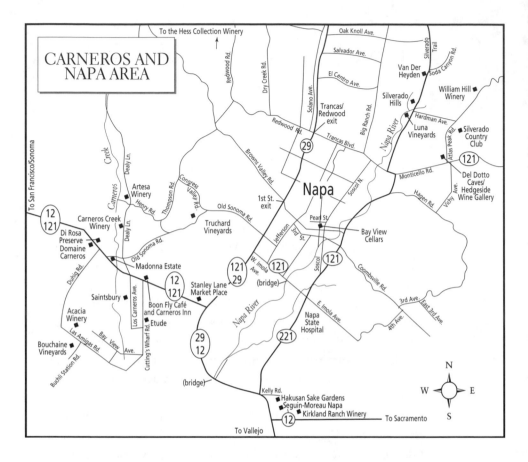

HOW TO GET TO THE CARNEROS DISTRICT

To get here from San Francisco, take the Golden Gate Bridge and Highway 101 north, turn east on Highway 37, left at Sears Point Raceway to Highway 12/121, and follow toward Napa. The Domaine Carneros château, vineyards, and sign on the right mean soon you will take an extremely sharp hairpin right onto Duhig Road and the first winery on our tour. From Oakland/Berkeley, take I–80 east, take Highway 37, north on Highway 29, and left on Highway 12/121. In about 1 mile Domaine Carneros and Duhig Road will be on your left. Before stopping at Domaine Carneros, however, you should make an appointment to visit the di Rosa Preserve, which is right across the way. When you see wooden cutouts of animals against the hillside and a newish corrugated metal building, turn right (north) into the di Rosa driveway.

WINERIES OF THE CARNEROS REGION

Wineries and grape growers in the area have created The Carneros Quality Alliance, an organization dedicated to improving and promoting the wines of Carneros with dignity and gusto. A small group, its members believe intensely in their mission and group individuality. In Napa Valley's part of the Carneros, you can visit Domaine Carneros, Acacia, Bouchaine, Saintsbury, Madonna Estate, Carneros Creek, Etude, and Artesa.

Just west of the wineries, though, you come to the fascinating **di Rosa Preserve: Art & Nature,** on the north side of Highway 12/121, a highly unusual and personal collection of unconventional and experimental indoor and outdoor art. These pieces are dramatically presented throughout Rene di Rosa's fifty-three-acre property, which includes the thirty-five-acre Winery Lake, the Gatehouse Gallery, the Main Gallery, and a 162-acre natural wildlife preserve, all under Napa County Land Trust open space protection.

Rene di Rosa collects San Francisco Bay Area artists' work and exhibits his 2,000-piece collection according to his own instincts, not according to curator's school standards. So you might find an unknown artist's work next to William Wiley's, an artist from San Jose next to Napa's Earl Thollander, or perhaps a lesser piece next to the drama of Joan Brown.

What many critics miss in describing Rene as a collector is the mission he feels to help artists. A former journalist who bought 460 Carneros acres when "experts" said you couldn't grow grapes here, di Rosa and his late wife, Veronica, took tremendous pleasure from helping artists by buying their work—a kind of sponsorship of the arts.

Veronica was the backbone of the restoration of the Napa Opera House. Tragically, she fell over a cliff in France while collecting flower seeds for her garden in Carneros. (Our mutual friend, the late Bob Ernest, who designed the di Rosas' chapel and some of the gardens, had told the di Rosas exactly where to find the seeds.) Veronica died as a result of the fall, just after Bob passed away.

Rene di Rosa sold most of his vineyards to Joseph E. Seagram & Sons in 1986 for a few million. He then created the Rene and Veronica di Rosa Foundation, part of whose mission is to support and inspire the work of Bay Area artists.

We guarantee that you will have an artistic experience at the di Rosa Preserve unlike any you will have in a museum—or anywhere else, for that matter. Di Rosa's collection of 2,000 works of art in all media by 750 artists will wake up your mind and your senses and stimulate your imagination as well as your funny bone.

Fine points: Call for a reservation to take the tours and for seasonal day hikes. The Gallery Tour of the four gallery buildings, including the former di Rosa Residence and the Tractor Barn, runs year-round. The House and Sculpture Meadow Tour is offered from June 1 through September 30. Both tours offer viewing of 150 pieces of outdoor sculpture. Private tours are also available. Everyone is welcome, and guides limit each group to twenty-five. Park in the lot below the corrugated-metal Gatehouse Gallery; the tours begin at the Gatehouse. Open your receptors and enjoy!

Di Rosa Preserve, 5200 Highways 12/121, Napa 94558; phone (707) 226–5991, Web site: www.dirosapreserve.org. Tours start at 9:25 A.M. and 12:55 P.M. Monday, Wednesday, and Thursday; 12:55 and 6:25 P.M. Tuesday; 9:25 and 10:25 A.M. Saturday. Admission is $12; free on first and third Wednesday of every month. Visa, MasterCard, and American Express. Wheelchair accessible.

The first winery you come to—and one of the grandest of Carneros—lies right across from di Rosa's property. The fabulous **Domaine Carneros** is owned by the Taittinger family of France.

In 1931 Pierre Taittinger acquired the venerable Champagne house Fourneaux, founded in 1734, and established Champagne Taittinger, which today is the last major French Champagne house still controlled by its founding family. Pierre Taittinger created a lighter Champagne wine, which now is the elegant wine that other producers emulate.

His son, Claude Taittinger, now president of Champagne Taittinger, selected this 138-acre parcel in Carneros in 1970 to build his American enterprise, a joint venture with Taittinger's distributor, Kobrand Corporation. Following his father's death in 1965, Claude Taittinger established the Prix Culinaire International Pierre Taittinger, now the ultimate recognition of a chef's skills.

Domaine Carneros was established in 1987. The building's design, inside and out, was inspired by the Taittinger family's French residence in Champagne, Château de la Marquetterie. Beautiful and slightly imposing, it is set on a knoll overlooking Carneros and the Napa Valley from the southwest.

Domaine Carneros's Entrance Deck

As you enter the elegant winery, a grand portrait of Madame de Pompadour greets you. Turn right to the tasting room, with its vast views of the di Rosa Preserve and Artesa. Enjoy well-known designer Mary Steer's interior decoration, featuring blue upholstered maple chairs, glass and brass tables, maple walls, an exquisite collection of wine and food books, and a warm and welcoming tasting bar.

If the ambience here seems familiar to you, there's an excellent reason: Winemaker Eileen Crane contributed to the design of both Domaine Carneros and Gloria Ferrer Champagne Caves in the Sonoma Valley part of the Carneros. An exceptional person who taught nutrition science in Venezuela, Eileen has a master's degree in nutrition and graduated both from the University of California at Davis enology program and from the Culinary Institute of America. She left Gloria Ferrer for Domaine Carneros to help design, develop, and lead this facility.

Domaine Carneros has added a tasting bar, or you can have a seat in the salon, and a server will explain the day's tastings. You may also indulge in a caviar plate ($25) or a cheese plate ($14) to accompany your wine.

Fine points: Mother's Day celebrations include music and treats with wine tasting. Winery tours hourly from 10:15 A.M. to 4:00 P.M. daily, April–October; same hours on Friday–Saturday, rest of the year; with tours at 10:15 and 11:00 A.M., noon, and 1:00, 2:00, 3:00, and 4:00 P.M. daily. Featured wines: Sparkling wines made in the *méthode champenoise,* including Brut, Brut Vintage, La Rêve Blanc de Blancs, Brut Rose, Merlot, and Famous Gate Pinot Noir. Tasting fees: $5.50–$10.00 a glass. Owner: Taittinger family. Managing President/Winemaker: Eileen Crane. Cases: 35,000 sparkling, 10,000 Pinot Noir. Acres: 138 here, 70 at Pompadour Vineyard.

Domaine Carneros, 1240 Duhig Road at Highway 12/121, Napa 94559; phone (707) 257–0101, Web site www.domainecarneros.com. Open 10:00 A.M. to 6:00 P.M. daily. Master-Card, Visa, and American Express. Wheelchair accessible from upper parking lot.

Chèvre and Herb Mousse

from Eileen Crane, President/Winemaker, Domaine Carneros, Napa

½ cup parsley leaves
½ tsp crushed garlic
1 bunch (about ¼ cup)
of tarragon leaves
1 cup chèvre (goat cheese)
1½ lbs cream cheese

Chop parsley leaves, crushed garlic, and tarragon leaves in a food processor, turning on and off in short pulses until finely minced but not liquefied. Remove to a small bowl. Blend the chèvre and cream cheese in the food processor until creamy and smooth. Add the herb/garlic mixture, and lightly combine the ingredients by turning on and off the processor in short pulses.

The mousse can be piped or spooned into a serving dish. Present with minitoasts, crackers, or bread. Makes 25 small ramekin-size servings. Serve with Domaine Carneros' Famous Gate Pinot Noir or sparkling wines.

As you come out of the Domaine Carneros driveway, turn right up Duhig Road. Follow it for about 2 miles, up the hill, down, and past Mondavi and Cardinale vineyards on the right. Turn left on Las Amigas at Beaulieu's vineyard, and in 0.3 mile turn left into the driveway of **Acacia Winery,** the Carneros sister of the Chalone Wine Group.

Acacia Winery is a surprise, located in a pleasant, adobe-colored stucco building with leaf-green trim. It is surrounded by cow pasture and Beaulieu

Vineyard across the road. On a clear day, you can see forever—including to the Bay. Enjoy the picnic table and lawn under young olive trees.

In 1986 Chalone Wine Group founder Dick Graf and Phil Woodward bought Acacia from Mike Richmond and partners, adding it to their Chalone Vineyard near Soledad, California; Edna Valley Vineyard near San Luis Obispo; Carmenet in Sonoma; Canoe Ridge Vineyard in eastern Washington; Sagelands (formerly Staton Hills) in Yakima, Washington; and Jade Mountain, Echelon, and Provenance vineyards in Napa. They sold everything to Domaines Barons de Rothschild in late 2004.

The Acacians, as Acacia's loyal and jovial staff members call themselves, stress their sensitivity to *terroir*, the French concept that each vineyard has a character different from others. That character emanates from its geography, geology, climate, and biological and sociological influences, and it should not be disturbed. Acacians call themselves "a friendly if a bit eccentric bunch" who "have never had a black tie event . . . and intend to keep it that way." The staff here are taught that no matter what the request, the answer is yes. The Acacians clearly enjoy themselves, their work, and their wine, and they will do everything possible to be sure that you do, too. But please, be sure to call ahead for reservations.

Acacia gives killer tours, with barrel tastings and technical tours. In the "sky's the limit" attitude Queen of Conviviality Margaret offers occasional bocce ball tournaments and general fun, all by appointment due to Napa County permit regulations.

Acacia Winery in Carneros

Fine points: Acacia has bottled its wines with private labels for Tra Vigne, Spago, the Mauna Kea Beach Hotel, Ruth's Chris Steak House, Burlingame Country Club, and the Claremont Country Club. Tasting fee: none, except $10 per person for Reserve tastings, which includes a keepsake glass. Featured wines: Chardonnay, Pinot Noir, Viognier, Brut, and Chardonnay Brandy. Owner: Domaines Barons de Rothschild. Winemaker/General Manager: Anthony King. Cases: 70,000. Acres: 120.

Acacia Winery, 2750 Las Amigas Road, Napa 94559; phone (707) 226–9991, Web site www.acaciavineyard.com. Open "by appointment" from 10:00 A.M. to 4:00 P.M. Monday–Saturday, noon to 4:00 P.M. Sunday. MasterCard, Visa, American Express, and Discover. Wheelchair accessible.

As you leave Acacia Winery, turn left on Las Amigas Road, and in about 1 mile turn right onto Buchli Station Road to **Bouchaine Vineyards,** a rapidly rising star of Los Carneros. Notice the late architect William Turnbull's winery design trademark of natural vertical wood on the winery's exterior, which in this case comes from recycled redwood wine tanks from the 1900s. Enjoy the colorful herb and perennial garden near the monogrammed gate.

According to the staff, *Bouchaine* is the French word for a person who puts corks in wine bottles. Residents of Delaware, Gerret Copeland is a Dupont, and Tatiana, his wife, is a native of Buenos Aires, Argentina, of Russian heritage.

In 1980 the Copelands purchased what was the Boon Fly ranch in the mid-1800s and completed the winery and tasting room renovations in 1997. It was once owned by the Garretto Brothers, who made sacramental wines and distilled Grappa and whiskey before and after Prohibition, delivering their stash on the back of a truck. Beringer bought the property from Boon and later sold it to the Copelands. Bouchaine is the longest continually operated winery in Carneros.

Now lovely sculpture, a cozy fireplace, living room furniture, a deck, and views of Carneros's rolling hills create a casually elegant but homey ambience.

Fine points: No tasting fee except for groups of ten or more; fee for Reserves. Featured wines: Pinot Noir, Pinot Gris, and Chardonnay. Owners: Gerret and Tatiana Copeland. Winemaker: Michael Richmond. Cases: 20,000. Acres: 105.

Bouchaine Vineyards, 1075 Buchli Station Road, Napa 94559; phone (707) 252–9065 or (800) 654–9463, Web site www.bouchaine.com.

Southwestern Spiced Chicken Sandwiches with Currant/Gewürztraminer Chutney

from Bouchaine Vineyards, Napa

CURRANT/GEWÜRZTRAMINER CHUTNEY:

1 cup red currants
$1/4$ cup sugar
1 cup Gewürztraminer wine
1 small red onion, chopped
$1/2$ cup white wine vinegar

SOUTHWESTERN SPICED CHICKEN:

1 cup extra virgin olive oil
1 clove garlic, minced
1 Tbs fresh cilantro, chopped
1 Tbs fresh thyme, chopped
1 Tbs fresh oregano (Mexican if available)
$1/2$ poblano chili, seeded and finely diced
salt and pepper to taste
4 boneless chicken breasts
4 thick red onion slices
8 slices French or Italian bread, lightly toasted
4 slices Pepper Jack cheese

Combine oil with all herbs, peppers, and spices. Mix gently and add in chicken breasts. Marinate chicken in seasoned oil for at least one hour but preferably longer.

After marinating, grill or panfry chicken on high heat until cooked through. Grill or panfry onion slices until soft and lightly charred. Place chicken breast on one toasted slice of bread, top chicken with onion slice and cheese. Broil briefly until cheese melts. Sprinkle with any leftover herbs if desired and serve with chutney on side. Serves 4.

Open from 10:30 A.M. to 4:00 P.M. daily. Visa, MasterCard, American Express, and Discover. Wheelchair accessible.

On the south side of the Carneros Highway (12/121), don't miss **Saintsbury,** renowned producer of Carneros Pinot Noir and Chardonnay. To get there, turn right (south) from the highway onto Los Carneros Avenue. Turn left (east) onto Withers Lane, then turn south into Saintsbury's driveway.

Saintsbury has a Ned Forrest–designed, elegant rural barn with gray stucco walls and beamed ceilings. An English garden of native plants and blonde pebbles provides a charming setting.

As you enter the Mexican tiled office and tasting area, you are struck with the quality of art everywhere, much of it from the San Francisco Museum of Modern Art Rental Center.

UC Davis enology classmates David Graves and Dick Ward discovered in 1977 that they liked "knocking back a decent glass of Morey-Saint-Denis." In 1981 they moved their wine friendship into a wine partnership. Original winemaker Bill Knuttel joined them in 1983, and Byron Kosuge came in as "Bill's right-hand man."

Dick and Dave both named their winery for "the old codger" George E. B. Saintsbury (1845–1933), a Scottish professor of literature at the University of Edinburgh and wine fan. In his *Notes on a Cellar Book,* first published in 1920, Saintsbury wrote: "Well! A cellar is an interesting place to fill, to contemplate when filled, and to empty in the proper way."

Dick and Dave believe, and hopefully they are correct, that Carneros is the Beaune of California. They were among the first wineries to produce 100 percent malolactic Chardonnay, which means that the wine goes through malolactic fermentation, in which the conversion of malic acid to lactic acid makes the wine softer and richer. While their first devotion is to their exceptional Pinot Noirs, their reality also includes the fact that, as Dick puts it, "You need to have something for the fish course."

Fine points: Featured wines: Carneros Chardonnay, Pinot Noir, Marc Brandy, and Vin Gris of Carneros Pinot Noir. Owners: Richard Ward and David Graves. Winemaker: Jerome Chery. Cases: 50,000. Acres: 55. Tasting fee: none.

Saintsbury, 1500 Los Carneros Avenue, Napa 94559; phone (707) 252–0592, Web site www.saintsbury.com. Open from 9:00 A.M. to 5:00 P.M. Monday–Friday by appointment only. Visa, MasterCard, and American Express. Wheelchair accessible.

Etude is the brilliant creation of Tony Soter, after two decades of serving as consulting winemaker for Araujo Estate, Dalla Valle, Moraga Vineyards, Niebaum-Coppola, Shafer, Spottswoode, and Viader. A philosophy graduate of Pomona

College in Claremont, California, Soter began his winemaking career in 1975 as a cellar worker at Stag's Leap Wine Cellars. Then as a postgraduate student in enology and viticulture at UC Davis, Soter joined Chappellet Vineyards, where he became winemaker in 1977. In 1980 Soter broke out as a consulting winemaker, a role he now plays at Etude since selling it to Beringer in 2003.

Soter created his own brand, Etude, which means "study" in French, in 1982. Ever the philosopher, Soter believes "that inspired grape growing diminishes the need for intervention by the winemaker, resulting in superior wines that are grown, not made," resulting in some of the most highly rated wines in the country.

With Beringer's investment, Etude now occupies huge French-looking facilities that used to house the RMS (Remy-Martin) Distillery, with a hospitality center in the future. RMS's tasting room has been converted to offices. Currently visitors may taste Etude's elegant wines by appointment, with special tastings in the cozy "winemaker's room" sitting around a table. What a way to go!

Fine points: Featured wines: Cabernet Sauvignon, Merlot, Pinot Noir, Heirloom Carneros Pinot Noir, and Pinot Blanc. No tasting fee. Owner: Beringer Wine Estates. Winemaker: Kevin Morrissey, with Tony Soter consulting winemaker. Cases: 13,000. Acres: 500.

Etude, 1250 Cutting's Wharf Road, Napa 94558; phone (707) 257–5300, Web site www.EtudeWines.com. Open noon to 4:00 P.M. Tuesday–Friday by appointment. Visa, MasterCard, and American Express. Wheelchair accessible.

On the north side of Highway 12/121 you will find three more wineries with vastly different and distinct personalities: Madonna Estate, Carneros Creek, and Artesa.

To get there from Napa, Cutting's Wharf Road, or Los Carneros Avenue, turn right off Highway 12/121 onto Old Sonoma Road. (If you decide to forgo Saintsbury and go there from Domaine Carneros, get back onto the highway and immediately turn left onto Old Sonoma Road.)

Madonna Estate, with its arched windows, is at the northeast corner of Old Sonoma Road and Highway 12/121, so turn right into its driveway. The Bartolucci family founded the winery in 1922 in the shadow of Mt. St. John near Oakville. They were among the first to plant premium grape varieties in the Napa Valley.

Madonna Estate

Andrea (Andy) Bartolucci came to the United States from Italy in 1913 expressly to make wine. He settled in St. Helena in 1919. In 1922 he purchased a twenty-four-acre vineyard and winery, where he made sacramental wines and sold grapes to home winemakers during Prohibition. He made his first table wine

Peachy Walnut Salad

from Madonna Estate, Napa

large bowl of mixed greens
2 ripe peaches, sliced
$^1/_4$ cup blue cheese, crumbled
$^1/_4$ cup toasted walnuts brushed with honey and broiled or baked until brown
1 small red onion, sliced thinly
$^1/_2$ cup cherry tomatoes
Toasted Walnut Grapeseed Oil
Late Harvest Riesling Vinegar

Drizzle Toasted Walnut Grapeseed Oil and Late Harvest Riesling Vinegar over ingredients and toss.

with his son Louis in 1933, selling the 5,000 gallons for 20 cents a gallon. Louis studied enology at UC Davis, began to modernize Madonna Winery, bought out his father, and began production of wines under the Mont St. John label. By 1947 Mont St. John Cellars was the twelfth-largest winery in California.

Louis's son, Andrea (Buck) Bartolucci, grew up in Louis's varietal-specific vineyards, studied viticulture and enology at Cal State University at Fresno, and came home in 1967 to work as assistant winemaker to his father. When Louis and his brothers sold the winery in 1970, Buck bought and planted 160 acres in the not yet "discovered" Carneros Region, which he still farms organically and dry—meaning nature runs things. Buck's Madonna Vineyards is one of the few vineyards in Napa County with the California Certified Organic Farmers Association designation and produces the fine pesticide- and herbicide-free wines of Madonna Estate. Buck believes that "herbicides and pesticides . . . are shortcuts that ultimately throw things in the vineyards out of balance, causing more problems down the road."

Buck's daughter, Brette, has joined the winery as director of public relations.

As you enter the tasting room with its wood-paneled walls and obviously linoleum floors, you instantly know that this is a casual, fun place with warm hospitality and humor. The staff's motto is "No question's too dumb; the only dumb question is the one unasked." Here you can purchase some of our favorites: Angelo's garlic-stuffed olives, garlic marinara sauce and salsa, mustard, Cuisine Perel pastas, grapeseed oils, Madonna Estate vinegars, such as orange, spicy peach, and black fig, olive oils, and Merlot blackberry grilling sauce. Don't miss the white truffle oil. You'll also find "Life Is a Cabernet" mouse pads, espresso shortbread cookies, and wine-country posters and books.

Truffle Risotto

from Madonna Estate, Napa

2 oz dry porcini mushrooms
½ stick butter (⅛ lb)
4 Tbs truffle oil
1 bunch scallions, chopped
3 carrots, minced
2 cups Arborio rice
2 cups grated Parmesan cheese

Add hot water to the dry porcini mushrooms and let stand 30 minutes. In another pan, melt butter, then add oil, scallions, and carrots. Cook for 10 minutes. Add the rice and cook for 5 minutes. Drain the porcini by slowly pouring the water over the rice. Simmer until the rice is tender but firm, about 25 minutes. When done, drizzle with a little extra truffle oil and sprinkle with Parmesan cheese.

Fine points: Reserve ahead to spend some entertaining time with Buck or other wine guys on their vineyard and tasting tours, particularly on the second and fourth Saturday of the month. These exceptionally personal and informative tours of organic farming and wine tasting cost $5.00 for tour and tastings. Featured wines (all estate-bottled): Chardonnay, Pinot Grigio, Merlot, Johannisberg Riesling, Gewürztraminer, Muscat di Canelli, Pinot Noir, and Cabernet Sauvignon. Owner: Andrea (Buck) Bartolucci. Winemaker: Buck Bartolucci. Cases: 10,000. Acres: 160 certified organic.

Madonna Estate, 5400 Old Sonoma Road, Napa 94559; phone (707) 255–8864, Web site www.madonnaestate.com. Open from 10:00 A.M. to 5:00 P.M. daily. Call for a tour appointment. MasterCard, Visa, and American Express. Wheelchair accessible.

Carneros Creek Winery is next on our tour. As you leave Madonna Estate, turn right up Old Sonoma Road. (If you skipped Madonna Estate, just continue up the road.) Turn left (west) onto Dealy Lane 0.3 mile from Madonna Estate, and travel west 1 mile. After you pass a private golf course, watch for the Irish and American flags near what looks like a yellow wood house, which it was before it became Carneros Creek. Turn left into Carneros Creek's parking lot at the flags.

An Irishman making wine? You bet! In fact, Carneros Creek Pinot Noir is the official wine of the Irish city of Cork, one of San Francisco's sister cities. Here's the story.

Founder Francis Mahoney's parents left County Cork in the 1920s for California. Their families, the O'Mahoneys and O'Riordans, still farm around Cork. In the 1960s Francis took off to work the family farms and travel the wine regions of France, Germany, and Italy. After carefully developing his affinity for Burgundian wines, Francis taught for a while, then decided to follow his true love: wine. He studied enology at UC Davis, worked at Connoisseur Wine Imports in San Francisco and as vineyard manager for Mayacamas Vineyards, and established his own winery in the Carneros district in 1972. His goal was to make wines that would stand up to French Burgundies. Eventually he cofounded the Carneros Quality Alliance.

In a brilliant move, Francis offered his land for a UC Davis field study to improve grape varietal quality. He selected the enology department's top student, Melissa Moravec, to lead the clonal research project. Francis learned along with

Carneros Creek Winery

the researchers, hired Melissa as enologist, then winemaker, and now sets a standard for Pinot Noir. The winery's thirtieth anniversary was marked in 2002. Four cats have taken over the tasting room's chairs with pride. Already fully utilizing its new production building, Carneros Creek will soon build a new hospitality center.

No surprise, but Carneros Creek's wines were served by President Clinton to then President Mary Robinson of Ireland.

Fine points: The tasting fee of $2.00 to $7.00 for vineyard designates goes toward your purchase of wine. Featured wines: Fleur de Carneros Pinot Noir, Mahoney Estate Chardonnay and Pinot Noir, and Cabernet Sauvignon. Owners: The Mahoney Family. Winemaker: Ken Foster. Cases: 35,000. Acres: 187.

Carneros Creek Winery, 1285 Dealy Lane, Napa 94559; phone (707) 253–9463, Web site www.carneroscreek.com. Open from 10:00 A.M. to 5:00 P.M. daily. MasterCard, Visa, American Express, and Discover. Wheelchair accessible.

Artesa's entrance and winery under native grasses

As you leave Carneros Creek, turn left onto Dealy Lane to visit **Artesa Vineyards & Winery** (formerly Codorniu Napa), an architectural and artistic heaven. After a curve in the road, turn left onto Henry Road and drive for about 0.5 mile. Turn left into Artesa's long driveway, well marked with gate and gray cement walls. No—the cute old house on the left is not it. Keep going. Notice the peaceful lake just below what appears to be a knoll topped by a mound of long grass. *That* is Artesa.

Designed by Barcelona architect Domingo Triay and assisted by Napa Valley architect Earl R. Bouligny, this local landmark features water cascading down the building and staircase edges, reflecting pools, smoky quartz-colored windows, an art gallery featuring exceptional Spanish and American artists (including the decorative glass and sculpture of permanent resident artist Gordon Huether), and winemaking artifacts. Barcelona craftspeople designed and built the custom furniture and fittings to express contemporary Catalán culture.

With their abundant resources the Raventos family built this remarkable winery. Part of a hill was removed and set aside while the production facility, offices, and visitor center were constructed. Then the complex was re-covered with the reserved earth, and the new winery's height was matched with the top of the original hill. Native grass was planted over the top so that the exterior changes with the seasons in tune with the surrounding hills, with the grass drip-irrigated from ponds on the estate. Talk about environmental sensitivity!

The family made the first *méthode champenoise* sparkling wine in Barcelona in 1872 and began making elegant and delicate California sparkling wine here in 1991. They have been making still wines in Spain since the 1500s and today are Spain's foremost maker of Cava. The renaming of Artesa signifies a winery move toward still wines, which they certainly make successfully. Artesa even provides a map and directions to its Codorniu Winery in Sant Sadurni, Spain.

Fine points: The Raventos family also owns other wineries, including Scala Dei in Catalonia and Septima in Argentina, as well as the Bach, Bodegas Bilbainas, Rondel, Le Garis, and Raimat wineries in Spain. Featured wines: Sauvignon Blanc, Chardonnay, Gewürztraminer, Pinot Noir, Brut, Reserve Cuvée, Merlot, Cabernet Sauvignon, Syrah, and Artesa Elements blend of Merlot and Cabernet Sauvignon. Tasting fee: $6.00 for six wines or $2.00 for two ounces, $10.00 for Reserves. No picnicking. Owners: The Raventos Family. Winemaker: Don Van Staaveren. Cases: 55,000. Acres: 350.

Artesa Vineyards & Winery, 1345 Henry Road, Napa 94559; phone (707) 224–1668, Web site www.artesawinery.com. Open from 10:00 A.M. to 5:00 P.M. daily. Tours at 11:00 A.M. and 2:00 P.M., or call ahead for large parties. MasterCard, Visa, and American Express. Wheelchair accessible by elevator at southern entrance.

Hungry travelers in Carneros have limited but contrasting opportunities to "dine." At the foot of Cutting's Wharf Road is **Moore's Landing,** where Napa is building a new boat launch and parking lot. If you want to hang out with a bunch of wine folks in their jeans and their elbows on the table and a view of the Napa River, this is the place.

Boon Fly Café at the new **Carneros Inn,** located on the north side of Highway 121 across from the junction with Cutting's Wharf Road, is another story. Once upon a time, just a few years ago, there was a trailer park on this site, where there also seemed to be an overabundance of Ford Pinto cars. Hence, Sonoma high school students commuting to Napa's Justin-Siena High School dubbed the trailer park "The Pinto Farm." With international investment and design of the Carneros Inn, locals are surprised at how much the eighty-six-room elegantly decorated metal buildings resemble the old trailer park. (Rooms $380 to $1,200 per night.)

The Carneros Inn development was highly controversial politically, with locals in the Carneros region actively campaigning against it, and now trying out Boon Fly Café with some skepticism. Located in one of the two metal buildings that border the highway, the Boon Fly is named for an early settler who bought land in Carneros way before anyone else saw the value of it. Carneros Inn also has a Hilltop Restaurant open only to hotel guests, although opening it to the public is a local political topic.

The Plumpjack Group, and enterprise owned primarily by Billy Getty and San Francisco mayor Gavin Newsom, bought the entire property in early 2005. Plumpjack's other holdings include Plumpjack winery in Oakville, and the Balboa Café and Plumpjack Wine Shop in San Francisco.

Chef Kimball Jones's food is excellent, and we expect the fun and quality of service to rise to the Plumpjack Group's reputation. Winery workers swear by the hamburgers and macaroni and cheese. At $10 for a small ramekin, this is definitely not your mother's mac and cheese. Heavy shells with melted white cheddar, topped with a tower of nearly taste-free bread crumbs, make this dish a wee bit unwieldy. Some grilled corned beef reubens with house sauerkraut were excellent and drippy, and others seemed dry. Try the baked onion soup ($6.00), the citrus cured salmon sandwich ($11.00), or the peppered Dakota organic ribeye steak ($25.00). Flatbreads (thin pizzas) are a deal at $6.00 to $9.00, with creative toppings such as bacon and blue cheese, coastal field mushrooms, or cured salmon with prosciutto di Parma and goat cheese. Kids will love their menu of corn dogs with fries, grilled cheese, fried chicken "thumbs," and cheese pizza the adults can't have.

Breakfasts are worth stopping by for, and are listed by price. Five Bucks for the Road could include a caggiano ham and gruyere cheese croissant, or a baker's dozen homemade Boon Fly doughnuts. As the price ascends, so do the intricacies of eggs, pancakes, breakfast pizzas, meats, and daily specials.

Boon Fly Café, 4048 Sonoma Highway (121), Napa 94559; phone (707) 299–4872, Web site www.carnerosinn.com. Open 7:00 A.M. to 10:30 P.M. daily. Beer and wine. Corkage fee: $15. Visa, MasterCard, and American Express. Wheelchair accessible.

Bill Wilcoxson's **Stanley Lane Market Place** is an ever-evolving secret home to locally produced gourmet foods, sandwiches, organic produce and coffees, and tastes galore. Located in the triangle where Stanley Lane meets Highway 121 just west of the highway's intersection with Highway 29, Stanley Lane Market sells organic pastas, local and Mediterranean cookbooks, Taylor Made organic and sustainably grown coffees and teas, including espresso drinks, Sweetie Pies cookies, biscotti, and other baked treats, French and local wines, Springhill cheeses, and bargain whole wine barrels ($17) or half cuts ($10), the best price anywhere for garden planters.

The sandwiches in the back case along with organic juices are excellent and miraculously under $5.00. We buy bananas and sustainably grown almonds here for less than supermarket prices. Depending upon the season, Wilcoxson grows and sells corn, pumpkins, and other veggies, always displayed with interesting flair along the highway.

Stanley Lane Market Place, 3100 Golden Gate Drive, Napa 94558; phone (707) 253–7512. Open 6:30 A.M. to 6:00 P.M. Monday–Friday, 8:30 A.M. to 6:00 P.M. Saturday–Sunday. Beer and wine. Visa, Master-Card, and American Express. Wheelchair accessible.

SOUTH OF NAPA

As you approach Napa on Highway 29 coming from Berkeley/Oakland or the East Bay, you may want to detour east for a mile to the Kirkland Ranch Winery or stop at three interesting places that most people miss: Hakusan Sake Gardens, Seguin-Moreau Napa cooperage, and Napa Ale Works. Kirkland is on Highway 12 (Jamieson Canyon Road) and Kirkland Ranch Road, while the other three, and a Lafitte cork production facility, are all in a newish industrial complex in a triangle formed by the Kelly Road cutoff between the junction of Highways 12 and 29. First we'll go to Kirkland Ranch Winery, certainly one of the most exciting tasting rooms in the Napa Valley.

Kirkland Ranch Winery is one of the few Napa Valley wineries where you are actually greeted by family members who host and work the property. Brothers Larry and Lonnie Kirkland bought the land, still a working cattle ranch and vineyard, in 1978 and became the second owners of the actual deed from General Mariano Vallejo.

As you approach this dramatic rustic cedar edifice atop a hill along Highway 12 (Jamieson Canyon Road), you will be struck by the dramatic stone, water fountain and tumbling waterfall, and lovely landscaping. Just wait until you get inside. It appears that no expense was spared to create a tasteful Wild West cattle ranching theme, with giant murals of the Kirkland family working the cattle

Crab Cake Salad

from George Meggers, wine educator for Kirkland Ranch Winery, Napa

FOR THE CRAB CAKES:

1 lb lumpy crabmeat

1 cup dry bread crumbs

3 Tbs mayonnaise

$\frac{1}{2}$ tsp Tabasco sauce

1 Tbs Dijon mustard

1 tsp salt

$\frac{1}{8}$ tsp fresh ground black pepper

$\frac{1}{2}$ cup flour

2 eggs, slightly beaten

2 Tbs extra virgin olive oil

FOR THE HONEY-LEMON VINAIGRETTE AND SALAD:

$\frac{1}{3}$ cup cider vinegar

$\frac{1}{4}$ tsp cracked black pepper

1 Tbs honey

1 Tbs fresh lemon juice

$\frac{1}{4}$ tsp salt

1 cup extra virgin olive oil

2 tsp grated lemon zest

1 package spring greens mix

1 Tbs capers, drained (optional)

For the crab cakes: Combine the crab, 3 Tbs bread crumbs, mayonnaise, Tabasco sauce, mustard, salt, and pepper in a bowl. Shape the mixture into twelve cakes, using about $\frac{1}{4}$ cup each. Dust the cakes with flour and dip them into the beaten eggs momentarily. Then roll the cakes in the remaining bread crumbs.

Heat the oil in a nonstick pan over medium heat. Add some of the crab cakes and fry until they are golden brown and crisp. Turn them over and fry them on the other side. Drain crab cakes on paper towels. Repeat with the remaining crab cakes.

For the vinaigrette and salad: Mix the vinaigrette ingredients and whisk until blended. Toss the spring greens in about half of the vinaigrette along with the capers. Lay two crab cakes on a bed of greens and drizzle a small amount of the vinaigrette over the crab cakes. Serves 6. Serve with Kirkland Ranch Block 13 Chardonnay.

on horseback and with a covered wagon coming out of the downstairs mural into the reception room. American flags decorate the balcony railing, and active military personnel get a 30 percent discount "to help them enjoy the finer things in life."

Take the elevator or stairs made of logs split by one of the Kirklands up to the tasting bar, and don't miss the viewing hall's three large windows through which you can see the bottling line, German tanks (wine, that is), and barrel rooms. The walls are lined with real family photos depicting local modern cattle ranching history. On the third floor is the Cedar Room, a corporate entertainment venue whose walls are covered with cedar.

Next, head back to the bar, made of rare reddish wood and surrounded by cowhide-covered chairs, red cedar tree trunks from Astoria, Oregon, for posts, and a veranda with tables and chairs for sipping and viewing the 2,600-acre ranch and beyond. Lots of barn siding lines the room, the central chandelier is made of forty pairs of naturally shed elk antlers, and all of the antiques are family heirlooms. There's even a large television, because Larry and Lonnie don't want to miss their favorite sports programs and assume you don't want to either.

Signs instruct COWBOYS LEAVE YOUR GUNS AT THE BAR. These people have thought of everything. A must visit, if only for the Wild West experience. Chris Kirkland Davison is vineyard manager and grows fruit for wines. Candace Redman, Chris's daughter, researches and buys all the wine accessories for the lobby shop. Check out the Web site for a virtual shop and tour of the winery.

Fine points: Tasting fee: $5.00. Featured wines: Chardonnay, Pinot Grigio, Sangiovese, Cabernet Sauvignon, Merlot, and Agape. Owners: Kirkland family. Winemaker: Rick Tracy (formerly of Far Niente). Cases: 32,000. Acres: 150 planted of 2,700.

Kirkland Ranch Winery, 1 Kirkland Ranch Road (formerly Lynch Road) at Highway 12–Jamieson Canyon Road, Napa 94558; phone (707) 254–9100, Web site www.kirklandwinery.com. Open from 10:00 A.M. to 4:00 P.M. daily. Visa, MasterCard, American Express, Diners Club, and Discover. Wheelchair accessible.

We highly recommend that you visit the **Seguin-Moreau Napa** cooperage to view the craft of making wine barrels in the French tradition from American oak. In the cooperage across from Seguin-Moreau's offices, you can watch from a walkway so close to the process that you can feel the heat of the flames and inhale the smoke and sawdust.

Huge signs explain the process, from cutting wood and stoking the fires with oak chips to the cooper's art of using water and dancing flames to mold the barrels. Like witches' cauldrons, the flames seem to toast the barrels and the coopers' hair, sending a vanilla aroma into the air. Watch the hammer blows shape the metal bands in the "barrel maker's dance."

Fine points: T-shirts, books, and other souvenirs are available here. Barrels: 80 per day.

Seguin-Moreau Napa, 151 Camino Dorado, Napa 94558; phone (707) 252–3408. Open from 8:00 A.M. to 5:00 P.M. Monday–Friday. Best time to watch: 9:00 and 11:00 A.M., 1:00 and 3:00 P.M. MasterCard and Visa. Wheelchair accessible.

2

In the City of Napa Itself

Good news, folks. Downtown Napa is undergoing an extensive makeover—a Mondavi-style makeover.

The Napa County seat, complete with historic courthouse, big post office, and excellent new library, has suffered predictably from the development of outlying shopping centers and discount chains in ticky-tacky big boxes, to say nothing of the Yountville earthquake. To the rescue, riding white stallions and wearing twenty-five-gallon white hats, have come Robert Mondavi and friends, including many city of Napa residents.

Until recently, private redevelopment of downtown storefronts and historic buildings had been slow because the Napa River has flooded drastically a few times in recent years, making any new investments vulnerable to disaster. In June 1998 Napa voters decided to spend $155 million to control the river's flooding. This was great news for everyone because investors began to feel that they can safely put money toward the redevelopment of the downtown without fear. Napa is turning itself around, with historic buildings renovated as attractive galleries and restaurants.

Even before the people of Napa cast this life preserver into the water, Robert Mondavi's powerful safety net had begun to spread. When the restoration of the Napa Opera House seemed to have bogged down, for example, he and his wife, Margit Biever Mondavi, pledged millions of dollars to finish the project. (Mondavi also pledged support to create the Oxbow School, a residential art school that opened in 1999.) And, aware that the "Up Valley" towns of Yountville, St. Helena, and Calistoga really couldn't bear any more tourism and that the city of Napa was dying on the vine, Mondavi

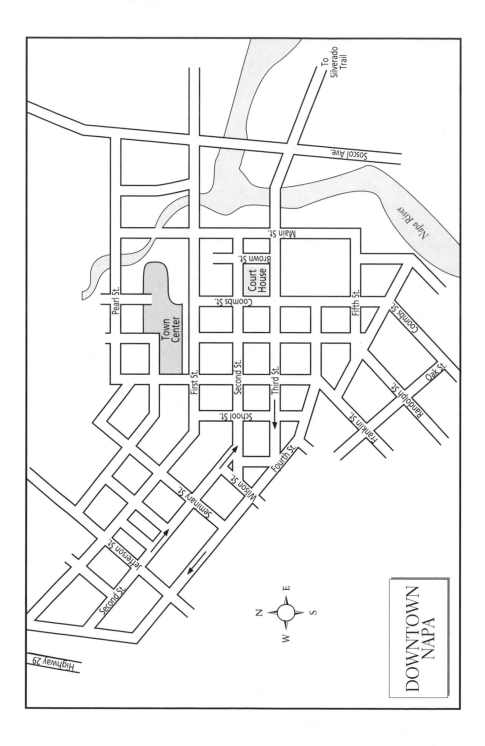

DOWNTOWN
NAPA

inspired, organized, and hired staff to raise funds to develop the enormous and fascinating American Center for Wine, Food and Art (also known as COPIA).

Located on thirteen acres on the banks of the Napa River on First Street, the center already enjoys support from the biggest names in American food and wine, including the late Julia Child. Its purpose is to promote the best of American culture and play a significant role in the advancement of America's achievements in wine, food, and the arts.

COPIA, the popular name of the American Center for Wine, Food and Art, is indeed the grandest improvement in downtown Napa. Aptly named for the Goddess of Abundance, COPIA is located on First Street just across the Napa River from the center of Napa and looks out on river bends. COPIA looks slightly like a Silicon Valley tech center unless you first see or smell the fabulous vegetable and herb gardens that line both sides of the street in front of the building.

At COPIA you can dine elegantly in Julia's Kitchen restaurant, a tribute to Julia Child but with which she had no involvement, and enjoy gourmet snacks in the American Market Café or take them to the center's three and one half acres of gardens. Shop for elegant books and gourmet foods, COPIA wines produced by West Coast wineries to support COPIA's education programs, and kitchen utensils in the Cornucopia exclusive gift shop; wander through the permanent, artist-in-residence, and special exhibits; or take a stroll through the extensive herb and vegetable gardens as well as the orchards and vineyards.

COPIA has carefully scheduled programs that appeal to local residents as well as visitors, and members gain free admission (memberships begin at $60 for two). Exhibitions have included the art, history, packaging, and recipes of "Forks in the Road: Food, Wine, and the American Table"; "A Fine Glass of Wine," featuring European and American drinking vessels; "Talking Turkey," with sculpture and artwork on turkeys; "The Artful Teapot"; "The Birth of Coffee"; and "Return Engagement: Art from Recycled Materials."

Public programs range from poet Francisco Alarcon and food writer Georgeanne Brennan to guest presenters such as chef and cookbook author Joyce Goldstein, Mexican chef Pablo Jacinto, author David Mas Masumoto, concerts by Beach Blanket Babylon's Val Diamond, Billy Philadelphia, Rhythmix, and Tango Number Nine, wine tastings from other regions, films, musical performances, new festivals, and guests such as Joey Altman and The Naked Chef.

At **Julia's Kitchen** you may select from the a la carte menu or from the executive chef Victor Scargle's Chef's Tasting Menu. Selections may include mouthwatering pan-seared Sonoma Valley foie gras ($14); Ahi tuna tartare ($13);

Liberty duck confit salad ($12); petrale sole or trout ($17); a chef's tasting menu ($40); or an Ahi tuna Nicoise salad ($12). Dinner entrees are slightly higher priced, with a chef's tasting menu at $60.

A great addition to encourage families to visit is a COPIA kids menu of $5.00 "full meals," including peanut butter and jelly.

Go ahead and order a fabulous dessert or two created by pastry chef Nicole Plue ($7.00 to $14.00). Our favorites are the bittersweet chocolate pâté with malted ice cream and Guinness glaze, a crème brûlée trio, or the fresh berry Napoleon. Specialty teas range from $4.50 to $6.50.

A must experience!

COPIA, 500 First Street, Napa 94559; phone (707) 259–1600 or (888) 51–COPIA, Web site www.copia.org. Open from 10:00 A.M. to 5:00 P.M. Wednesday–Monday. Julia's Kitchen is open from 11:30 A.M. to 3:00 P.M. Wednesday–Sunday and 5:30 to 9:30 P.M. Thursday–Sunday. Admission: $12.50 for adults, $10.00 for students and seniors, $7.50 for children ages 6–12. Members free. Corkage fee: $15, waived with purchase of bottle. Visa, MasterCard, and American Express. Wheelchair accessible.

All of this activity suggests a very exciting future for Napa.

Of course, the present isn't all that bad, either.

MAIN STREET, FIRST STREET, AND NAPA TOWN CENTER

Most of what you will want to visit on foot or wheelchair is along Main Street, First Street, and adjoining Napa Town Center, a collection of mall stores that snake around older buildings. Here is where most of Napa's interesting shops and restaurants are clustered, along with the Napa Firefighters Museum and some intriguing import shops.

The most exciting development project in central downtown Napa is Harry Price's renovation of the historic landmark Napa Mill, built in 1884. The mill complex includes the casually elegant Napa River Inn; Sweetie Pies fabulous baked goods and coffee; Greg Cole's recently moved Celadon restaurant; Bettina, Claudia, and Claude Rouas's Angele restaurant; Mill and Jim Brandt's Napa General Store; and Aprile and Angelino Sandri's Gondola Servizio, to say nothing of the remarkable indoor and outdoor entertainment venues. Even the Napa

Valley Shakespeare Festival has moved here, performing on the Riverbend Plaza's outdoor stage.

Greg Cole and his wife, Elizabeth Fairbairn, opened **Celadon** in Napa specializing in "global comfort food" and quickly became recognized as one of *Wine Spectator*'s "hottest young chefs." Specialties include Maine crab cakes ($11.00), flash-fried calamari ($9.00), Celadon BLT with house-cut fries ($11.00), burger with sun-dried tomato mayo ($10.00), and filet mignon with horseradish mashed potatoes ($23.00). Celadon also enjoys *Zagat Survey*'s Award of Distinction, *Wine Spectator*'s Award of Excellence, and *USA Today*'s recognition as one of the "ten great places to dine at the bar." In this new location, we enjoy shaded outdoor seating as well as a redesigned dining room and bar. All this and fabulous food, too, at reasonable prices. Without question, we highly recommend Celadon as one of our favorites.

> *Celadon, 500 Main Street, Napa 94559; (707) 254–9690. Open from 11:30 A.M. to 2:00 P.M. daily, 5:00 to 9:00 P.M. Monday–Thursday, and 5:00 to 10:00 P.M. Friday–Saturday. Full bar. Visa, MasterCard, and American Express. Wheelchair accessible.*

The Napa General Store, (707) 259–0762, presents a large space with "gourmet-to-go" food as well as dining inside and on the riverside terrace. Enjoy Bonavita coffees, a wine bar (which offers tastings 11:00 A.M. to 6:00 P.M. daily), and a delicatessen, as well as retail gourmet picnic baskets and specialty offerings. Breakfast includes bagels, muffins, scones, fritattas, Napa General Store granola, and fruit cups, and lunch offerings include East Coast sandwiches featuring meats baked in the brick oven, excellent brick-oven pizzas, rotisserie chicken, and salads.

Napa General Store has added a Pan-Asian dinner menu created by Chef Nam Phan and Pastry Chef Judy Takasaki. Try the Pho beef noodle soup ($9.75), sautéed squid with cellophane noodles ($8.25), Coca-Cola braised beef short ribs ($12.25), or diced chicken with shiitake mushrooms ($9.25). Open 9:00 A.M. to 7:00 P.M. Sunday–Tuesday, 9:00 A.M. to 9:00 P.M. Wednesday–Saturday. 540 Main Street; Web site www.napageneralstore.com.

Gondola Servizio, (707) 257–8495, offers personal cruises on the Napa River in authentic Venetian gondolas, of which co-owner Angelino Sandri spent fifteen years studying construction and operation in Venice before bringing them to the United States. Passengers will be treated to his costumes and serenades of

Maine Crab Cakes with Sweet Corn and Peppers and Grainy Mustard Sauce

from Chef Greg Cole, Celadon, Napa

CRAB CAKES:

½ lb Maine crabmeat, cleaned

¼ cup mayonnaise

2 eggs

1½ cups fresh white-bread crumbs

1 tsp Worcestershire sauce

½ tsp Tabasco sauce

½ tsp salt

pinch black pepper

2 Tbs salad oil

Combine all the ingredients except salad oil and mix well. Divide the crab-cake mixture into twelve even portions. Panfry in salad oil until golden brown on both sides. Remove onto absorbent paper and drain. Serve with Grainy Mustard Sauce. Serves 4.

SWEET CORN AND PEPPERS:

1 Tbs olive oil

1 medium onion, finely diced

2 celery ribs, finely diced

1 ear white corn, husked, cut off cob

1 tsp garlic

1 red bell pepper, finely diced

1 Tbs Italian parsley, chopped

zest of ½ lemon

Heat the olive oil in a small skillet and sauté the onion, celery, and corn kernels for 3 minutes. Add the garlic and cook for 1 minute. Add the red bell pepper and cook for an additional minute. Remove from heat and add the Italian parsley and lemon zest. Allow to cool. Serves 4.

GRAINY MUSTARD SAUCE:

1 cup sour cream

¼ cup white wine

3 Tbs whole grain mustard

pinch salt and black pepper

Combine all ingredients and mix well.

Italian folk songs and opera. Ride packages cost $55 for a half hour and $125 for a full hour. Watch for romantic packages including picnics from the Napa General Store.

Angele is a family project of renowned restaurateur and hotelier Claude Rouas and his daughters, Bettina and Claudia. A native of Algeria, Claude Rouas was discovered as a headwaiter at Ernie's Restaurant in San Francisco by Dolly Fritz McMasters Cope, owner of the Huntington Hotel. She lured Claude and fellow headwaiter Henri Barberis to reopen the seemingly jinxed L'Etoile Restaurant in her hotel. (As full disclosure, Kathleen did public relations for L'Etoile.) Claude Rouas moved on eventually to launch the Piatti restaurant chain, as well as Auberge du Soleil in Rutherford.

Managing partner Bettina Rouas served as manager at the French Laundry and general manager of Bistro Jeanty, as well as at Bistro Don Giovanni. Sister and partner Claudia Rouas is vice president of retail operations at Niebaum-Coppola Estate Winery in Rutherford. French native and Executive Chef Christophe Gerard did an apprenticeship at Relais des Hussards in Coulombs and worked at three-star Taillevent in Paris, Restaurant L'Auberge in Albany, New York, and was sous chef at Lespinasse in New York's St. Regis Hotel. He also worked at Café Pierre in the Pierre Hotel.

Angele's food is superb, although some servings are quite small. Temptations include oxtail roulade with frisee salad ($10.00), a charcuterie plate of Parisian ham, duck rillettes, and rosette de Lyon ($11.00), pan-seared sweetbreads ($12.00), classic French onion soup ($8.50), a huge Croque Monsieur with grilled Parisian ham and gruyere with green salad ($9.00), braised lamb shank with butter bean stew ($21.00), seared halibut ($19.00), double-cut pork chop with caramelized Brussels sprouts, lardoons, and prunes ($19.50), a great hamburger with French fries ($11.00), or a risotto confit of tomatoes, wild mushrooms, and Reggiano Parmesan cheese ($16.00). Check out the truly French feeling back room for larger parties, and enjoy the patio overlooking the Napa River.

Angele, 540 Main Street, Napa 94559; phone (707) 252–8115, Web site www.angele.us. Open 11:30 A.M. to 10:00 P.M. daily. Full bar. Visa, MasterCard, and American Express. Wheelchair accessible. Parking lot.

The **Napa River Inn** is the centerpiece of the Napa Mill project and features sixty-six luxury rooms with full breakfast at Sweetie Pies Bakery. Greenhaus spa on the property offers full health and beauty spa treatments. Visitors may arrive by either boat or car. We highly recommend a visit.

> *Napa River Inn, 500 Main Street, Napa 94559; (707) 251–8500 or (877) 251–8500; Web site: www.napariverinn.com. Wheelchair accessible.*

Beginning at Main Street's south end, visit the Napa River Inn in the redeveloped old Hatt Market building. Then, from Second Street on Main heading north, you might want to try one of several small restaurants, such as Pilar, P. J.'s at the corner of First Street, Peking Palace, ZuZu, and Downtown Joe's.

Pilar is the newly born baby of renowned chefs Pilar Sanchez and her husband, Didier Lender, who met at the now late Ernie's Restaurant in San Francisco, where he was sous chef.

Lunch at Pilar may offer a light celery root slay with whole grain mustard and herbs ($9.00), a seafood stew of salmon, halibut, mahimahi, oysters, fennel, saffron, and basil ($13.00), sea scallops with potato gratin and Swiss chard ($14.00), grilled hanger steak with French fries ($16.00), lamb chops ($16.00), or a creamy carrot risotto ($12.00).

Dinner varies slightly, adding free-range veal rib chop ($26.00), Colorado lamb rack with pearled barley and figs ($27.00), venison flank steak or Muscovy duck breast ($23.00), a "golden bouillabaisse' ($19.00), and sea scallops ($26.00). Desserts are $6.00 at lunch and $8.00 at dinner, including a slow-baked chocolate mousse with Scharffen Berger chocolate gelato, carnaroli rice pudding with Moscato poached raisins, warm apple tart with vanilla ice cream, or a blue cheese tart with figs. Do try, for fun and food!

> **Pilar,** *807 Main Street, Napa 94559; phone (707) 252–4474. Open 11:30 A.M. to 2:30 P.M. and 5:30 to 9:30 P.M. Tuesday–Saturday. Beer and wine. Visa, MasterCard, and American Express. Wheelchair accessible.*

Napa's hottest new restaurant is **Bounty Hunter** in the 1888 Semorle building, enhancing Mark Pope's wine shop with Jake Southworth's jazzy food, like beer-can chicken ($18.00), ribs, mac and cheese ($4.00), pizzas, and some sensational wines.

Bounty Hunter, 975 First Street (east of Main), Napa 94559; (707) 255–0622. Open 11:00 A.M. to 10:00 P.M. Sunday–Thursday, til midnight Friday–Saturday. Beer and wine. Visa, MasterCard, American Express. Wheelchair accessible.

ZuZu is Napa's hot little tapas restaurant in a thankfully revamped small space right on Main Street north of the Napa River Inn and Mill restaurants. Chef Angela Tamura offers small plates of cold and hot tapas, ranging from a dish of Mediterranean olives ($3.00) to Spanish white anchovies with roasted tomatoes and peppers ($6.00), sizzling prawns ($9.00), Bacalao of Salt Cod with Truffle Oil ($8.00), Moroccan barbecue lamb chops ($13.00), and Argentine marinated Flat Iron steak with chimichurri ($9.00). Most interesting are the port and wine selections from Spain, Australia, Italy, and Argentina, plus of course Napa, Carneros, and Sonoma.

ZuZu, 829 Main Street, Napa 94559; (707) 224–8555; Web site www .zuzunapa.com. Open from 11:30 A.M. to 10:30 P.M. Monday–Friday, 4:30 to 10:30 P.M. Saturday–Sunday. Full bar. Corkage fee: $10 per 750 ml bottle. Visa, MasterCard, and American Express. Downstairs is wheelchair accessible.

Downtown Joe's, named for owner Joe Peatman, has been voted "Best Outdoor Dining," "Best Bar," "Best Night Spot," and "Best Place to Meet the Opposite Sex" by Napa residents. Downtown Napa's only microbrewery/restaurant, the restaurant and outdoor dining area look out over the river, a Napa park lawn, and Main Street action (such as it is). We enjoyed the best brewpub grub we've ever had here, ranging from a roasted-garlic Caesar salad and pulled pig to burgers, grilled veggie panini, flank-steak sandwich, pastas, and pizzas.

Fine points: Featured beers: Lickety Split Lager, Ace High Cream Ale, Dancin' Feet Red Wheat Beer, Past Due Dark Ale, Golden Thistle Bitter Ale, and Slipknot Stout. Owner: Joe Peatman. Brewmaster: Lance McLaughlin. Chef: Paul Croshal. Barrels: 1,000.

Downtown Joe's, *902 Main Street, Napa 94559; phone (707) 258–2337. Open from 11:00 A.M. to 11:00 P.M. daily, Sunday brunch from 8:30 A.M. Full bar. Visa, MasterCard, American Express, Discover, and JCB. Wheelchair accessible.*

La Gondola is a new kid on the block in the heart of downtown Napa, with reasonably priced Italian specialties that appeal to locals and county workers in nearby court buildings.

Enjoy a wide range of salads with spinach, chicken, Gorgonzola, and other accoutrements, and ever-present minestrone soup, all under $10. Panini come with fries, soup, or salad and may included chicken, portobello mushrooms, grilled eggplant or steak, and cheeseburgers, again all under $10. Pastas are all $9.95 and come with soup or mixed green salad. Chicken piccata, scaloppini, or dorato substitute for veal dishes, and calamari, fillet of sole, scallops Marsala, and snapper Livornese complete the menu (all under $12). Enjoy!

> *La Gondola, 1001 Second Street, Napa 94559; phone (707) 224–0607. Open 11:00 A.M. to 10:00 P.M. Monday–Friday, 1:00 to 10:00 P.M. Saturday, 4:00 to 10:00 P.M. Sunday. Beer and wine. Visa, MasterCard, and American Express. Wheelchair accessible.*

A couple of doors north on Main Street is one of Napa's best coffee places, the **Napa Valley Coffee Roasting Company,** where you can inhale the mouthwatering aromas of roasting coffee, sit and read while you enjoy a cup, nibble on light foods, and feel slightly urban.

Our only complaint is that the place closes at 6:00 P.M. But you can enjoy the newish Café Society later into the evening (see p. 33).

> *Fine points:* Enjoy the Roasting Company's other cafe in St. Helena, at Oak and Adams Streets, 1 block west of St. Helena's Main Street (Highway 29).

> *Napa Valley Coffee Roasting Company, 948 Main Street, Napa 94559; phone (707) 224–2233. Open from 7:00 A.M. to 6:00 P.M. daily. No credit cards. Wheelchair accessible.*

You might want to try **Tuscany** restaurant, across Main Street, which opened in June 2000. Chef Aram Chakerian, most recently head chef at now-closed Piatti's, offers antipasti, including creative salads, panini ($8.50 to $10.00), steamed Prince Edward Island mussels ($10.00), a seafood fritto misto ($10.00), yummy cannelloni ($15.00), pizzas ($8.00 to $13.00), salmon ($13.00), ravioli stuffed with Dungeness crab and rock shrimp mousse with tomato brandy sauce ($14.50), veal scaloppine picatta (yes, all in one) at $18.00, thick-cut pork loin ($20.00), two semi-boneless quail with braised endive ($20.00), steak, and seafood of the day. The open kitchen, counter seats, and windows open to Main Street add to the fun. Choose beer and wine from an extensive list.

Tuscany, 1005 First Street, Napa 94559; phone (707) 258–1000. Open from 5:00 to 11:00 P.M. daily. Corkage fee: $15 per bottle, waived if you purchase a bottle. Visa, MasterCard, and American Express. Wheelchair accessible.

Café Society is one of the most fun new spots in Napa in a long time, especially for Berkeley-Sorbonne graduates, as owner Joan Osburn and author Kathleen Hill are. Joan and Steve Osburn recently opened this northern exposure of their Café Society Showroom at the San Francisco Design Center with inviting additions. In one space, Joan offers French woven Gatti cafe chairs (she has the exclusive in the United States); cafe, aperitif, and street signs; a cafe with gelato, desserts, and Angelina's hot chocolate; poetry readings, with desserts on weekend evenings; monthly L'Alliance Francaise meetings; live and recorded music; book signings; and an interior design studio in the back. You may not be able to resist the French furniture, to say nothing of the fine coffee. Joan says she features "cafe and wine related art, antiques, collectibles, accoutrements, and whimsy." She is right! Retail and to the trade.

Croque Monsieur

from Joan Osburn, Café Society, Napa

2 slices of brioche bread, about ¼-inch thick
3 oz Gruyère cheese, sliced thin
3 slices prosciutto
2 thin slices of tomato
Small tossed salad

Place brioche slices on a baking sheet. Top one half with 1 oz cheese and folded slices of prosciutto. Top the other half with 1 oz cheese. Bake for about 2 minutes at about 350 degrees.

Remove from oven and place the side with just cheese on top of the other slice. Top with two slices of tomato. Slice remaining 1 oz cheese into small strips lengthwise and place in a lattice-work style over the top of the tomatoes. Bake for another 2 minutes, or until cheese has melted and the tomatoes look cooked.

Place whole sandwich on a large clear glass plate and garnish with cornichons, olives, and a small salad.

Osburn has expanded both the food and music menus. She now offers real French sandwiches and salads, soups, and excellent coffee beverages, using Bouchon Bakery specialties and breads exclusively.

. Enjoy live music Friday and Saturday nights, with special cabaret presentations ($20) monthly, with most talent coming directly from Yoshi's in San Francisco.

Café Society, 1000 Main Street, Napa 94559; phone (707) 256–3232, Web site www.cafesocietystore.com. Visa, MasterCard, and American Express. Wheelchair accessible.

Main Element is a gallery offering one-of-a-kind and limited-edition home furnishings, masks, gifts, and work of local artists, some of whom are featured at Friday night openings. Reasonable prices.

Main Element, 1006 Main Street, Napa 94559; phone (707) 254–7131. Open from 10:00 A.M. to 6:00 P.M. Monday–Wednesday, 10:00 A.M. to 8:00 P.M. Thursday–Saturday, and 11:00 A.M. to 4:00 P.M. Sunday. Visa, MasterCard, American Express, and Discover. Wheelchair accessible.

After years of fund-raising, diverting the Napa River, and earthquake bolstering and reconstruction, the little **Napa Valley Opera House** finally reopened in June 2002 as a resounding success. Designed by Samuel and Joseph Newsom in the Italianate style and first built in 1879, this historic landmark once featured readings by Jack London and performances by John Philip Sousa's band, vaudeville, operetta, political rallies, and local dance recitals. That Napa Valley Opera House closed in 1914 due to earthquake damage, the decline of vaudeville, and the advent of motion pictures.

In its newest incarnation, the Opera House's first floor is the Café Theatre, which offers performances including popular, jazz, blues, Latin, world, and chamber music, and comedy. For its inaugural concert June 14, 2002, the Napa Valley Opera House opened with a concert by Dianne Reeves, 2001 Grammy award winner for best jazz vocalist. The Margrit Biever Mondavi Theatre upstairs seats 500 attendees and presents plays, musical theater, opera, dance, chamber music, jazz, and special family programs. Call ahead or check the Web site for the current schedule.

Napa Valley Opera House, 1040 Main Street, Suite 100, Napa 94559; phone (707) 226–7372, Web site www.napavalleyoperahouse.org. Visa, MasterCard, and American Express. Wheelchair accessible.

Just across a narrow part of Napa Creek, Greg Cole and Elizabeth Fairbairn opened **Cole's Chop House,** a Napa version of the old American steak house. More elegant than anything your parents habituated, Cole's Chop House was an instant hit in the renovated 114-year-old native stone Williams-Kyser building, which features a Douglas fir floor and vaulted ceiling.

Open only for dinner, Cole's offers a great Chop House Caesar salad ($7.00), iceberg wedge with Maytag blue cheese ($6.00), portobello mushroom caps entree ($15.00), and an array of finest quality beef, veal, lamb, and pork chops, with New York steak ($37.00), porterhouse ($42.00), and Atlantic salmon ($16.00). All vegetables and sauces cost extra. Be sure to leave room for lots of Sweetie Pies desserts. This is a great complement to the Coles' Celadon.

Cole's Chop House, 1122 Main Street, Napa 94559; phone (707) 224–6328. Open from 5:00 to 9:00 P.M. Sunday–Thursday, 5:00 to 10:00 P.M. Friday–Saturday. Full bar. Visa, MasterCard, and American Express. Wheelchair accessible.

Belle Arti is as close to a "trattoria Siciliana" as you might find in Napa. Located behind Congressman Mike Thompson's district office just north of Cole's Chop House, Belle Arti occupies the triangular dining room where Celadon started. Great location for before or after Napa Valley Opera House performances or movies on the other side of the bridge.

Owner Rosario Patti began his first restaurants in Arkansas, where he won awards as the Best Italian Restaurant in Arkansas! Then he branched out to New York, which didn't work, and migrated westward to the Napa Valley.

All of Patti's salads are light and airy, perhaps due to his oil and lemon dressing. The house salad is plenty for two to share, as is the spinach salad with warm goat cheese ($5.75 to $9.50). The Penne alla Norma with dry ricotta cheese and sautéed eggplant is spectacular, as are the thick egg spaghetti with Shiitake mushrooms and Parmesan, and the pasta with wild fennel and sardines ($11.50 to $17.75). Main plates may include veal with Gorgonzola cheese and green onions, or with capers, olives, tomato, and basil (each $18.50), or the grilled lamb chop marinated in mint sauce ($21.00) and the simple filet mignon with sautéed fresh mushrooms ($25.00). Short list of Italian wines only. Great deck overlooking the creek.

> *Belle Arti, 1040 Main Street, Suite 104, Napa 94559; phone (707) 255–0720. Open 11:00 A.M. to 2:00 P.M. for lunch, 4:00 to 10:00 P.M. Monday–Thursday, 4:00 to 11:00 P.M. Friday–Sunday. Beer and wine. Visa, MasterCard, and American Express. Wheelchair accessible.*

Continue up Main Street to explore exciting new Napa additions. Linda Kloos' **Napa Valley Furniture Company** is a fabulous treasure trove of funk and imaginative furniture, some of which is old, painted, practical, and whimsical. Great prices.

> *Napa Valley Furniture Company, 1138 Main Street, Napa 84559; phone (707) 252–3626. Open from 10:30 A.M. to 6:00 P.M. Monday–Saturday (until 6:00 P.M. Thursday for Farmers' Market), noon to 5:00 P.M. Sunday. Visa and MasterCard. Wheelchair accessible but crowded.*

Sweet Finale Patisserie is actually an improvement over its predecessor at this location, House of Breads, if that is possible, and bakes for Oakville Grocery, Dean & DeLuca, and Sunshine Foods.

Joan and Tim Ketchmark combine their talents. Joan graduated from the professional pastry program at the California Culinary Academy and also has an associates of science degree in hotel and restaurant management. She worked at Grace Baking in Oakland, Draegers' Gourmet in Menlo Park, and Model Bakery in St. Helena.

Tim worked at the world-renowned Masa's restaurant in San Francisco, Sutter 500, Auberge du Soleil, the late East Side Oyster Bar and Grill and Babette's in Sonoma, the All Seasons Café in Calistoga, and on the Napa Valley Wine Train. Tim draws pictures of desserts they are creating that are so popular that they hang in restaurants and here in the patisserie. Sandwiches and salads, as well as small pizzas, make light lunches. Great self-serve soups and chilies combine with Halloween "wicked witch of the West" and pumpkin cookies to happily overwhelm the senses.

Sweet Finale also features Illy coffees, Harney & Sons English teas, organic ice creams, and a strawberry Grand Marnier ice cream, plus sorbets like nectarine-cantaloupe all made on the premises.

Occasionally Joan offers High Tea by reservation with seatings at 1:00, 1:30, 3:30, and 4.00 P.M. Do not miss this opportunity, featuring gingerbread scones with lemon curd, cream of Shiitake mushroom soup, salmon gravlax, chicken salad in puff pastry, English cucumber and potted ham tea sandwiches, and a dessert sampler plate. High Tea is $25 per person, while Royal High Tea, including Hagafen Sparkling wine, mini cookies, and chocolate truffles, is $35.

Sweet Finale, 1146 Main Street at Pearl, Napa 94559; phone (707) 224–2444, Web site www.sweetfinale.com. Open 7:00 A.M. to 6:00 P.M. Wednesday–Saturday, 8:00 A.M. to 6:00 P.M. Sunday. Visa and Master-Card. Wheelchair accessible.

If you like Mexican food, take a chance on **Taqueria Rosita** one door up in the next block of Main Street. Chef Daniel Lopez Pelayo of El Grullo Jalisco, Mexico, creates reliable, hearty Mexican food that is a favorite of Napans. The place is always packed, and locals line up next door at Rosita's take-out annex. You can have a great lunch for $5.00, $6.25 for an entree, including excellent carne asada with pico de gallo ($7.75). All selections are available with chicken, beef, pork, carne asada, or carnitas (fried shredded pork).

Taqueria Rosita, 1210 Main Street, Napa 94559; phone (707) 253–9208. Open from 10:30 A.M. to 8:00 P.M. Monday–Wednesday, 10:30 A.M. to 9:00 P.M. Thursday–Saturday. Beer and wine. Visa and MasterCard. Wheelchair accessible.

Down at the end of the next block from Taqueria Rosita is every cook's dream: **Shackford's** discount kitchen store. Owners John and Donna Shackford call it "Napa's one-stop kitchen shop," and it should be everyone's. We have never seen such deals on everything to use in your kitchen, from restaurant salt shakers for less than $1.50 to great cookbooks, the latest gadgets, an individual bean slicer, huge piggy banks, and their locally popular Jackass Calendars. Not to be missed for cooks, home or professional.

Shackford's, 1350 Main Street, Napa 94559; phone (707) 226–2132. Open from 9:30 A.M. to 5:30 P.M. Monday–Saturday. Visa, MasterCard, American Express, and Discover. Wheelchair accessible, but a little tight.

The Vintners' Collective Tasting Room across Main Street is an elegant tasting room for boutique wineries that don't have their own tasting rooms. The historic Pfeiffer Building was the first stone building erected in Napa and the oldest commercial building in town, first occupied by a brewery in 1875. It also housed a saloon and the Sam Kee Laundry.

Wineries participating in the tasting room include Ancien, Buoncristiani, Caldwell, D Cubed, Elan, Gregory Graham, Judd's Hill, Longfellow, Melka, Mi Sueno, Patz & Hall, Richard Perry, Phelan, Showket, Strata, and Vinoce.

Tasting fees are a cut above those at wineries but include a selection of tasting flights ranging from $10 to $75 and including several wines from different wineries.

> *Vintners' Collective Tasting Room, 1245 Main Street, Napa 94559; phone (707) 255–7150, Web site www.vintnerscollective.com. Open 11:00 A.M. to 6:00 P.M. Wednesday–Monday. Visa, MasterCard, American Express, Discover, and JCB. Not wheelchair accessible.*

Be sure to take the time to cross Main Street and visit the **Napa Firefighters Museum,** which really should be called the International Firefighters Museum. A volunteer staff has collected donations of antique fire engines, equipment, uniforms, photos, carriages, badges, hats, and stories from around the world. The collection grows constantly as firefighters from everywhere hear of the museum and send contributions. Following the September 11, 2001, attack, the museum added a mannequin clad in a New York Fire Department uniform to honor fellow firefighters' efforts and sacrifices.

> *Napa Firefighters Museum, 1201 Main Street, Napa 94559; phone (707) 259–0609. Open from 11:00 A.M. to 4:00 P.M. Friday–Sunday. No admission fee. Wheelchair accessible.*

Now go back to First Street, heading west from Main Street. Significant places to stop include Rod Covington's Napa Wine Merchants (1146 First Street), where you can find the best wines of the Napa Valley, in case you don't have time to explore the wineries yourself, and Bookends Bookstore at 1014 Coombs Street between First Street and the Napa Town Center.

Bombay Bistro offers both northern and southern Indian cuisines, reflecting the origins of its two owners. Favorite dishes include Tandoori roasted salmon, prawns Sandhu in tomato cashew and cream sauce, and Chicken Tikka

Masala, chicken breast cooked in the Tandoori oven and served in a sauce of tomatoes, garlic, cream, and cashews. All entrees, including a Tandoori rack of lamb, range from $10.00 to $16.00 (prices vary daily), with a buffet for $10.50. Lunch buffet, 11:30 to 2:30 Monday–Friday ($8.99), includes all-you-can-eat Dal soup, Tandoori chicken, chicken curry, Naan bread, and two vegetarian dishes that vary daily.

Bombay Bistro also offers several vegetarian selections such as Channa Masala, Bangan Bharta, and Saag Paneer. Right next door is Cork & More Tasting Bar and fine wine and cheese shop.

Bombay Bistro, First Street at Main Street, Napa 94559; phone (707) 253–9375. Open for lunch 11:30 A.M. to 2:30 P.M. Monday–Friday and dinner 5:30 to 9:00 P.M. Monday–Saturday. Beer and wine. Corkage fee: $10. Visa, MasterCard, American Express, and Diners Club/Carte Blanche.

Continuing our walk north on Main Street, a little Berkeley-style import shop called **Inti,** named for the Peruvian sun god, sells pottery, jewelry, tapestry bedspreads, candles, incense, scarves, beads, and masks.

Inti, 1139 First Street, Napa 94559; phone (707) 258–8034. Open from 11:00 A.M. to 6:00 P.M. Monday–Saturday; 11:00 A.M.–5:00 P.M. Sunday. Visa and MasterCard.

On the south side of First Street, check out the Napa Valley Historical Society's Research Library and Museum in the historic Goodman Building; Napa Children's Book Company with toys, stuffed animals, books, and author readings; Copperfield's Books, an excellent North Bay independent book chain featuring used and new books; and Anette's Chocolate and Ice Cream Factory for Bud's Ice Cream, old-fashioned handmade candies, and espresso drinks. Venture up the block to the pink Neighborhood Collective Antiques, where fifty dealers offer their best.

Small World Deli on First Street offers excellent sandwiches, and its original, Small World Restaurant, is around the corner on Coombs Street. Great sandwiches, homemade soups, a salad bar, and fresh fruit smoothies are offered.

Small World Deli, 1149 First Street, Napa 94559; phone (707) 224–4500. Open 11:00 A.M. to 4:30 P.M. Monday–Saturday. No credit cards.

Even better is **Small World Restaurant,** which features food from Israel, specifically Nazareth, and around the world. Enjoy terrific falafel, lambo gyro, tri-tip pitas, thick smoothies, gourmet coffees, fresh pastries, and more in a slightly funky, comforting atmosphere.

> *Small World Restaurant, 928 Coombs Street, Napa 94559; phone (707) 224–7743. Open 8:30 A.M. to 5:30 P.M. Monday–Friday and 9:30 A.M. to 4:30 P.M. Saturday. Closed Sunday. No credit cards.*

SIGNIFICANT OTHERS

The immediate downtown center is not the only place in the city of Napa for good shopping and dining. Listed alphabetically, here are some other choice spots worth looking for.

Alexis Baking Company and Cafe is a hidden treasure in downtown Napa. Few visitors find it, but it is worth searching for. Alexis is a popular place to drop in for breakfast pastries and breads, teatime pastries and cakes, lunchtime daily special salads and soups, and adventurous burgers (love that gorgonzola!). The same informal goodies and two tasty specials ($10–$11) are offered for dinner Thursday and Friday. Alexis is a great place to stop before or after a movie at the downtown Uptown Theater.

> *Alexis Baking Company and Cafe, 1517 Third Street, Napa 94559; phone (707) 258–1827. Open from 6:30 A.M. to 6:00 P.M. Monday–Wednesday; 6:30 A.M. to 8:00 P.M. Thursday–Friday; 7:30 A.M. to 3:00 P.M. Saturday; 8:00 A.M. to 2:00 P.M. Sunday. No credit cards. Wheelchair accessible.*

The **Atlas Peak Grill** is everyone's favorite secret steak house, especially for those of us who claim that we no longer eat meat. At the northeast side of old Napa and near the Silverado Country Club, Atlas Peak is in a charming storybook cottage surrounded by flowers and greenery. Here you can sink your teeth into juicy, corn-fed beef that reflects another era, when Americans cared about whether their steak cuts were in the New York or Chicago style. Everything carnivorous here is perfect, from pork loin to filet mignon. Famous also for its perfect martinis, Atlas Peak provides an excellent chance to enjoy the best of Napa Valley's wines.

Atlas Peak Grill, 3342 Vichy Avenue at Monticello Road (Highway 121), Napa 94559; phone (707) 253–1455. Open for dinner only at 5:30 P.M. daily, summer; Wednesday–Sunday, winter. Full bar. Visa and American Express. Wheelchair accessible.

Posticino replaced longtime favorite Café Lucy with a casually elegant Italian restaurant in this intimate triangular room in an old house. The garden patio in front is a great place to sip, nibble, and watch shoppers go by. Chef/owner Marco Fiorini worked at the memorable Blue Fox in San Francisco and helped open the first Piatti in Yountville. At Posticino, Fiorini proudly serves all-natural, hormone and antibiotic-free beef and seafood in re-creating the cuisines of Emilia-Romagna, Lombardia, and Piemonte.

Antipasti include raw ahi tuna marinated with sweet onions, sun-dried tomatoes, and capers ($10.00), a soup of tortellini filled with prosciutto di Parma, mortadella, and Parmigiana Reggiano in chicken and beef broth ($9.00), and a Tuscan tomato and bread soup ($8.00).

Lunch salad specials are marinated tomatoes with cucumbers, sweet onions, soft croutons, and shaved Parmigiana Reggiano ($7.00), a tasty pulled-chicken spinach salad ($11.00), and a salad of grilled king salmon ($15.00). Panini, risotto, creative hand-crafted pastas, steaks, lamb loin chops, and fish of the day are added at dinner ($11.00 to $28.00). Interesting imported beers and wines.

Posticino, 1408 Clay Street, Napa 94559; phone (707) 255–9470, Web site www.posticinonapa.com. Open 11:00 A.M. to 10:00 P.M. Monday–Friday, noon to 10:00 P.M. Saturday. Beer and wine. Wheelchair accessible.

The **Depot Hotel** is something else entirely. The "longest continuously serving restaurant in Napa," this Depot Hotel (in contrast to the elegant one in Sonoma) is a T-shirt and elbows-on-the-table, after-work-on-Friday-night kind of place. The main dining-room walls have olive-green, floral-print wallpaper above fake wood paneling and green-squares linoleum on the floors. Waitresses who have been serving and living for a while engage in brief, matter-of-fact conversation and bring your dinner Italian "family style," which here means bowls of thick minestrone accompanied by Parmesan cheese, a bare-bones salad, a choice of pastas (try the malfatti or paper-thin ravioli, or both), and an entree (choices range from veal marsala to chicken livers, lamb chops, and steaks). And the whole dinner costs just $12.

Petto di Pollo in Crosta
(Breast of Chicken in Crust)

from Marco Fiorini, Posticino, Napa

FOR THE MEAT:

1 Tbs butter

2 Tbs olive oil

4 chicken breasts, boneless and skinless

sea salt and black pepper to taste

4 oz fresh porcini mushrooms, cleaned and sliced (substitute reconstituted dry porcini or other mushrooms)

2–4 oz parmigiano reggiano cheese, shaved thinly with a vegetable peeler

FOR THE VEGETABLES:

1 Tbs olive oil

2 fresh garlic cloves, chopped

$^1/_2$ lb fresh spinach

Pinch sea salt

Pinch black pepper

FOR THE SAUCE:

$^1/_2$ cup white wine

$1^1/_2$ Tbs butter

Preheat oven to 450 degrees. Heat large ovenproof skillet on stovetop to medium heat and add butter and oil.

Season chicken breasts on both sides with salt and pepper and place into skillet top side down. Continue to cook on the same side until the breasts are well browned and about halfway cooked through. Turn breasts over and continue to cook over medium heat. Arrange mushrooms over tops of breasts, covering most of the surface area. Then top with shaved parmigiano cheese, covering mushrooms and chicken completely; this will be your crust or "crosta."

Place skillet in oven and cook until chicken is cooked thoroughly and cheese has formed a nice brown crust. Remove skillet from oven and place onto stovetop.

In a separate skillet heat olive oil and garlic until garlic is lightly toasted. Add fresh spinach and sauté briefly until spinach just begins to wilt. Season with salt and pepper and place onto plate. Remove chicken breasts from skillet using a spatula and place on spinach. Return skillet to stovetop over medium heat and add wine. Continue cooking until wine has reduced by half. Add butter and whisk in until butter has completely dissolved. Remove from heat and pour reduction over top of chicken breast. Serve with Sauvignon Blanc or Chardonnay.

You can't miss here if you want to run into lots of locals mixed with winery owners having a good time. The wine list is local, limited, and inexpensive, offering Robert Mondavi Pinot Noir at $18.00, Louis M. Martini Cabernet Reserve at $10.00, and Sutter Home White Zinfandel at $9.50.

Depot Hotel, 806 Fourth Street, Napa 94559; phone (707) 252–4477. Open for dinner daily. Full bar. No credit cards. Not wheelchair accessible.

Many locals go to Jerry Shaffer's **Foothill Cafe** for his baby back ribs, said by many Napa and Sonoma chefs to be the best in the country. But everything on the menu is tantalizing. Located in an unlikely little strip mall northeast of many Carneros wineries on Old Sonoma Road, Foothill Cafe is open only for dinner, alas, and is "closed for therapy Monday and Tuesday."

Jerry's humor shows everywhere, from decor to menu. The walls are bright mustard yellow with silver grape leaves. Round mirrors seem to enlarge the tiny room, and a red-framed window hangs free just inside the door. The total effect is to suggest you are going to have fun here. Jerry suggests in print, "If our food, drinks and service aren't up to your standards . . . please lower your standards."

Be sure to try the "world renowned baby back ribs" ($15.50), half smoked chicken ($12.00), or braised lamb shank ($14.50). The Thai spinach and Caesar salads are excellent ($7.50 each). Desserts such as crème brûlée, cobblers, crisp, and chocolate indulgences are each $5.00. Enjoy—but be sure to call for reservations in advance.

Foothill Cafe, 2766 Old Sonoma Road, Napa 94559; phone (707) 252–6178. Open from 4:30 to 9:30 P.M. Wednesday–Sunday. Wine and beer. "We like cash and take Visa, MasterCard, American Express, and checks that don't bounce." Wheelchair accessible.

Genoa Delicatessen & Ravioli Factory is one of our favorites and has been ever since Kathleen was growing up in Berkeley and her mother used to go to the original Genoa Deli in Oakland (here since 1926) to get ravioli. Located in a strip mall on Trancas Boulevard, Genoa is worth tracking down for picnic supplies or an informal lunch or dinner. Here you will find the best in deli salads, minestrone and other soups, roasted chicken with garlic bread ($4.29), pastas, an excellent espresso and juice bar, and a wine shop with Napa Valley's best. Oh yes, and huge sandwiches ranging from $4.50 to $5.25, featuring maple turkey, Virginia baked ham, crab salad, head cheese, domestic prosciutto, bresaola, beef tongue, coppa Veneziana, and just about anything else you can imagine (but no peanut butter). Delivery is available.

Genoa is also a great place to buy dried pastas and olive oils, and it sells its famous pastas and sauces, frozen, in a case against the wall. Long live the DeVincenzi family, please!

> *Genoa Delicatessen & Ravioli Factory, 1550 Trancas Street, Napa 94558; phone (707) 253–8686. Wine and beer. Open from 9:00 A.M. to 6:30 P.M. Monday–Saturday, 9:00 A.M. to 5:00 P.M. Sunday. Visa, MasterCard, Diners Club, and JCB. Wheelchair accessible.*

While you're at the Napa Valley Airport, don't miss **Jonesy's Famous Steak House** and its sidekick cafe. Often rated the "Best Beef in the Napa Valley" (read: steaks) by locals, Jonesy's takes us fifty years back to another era, when it was cool to smoke and drink Manhattans. You can actually order a cottage cheese and peaches salad (small or large), shrimp Louies, Caesar salads, shrimp cocktails, or calamari ringers.

So many locals come here for lunch that tables in the lounge are reserved for the cafe's overflow crowd. For a real steak-house experience, eat in the dining room, where you'll find linen tablecloths. Jonesy's Famous Steak Dinners are "Hand-carved on Premises." Top sirloin steak starts at $12.95, including tossed green salad with Jonesy's bleu cheese dressing or soup and choice of potato or rice pilaf. Other steak meals are on the menu, as well as chicken and seafood dishes ($6.95–$24.95). You can even have a grilled ham and cheese sandwich ($5.95). The children's menu is equally generous, from grilled cheese sandwiches ($3.75) to steak ($5.75) with salad or soup, french fries, and Jell-O included.

A short but well-selected local wine list ranges from Hakusan Sake ($6.50) and Beringer Gamay Beaujolais ($12.00) to exceptional Silver Oak Cabernet Sauvignon ($45.00).

> *Jonesy's Famous Steak House, 2044 Airport Road (in the airport building), Napa 94558; phone (707) 255–2003. Open from 11:30 A.M. until people leave Tuesday–Sunday. Full bar. Corkage fee: $7.00. Visa, MasterCard, and American Express. Wheelchair accessible.*

Local favorite **Pearl** is a great, funky bistro with fun attitude and people. Nickie and Pete Zeller oversee everything in the triangular restaurant and casual patio, assisted by cochef Jose Bravo Guzman, with Jill Castro on desserts.

Immediately after ordering, you receive steaming hot focaccia (flat Italian bread) to die for. We like the special halibut soft tacos ($6.95), ahi tuna sandwich on a potato bun ($10.75), chicken verde with lime cream and house tortillas ($12.95), and New York Steak au poivre with blue cheese ($21.95). Don't miss the hex signs painted by local artist Kathy Dennett—they say everybody needs one to "protect your homes, crops and barns. . . ." There are also metal sculptures by Richard Mendelson, patio tables painted by Thea Witsil, and handmade pottery by Sherry Fournier, all local artists. Excellent short wine list. Along with the usual best places and travel guide recommendation stickers, Pearl proudly posts a Guide Dogs for the Blind Friendly Places sticker.

Pearl, 1339 Pearl Street, Suite 104, Napa 94559; phone (707) 224–9161. Open for lunch 11:30 A.M. to 2:00 P.M. and dinner 5:30 to 9:00 P.M. Tuesday–Saturday. Wine and beer. Corkage fee: $12.00 per 750 ml bottle, $6.00 of which is donated to the Humane Society of Napa County New Shelter Fund. Visa and MasterCard. Wheelchair accessible.

Uva Trattoria is well worth walking a half block up Clinton from Main Street. Local inhabitants Sean Pramuk and Giovanni Guerrera, Justin Siena High School classmates, have renovated and revitalized Uva. Sean and Giovanni bumped into one another as co–best men at a wedding, chatted about life goals in restaurants, bonded, and here is the result. Sean paid his dues working the front of the house at The French Laundry and Piatti, while Giovanni once owned the renowned Sam's Pizza in Napa, the site of the current Mary's Pizza Shack. Chef Jude cooked at Sonoma Piatti and Tra Vigne.

Working with huge rooms, Sean and Gio have hung green velvet panels to separate the bar from the largest room, improving acoustics and the ambience, and artfully use Fiesta ware plates, selecting colors to go with artwork hanging on the walls. Check out the fabulous collections of movie and star posters and photos, as well as old typewriters. The Bar@Uva offers inexpensive samples of antipasti, calamari fritti, clams, calamari salad, and other little tastes for less than $7.50.

The rest of the restaurant offers great salads and Italian appetizers, terrific homemade pastas, pizzas, and panini (most under $12.00), and excellent veal piccata ($16.50), grilled double-cut pork chops ($16.75), roast chicken, and steaks. Specials might include a risotto of Teleme cheese and green onions, grilled prawns and pancetta ($16.50), trout saltimboca with prosciutto di Parma

Arancini

from Giovanni Guerrera, Uva Trattoria, Napa

2 Tbs olive oil
¼ cup onions, diced small
1 bay leaf
1 cup Arborio rice
1 Tbs white wine
2 cups fresh chicken stock (homemade is always best)
1 tsp salt
¼ cup butter
¼ cup grated Parmesan cheese
pinch black pepper
¼ cup chopped parsley
¼ cup basil pesto
Teleme cheese
2 eggs
1 cup fine bread crumbs
olive oil

In a large saucepan, heat olive oil, sweet onions with bay leaf, and add rice. Stir 2 minutes, add white wine, and reduce heat. Stir and add ¼ cup chicken stock. Wait for the rice to absorb the liquid. Continue to add stock in ¼-cup portions until rice is done (about 20 minutes) and takes on a creamy consistency. Turn off heat. Add butter and Parmesan cheese. Stir until all is melted. Add basil pesto. Immediately spread out onto a sheet pan and let cool overnight.

With a large soup spoon, scoop risotto and shape into a ball. Form a small well in the ball with your finger, add small piece of Teleme, and pinch the well opening closed. Shape into a ball once again.

Beat eggs. Coat balls with egg mixture, then with bread crumbs. Let set overnight ("they sauté better when firm").

In a large sauté or saucepan, add olive oil until about 3 inches deep. Bring up to 350 degrees and gently add balls, a few at a time, into oil for 6–7 minutes or until golden brown. Serve with a dipping sauce such as marinara. Serve with Chardonnay.

($16.50), spinach and asparagus ($17.50), or Black Mission Fig and Arugula Salad with prosciutto di Parma ($7.00). Music five nights.

Uva offers rare Italian wines from Sicily, Puglia, and Campagne.

Uva Trattoria, 1040 Clinton (at Brown), Napa 94559; phone (707) 255–6646. Open from 11:30 A.M. to 10:00 P.M. Tuesday–Friday, 5:00 to 10:00 P.M. Saturday, and 4:00 to 9:00 P.M. Sunday. Full bar. Corkage fee: $10 waived with bottle wine purchase. Visa, MasterCard, and American Express. Wheelchair accessible.

3

Highway 29 (The St. Helena Highway)

W e will now take you up Highway 29—known locally and more fashionably as the St. Helena Highway. Road signs say 29, but merchants prefer to use St. Helena Highway in their addresses. Try not to be confused by the fact that Highway 29 is also called South St. Helena Highway, Main Street in St. Helena, St. Helena Highway North, and North St. Helena Highway. It's all the same road. If you don't want to explore the Napa Valley's wineries, restaurants, towns, and galleries quite this thoroughly, and decide to cut the tour short and head down the other side, just leap ahead in the book to the winery or restaurant you want.

We must emphasize the danger of turning left across Highway 29. Please make the crossing as few times as possible.

NAPA TO YOUNTVILLE

Four and a half miles north of the intersection of Highways 121 and 29, you'll come to a stoplight at an intersection, announced on overhead signs as Trancas Boulevard. What it doesn't tell you is that Trancas goes east from Highway 29, and Redwood Road heads west.

Take Redwood Road to the fabulous **Hess Collection**—the ultimate expression of owner and Swiss entrepreneur Donald Hess's two passions, wine and art. Get into the left lane so that you can ease left in 0.9 mile. Continue up Redwood about 4.5 miles and turn left into The Hess Collection and Mont La Salle Christian Brothers Monastery and Retreat House. The Hess Collection is just beyond the

Entrance to The Hess Collection

monastery. It belonged to the Christian Brothers until Donald Hess bought the facility in 1985.

The Hess Collection is an *absolutely do not miss!* destination. The architecture, the art collection, and the wines are among the best in California.

There's a bike rack for cyclists in the upper parking lot. Follow the wide brick path lined with oleander trees to the visitor center entrance on the right at the back of the courtyard. You will be struck by the elegant vestibule, with white walls and railings and blonde wood floors. The round window in the stairway between the second and third floors evocatively frames the round tops of the punch-down fermentation tanks, and the windows in the shop and tasting room frame the wine barrels.

Explore the art collection, which rotates, showing about 25 percent of Hess's private collection at a time. It includes works by Francis Bacon, Robert Motherwell, Georg Baselitz, Magdelena Abakanowicz, Franz Gertsch, Bruce Robbins, Henri Michaux, Emilio Vedova, Frank Stella, and many other great artists.

Hess Holding has an extended family of prominent wineries on other continents, including Glen Carlou and Impala in South Africa, Castello Vicchiomaggio in Italy, and Bodega Norton in Argentina.

Fine points: You *must* visit the shop here; it is the best in the wine country. The tasting fee is $5.00, $10.00 for Reserves. Featured wines: Chardonnay, Cabernet Sauvignon, Meritage, Zinfandel; from South Africa, Chardonnay and Gran Classique Reserve. Owner: Hess Holding. Winemaker: Dave Guffy. Executive Chef: Chad Hendrickson. Cases: 300,000. Acres: 400.

The Hess Collection, 4411 Redwood Road, Napa 94558; phone (707) 255–1144, Web site www.hesscollection.com. Open from 10:00 A.M. to 4:00 P.M. daily. Visa, MasterCard, and American Express. Wheelchair accessible.

As you leave The Hess Collection driveway, turn right down Redwood Road to Highway 29, and turn left (north).

Now we have you traveling northward on Highway 29, barely out of town, and if you're already hungry for lunch, stop immediately at one of our favorites, **Bistro Don Giovanni.** As soon as you see the mud-colored building on the right, turn off Highway 29 into the driveway. As you walk onto the restaurant's deck from the parking lot, you can decide whether to choose an outdoor table or to walk inside. The deck wraps around the northern and eastern sides of the building, away from highway traffic. Wine-industry locals hang out here to see who's arriving with whom.

When we ask locals for their favorite restaurants, nearly everyone starts the list with Don Giovanni, and for good reason. When you walk in, you're greeted by unpretentious hosts in an unpretentious atmosphere that reeks of confidence in taste and style. Don't miss the large painting on Italian newspapers of a cutlery set hanging against soft yellow walls in one corner of the dining room. Gigantic arrangements of blue, yellow, and white flowers set the tone.

Owners Donna and Giovanni Scala were opening chefs at the original Piatti in St. Helena and basically set the chain's standard for Claude Rouas and his partners. Here at their own bistro, they have the luxury of doing it their own Italian-French way. What a relaxing pleasure! The staff is terrific, too.

The wood-burning oven and pantry fill one corner in the room, with the mesquite grill and rest of the kitchen behind glass, off to the side. Donna serves the perfect Caesar salad ($8.75), complete with an actual anchovy and large enough to share as an appetizer; and the beet and haricots verts salad ($8.50) is always a memorable treat. The Maine crab cakes ($10.00) are elegantly

Entrance to Bistro Don Giovanni

Silk Handkerchiefs al Pesto

from Giovanni and Chef Donna Scala, Bistro Don Giovanni, Napa

FOR THE SILK HANDKERCHIEFS:

1 lb all-purpose flour
5 eggs
2 Tbs dry white wine

FOR THE PESTO:

2 cups clean basil, stems removed
1¼ cups extra virgin olive oil
1 clove garlic
3 Tbs toasted pine nuts
Salt to taste
½ cup Pecorino cheese
3 Tbs Grana Padano cheese

OTHER:

½ lb haricots verts (green beans), ends removed and par-cooked
6 small yellow new potatoes (boiled in salted water, peeled, and diced)

For the silk handkerchiefs: Knead all ingredients until dough is smooth and silky. Let rest for 1 hour. Roll out thin sheets of dough and cut into 3" to 4" squares.

For the pesto: Puree basil, oil, garlic, pine nuts, and salt in a blender or mortar and pestle until smooth. Fold in cheese.

For the pasta: Cook dough squares in boiling salted water. Add beans and potatoes to the water to warm briefly. Drain squares, beans, and potatoes and toss in a bowl to coat with pesto, butter, and a little of the pasta water to emulsify the sauce. Serve and garnish with a little of the Pecorino cheese. Serves 2–4. Serve with Sauvignon Blanc.

light—topped with avocado salsa and accompanied with a fennel slaw dressed in oil and vinegar. Kathleen's favorite forget-the-cholesterol is the fritto misto of calamari and rock shrimp ($9.75). Even if you usually don't like clams, try Donna's Linguini and Clams ($17.75), a dish she prepared for Giovanni's mother in Naples—who exclaimed that they were actually better than her own! All pastas and breads are housemade. The Sonoma duck confit risotto ($19.50) is to die for. Don't miss the roasted whole fish if it is offered. Steak frites ($28.00) is always reliable. Kids like the Pizza Per Bambini with tomato and cheese, with fries and "no green stuff" ($10.75). We have friends who come here for drinks in the evening and happily make a meal of appetizers with terrific celebrity sightings.

> *Bistro Don Giovanni, 4110 Howard Lane, off St. Helena Highway, Napa 94558; phone (707) 224–3300, Web site www.bistrodon giovanni.com. Open for lunch and dinner daily. MasterCard, Visa, and American Express. Wheelchair accessible.*

Trefethen Estate Vineyards is the first winery you come to north of here; it is also one of the most congenial and fun. To get here, turn east onto tree-lined Oak Knoll Avenue off Highway 29. One-half mile later, turn left onto Eshcol Drive, named for the Eshcol Ranch vineyard and winery located here from 1886 to 1940. Notice the labels on vineyards to help you know what varietals you're passing and the one hundred sycamore trees, planted in the late 1990s, whose shade we will welcome someday. Turn left at the large oak tree onto Trefethen Lane, and continue until you reach the pink wood winery with brown trim.

   As you get out of your car, enjoy the large, 500-year-old valley and cork oak and the gardens full of old farming equipment, along with marked and identified

Trefethen Estate Vineyards

Riesling Spring Rolls

from Janet Trefethen, Trefethen Estate Vineyards, Napa

NOTE: Janet Trefethen served these Riesling Spring Rolls as an hors d'oeuvre when Julia Child came to Trefethen Estate Vineyards in 1992 to film Christmas dinner for ABC's *Good Morning America.*—Kathleen Hill

FOR THE SPRING ROLLS:

1 lb crabmeat, cooked and chopped

4 small yellow onions, peeled and chopped fine

2 cups bean sprouts

$\frac{1}{2}$ cup green cabbage, shredded

4 nam prik or jalapenos, seeded and chopped

4 garlic cloves, minced

4 Tbs fish sauce

4 Tbs soy sauce

2 Tbs sugar

1 bunch cilantro, chopped

1 bunch mint, chopped

8 8-inch rice papers

$\frac{1}{2}$ cup Trefethen Estate Dry Riesling

$\frac{1}{2}$ cup cold water

FOR THE GINGER SESAME DRESSING:

2 cups seasoned rice vinegar

2 Tbs soy sauce

5 Tbs finely chopped fresh ginger

3 Tbs toasted sesame seeds

4 green onions, trimmed and minced

4 Tbs sesame oil

For the spring rolls: Mix all ingredients together except rice papers and wine. Soak rice papers in Riesling and cold water for 4 minutes. Place equal amounts of mixture into each rice paper and roll up, egg-roll style, tucking in sides to enclose filling.

For the dressing: Blend together all ingredients except oil. Add oil slowly, drip by drip, whisking well with each addition. Use immediately or refrigerate. Whisk thoroughly before using.

Drizzle dressing on top of spring rolls and serve extra dressing on the side for dipping. Makes 8 servings. Serve with Trefethen Estate Dry Riesling.

plants and rows of herbs, from anise to rosemary. Built by James and George Goodman and designed by Captain Hamden McIntyre in 1886, the winery is listed in the National Register of Historic Places.

While Gene Trefethen was still president of Oakland's Kaiser Industries, he and Katie spotted this run-down old treasure and couldn't resist. Gene had only overseen construction of Hoover Dam and the San Francisco–Oakland Bay Bridge—that's all! So what was a mere 600 acres to replant, rebuild, and organize? After son John got his MBA at Stanford, he and his wife, Janet, joined the winery. Both serve as managing director, making Trefethen the largest contiguous family-owned and -operated vineyard acreage in the Napa Valley.

The brick floors and cedar walls in the tasting room set the mood, framing an excellent selection of cookbooks and guidebooks. The Trefethens attract cooking celebrations and classes, and Julia Child even cooked Christmas dinner here for *Good Morning America* in 1992. Reflecting the Trefethens' community and political involvement, their wines were served at Reagan and Clinton White House dinners for Queen Elizabeth II, the queen of Thailand, and a French president. Trefethen remains the only wooden gravity-flow winery and the largest estate-vineyard winery in the Napa Valley.

Aside from the wine biz, John is a pilot and motorcyclist. Once a Miss Rodeo California, Janet is an expert in food and wine matching, a leader of the quest for a local appellation designation, and an occasional speaker at the Culinary Institute of America's Hyde Park, New York, campus.

Under Janet Trefethen's leadership, the Napa Valley Cooking Class, featuring great chefs from around the United States, has taken place at the winery since 1973. For Trefethen's thirtieth anniversary in 1998, Trefethen held a cooking class given by four thirty-year-old chefs teaching thirty students, sponsored a Club 30 Recipe Contest for culinary professionals, and celebrated dinners honoring some of the country's top chefs' thirty-year-old protégés, with all proceeds from the dinners benefiting charitable causes fighting world hunger.

Oh yes, the wine. To hint at the quality, Trefethen's 1976 Chardonnay ranked number one in the world at the 1979 World Wine Olympics, sponsored by the French magazine *Gault Millau*. The next year Burgundy winemaker Joseph Drouhin challenged the '79 results, resulting in a second competition, this time at the esteemed Hospice de Beaune. Guess what? Trefethen won again, much to the disappointment of Monsieur Drouhin (who also once challenged the results when Oregon's Eyrie Pinot Noir finished in the top three at a Paris blind tasting. After Eyrie's wine finished a close second in retasting, Drouhin opened his own winery in Oregon's Dundee Hills.)

Fine points: Featured wines: Chardonnay, Dry Riesling, Cabernet Sauvignon, Cabernet Franc, Merlot. Tasting fee: $10, $20 for Reserves. Owners: Trefethen family. Winemaster: David Whitehouse Jr. Winemaker: Peter Luthi. Cases: 65,000. Acres: 600.

Trefethen Estate Vineyards, 1160 Oak Knoll Avenue, Napa 94558; phone (707) 255–7700 or (800) 556–4847, Web site www.trefethen.com. Open from 10:00 A.M. to 4:30 P.M. daily. MasterCard, Visa, and American Express. Wheelchair accessible.

Back to Highway 29. Just north of Trefethen and on the other side of Highway 29 you will find **Koves-Newlan Vineyards & Winery** on Solano Avenue, which parallels the highway. Newlan is definitely a family affair, with founder Bruce Newlan and winemaker Glen Newlan almost always available to talk about their exciting wines.

To get here, turn left across Highway 29 at Oak Knoll (or straight across the divided highway, ½ highway at a time please, from Trefethen) and turn north (right) onto Solano Avenue. Or turn west (left) from Highway 29 onto Darms Lane and left again onto Solano.

Bruce told us, "It doesn't take a rocket scientist to make wine," with an enticing twinkle in his eye. Yes, he was a rocket scientist for Lockheed Missiles in Sunnyvale. He worked on the *Polaris, Poseidon,* and *Trident* programs. Ultimately, his family's farm roots grow deeper, though. Bruce and son Glen, the current winemaker, used to buy grapes near Gilroy and ferment them in the garage. After working as a computer whiz in Santa Clara, Glen moved to Napa with his wife, Jerri-Lynn. Their young son, Ryan, is "a train fanatic who watches the Wine Train ride by the vineyard every day."

The Newlans bought their first acreage in Napa Valley in 1967 and turned the thirteen-acre mess of a walnut orchard into a Cabernet Sauvignon vineyard. Bruce took courses at UC Davis, read viticulture texts, and soon began selling his grapes to Inglenook, Clos du Val, and Robert Mondavi. When he discovered that his grapes usually ended up in the wineries' reserve or cask bottlings, he decided that he should make his own wine, if they were that good. Recently the Newlan family was joined by the Sato family, creating Koves-Newlan wines.

As you enter the California-style stucco building, you immediately run into a railing, which overlooks the small winery and the cozy tasting room. You are at eye level with wine barrels. Walk down the few stairs to the left to see everything.

Fine points: Newlan's Cabernet Sauvignon and Zinfandel have been rated in the 90s by Robert Parker Jr., and Jerry Mead, creating a great demand nationally. Every part of the winemaking process here is "simple and slow." Tasting fee: $5.00 to $7.00, including keepsake glass. Featured wines: Chardonnay, Pinot Noir, Cabernet Sauvignon, Zinfandel, Late Harvest Riesling, Merlot. Owner: Newlan and Sato families. Winemaker: Glen Newlan. Cases: 15,000. Acres: 43.

Koves-Newlan Vineyards & Winery, *5225 Solano Avenue, Napa 94558; phone (707) 257–2399 or (800) 500–9463, Web site www.kovesnewlanwine.com. Open from 10:00 A.M. to 5:00 P.M. daily with tours at 2:00 and 4:00 P.M. MasterCard and Visa. Not wheelchair accessible.*

South of Koves-Newlan is the brightest new winery addition to the Napa wine scene, **Laird Family Estate,** a true family endeavor. Ken and Gail Laird have been growing great grapes for other vintners since 1970 and are the largest landowners in the Napa Valley. Daughter Rebecca serves as general manager. Laird Family wines have earned three 92 ratings from *Wine Spectator* magazine.

Striking even from Highway 29 is the pyramid-shaped berm, cooled by nature, in which wine is stored. Twenty-two tenant wineries form a custom crush cooperative here, including Merryvale's 67,000 cases and well-known winemakers such as Ann Colgan and Paul Hobbs. The Lairds never expect their own wines to comprise more than 5 percent of the total they will produce, genuinely wanting to offer independent winemakers a place to perform their art and craft. They also use only 2.5 percent of the grapes they grow in their own wines, selling the rest to other wineries.

Enjoy some of the best wine accoutrements at the best prices, including shirts, glasses, and books. Laird reeks elegance and good taste. Enjoy! Picnics are welcomed.

Fine points: Featured wines: Estate-grown Laird and Bayview Vineyards Chardonnay, Merlot, Cabernet Sauvignon. Owners: Ken and Gail Laird. Winemaker: Paul Hobbs. Cases: Laird: 3,300; 120,000 for others. Acres: 2,000, lease 600 more.

Laird Family Estate, 5055 Solano, Napa 94558; phone (707) 257–0360 or (877) 297–4889, Web site www.lairdfamilyestate.com. Open from 10:00 A.M. to 5:00 P.M. daily by appointment (make it here). Tasting fee: $7.00 to $10.00. Visa, MasterCard, and American Express. Wheelchair accessible.

Your next stop could be Yountville, or you can just drive north on Solano Avenue and cross California Drive at the Veterans' Home to visit Domaine Chandon.

YOUNTVILLE

Just over 4 miles north of the Highway 29–Trancas Boulevard intersection, take the Yountville exit for elegant small-town wine-country shopping, dining, wine tasting, and the Napa Valley Museum and newly renovated Lincoln Theater on the grounds of the California Veterans' Home. As you turn off the highway to the right, turn right again and then immediately left at the stop sign and Washington Street to tour "downtown" Yountville. New resort hotels abound, as Yountville has made a decision to welcome visitors with open arms.

A historic town along the wine trail, Yountville is now known for its outstanding restaurants, such as The French Laundry, Bistro Jeanty, Bouchon, Domaine Chandon, Pacific Blues Cafe, the Napa Valley Grille, Gordon's Cafe and Wine Bar, Cucina à la Carte, and Compadres. The California Veterans' Home was established here in 1882 by veterans of the Mexican and Civil wars as a home for all veterans west of the Rocky Mountains. In 1900 the state of California bought it for a twenty-dollar gold piece. You can visit the Veterans' Home Museum as well as the Napa Valley Museum here.

On the west side of Highway 29 in Yountville is the open-to-the-public golf course and restaurant called **Lakeside Grill.** Locals say the grill's breakfast is the best in Yountville, with large portions, fresh ingredients, and great views of the small lake, golf course, and mountains that line the Napa Valley.

Lunch and dinner include burgers, steak sandwiches, grilled fresh albacore on focaccia with chipotle aioli, a club sandwich, a BLT of applewood-smoked bacon and crab salad, a Southwestern Caesar salad with blackened chicken and shaved Parmesan cheese, Bay shrimp or calamari salads, grilled salmon, and rib-eye steak. Everything is under $10.

The golf course is lush and the fees are inexpensive, ranging from $10 early bird (before 8:00 A.M.) and $12 for Napa Valley residents to $18 to play nine holes, $16 to $24 for eighteen holes. Golf carts range from $12 to $24.

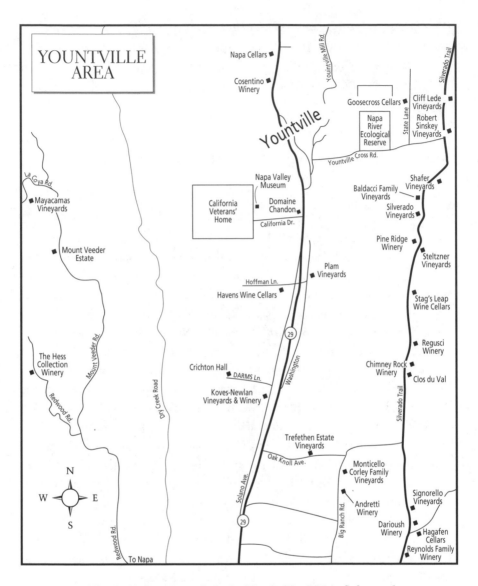

Yountville Golf Course and Lakeside Grill, 7801 *Solano Avenue, Yountville* 94599; *phone* (707) 944–1992. *Open from* 7:00 A.M. *to* 8:00 P.M. *daily. Full bar. Visa, MasterCard, and American Express. Wheelchair accessible.*

Yountville's new Yountville Inn and Villagio Inn and Spa are among Napa Valley's most convenient and pleasant accommodations (see chapter 5, Where to Stay in the Napa Valley).

The new **Wine Garden Food & Wine Bar** replaced The Diner, a Yountville institution that closed a couple of years ago.

Will and Julie Nord, of the highly respected Nord family and innovators in sustainable vineyard farming, lured Executive Chef Michael Bilger away from Carneros Restaurant at The Lodge at Sonoma in Sonoma to create a fun "small plates" restaurant in the Napa Valley.

The Wine Garden's menu is divided into sections called Ocean & Stream, Field & Farm, Ranch & Range, Sweet Finales, Additions, Hops & Barley, Beans & Leaves, and Boys & Girls (kids 15 and under). At the top of the menu is the lure of a Napa Valley Shooter, which here includes California Osetra Caviar, a Shot of Mumm DVX, and fresh raspberry ($10.00).

Four Hog Island Oysters from Tomales Bay come on the half shell, crispy in cornmeal with chili aioli, or hickory smoked with bacon and molasses BBQ sauce ($10.00).

"Small plates" means small portions are served on salad or bread and butter plates, with the intention that visitors share tastes and order lots of small plates since none is large enough to satisfy one person.

Here you can sample Dungeness crab Louis, Day Boat scallops, trout almandine, mussels, Florida rock shrimp, crispy sopitos with Alaskan halibut, liberty duck tamales, salads, macaroni gratin, stuffed quail, Berkshire Farms pork pozole with morel mushrooms, sweetbreads, organic hanger steak, Smithfield ham wrapped venison with New York huckleberries and mustard spaetzle, french fries with house-made ketchup, and even an Ode to the Diner, which includes two buttermilk milkshakes with candied cherries, and the Real American Cheese Plate with the best organic cheeses around. All small plates range from $6.00–$15.00.

The wine list is an exceptional collection of sustainably grown wines, all of which contain grapes tended by the Nords' Nord Coast Vineyard Service (NcVs) and are available retail to take with you in the wine shop just to the right as you enter the restaurant. Enjoy the "wine bottle bathrooms," which are worth the trip, jazz on Saturday evenings (indoors or out), and special flights of wine tasting.

Wine Garden Food and Wine Bar, 6476 Washington Street, Yountville 94599; phone (707) 945–1002, Web site www.napawinegarden.com. Beer and wine. Open 11:30 A.M. to 9:00 P.M. Sunday–Thursday, 11:30 A.M. to 11:00 P.M. Friday–Saturday. Visa, MasterCard, and American Express. Wheelchair accessible.

The local phenomenon **Ranch Market Too** supplies locals and transients with basic food needs such as blood oranges and a few veggies, brooms, soap, and other sundries. Many office workers slip in the side door facing Bistro Jeanty's parking lot for a deli sandwich ($3.65) and Bud's ice cream. A true country store with red-and-white checked curtains, Ranch Market makes you feel as if you're really on vacation.

> *Ranch Market Too, 6498 Washington Street, Yountville 94599; phone (707) 944–2662. Open from 6:00 A.M. to 10:00 P.M. No credit cards. Wheelchair accessible.*

One door up the street is **Bistro Jeanty,** the creation of former Domaine Chandon executive chef Philippe Jeanty, who enjoys one of the greatest followings in the Napa Valley. The Champagne native shed the corporate umbrella to strike out on his own and give birth to a "homey place where my little daughter can come in anytime." Philippe is often back in the tiny kitchen, to the good fortune of his new and loyal customers, although his time is now divided by the Bistro, Père Jeanty steakhouse up Washington Street, and Jeanty at Jack's, his version of the original Jack's started in 1864 at 615 Sacramento Street, San Francisco (415–693–0941; www.jeantyjacks.com).

One of the greatest benefits of this bistro is that we can enjoy Philippe's food at prices lower than at Domaine Chandon. He truly wants you to come by regularly, be comfortable, and greet your friends. On the door facing Washington Street, Philippe has handwritten the hours and specials, making the whole greeting reminiscent of a Paris neighborhood bistro, with half curtains and little floor tiles. Outdoor tables face south and the parking lot, while French antiques fill the dining rooms. Terra-cotta flower pots planted with miniature roses decorate the tables. Framed French posters hang on the walls, and recorded Edith Piaf warbles reach even the patio tables, creating an even greater allure to us than spraying garlic into the fans. A small sign on the door proclaims CHIEN LUNATIQUE (mad dog) to all who should not be here.

You enjoy the same menu at lunch and dinner, featuring appetizers of smoked trout and potatoes in olive oil ($10.50), rabbit pâté with celery root salad ($10.50), pigs feet with haricots verts (green bean) salad ($9.50), beet salad with feta and asparagus ($8.50), and tomato soup in puff pastry ($8.50). Main courses may include mussels in red wine ($16.50), classic sole meunière ($18.50), veal kidneys with peppercorn sauce ($21.50), steak tartare ($16.50), and cassoulet

Bistro Jeanty Tomato Soup

from Pierre Jeanty, Bistro Jeanty and Père Jeanty, Yountville

$^1/_2$ cup plus 2 Tbs unsalted butter
$^1/_2$ lb yellow onions, sliced
$2^1/_2$ lbs tomatoes, ripe, cored and quartered
6 garlic cloves
$^1/_4$ cup tomato paste
1 bay leaf
$^1/_2$ Tbs whole black peppercorns
1 tsp dried thyme
1 cup water (use only if tomatoes are not ripe and juicy)
4 cups heavy cream
Salt and pepper to taste
$^1/_2$ tsp ground white pepper
1 lb puff pastry, defrosted if frozen
1 egg, beaten with 1 Tbs water

Melt $^1/_2$ cup butter in a large stockpot over medium-low heat. Add the onions, cover, and cook for about 5 minutes. Do not let the onions color. Add the tomatoes, garlic, tomato paste, bay leaf, peppercorns, thyme, and water if needed. Simmer over low heat for 30–40 minutes, until the tomatoes and onions are very soft. Puree in a blender (working in batches) or use a handheld immersion blender and strain.

Return the soup to the pot. Add cream, salt, pepper, white pepper, and the remaining 1–2 Tbs butter to taste. Bring soup back to boil. Let the soup cool for two hours or overnight in the refrigerator.

Divide soup among six 8-oz. soup cups or bowls.

Roll out the puff pastry to $^1/_4$ inch. Cut 6 rounds slightly larger than the cups or bowls for the soup. Paint the dough with the egg wash and turn the circles egg-wash side down over the tops of the cups, pulling lightly on the sides to make the dough tight like a drum.

Preheat oven to 450 degrees.

Lightly paint the top of the dough rounds with egg wash without pushing the dough down. Bake for 10–15 minutes until the dough is golden brown. Do not open the oven door in the first few minutes or the dough will fall. Serve immediately. Serves 6.

($22.50). Desserts and dessert wines, ports, cognacs, and brandies are all very special.

> *Bistro Jeanty, 6510 Washington Street, Yountville 94599; phone (707) 944–0103. Open from 11:30 A.M. to 10:30 P.M. daily. Full bar. Corkage fee: $15 (one corkage waived for every bottle bought from the extensive wine list). MasterCard, Visa, and American Express. Wheelchair accessible.*

Next door, to the north of Bistro Jeanty, is the **Antique Fair,** a collection of interesting French antiques and furnishings, some from estates in Lyon and Paris. This is a great spot to find interesting old beds, silverware, armoires, jewelry, and figurines. Locals and visitors have found the antiques here intriguing for almost thirty years. Browse with care. Be sure to catch the Noël Française here from Thanksgiving to December 31, 10:00 A.M. to 9:00 P.M., during Yountville's Festival of Lights.

> *Antique Fair, 6512 Washington Street, Yountville 94599; phone (707) 944–8440, Web site www.antiquefair.com. Open from 10:00 A.M. to 5:00 P.M. daily. MasterCard, Visa, and American Express. Wheelchair accessible.*

Hurley's Restaurant & Bar filled a void and oft empty restaurant here. A fun "family restaurant," Hurley's has lots of promotional events, such as "fish Fridays" in July and August, music on the patio in September, Oktoberfest guess when, and Wild Game Week November 1–6 featuring wild boar, pheasant, buffalo, venison, caribou, sailfish, and antelope, followed by a crab festival with Dungeness crab prepared "every which way" November 22–December 4, except for Thanksgiving Day, when they offer a $35 prix fixe Thanksgiving feast.

Owner Bob Hurley and general manager Jerry Lampe are both distinguished alumni of the now defunct Napa Valley Grille, which was just up the road.

Try the Bell River crab cakes with watercress and molasses vinaigrette ($11.00); butternut squash ravioli with prosciutto and reggiano cheese ($16.00); steamed mussels with Caggiano chorizo and red wine ($9.00); house cured gravlax ($10.00); Delta crayfish risotto ($17.00); Blue Nose sea bass ($20.00); roasted chicken with lemon preserve, caramelized pearl onions, and broccoli rabe ($18.00), pork chops with cranberry and crowder beans and ham hock ragout ($18.00); spicy vegetarian Moroccan Tagine with eggplant, roasted peppers, tomatoes, and couscous ($14.00); and grilled rib eye steak or lamb chops with

My Mother's Strawberry Shortcake

from Bob I lurley, Hurley's Restaurant & Bar, Yountville

FOR THE BISCUIT:

4 cups all-purpose flour
¼ cup sugar
2 Tbs baking powder
1 tsp salt
2 sticks cold butter, cubed
1½ cups cream

FOR THE STRAWBERRIES:

2 baskets strawberries, washed and cut
3 Tbs sugar
whipped cream

Preheat oven to 350 degrees.

For the biscuits: Sift all dry ingredients into a bowl and mix well. Work butter into mixture until it is the size of peas. Work in cream until it comes together. Do not overmix. Spread mixture onto floured surface, roll to 1-inch thickness, cut out circles with cutter, and place on lightly oiled baking sheet. Brush tops lightly with cream and sprinkle with sugar. Bake for 25–30 minutes. Let cool 20 minutes.

For the strawberries: Put strawberries in a bowl, add sugar, and stir gently.

Cut biscuits in half, spread with butter, sprinkle evenly with sugar, and place under broiler until they bubble lightly. Put equal amounts of strawberries on each half and spoon on a generous dollop of whipped cream. Sprinkle with powdered sugar and garnish with a sprig of mint. Makes 8.

orzo, baby carrots, oil cured olives, and roasted shallot jus (each $28.00). Then there's always the Black Angus burger with Vermont cheddar and fries ($10.00), grilled mozzarella on ciabatta bread ($10.00), and their signature poached tuna pan bagnat ($12.00). Great value side orders include grilled asparagus, buttermilk mashed potatoes, a bowl of french fries, or macaroni and cheese (all $3.50).

Hurley's Restaurant & Bar, 6518 Washington Street, Yountville 94599; phone (707) 944-2345, Web site www.hurleysrestaurant.com. Open 11:30 A.M. to 10:00 P.M. daily. Full bar. Corkage fee: $10, waived with bottle purchase. Visa, MasterCard, and American Express. Wheelchair accessible.

Bouchon was created by the Keller brothers of The French Laundry (Yountville) and Fleur de Lys (San Francisco) as a bistro where people in the restaurant business could go for great food after work, but we are not sure just how often restaurant staff could actually afford to dine here.

Be sure to try Bouchon if you can't get into The French Laundry, which usually requires reservations months ahead. The food is sublime and less formal than its parent's but equally adventurous. The menu is the same day and night.

Appetizers range from pâté de campagne ($10.50) to excellent classic onion soup ($8.50), a *terrine de foie gras de canard* with toasted baguette ($45.00 for 5 oz), and sheep's, cow's, and goat cheese tastes ($9.50–$14.25).

Select from a whole *fruits de mer* menu featuring six shellfish or a *petit* or *grand plateau* combination ($45.00–$85.00), truly French salads, six cheeses, and entrees from an open-faced sandwich or croque madame ($14.95), pan roasted trout aux amandes ($22.00), to white sausage with potato puree and sautéed prunes ($17.50), flatiron steak frites ($21.50), or leg of lamb with flageolets ($23.50).

Here, too, you can combine sides of french fries, cauliflower gratin, potato puree, sautéed spinach, and olives, all in the $4.50–$5.50 range.

Bouchon, 6534 Washington Street, Yountville 94599; phone (707) 944–8037. Open from 11:30 A.M. to 2:30 P.M., 5:30 to 10:30 P.M., with limited menu in the afternoon and until 12:30 A.M. daily. Full bar. Visa, MasterCard, and American Express. Wheelchair accessible.

Thomas Keller of The French Laundry and Bouchon here in Yountville has created an instant hit with **Bouchon Bakery,** which shares a casually elegant garden courtyard with his Bouchon restaurant. Here you will find the most sumptuous "Madeleines" this side of France, braided breads, baguettes, levain, pain au lait, walnut bread (as well as currant and cranberry, flax with sesame seeds, and herb-roasted olive), brioche, croissants, muffins, scones, flavored macaroons and other cookies, tarts, coffee drinks, and divine sandwiches such as the ham and Gruyère cheese on a baguette, tomato and mozzarella on ciabatta bread, and roast turkey on potato chive bread.

Get there early for Bouchon's signature Chocolate Bouchon brownie. "Bouchon" means cork, so the chocolate Bouchon is shaped like a stand-up wine cork and made of and filled with Valrhona chocolate that makes it gooey heaven and messy to eat with your fingers. Everyone working at Bouchon Bakery can answer questions. Enjoy Illy coffees as the perfect companion to Bouchon treats.

Bouchon Bakery, 6528 Washington Street, Yountville 94599; phone (707) 944–BAKE. Open 7:00 A.M. to 7:00 P.M. daily. Visa, MasterCard, and American Express. Wheelchair accessible but tight.

North of Bouchon, wander among a small complex of shops and galleries in Beard Plaza, including Images Fine Art, Artistry in Gold, Raku Ceramics, Raspberry's Art Glass Gallery, and Visions-Nature's Art.

Just for the heck of it, visit fun and charming Peggy Murray at her **Mosswood,** a shop to enhance your garden. Peggy left the fast-paced world of public relations to own Mosswood, where she offers exquisite garden sculpture and statuary.

Mosswood, 6550 Washington Street, Yountville 94599; phone (707) 944–8151. Open from 10:00 A.M. to 5:30 P.M. daily. MasterCard, Visa, American Express, and Diners Club. Wheelchair accessible.

If you're ready for a splurge, make reservations to have lunch or dinner at **The French Laundry,** another block north on Washington Street at Creek Street, in a century-old, two-story stone house with no sign. The James Beard Foundation named owner/chef Thomas Keller the best chef in the United States in 1997.

The French Laundry

Keller's wry humor means to deceive and intrigue with occasional simplified names attached to complex dishes.

Keller has expanded his empire with the new and highly respected Perse in New York's Time Warner Center Complex at Columbus Circle, Bouchon Las Vegas in the Venetian Resort-Hotel Casino's Venezia Tower, and Bouchon Bakery right here in Yountville.

Originally a bar and brothel and then (yes) a French laundry, the building and exquisite tranquil gardens with raised beds of daffodils and vegetables melt away any anxiety if you have to wait for your table. Reservations are mandatory for the eleven-table dining room. You may select from the five-course regular or vegetarian menus or the nine-course degustation (tasting) menu. Dress code of no jeans or tennis shoes and coats and ties required for men is enforced.

The nine-course Chef's Tasting Menu is $150. The nine-course Vegetarian Tasting Menu costs $125, and the five-course menu is $135.

Lunch is served only Friday through Sunday. The nine-course orgy may include Sabayon pearl tapioca with Baga duce oysters and Iranian Osetra caviar, salad of asparagus and black truffles, grilled pavé of Hawaiian tuna Nicoise, poached Maine lobster, chicken and dumplings, roasted braised Swiss chard and Walla Walla shallot purée, and much more.

The French Laundry is a member of two prestigious French organizations, Relais & Chateaux and Relais Gourmands.

The French Laundry, 6640 Washington Street, Yountville 94599; phone (707) 944–2380, Web site www.frenchlaundry.com, reservations through www.opentable.com. Open for lunch 11:00 A.M. to 1:00 P.M. Friday–Sunday, dinner 5:30 to 9:00 P.M. nightly, except Sunday. Book reservations two months ahead. MasterCard, Visa, and American Express. Wheelchair accessible.

Jessup Cellars has opened an exciting new tasting room in "downtown" Yountville, well located between The French Laundry and Gordon's Cafe and Wine Bar, and across from Pere Jeanty steakhouse.

With Volakis Art Gallery sharing the new small adobe-looking complex, Pam Jessup has her offices next door in Yountville's tiny original jail.

Both Pam and Mark Jessup grew up in Napa, which is unusual in these parts and in the Napa Valley wine business. Mark is a first-generation winemaker, meaning they saved their money, bought their land, learned the business, and have done it all themselves, unlike others in the valley whose fathers and grand-fathers left a legacy. He also worked at Mondavi, and Pam pursued activism and a career as a family disability specialist.

Designed by architect John Kaston, the small, elegant tasting room is lots of fun, with memorabilia of uncle Bill Jessup's career with the San Francisco 49ers football team, lots of artwork, and unusual palate cleansers of mini-'Nilla Wafers to dip in Jessup's Zinfandel Chocolate Port Sauce.

Jessup's wines are unfiltered and estate-grown with low sulfur. Enjoy the outdoor fireplace facing the street and Pere Jeanty with weekend jazz and appe-tizers before dinner at one of Yountville's renowned restaurants.

Fine points: Featured wines: Zinfandel, Merlot, Cabernet Sauvignon, Zinfandel Port. Owners: Pam and Mark Jessup. Winemaker: Mark Jes-sup. Cases: 4,000. Acres: 50.

Jessup Cellars, 6740 Washington Street, Yountville 94599; phone (707) 944–8525, Web site www.jessupcellars.com. Open 11:00 A.M. to 6:00 P.M. daily. Visa and MasterCard. Wheelchair accessible.

On a more economical but still high culinary level, don't miss **Gordon's Cafe and Wine Bar,** another block north on Washington. The sign says Gordon's Market.

Sally Gordon first visited the store run by the Tenaci family in 1967. She moved to the Napa Valley in 1977. We first met her as the public relations direc-tor at Domaine Chandon when we accompanied M. F. K. Fisher there for lunch every year to celebrate her birthday and Bastille Day.

Gordon's is immensely popular with locals at breakfast and lunch, and its Friday dinners sell out every week. When you walk in, you feel as if you're enter-ing a cozy country store. On your right, Chef Mari Tola, formerly of Mustards Grill and Table 29 (now Bistro Don Giovanni), and friends cook right in the room, and to the left shelves of well-selected delicacies line the wall. You will find Tazo teas, Potluck Studios bowls, V. G. Buck olive oils, The French Press Virgin Filbert Oil, Sparrow Lane vinegars, the *San Francisco Chronicle,* and the *New York Times.* Along the back of the left wall is an admirable collection of local wines for sale. And, miracle of miracles, when you select a bottle to accompany your Friday dinner, Sally sells it to you at the shelf price, without the customary restau-rant increase.

Gordon's sells and uses our favorite della Fattoria and Acme breads and serves elegant sandwiches and salads ($8.50). If it happens to be on special, try the sandwich of roasted eggplant with sweet red peppers; Italian tomato, sausage, and lentil soup; corned beef and Gruyère on rye; and always the genuine *croque monsieur*, a grilled ham-and-cheese sandwich made with French toast. The homemade raspberry lemonade is a must-try. Locals play chess or cards while eating huge bowls of oatmeal at 1:30 P.M., and we love the espresso bar beyond the kitchen. Sally cooks and bakes on weekends. Try the perfect breakfasts such as the house omelette with Gruyère, white cheddar, or goat cheese and fresh herbs ($8.95). Not to be missed is the *croque madame* with grilled ham and cheese and two eggs on top, served with home fries ($9.95).

Fine points: If you need a stiffer drink than wine, there's always Pancha's bar next door.

Gordon's Cafe and Wine Bar, 6770 Washington Street, Yountville 94599; phone (707) 944–8246. Open from 7:30 A.M. to 6:00 P.M. Kitchen closes at 3:00 P.M. Tuesday–Saturday, later Friday, 7:30 A.M. to 5:00 P.M. Sunday. Beer and wine. MasterCard, Visa, American Express, and Discover. Wheelchair accessible.

Père Jeanty is the latest Napa Valley effort of Philippe Jeanty, the jovial French chef. Jeanty snapped up the location of a former glorified local Italian restaurant, Frankie & Johnnie & Luigi Too. After yet another Provencal restaurant didn't quite go here, Jeanty is retooling it into an upscale steak and chop house, with Kobe short ribs, veal chops, and porterhouse and cowboy steaks, ranging from $22.50 to $68.00 for a 38-ounce porterhouse steak for two. Père Jeanty is now closed for lunch, so call before visiting.

Père Jeanty, 6725 Washington Street, Yountville 94559; phone (707) 945–1000. Open 5:30 to 10:00 P.M. nightly. Full bar. Visa, MasterCard, and American Express. Wheelchair accessible. Parking lot.

At this point, Washington Street veers leftish and back to Highway 29. If, instead of going left with it, you decide to go straight ahead (north) on Lincoln, you can explore **Yountville Park** and a bit of Yountville history at the George C. Yount Pioneer Cemetery & Ancient Indian Burial Grounds.

Yountville Park offers colorful children's play equipment, good barbecues, public restrooms, and lots of grass to play or lounge on.

Yountville Park, Washington and Lincoln Streets, Yountville 94599. Open from 6:00 A.M. to 10:00 P.M. No pets or motor vehicles.

Just beyond the park, **George C. Yount Pioneer Cemetery & Ancient Indian Burial Grounds** gives a short and fascinating history of Yountville, as do most old cemeteries. Ironically, George Yount was the first white settler in the Napa Valley and is buried here with Napa and Pomo Indians and some much more current immigrants.

George C. Yount Pioneer Cemetery & Ancient Indian Burial Grounds, Lincoln and Jackson Streets, Yountville 94599.

Just south is the intriguing Burgundy House five-room inn. Once a brandy distillery built in 1891, the rich little building's 22-inch thick local stone walls keep it cool in the summer, perfect for sipping the decanter of wine that greets you in your antiques-furnished room on arrival. (See chapter 5, Where to Stay in the Napa Valley.)

Compadres Mexican Bar & Grill is the only Mexican restaurant in Yountville, so if you truly have the urge, this is it. Compadres bills itself as "A Great Place to Party" for breakfast, lunch, and dinner, and it is. If that's your goal, go for it. This place is super-California and huge, with loads of indoor and outdoor seating. Watch for the daily fish specials, seafood tacos, enchiladas galore, and several Jaliscan specialties. Margarita variations abound, but we prefer the originals.

Yountville's Farmers' Market takes place in Compadres' parking lot Wednesdays from 4:00 to 8:00 P.M.

Compadres Mexican Bar & Grill, 6539 Washington Street, Yountville, 94599; phone (707) 944–2406. Open from 8:00 A.M. to 10:00 P.M. Sunday–Thursday, 8:00 A.M. to 11:00 P.M. Friday–Saturday. Master-Card, Visa, and American Express. Wheelchair accessible.

Before we get you inside the Vintage 1870 complex, we want to introduce you to **Pacific Blues Cafe,** named "Best New Restaurant of Napa Valley" in 1997.

Jeff Steen, formerly of Piatti and Compadres, has created the most fun casual restaurant in the Napa Valley. He serves consistently hearty "maverick American" taste surprises in what was once the train station. Hence the train and blues themes, which carry into the old train posters on the walls and train names on the menu, while blues music pipes softly through the restaurant and deck facing Vintage 1870 during the week, replaced by live blues bands on the weekend. Portions are large and prices small. Chef Nan Hernandez shakes up culinary snobbery with downright good food fun.

Breakfasts are classic and innovative, from Flatcar Flapjacks with whipped orange butter and hot maple syrup ($1.95 each) and vanilla-cinnamon French toast with bananas and walnuts ($7.25), to the Rocky Rail Scramble of turkey, spinach, onions, and egg whites ($8.25), the Engineer's Hearty Breakfast of grilled New York steak with eggs and hash browns ($13.99), and Julio's great chorizo and eggs ($8.75).

Lunch and dinner offer rib eye and other excellent steaks, several veggie specialties (from fancy baked potatoes to dim sum and hot veggie chili and veggie pastas), humongous double-layered, tricolored nachos ($8.95) or with grilled chicken or steak ($11.25), grilled cheese ($5.75), or $6.95 with Black Forest ham or bacon added, Julio's Black Beans with Chicken Breast ($13.95), Caesar and spinach salads, a fab iceberg-lettuce wedge with thick, creamy, chunky bleu cheese dressing ($5.95), burgers galore, finger-licking ribs, and Kathleen's favorite—the Blues Burger, with ground turkey, bleu cheese, and jalapeño jam, served with perfect slaw or french fries (go for the garlic ones with fresh, crushed garlic) ($10.25). Outlandish desserts and a children's menu make this a place we come back to again and again. Try the new Snappin' Cracklin' Rice Krispies Trash Treats with Carmel and Hot Fudge Dipping Sauce ($6.50). All soft drinks are $2.00 and bottomless. Pacific Blues also has one of the best-selected local wine lists and good espresso drinks. Children's lunch and dinner are all $4.99 from the kids' menu, with healthy breakfasts ($3.50).

Great blues music on Saturday.

Pacific Blues Cafe, 6525 Washington Street, Yountville 94599; phone (707) 944–4455. Open 8:00 A.M. to 10:00 P.M. Monday–Saturday. Beer and wine. MasterCard, Visa, and American Express. Wheelchair accessible.

The large brick building across the patio is **Vintage 1870,** loaded with specialty shops and art galleries. Originally the Groezinger Wine Cellars, the building is listed in the National Register of Historic Places and is built on the original land grant made to Salvador Vallejo by the Mexican government in 1838. In 1870 G. Groezinger purchased it from George C. Yount's estate for $250 in gold coins, and it was used as a winery to 1954.

Vintage 1870 offers refreshingly high-quality businesses, one of the most tempting of which you encounter just to the right of the door. Gillespie's Ice Cream & Chocolates serves Double Rainbow ice cream and made-before-your-eyes chocolates, including sugar-free peanut clusters. Smoothies, shakes, and sundaes steel you for shopping till you drop. Cravings Gourmet & Cookware sells wine stuff such as drip stoppers, cookbooks, cool drinks, and picnic baskets. Kinyon! Restaurant invites you in with hardwood floors, colored napkins, and cobalt-blue glasses, to say nothing of the Thanksgiving turkey sandwich ($9.75), Holy Cow roast beef on French roll, a grilled chicken sandwich called Last Mango in Paris, a veggie Griller Thriller, To Brie or Not to Brie, salads galore, and a Here's the Skinny menu.

Notice the plaque marking the old Chutney Kitchen's cutting board. You can still get the once-famous chutney at Cravings. Mira Boutique sells replica jewelry. The Toy Cellar carries trains, stuffed Breyer bears and other animals, toys, Beanie Babies, yo-yos, everything Madeline, and a 1-cent box of goodies. Gallery 1870 represents world-renowned contemporary artists.

We especially like Generations, a fine art gallery, with interestingly designed space and involvement in the community. Generations features art of the West, Judith Gaulke's (former food editor of *Sunset* magazine) French waiter series, Mikki Senkauk, and other Northern California artists. Also on the first floor are Rosalia's for Shoes and Touch of Gold Bath Shop. Be sure to check out Starz Gallery of celebrity art and memorabilia.

> *Vintage 1870*, *6525 Washington Street, Yountville 94599; phone (707) 944–2451. Open from 10:00 A.M. to 5:30 P.M. daily. Credit cards vary by shop.*

Cucina a la Carte bills itself as a "Franco-Italian Marketplace" offering Ceruta ceramic tableware and loads of Italian foods, available for casual dining here or to go. Cucina a la Carte is part of the Villagio Inn Spa and Vintage Inn group and replaces the former Bocconcini restaurant at this site in the back of the Vintage 1870 complex.

Cucina a la Carte has reduced its seating and improved its food. New starters include edame of steamed soy beans ($4.00) and dim sum steamer basket ($7.00); salads include good versions of standards such as mesquite turkey Cobb salad ($11.00), chicken and Nappa cabbage with Asian vegetables ($10.00), spicy tuna and asparagus tempura roll with soba noodles and shiitake mushrooms ($13.00), and a shrimp and Bay scallop salad with avocado ($12.00).

Sandwiches range from a tuna wrap to hot pastrami, French dip, grilled cheese, and a great Dungeness crab burger ($9.00–$11.00).

Main plates include Mongolian baby back pork ribs, pad Thai, pizzas, and pastas ($6.00–$13.00). The deck is fabulously shady and comfortable, with yellow umbrellas and a rustic feel. Pick up excellent coffee, breakfast, and pastries in the morning.

Cucina a la Carte, 6525 Washington Street (behind Vintage 1870), Yountville 94599-1300; phone (707) 944–1600, option 1. Open from 11:00 A.M. to 7:00 P.M. daily. Full bar. Corkage fee: $15 per bottle. Visa, MasterCard, and American Express. Wheelchair accessible.

Just south of Vintage 1870, and across the street at the junction of Oak Leaf and Washington, stop at the Whistle Stop Center, a collection of shops in another train station beside a collection of railroad cars that make up the Napa Valley Railway Inn (see chapter 5, Where to Stay in Napa Valley).

If you like leather, the **Overland Sheepskin Company** in the Whistle Stop Center is a must-see for waxed coats, sheepskin pelts, purses, briefcases, bicycle-seat covers, suede skirts and vests, slippers, Western belts, and wallets. While it is one of twelve stores, this Overland at least feels local.

Overland Sheepskin Company, 6505 Washington Street, Yountville 94599; phone (707) 944–0778. Open from 10:00 A.M. to 7:00 P.M. Monday–Thursday, until 8:00 P.M. Friday, and until 6:00 P.M. Sunday. MasterCard, Visa, and Discover. Wheelchair accessible.

Upstairs, visit Galerie Bacchus for vintage posters from La Belle Epoque and heirloom tapestries.

Go under the highway at the south end of Yountville and up California Drive to the Veterans' Home, Napa Valley Museum, and Domaine Chandon winery and restaurant, all of which are off this main road and within pea-shooting distance of one another. While only a chain-link fence separates the Napa Valley Museum and Domaine Chandon, their staffs rarely visit each other in this cozily nestled complex.

Just before the Veterans' Home entry post, you will see **Domaine Chandon**'s arch over California Drive. Turn right and follow the signs to the parking lot. You can park in the first lot, cross the little bridge over peaceful ponds with waterfalls and lilies, and walk into Domaine Chandon's dramatic entrance, or you can drive

Domaine Chandon

to a lot above and enter at the restaurant level. Ramps and elevators help you get from floor to floor.

Domaine Chandon deserves attention for both its winery and the restaurant. California's early Champagne wine prospects turned sharply better in 1973, when Moët-Hennessy of France built this dramatic, state-of-the-art sparkling-wine facility, which it now owns with Louis Vuitton. Moët & Chandon, the French Champagne house founded in 1743 and parent company of Domaine Chandon, uses the same methods that the monk Dom Perignon discovered as cellarmaster at the Benedictine Abbey in Hautvillers in 1690.

Domaine Chandon has integrated modern innovations with those traditional methods, including sustainable agriculture in its Carneros and Mt. Veeder vineyards. According to the 1920 Treaty of Madrid, which the United States did not sign during Prohibition, only sparkling wines made from Chardonnay, Pinot Noir, and Pinot Meunier grapes grown in Champagne and using *méthode champenoise* could be called Champagne. "Sparkling wine" applies to all wines containing effervescence created by natural fermentation. Out of deference to its French founders, Domaine Chandon calls its California product sparkling wine, even though it is made by the same methods as are their Moët & Chandon French Champagnes and legally can be called Champagne.

As you enter the winery, you can enjoy a vast shop of Domaine Chandon wines, beautiful books, aprons, glasses, wine goodies, mustards, shortbread cookies, and shirts even in kids' sizes. Along the hallway is a museum-style, lighted instructional display of the Champagne-making process, and stairs or elevators take you up to the next level.

On the mezzanine visit the Pavillion, an elegant, glassed-in tasting bar and the restaurant. The menu changes weekly and may include soft-shell crab salad, oestra caviar, hot and cold foie gras, hamachi and smoked salmon carpaccio, salmon, halibut, tuna, Watson Ranch baby lamb two ways, and mesquite-grilled pork chop.

Winemaker Wayne Donaldson makes regular visits to Moët & Chandon in Epernay, France, and consults to Moet's Australian winery.

Fine points: In the restaurant, you may want to try the Tasting Menu, at $90 or $135 with wine. In 1998 Domaine Chandon released its first still wines—Pinot Meunier, Pinot Noir, and Pinot Blanc—all made in small lots and available only in its shop, restaurant, and by direct mail. Featured wines: Brut Cuvée, Carneros Blanc de Noirs, Reserve Cuvée, Etoile Cuvée, Chardonnay, Chandon Pinot Meunier, and Pinot Noir. Owners: Moët-Hennessy-Louis Vuitton. Winemaker: Wayne Donaldson. Executive Chef: Ron Boyd. Cases: 450,000. Acres: 1,600.

Domaine Chandon, 1 California Drive, Yountville 94599; phone (707) 944–2280, Web site www.dchandon.com. Winery open from 10:00 A.M. to 5:00 P.M. in winter, 6:00 P.M. May–October, tours on the hour from 11:00 A.M. to 5:00 P.M., departing from the bottom of the stairs in the entry hall. Tasting fee: three for $9.00 to $14.00 or five for $12.00, complete with logo glass. Restaurant open for lunch from 11:30 A.M. to 2:30 P.M. daily April–October, dinner seatings from 6:00 P.M. Wednesday–Sunday except January. Winery and restaurant are closed Monday and Tuesday November–April. MasterCard, Visa, American Express, Diners Club, and Discover. Wheelchair accessible.

Just up the tree-lined divided road, about half a block from Domaine Chandon's entrance, is the **Napa Valley Museum.** The state-of-the-art edifice, designed by architects Fernau and Hartman to resemble two-thirds of a farm shed, serves as a regional museum that features wine-industry history, art, and local culture.

Here you can visit the $1.5 million "California Wine: The Science of an Art" exhibit, which was moved here from the earthquake-unsafe California Museum of Science and Industry in Los Angeles and redesigned by Academy Studio for the Industry Gallery of the Napa Valley Museum. Explore the information provided on twenty-six video disc players, nine microcomputers, twenty-four monitors, and eleven audio speakers for a definitive wine-history experience.

Collections include works of Napa Valley painter Sofia Alstrom Mitchell, the Johnson Collection of Minerals and Fossils, Native peoples of the Napa Valley including Wappo relics and folk culture, local viticultural materials, and historical and contemporary works by artists who live or have lived in the Napa Valley or use the Napa Valley as subject matter. We particularly enjoy the work of Earl Thollander, a favorite book illustrator for *Gourmet* and *Sunset* magazines.

Fine points: Be sure to visit the museum shop downstairs. It has one of the best collections of Napa history books and souvenirs anywhere.

Napa Valley Museum, 55 Presidents Circle, Yountville 94599; phone (707) 944–0500, Web site www.napavalleymuseum.org. Adults $4.50; seniors 60 and up and students 18 and up, $3.50; children 7–17, $2.50; under 7 free. Free admission for everyone every Monday. Open from 10:00 A.M. to 5:00 P.M. Wednesday through Monday; closed Tuesday and major holidays. Wheelchair accessible.

As you visit the museum, you are surrounded by the **California Veterans' Home,** established in 1882 by veterans of the Mexican and Civil Wars as "a home for all veterans west of the Rockies." Sold in 1900 to the state of California for a $20 gold piece, the vast home has been remodeled and updated (sort of) and has served veterans of the Mexican, Civil, Indian, Spanish-American, Korean, and Vietnam Wars, as well as World Wars I and II.

Fine points: The fascinating little museum behind the main building is open only on Friday from noon to 2:00 P.M. You might see interesting rotating exhibits of historic uniforms, weapons, documents, models, and photographs. Be sure to visit the newly renovated Lincoln Theater, home of the Napa Symphony.

California Veterans' Home, 180 California Drive, Yountville 94599; phone (800) 404–8387, Web site www.blink.com/vets.

As you work your way northward on Highway 29 from Yountville, four interesting stops on the west side of the highway break our first recommendation of not turning left across this two-lane highway. Brix, Mustards Grill, Cosentino Winery, and Napa Cellars all tempt.

General Manager Curtis Jones and the **Brix** staff set the casually elegant tone in a restaurant where warm, comforting yellows and woods with beamed ceilings and large windows frame vegetable gardens, vineyards, and the Mayacamas Mountains. Brix makes olive oil from its trees' olives, grows vegetables and herbs for your meal, and maintains ten acres of Chardonnay and Cabernet Sauvignon grapes (which it sells to Caymus Vineyards).

At lunch, Chef Ryan Jackson's starters may include ahi tuna sashimi with cucumber salad ($13.00), Chanterelle mushroom soup and foie gras mousse ($9.00), Dungeness crab and artichoke beignets ($11.00), wood-fired pizza ($10.00), and roasted Creole shrimp with creamy polenta ($12.00). Main courses range from prosciutto and basil-crusted chicken breast with chive potato purée ($17.00), Nicoise salad ($14.00), a burger with white cheddar, bacon, and fries ($11.00), duck breast salad ($18.00), and lobster risotto ($19.00), to filet mignon sandwich with caper aioli, Gruyère, and grilled onions ($15.00).

Dinner additions include pastas, steaks, racks of lamb, roasted duck breast, sea bass, scallops, and pork chops ($21.00–$36.00).

Sunday brunch buffet is terrific and includes eggs cooked to order, meats, quiches, pizzas, desserts, charcuterie and patés, cheese, vegetables, fritters, and beignets ($22.95 adults, $10.95 children 5–12, under 5 free).

Fine points: The wine list is exceptional. Be sure to stop in at the interesting gift shop with wine-country goodies and excellent travel and cook/food books. Feel free to stroll through the vegetable gardens and vineyards.

Brix, 7377 Highway 29, Yountville 94599; phone (707) 944–2749, Web site www.brix.com. Open for lunch 11:30 A.M. to 2:00 P.M., dinner 5:00 to 9:30 P.M. Monday–Saturday; Sunday brunch 11:00 A.M. to 2:00 P.M., dinner 4:00 to 9:00 P.M. Full bar. Corkage fee: $15.00 per 750 ml bottle. MasterCard, Visa, American Express, Diners Club, Discover, Carte Blanche, and JCB. Wheelchair accessible.

Practically next door to mustard-colored Brix, the better-known and noisier white **Mustards Grill** is the original outpost of the Real Restaurants group, which now includes Fog City Diner, Tra Vigne, and Tomatina in St. Helena and elsewhere, and the Buckeye Roadhouse in Mill Valley. The group has opened

Miramonte at what was Showley in Miramonte next to Terra in St. Helena. Look for their New Diner in downtown Yountville.

Mustards' roadside signs claim COCKTAILS, PORK CHOPS—ALMOST A MILLION SOLD, WAY TOO MANY WINES, GARDEN PRODUCE, CHOPS, RIBS. Just to the left of the front door is a small patio labeled MUSTARDS CIGAR & WILDLIFE PRESERVE, so park your stogies and stogie smokers here.

A fast-paced, clanking restaurant with attractive art, Mustards serves good-size portions of hearty and occasionally healthy comfort food (speaking of which, you must try the off-the-diet stacks of crisp, thin onion rings with homemade ketchup). White walls, dark wood, and white tile floors give the feel of a city bistro.

The Caesar salad is good at $8.95, the lemon-and-garlic chicken with mashed potatoes ($15.95) is excellent, and the half-slab of barbecued baby back ribs with crispy yams and creamy slaw ($19.95) can be terrific. If you eat such things, try the grilled Mongolian pork chop with garlic mashed potatoes ($21.95) or the Niman Ranch calf's liver Diablo with applewood-smoked bacon and griddled polenta ($13.95). The wild-mushroom "burger" with creamy potato salad and the regular Niman Ranch hamburgers are deals at $10.95, as is the ahi tuna steak sandwich with basil mayonnaise and ginger for $11.95. Try the new sweet corn tamales with wild mushrooms ($9.50) and the huge stack of onion rings ($6.25), not necessarily together!

Be sure to try Cindy Pawlcyn's Cindy's Backstreet Kitchen in St. Helena (see p. 158).

Fine points: The "New World" wine list includes twelve pages of fun reading and excellent wines, even some of Oregon's best Pinot Noirs. No photos of the restaurant without permission from manager Michael Kim Wolf personally.

Mustards Grill, 7399 St. Helena Highway, Napa 94558; phone (707) 944–2424. Open 11:30 A.M. to 9:30 P.M. Sunday–Thursday, 11:00 A.M. to 10:00 P.M. Friday–Saturday. Full bar. Corkage fee: $12. MasterCard, Visa, and Discover. Wheelchair accessible.

Immediately next door, to the north, is charming and small **Cosentino Winery,** the pride and joy of onetime assistant golf pro and wine distributor Mitch Cosentino. Possibly the only vintner to sell golf balls in his tasting room, Mitch plays golf in the Napa Valley with pals and pros, including Miller Barber and Walter Morgan.

Cosentino's Pinot Noir and Chardonnay are highly rated by most critics. It is one of the few wineries that prints and offers visitors the whole list of its *Wine Spectator* ratings and wine awards so that you can learn other people's opinions of its wines.

Fine points: Cosentino's "Art Series," which include "The Sculptor," "The Poet," and "The Novelist," are all "stylistically more 'old world' European than the California wines of that day. Each name was chosen to honor a type of artist whose approach to his medium best reflected the winemaker's approach to the development of these individual wine types." Cosentino offers two additional labels: CE2 V and Crystal Valley (Lodi) Cellars. Tasting fee: $5.00 for three current wine tastes, $10.00 for three Reserves (you keep the glass). Featured wines: Chardonnay, White Meritage/Sauvignon Blanc, Gewürztraminer, Viognier, Pinot Grigio, Nebbiolo, Pinot Noir, Merlot, Cabernet Sauvignon, Red Meritage, Zinfandel, Cabernet Franc, and Late Harvest Viognier. Founder and winemaker: Mitch Cosentino. Cases: 40,000. Acres: 163.

Cosentino Winery, 7415 St. Helena Highway, Yountville 94599; phone (707) 944–1220, Web site www.cosentinowinery.com. Open from 10:00 A.M. to 5:30 P.M. November–March, and by appointment only April–October. Visa, MasterCard, and American Express. Wheelchair accessible.

Now, walk next door to **Napa Cellars** in the interesting six-sided wooden building. As you enter, you face a corner of the tasting counter. Permanent Christmas-tree lights and dried flowers dangle over the six-sided bar. Enjoy the excellent book selection on the table to the left as you enter as well as the new Cabernet Sauvignon Vineyard around the tasting room.

Napa Cellars is an endeavor of Koerner Rombauer of Rombauer Vineyards and former Academy of Motion Pictures president Richard Frank, who are also involved in ownership of Hanns Kornell Champagne Cellars. Frank-Rombauer suffered a horrible warehouse fire June 15, 2000, and lost its rare vintages. They are back making all of their wines again, fortunately. Try the wines and stay tuned.

Dungeness Crab Cioppino

from Napa Cellars, Oakville

2 whole fresh crabs, cracked and cleaned

1½ lb fresh firm white fish (cod, snapper, sole) cut into 2-inch cubes

6–8 clams in shell, scrubbed and cleaned

½ lb fresh shrimp (prawns), cleaned and deveined

2 cans clams with juice

2 cans bay shrimp, drained

3 Tbs olive oil

1½ cup onions or shallots, chopped

3 cloves garlic, minced (more if you like)

2 16-oz cans whole tomatoes

1 16-oz can tomato sauce

1 8-oz bottle clam juice

1 bay leaf

3 Tbs fresh parsley, finely chopped

3 Tbs fresh basil, finely chopped (or 1 Tbs dried basil)

1½ cups Napa Cellars Chardonnay

salt and pepper to taste

3 drops Tabasco (more if you like)

Remove the meat from the crab bodies and a few legs, and set it aside with the clams, fish, and shrimp.

Sauté the onions in olive oil for about 8 minutes, and add the garlic. Cook together for another 2 minutes, then add tomatoes, tomato sauce, clam juice, herbs, and wine. Cover and let cook for 25–30 minutes at medium heat. Stir occasionally.

Add the crab legs and meat, fish, canned clams, and canned shrimp, and let simmer on low heat for 25 minutes.

Add fresh shrimp and clams, and let cook for 10 more minutes, discarding any unopened clams.

Add salt, pepper, and Tabasco to taste. Serve with tossed green salad, lemon wedges, and lots of French bread to soak up the sauce. Serves 6.

Napa Cellars

Fine points: Marc Chagall and Guy Buffet posters decorate the walls. Tasting fee: $5.00, refunded with any purchase. Featured wines: Chardonnay, Merlot, Cabernet Sauvignon, Zinfandel, Fie Doux (Late Harvest Semillon), Syrah, Sparkling Rose, and late harvest Zinfandel. Owners: Partnership including Koerner Rombauer and Richard Frank. Winemaker: Todd Graff. Cases: 10,000. Acres: 50.

Napa Cellars, 7481 St. Helena Highway, Oakville 94562; phone (707) 944–2565 or (800) 535–6400, Web site napacellars.com. Open from 10:30 A.M. to 5:00 P.M. daily. Visa, MasterCard, and American Express. Wheelchair accessible.

Across Highway 29, just north of Napa Cellars, visit **Cardinale Estate,** home also to Lokoya Cabernet Sauvignon and Atalon Cabernet Sauvignon and Merlot. All are owned by Jess Jackson. To get there, turn right (east) at the Cardinale sign, proceed for 0.4 mile, and turn right up the hill to cement-block and then stone buildings. (You enter the tasting room from the parking lot.) Jackson is filling in his own reservoir to build a winery with barrels underground. Enjoy the lovely new tasting room featuring blonde wood, marble floors, and a dining table.

Jess Jackson established Cardinale to make Cabernet Sauvignon and Merlot in Oakville, in the heart of the Napa Valley, to use the exceptional hillside and benchland vineyards in Napa and Sonoma Counties. Cardinale's handcrafted and unfiltered wines are aged 100 percent in French oak barrels.

Since 1966, Robert Pepi has grown and produced outstanding Sangiovese and Sauvignon Blanc from Pepi's original cuttings of Sangiovese Grosso, brought from Italy's Tuscany region. Pepi's Colline di Sassi comes from the "Hill of Stones" on the Pepi property. Jess Jackson bought the Pepi vineyard in 1994 from Robert Pepi.

Fine points: The new tasting room is spectacular, with fabulous views of the Napa Valley. Tasting fees: $3.00 to $15.00 for tastes, $20.00 to $30.00 for flights. (A "flight" of wines is a lineup of various vintages or sources of a type of wine, tasted in sucession for comparison purposes.) You will find a limited but excellent selection of wine and cookbooks here, as well as handsome hand-carved wooden bottle stoppers. In *The Wine Advocate*, Robert M. Parker Jr. rates Cardinale's Cardinale Red a 90–92. Featured wines: Cardinale: Red Wine; Lokoya: Cabernet Sauvignon; Atalon: Cabernet Sauvignon, Merlot. Cases: 3,000. Owner: Jess Jackson. Winemakers: Cardinale and Lokoya: Christopher Carpenter; Atalon: Thomas Peffer. Cases: 8,600. Acres: 450+, and is the largest purchaser of Cabernet Sauvignon grapes in Napa Valley.

Cardinale Estate, 7585 Highway 29, Oakville 94562; phone (707) 945–1391, Web sites www.cardinale.com, www.lakoya.com, and www.atalon.com. Open by appointment 10:30 A.M. to 4:00 P.M. MasterCard, Visa, and American Express. Wheelchair accessible.

North of Cardinale the Oakville Grade heads west from Highway 29 and winds almost treacherously to Glen Ellen in Sonoma County. There are several good reasons to make this turn: Pometta's Deli, an Episcopal church, the Carmelite House of Prayer and Religious Shop, and Diamond Oaks Winery. Many more signs guide you to the Carmelite mission than to any of the other attractions.

As you continue westward on the flat part of the Oakville Grade through acres of vineyards, notice the historic little St. Stephen's Episcopal Church on the right. It's worth getting out of the car if you're interested in local history. The next stop is also religious: the Carmelite House of Prayer and Carmelite Religious Store. Turn right up Mount Carmel Drive, and stations of the cross shrines lead you up the mission's driveway. Park at the top, respect the quiet, and explore the historic chapel to your left, the mosaics, and the popular shop.

Another 500 feet up the winding grade, turn left into **Diamond Oaks Winery.** After twenty-five years of growing grapes and acquiring more land in Napa and Sonoma Counties, thoroughbred horse breeder Dinesh Maniar purchased La Famiglia di Robert Mondavi Winery from the legendary Robert Mondavi and renamed it Diamond Oaks. The deal was completed in March 2003, and Diamond Oaks opened to the public that July in the lovely hilltop building left by the Mondavi clan, well before Mondavi sold to giant Constellation brands of New York for $1.3 billion in early November 2004.

Nearly every winery worker and winemaker suggests a visit to Diamond Oaks. It is definitely worth the trip.

Fine points: Featured wines: Chardonnay, Pinot Noir, Merlot, and Cabernet Sauvignon. Owner: Dinesh Maniar. Winemaker: Ron Brown. Cases: 25,000. Acres: 550.

Diamond Oaks Winery, 1595 Oakville Grade, Oakville 94562; phone (707) 948-3000, Web site www.diamond-oaks.com. Open 10:00 A.M. to 5:00 P.M. daily. Tasting fee: $7.00. Visa, MasterCard, and American Express. Wheelchair accessible.

From Diamond Oaks turn left on Oakville Grade and then left again on Mt. Veeder Road to **Chateau Potelle Winery** 1,800 feet above the valley in the forest. You can also get to it by taking Redwood Road west from Highway 29 in Napa, and following it as it winds up the hills about 5 miles and turns into Mt. Veeder Road.

Chateau Potelle is a highly respected winery located on top of the Napa world, with 360-degree views. Jean-Noel and Marketta Fourmeaux came to California in 1980 as official wine tasters for the French government to learn about California winemaking and wines. What a way to go! After tasting 2,000 wines in six months, the Fourmeaux sent a telegram home saying, "Looks good, we stay"; they went back to France, picked up their young daughters, Mariette and Clarisse, and moved to California in 1983.

Most Chateau Potelle wines are available only at the winery.

Fine points: Featured wines: Chardonnay, Sauvignon Blanc, Cabernet Sauvignon, Zinfandel, Zinie de Potelle (Port), and Riviera. Owners: Jean-Noel and Marketta Fourmeaux. Winemaker: Marketta Fourmeaux. Cases: 20,000. Acres: 202.

Chateau Potelle, 3875 Mt. Veeder Road, Napa 94558; phone (707) 255–9440, Web site www.chateaupotelle.com. Open 11:00 A.M. to 6:00 P.M. daily April 15–October 31, 11:00 A.M. to 5:00 P.M. daily November 1–April 14. Visa and MasterCard. Wheelchair accessible.

OAKVILLE

As you come into Oakville, please slow down, both for your safety and for that of pilgrims gathering at the Oakville Grocery Mecca.

At the southern end of this three-building metropolis is **Napa Wine Company,** which is not in most books but is fun to visit. Turn right onto the Oakville Crossroad just before the Oakville Grocery and right again into the winery's driveway.

The original winery on this site was built in 1877 by Adolph Brun and Jean Chaix as Nouveau Medoc Winery and California Bonded Winery No. 9. After passing through many winemaking hands before and after Prohibition, the property was bought by Heublein in 1986 and turned into Inglenook's Chardonnay Cellar. It closed three years later. The northwest corner building was built in 1892 for the Bartolucci Brothers' Modanna Winery, also passing through several hands and ending up with Heublein. The Andrew Pelissa family bought the whole works in 1993 and reopened under the name Napa Wine Company.

This is an unusual, custom-crush facility to which seventy-five small wineries bring their own winemaker, grapes, and barrels and use the equipment and space to crush, ferment, age, and bottle their wines. The renowned Heidi Barrett makes some of her wines here. Here in the gorgeous remodeled tasting room, called The Cellar Door, you can sample and buy handcrafted wines from family wineries whose wines are rarely available in stores or restaurants, including a 1985–1994 vertical Marilyn Merlot for a mere $6,750. In this case, "vertical" refers to one bottle of each vintage, and not to Ms. Monroe.

Fine points: If you have ever fantasized about starting your own small winery, check this out. It's full of learning opportunities. Tasting fee: $5.00. Wines from wineries you might sample and purchase in the salesroom here include Fife Vineyards' Cabernet Sauvignon, Merlot, Petite Syrah, and Zinfandel; Lamborn Family Vineyards' Zinfandel and Port; Mason Cellars' Merlot and Sauvignon Blanc; Napa Wine Company's Sauvignon Blanc, Pinot Blanc, and Cabernet Sauvignon; Nova

Wine Group's Marilyn Merlot and Marilyn Cabernet Sauvignon with luscious Marilyn portraits on the labels; Pahlmeyer & Co. Chardonnay and Merlot; Tria Winery's Pinot Noir, Zinfandel, and Syrah; Madrigal's Petite Syrah, Merlot, and Cabernet; Larkmead Vineyards' Cabernet and Merlot; Mason Cellars' Merlot, Sauvignon Blanc, and Cabernet Sauvignon; Michael Pozzan's Cabernet, Chardonnay, Marianna, Syrah, Regalo, Sangiovese, Sauvignon Blanc, and Pinot Noir; and wines of Oakford Vineyards, Pari, Showket, and Vinum. Owners: Andy Hoxsey, Dawne Dickenson, and the Harris family. Winemaker for Napa Wine Company: Rob Lawson. Cases: 1,000,000. Acres: 650.

Napa Wine Company, 7840 St. Helena Highway, Oakville 94562; phone (707) 944–1710, Web site www.napawineco.com. Open from 10:00 A.M. to 4:30 P.M. daily. MasterCard, Visa, American Express, and Discover. Wheelchair accessible.

Next door to Napa Wine Company is the **Oakville Grocery,** a fabulous place for food lovers and lovers of food lovers. Built in 1881 by James and Jennie McQuaid as the "mercantile" for the bustling town of Oakville, Oakville Grocery supplied essentials to locals for generations. Listed in the National Register of Historic Places, the store was owned from 1978 to 1980 by vintner Joseph Phelps, who sold it to current CEO Steve Carlin and partners.

It is worth braving the crowds for tastes of oils and Artisan, Panorama, Bouchon, Oakville Grocery, and Acme breads; classic sandwiches to go, from Mediterranean chicken and smoked turkey and brie to Ozark peppered ham, vegetarian, turkey pesto, roast beef and blue cheese, and mom's tuna salad; or focaccia sandwiches of turkey pesto, roast beef, and blue cheese, or house-roasted pork loin. All are under $7.00. Feast your eyes upon eight Italian pastas, Chinese noodle salad, citrus chipotle salsa, twenty kinds of olives, crab cakes with remoulade sauce, and chocolate-covered apricots. You might want to indulge in the House Salmon Pâté ($17.95/lb.).

Don't leave without a sweet from Napa patisseries Sweetie Pies, Sweet Finale, Bouchon, and La Grossiossa. Of course Ben & Jerry's supplies vanilla with Heath toffee and cookie dough Peace Pops.

Oakville Grocery sells hard-to-get half bottles of local wines as well as a vast array of excellent local and imported full bottles.

Oakville Grocery and U.S. Post Office

Be sure to notice the wines in the back, especially the unusual collection of splits of local wines, as well as Oakville Grocery's own oils, vinegars, mustards, preserves, honeys, and wines.

Fine points: The Oakville U.S. Post Office is still in the building, as are public telephones.

Oakville Grocery, 7856 St. Helena Highway, Oakville 94562; phone (707) 944–8802, Web site www.oakvillegrocery.com. Open from 9:00 A.M. to 6:00 P.M. daily; espresso bar open from 7:00 A.M. to 6:00 P.M. Monday–Friday, 7:30 A.M. to 6:00 P.M. Saturday, 8:00 A.M. to 6:00 P.M. Sunday. Beer and wine. MasterCard, Visa, and American Express. Wheelchair accessible, but difficult to get around due to closeness of aisles.

The greatest concentration of wineries is between Oakville and St. Helena, which means that you might want to plan your route carefully, with full awareness that some of your favorites might be between St. Helena and Calistoga or on the Silverado Trail.

Oakville Polenta Crostini with Sun-Dried Tomato Pesto

from Oakville Grocery, Oakville

3 cups water
1 cup milk
1 tsp salt
1 cup Oakville Grocery Organic Polenta
2 Tbs McEvoy Ranch extra virgin olive oil
³/₄ cup grated Vella Dry Jack cheese (can substitute Parmesan cheese)
2 Tbs Italian parsley, chopped
pinch of freshly ground black pepper
1 9½-oz jar Bella Cucina Sun-Dried Tomato Pesto

In a medium-size saucepan, combine the water, milk, and salt and bring to a boil. Sprinkle the polenta slowly into the boiling liquid and stir with a whisk until fully incorporated to avoid lumps. Lower the heat so that the mixture simmers slowly rather than boils. Switch to a wooden spoon and stir frequently for 20–25 minutes. The polenta should be very thick and smooth and free of lumps. When the grains are tender, add olive oil, ¼ cup of cheese, parsley, and pepper to taste. Stir until incorporated.

Carefully pour the polenta into a rectangular 8-by-12-inch cake pan that has been brushed lightly with olive oil. Spread polenta with a spatula until it is about ½ inch thick. Cover with plastic wrap and allow to cool for 2 hours.

Cut into 24 2-inch squares and arrange on lightly oiled cookie sheets. Brush tops with oil and set under preheated broiler until the tops brown lightly. Top each square with a dollop of pesto and sprinkle with reserved cheese. Place back in broiler to warm and serve immediately. Serves 6–8.

OAKVILLE TO RUTHERFORD

Opus One Winery is the perfect child created by Robert Mondavi and the late Baron Philippe de Rothschild of Bordeaux's Chateau Mouton-Rothschild, combining France's best with California's champion of wine. Open for tasting and tours by appointment only, Opus One's secrecy and mystery, and Robert Mondavi's unequaled skills at promotion, have contributed to wine fans' heightened desire to gain admission to this shrine. To get here, turn east (right) off Highway 29 into Opus One's driveway, 0.4 mile north of Oakville.

Opus One Winery

Designed by Johnson, Fain & Perreira of Los Angeles, who also designed San Francisco's once controversial TransAmerica Pyramid, the building resembles a cross between a Mayan temple and a spaceship. Partially buried by grasses and plantings, the redwood and limestone winery was built in 1991 for about $26.5 million. It has a dramatic courtyard entrance and a breathtaking open pavilion overlooking Napa Valley's finest vineyards.

Fine points: Old World traditional gravity-flow methods merge with advanced California technology here to produce some of the finest wines anywhere. This is one appointment worth making ahead to plan your trip around. While the tasting fee is the highest we know of ($25–$50), it is also worth it. (The wines you taste here sell for about $65 per bottle.) Featured wines: Opus One (Cabernet Sauvignon, Cabernet Franc, and Merlot blends) and Overture. Owners: Constellation Brands, Inc. Winemakers: Tim Mondavi and Patrick Leon. Cases: 30,000. Acres: 144.

Opus One Winery, 7900 St. Helena Highway, Oakville 94562; phone (707) 944–9442, Web site www.opusonewinery.com. Open from 10:30 A.M. to 3:30 P.M. by appointment only. MasterCard, Visa, and American Express. Wheelchair accessible.

The next winery as we progress northward on Highway 29 is **Robert Mondavi Winery,** on the west side of the road. Robert Mondavi is both the man and the winery. He is completely tied to his winery's image because he promoted it and developed it, while also warning loudly of his perception of a new Prohibition coming from America's political right. His sons Michael and Tim now run the winery, while Robert continues, in his late eighties, to educate consumers and promote wine.

Upon leaving the Mondavi family–owned Charles Krug Winery, Robert Mondavi built and began his own winery in what was, in 1966, an avant-garde California–Italian building that stood out dramatically from the undeveloped, natural surrounding landscape.

Chèvre-Stuffed Radicchio

from Executive Chef Annie Roberts, Robert Mondavi Winery, Oakville

1 large (about 10 oz) head radicchio
11 oz Chèvre cheese
2 Tbs Balsamic vinegar
2 Tbs sherry vinegar
½ cup extra virgin olive oil
¼ cup minced shallots
Salt and ground pepper

Preheat the broiler.

Core the radicchio and carefully remove the leaves. Rinse and dry them in a lettuce spinner.

Divide the Chèvre into 16 small pieces and roll each piece into a ball shape. Put each ball of Chèvre in a radicchio leaf. Roll the leaf around the Chèvre, tucking the edges as best you can, secure with toothpicks, and set on baking sheet. Repeat until all cheese and radicchio are used and placed on a baking sheet.

Combine the Balsamic and sherry vinegars in a small bowl. Gradually whisk in the olive oil to make an emulsion. Season well with salt and pepper.

When ready to serve, brush some of the vinaigrette over the radicchio packages. Place the baking sheet 5–6 inches from the broiler and cook until radicchio is browned, about 4 minutes, turning the packages two or three times with tongs. Place the radicchio packages on a serving platter and remove the toothpicks. Dress with remaining vinaigrette and sprinkle with the shallots. Serve immediately. Serves 6–8 as an hors d'oeuvre. Serve with Robert Mondavi Winery Chardonnay or Pinot Noir.

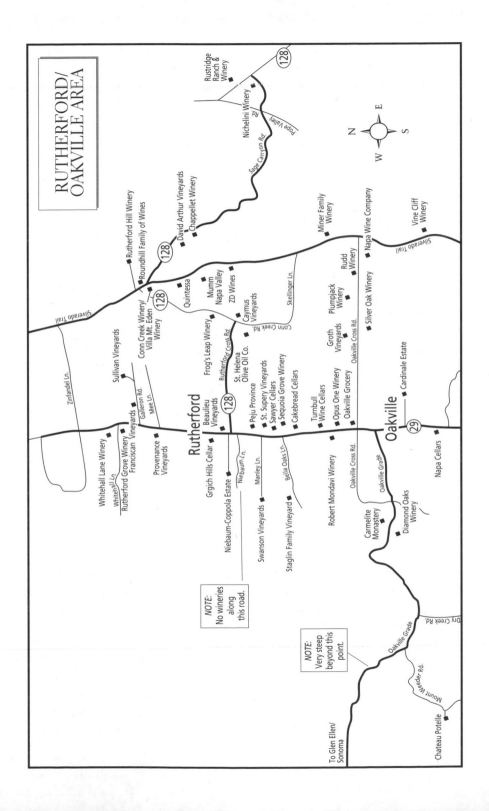

RUTHERFORD/
OAKVILLE AREA

N
W E
S

128
Rustridge Ranch & Winery
Nichelini Winery
Pope Valley Rd.
Sage Canyon Rd.

Rutherford Hill Winery
Roundhill Family of Wines
128
David Arthur Vineyards
Chappellet Winery

Silverado Trail

Conn Creek Winery/
Villa Mt. Eden Winery
Sullivan Vineyards
128
Quintessa
Mumm Napa Valley
ZD Wines
Caymus Vineyards
Conn Creek Rd.
Skellinger Ln.
Miner Family Winery
Napa Wine Company
Silverado Trail
Vine Cliff Winery

Zintandel Ln.

Rutherford

Frog's Leap Winery
Rutherford Cross Rd.
Groth Vineyards
Plumpjack Winery
Rudd Winery
Silver Oak Winery

Galleron Rd.
Mee Ln.
Whitehall Lane Winery
Rutherford Grove Winery
Franciscan Vineyards
Provenance Vineyards
Whitehall Ln.

Beaulieu Vineyards
128
St. Helena Olive Oil Co.
Peju Province
St. Supery Vineyards
Sawyer Cellars
Sequoia Grove Winery
Cakebread Cellars
Turnbull Wine Cellars
Opus One Winery
Oakville Grocery
Oakville Cross Rd.
Cardinale Estate

Grgich Hills Cellar
Niebaum Ln.
Manley Ln.
Bella Oaks Ln.

Niebaum-Coppola Estate

NOTE:
No wineries along this road.

Swanson Vineyards
Staglin Family Vineyard
Robert Mondavi Winery
Oakville Cross Rd.
Oakville Grade

Oakville
29
Napa Cellars

Carmelite Monastery
Diamond Oaks Winery

NOTE:
Very steep beyond this point.

Oakville Grade

Dry Creek Rd.

To Glen Ellen/
Sonoma

Mount Veeder Rd.

Chateau Potelle

In early November 2004, Constellation Brands, Inc., bought The Robert Mondavi Corporation for $1.35 billion.

The winery includes an elegant art gallery and dining rooms, reserve tasting room, and learning rooms, in addition to winemaking facilities. The layout resembles a California mission.

Besides its vast array of interesting wines, special events here are exceptional and well worth your attention. Robert and Margrit Mondavi and family worked to fulfill their goal of educating the public about wine and "its role as a mealtime beverage of moderation and to promote a gracious way of life."

The summer music series has included the biggest names in American music. Kathleen particularly likes The Great Chefs at Robert Mondavi Winery series, which since 1976 has included Simone Beck, Jean Troisgros, Roger Verge, Gaston Lenotre, Julia Child, Paul Prudhomme, Larry Forgione, Paul Bocuse, Wolfgang Puck, Barbara Kafka, Alice Waters, Diana Kennedy, Paula Wolfert, Martha Stewart, Jeremiah Tower, Joyce Goldstein, Giuliano Bugialli, Lydia Shire, Marion Cunningham, Marcella Hazan, Charlie Trotter, Joachim Splichal, Roy Yamaguchi, and Jacques and Claudine Pepin.

Mondavi Picnics in the Vineyards begin at 10:00 A.M. on Monday from May to October. They require reservations forty-eight hours in advance. The picnics are limited to ten people ($30 each) and include a four-hour tour and tasting, focusing on viticultural practices and tastings of wines selected to complement the day's picnic lunch.

Fine points: Mondavi has added two lovely tasting rooms for your tasting pleasure: The To-Kalon Room for Reserve-wine tasting, cigars, and Riedel Sommelier crystal stemware, and the Appellation Room for district wines. Enjoy the Rose Garden for new releases outdoors (weekends June–October). Call the winery for tour information and reservations. Tasting fees range from $5.00 to $15.00. Featured wines: Chardonnay, Fumé Blanc, Sauvignon Blanc, Cabernet Sauvignon, Merlot, Zinfandel, Pinot Noir, Moscato d'Oro, and La Famiglia di Robert Mondavi wines. Owner: Constellation Brands, Inc. Winemaker: Genevieve Janssens. Cases: 600,000. Acres: information not available.

Robert Mondavi Winery, 7801 St. Helena Highway, Oakville 94562; phone (707) 226–1335 or (800) 666–3284, Web site robertmondavi.com. Open from 9:00 A.M. to 5:00 P.M. daily May–October, 9:30 A.M. to 4:30 P.M. November–April. MasterCard, Visa, and American Express. Wheelchair accessible.

Turnbull Wine Cellars

Just north of the Oakville Cross Road on the east side of Highway 29, in a building with striking vertical redwood siding, is **Turnbull Wine Cellars,** founded in 1979 by famed architect William Turnbull, who died in 1997. Turnbull sold the winery in 1993 to publisher Patrick O'Dell, who rotates exhibits of his vast personal collection of works by Ansel Adams, Edward and Brett Weston, Yousef Karsch, and other photographers in the tasting room.

A 1998 addition to the winery on its southwest side was designed in the same style as the winery in homage to Bill Turnbull. Don't miss the small old Ford truck collection in the parking lot. On the first Sunday of April, May, and June, winemaker Jon Engelskirger hosts a preview of soon-to-be-bottled wines, from 1:00 to 4:00 P.M.

Fine points: There is a tasting fee of $5.00, which is refundable with a purchase. Featured wines: Sauvignon Blanc, Cabernet Sauvignon, and Merlot. Owner: Patrick O'Dell. Winemaker: Jon Engelskirger. Cases: 25,000. Acres: 380.

Turnbull Wine Cellars, 8210 St. Helena Highway, Oakville 94562; phone (707) 963–5839 or (800) 887–6285, Web site www.turnbullwines.com. Open from 10:00 A.M. to 4:30 P.M. daily. Visa, MasterCard, American Express, and California checks. Wheelchair accessible.

As you leave Turnbull, turn right and go 0.4 mile to **Cakebread Cellars,** one of the most upbeat and friendly wineries in the entire Napa Valley. Turn into Cakebread's driveway when you see vertical redwood siding like Turnbull's, but where the address number 8300 is written in red on a stone wall. There is no Cakebread sign.

Having left their mechanics garage in Oakland for greener vineyards, charming Jack and Dolores Cakebread bought the Sturdivant Ranch and started this winery in 1973. Bunches of friends helped them pound nails, trim roses, and generally build and fix up the place. Dolores cooked dinner for the weekend volunteer troops for several years, as the list of food and wine enthusiasts grew. Seven Cakebreads are now involved with the winery.

Belgian Endive with Smoked Chicken Sausage, Apple, and Whole-Grain Mustard

from Cakebread Cellars, Oakville

¼ cup water

¼ cup sugar

¼ cup apple cider vinegar

½ large Granny Smith apple, minced

¼ red onion, minced

½ tsp whole-grain mustard

½ tsp fresh dill, chopped

2 smoked chicken sausages, finely diced

2 tsp extra virgin olive oil

3 whole Belgian endives

In a small stainless steel saucepan, boil water and sugar over medium heat. Continue cooking until sugar turns to caramel. Remove from heat and add apple cider vinegar. Return to heat and stir to dissolve caramel. Reduce by half until mixture begins to thicken. Place minced apple and red onion in a stainless steel bowl. Pour apple cider vinegar mixture over apple and red onion. Add mustard and stir to coat. Allow to cool and then stir in chopped dill and reserve.

Sauté smoked sausage in olive oil over high heat until brown and crispy. Cut off the ends of the Belgian endive and cut each spear into 2-inch serving size. Reserve the center for another use. Place 1 tsp of sausage on the end of each endive spear. Top with ½ tsp of the apple and whole-grain mustard relish and serve. Makes 24 appetizer servings.

Enjoy with a glass of Cakebread Cellars Rubaiyat.

Culinary Director Dolores Cakebread hosts the annual fall American Harvest Workshop, featuring five chefs giving public classes. A winery with five kitchens and the tiny Cakebread Cellars Produce Center (which sells the extras from Dolores's one-and-a-half-acre vegetable and herb garden), Cakebread produces excellent wines. Instead of selecting a wine to go with food, the Cakebreads prefer to choose a wine and "cook to it."

As you walk into the barrel room, the tasting bar is to your left.

Fine points: The Cakebreads have assembled two exquisite binders containing Napa Valley restaurants' menus and chefs' histories for the convenience of visitors and staff. The binders are placed on two wine barrels in the back of the tasting room. Be sure to get on the mailing list for cooking classes, new wines, and special events. Cakebread's own little cookbook, created to celebrate their first twenty-five years, is yours free for the asking. Cakebread enthusiastically serves alternative beverages to designated drivers. Tasting fee: $5.00 cellars tastings; $10.00 "vintners' tasting." Featured wines: Sauvignon Blanc, Chardonnay, Cabernet Sauvignon, Rubaiyat, and Merlot. Owners: Jack and Dolores Cakebread. Winemaker: Julianne Laks. Chef: Brian Streeter. Cases: 95,000. Acres: 82.

Cakebread Cellars, 8300 St. Helena Highway, Rutherford 94573; phone (707) 963–5221 or (800) 588–0298, Web site www.cakebread.com. Open from 10:00 A.M. to 4:30 P.M. daily. Cellar tours by reservation. Visa, MasterCard, and American Express. Wheelchair accessible.

Just 0.1 mile up the line is **Sequoia Grove Winery,** the baby of Jim Allen, who holds degrees in psychology and political science; mined gold in Alaska; served as an interpreter for the United Nations in Germany, Australia, and Greece; worked as a correspondent for UPI in Europe; and taught at a college in Santa Fe, New Mexico.

Having thoroughly sipped and researched wine everywhere his travels took him, Jim is joined in this adventure of the soul by his brother, Stephen, and their wives, children, and mother. Turn right at the carved redwood burl sign.

The "sequoia grove" consists of seven trees surrounding the modest barn. Walking into the barn/tasting room, you will find the tasting bar to the right, barrels and hoses everywhere, and a welcoming committee of a couple of house dogs waddling through.

Sequoia Grove Winery

The personality and sociology of a winery really do contribute to the wine and aura of the endeavor—to say nothing of the local "Rutherford Dust" believed to yield the outstanding Cabernets grown on this Rutherford bench. (Hence the local effort to get the Bureau of Alcohol, Tobacco and Firearms to establish a Rutherford Bench appellation.)

With his robust, earthy energy, Jim transformed a more than century-old farmhouse into a winery whose wines have received platinum, gold, and silver medals throughout France and the United States. He also built "the first completely underground cellar in the floor of Napa Valley" to create perfect conditions for aging his wines—enduring criticism because of Napa's high water table but resulting in excellent wines stored and cooled naturally at 55°F.

The winery was sold in 2004 to Kobrand Corporation, the New York–based distributor, which installed Sequoia Grove's veteran winemaker Michael Trujillo as president of the Winery.

Fine points: Wine writer and critic Dan Berger named Sequoia Grove the 1988 American Winery of the Year, just twenty years after the winery's beginning. Wine writers from *Wine Spectator* and from Berger to Jerry Mead, Joe Pollack, and Bob Thompson rave about Sequoia Grove's Cabernet Sauvignon and Chardonnay. Tasting fee: $5.00 for four tastes. Featured wines: Cabernet Sauvignon, Chardonnay, Shiraz, and Gewürztraminer. Owner: Kobrand Corporation. Winemaker: Michael Trujillo. Cases: 30,000. Acres: 25.

Sequoia Grove Winery, 8338 St. Helena Highway, Rutherford 94573; phone (707) 944–2945, Web site www.sequoiagrove.com. Open from 10:30 A.M. to 5:00 P.M. daily; tours 11:30 A.M. and 2:00 P.M. Friday–Sunday. MasterCard, Visa, and American Express. Wheelchair accessible.

Just north of Sequoia Grove, don't miss what looks like an old barn and is— **Sawyer Cellars.** When you walk in the door, you immediately smell the elegant old Inland Cedar walls used to restore the barn and set a cool, calm, and delightful ambience and creative environment.

Joanne and Charlie Sawyer started coming to the Napa Valley from Jacksonville, Florida, in the 1980s, enjoying the Napa Valley Wine Auction almost every year. Like many other wine aficionados, the Sawyers began spending more and more of their time here, and they realized that they had to farm and make wine in the valley to "chase our dream." Sawyer is one of the few winery owners whom you might see working the vineyards with the crew.

After purchasing the property from Jaeger Vineyards in 1994, Sawyer, in one of his smartest moves, hired twenty-eight-year Robert Mondavi veteran Brad Warner as vice president and winemaker. Brad is often in the tasting room and will gently answer any questions you may have with deep knowledge of the Napa Valley.

You will also find terrific prices on hats, shirts, and leather totes, to say nothing of sensational wines.

Fine points: Tasting fee: $5.00 for three tastes. Featured wines: Estate-grown Cabernet Sauvignon, Merlot, Meritage, and Sauvignon Blanc. Tours and tastings available by appointment. Owners: Charles and Joanne Sawyer. Winemaker and vice president: Brad Warner. Cases: 4,200. Acres: 50.

Sawyer Cellars, 8350 St. Helena Highway, Rutherford 94573; phone (707) 963–1980, Web site www.sawyercellars.com. Open by appointment from 10:00 A.M. to 5:00 P.M. daily. Visa, MasterCard, and American Express. Wheelchair accessible.

Next up the line is the **St. Supery Vineyards & Winery Discovery Center,** 0.2 mile north of Sequoia Grove. In stark contrast to Sequoia, St. Supery is a highly technical and marketed establishment owned by French agribusinessman Robert Skalli, who bought the property once owned by Edward St. Supery. Skalli built the winery next to Atkinson House, the white Queen Anne Victorian house built by Joseph Atkinson more than a hundred years ago. St. Supery is a Napa Valley leader in sustainable farming.

As you drive into St. Supery, the Victorian and an educational vineyard are to your right, and the winery and Discovery Center are straight ahead. Offices

Grilled Filet Mignon with Cabernet and Balsamic Vinegar Reduction Sauce

from Resident Chef Ron Barber, St. Supery Vineyards & Winery, Rutherford

FOR THE FILET MIGNON:

4 8-oz filet mignons
1 clove garlic
1 Tbs fresh thyme leaves
$^1/_2$ tsp cracked black pepper
$^1/_4$ cup extra virgin olive oil
1 Tbs Balsamic vinegar
salt and pepper

FOR THE CABERNET SAUCE:

2 Tbs olive oil
$^1/_2$ cup chopped onion
$^1/_4$ cup chopped carrots
$^1/_4$ cup chopped celery
3 cloves garlic, crushed
1 bay leaf
$^1/_4$ cup Balsamic vinegar
1 cup St. Supery Cabernet Sauvignon
1 qt veal or chicken stock
salt and pepper

For the filet mignon: Place the filets, garlic, thyme, pepper, oil, and Balsamic vinegar in a Ziploc bag and refrigerate overnight. Remove the steaks 30 minutes before you are ready to grill. Wipe steaks with a paper towel, then season with salt and pepper. Grill to desired doneness. Serve with Cabernet sauce (below).

For the Cabernet sauce: Heat the olive oil in a medium-size saucepan and cook the onions, carrots, and celery until lightly browned. Add the garlic, bay leaf, vinegar, and wine. Bring the mixture to a boil and simmer until reduced by one-half. Add the veal or chicken stock and bring to a boil. Simmer until the sauce is reduced by two-thirds. Strain through a fine-mesh strainer. Return the sauce to the heat and simmer until it lightly coats the back of a spoon. Season with salt and pepper and serve over or with the steaks. Serves 4. Serve with St. Supery 2000 Elu (a red Meritage blend).

St. Supery Vineyards & Winery

are in a charming old wood pump house to your left. Notice the wine bottle collection dating to 1884 just inside the front door of the Winery Discovery Center.

St. Supery's self-guided and guided tours are famously popular—including the SmellaVision Tour, where you can learn to discern those elusive "cherry" and "chocolate" flavors that cause wine writers to rhapsodize, and the Garden Tour of designated flowers. Galleries of panoramic murals, photos, models, and interactive displays illustrate wine lore, to the delight of children and grown-ups alike.

CEO Michaela Rodeno came to St. Supery in 1988 after fifteen years with Domaine Chandon. Michaela is founder of Women for WineSense. She chaired the 1998 Napa Valley Wine Auction and holds an M.A. in French literature and an M.B.A. from UC Berkeley. She lives on a vineyard in Oakville with her husband, Gregory, and their two children, and grows grapes in Pope Valley. Michaela's mission is to take the snobbishness out of wine and make it fun.

In one of the busiest tasting rooms anywhere, you will find not only great wines but also olive oils, dipping sauces, mustards, aprons, Gil's olives, Elena's pastas, books galore, corks, and videos. You can sit outside on the patio on green iron tables and chairs.

Fine points: Enjoy visiting chefs' and artists' work throughout the summer. Be sure to get on the winery's mailing list for the funniest newsletter in the wine business. Tasting fee: $10 for "lifetime tour and tasting pass"; $15 for special Reserve tastings in the Victorian home. Featured wines: Sauvignon Blanc, Chardonnay, Merlot, Cabernet Sauvignon, Meritage Red, Meritage White, Cabernet Franc, Moscato, Semillon, and Syrah. Owner: Skalli family. CEO: Michaela Rodeno. Winemaker: Michael Beaulac. Chef: Ron Barber. Cases: 110,000. Acres: 535 planted.

St. Supery Vineyards & Winery Discovery Center, 8440 St. Helena Highway, Rutherford 94573; phone (707) 963–4507, Web site www.stsupery.com. Open daily from 10:00 A.M. to 5:30 P.M. summer, 10:00 A.M. to 5:00 P.M. winter. Guided and self-guided tours. Visa, MasterCard, and American Express. Wheelchair accessible.

Next door, to the north, is **Peju Province,** a lovely garden and winery that make you feel as if you have just walked into a home winery in Provence. What do you know? Madame Peju calls the trees down the driveway "Peju sycamores" because

Peju Province

HP's Capellini Salad

from Herta Peju, Peju Province Winery, Rutherford

$^1/_4$ lb capellini (angel hair pasta), cooked in boiling water for 2 minutes
1 small red onion, sliced thin
1 red bell pepper, seeded and quartered, sliced thin
1 zucchini; sliced round and paper thin
1 carrot, sliced very thin
$^1/_2$ jalapeño pepper
$^1/_4$ cup pine nuts, preferably toasted
pinch ginger, freshly ground
salt and pepper to taste
balsamic vinegar to taste
olive oil to taste

Mix all ingredients in a large bowl. Toss occasionally until oil, vinegar, and spices are absorbed into the pasta. Usually tastes best the next day. Serves 4 as small salad. Serve with Peju Province Table Wine.

Peju Cranberry Pie

from Herta Peju, Peju Province Winery, Rutherford

2 cups cranberries
$^1/_3$ cup Later Harvest wine or Grand Marnier
$1^1/_2$ cups sugar
$^3/_4$ to 1 cup chopped walnuts
2 beaten eggs
$^3/_4$ cup melted butter
1 cup flour
1 tsp almond flavoring

Soak fresh cranberries in wine for several hours, then drain excess. Butter a 10-inch pie plate and preheat oven to 325° F. Put cranberries on bottom of pie plate and layer with $^1/_2$ cup sugar and nuts.

Mix 1 cup sugar, eggs, melted butter, flour, and almond flavoring well and pour over cranberries and nuts. Bake for 35 to 45 minutes until top is golden brown. Serve warm with whipped cream or vanilla ice cream. Serve with Peju Province Late Harvest Sauvignon Blanc. Serves 8.

her husband trims the sycamores to look like a strong mistral wind blew the leaves and branches off one winter.

Notice Mendocino sculptor Welton Rotz's statuary in the parking lot and throughout the grounds. Enter through the brass-and-iron gate and enjoy the fountain and bell, Herta Peju's much-photographed, multicolored flowers, and French sculptured gardens.

Named the "Top Artisan Winery of the Year" in 1994 by *Wine & Spirits* magazine, its 1994 Cabernet Sauvignon was in the "100 Best Wines of the Year" at the 1997 World Wine Championships and among the "50 Best American Red Wines" chosen by *Wine & Spirits Buying Guide–1998*; Peju should be on your must-stop list.

Anthony Peju grew up in Aix-en-Provence, studied film direction at UCLA, and owned an extremely successful nursery and garden supply business in Los Angeles. Tony and his wife, Herta, from Salzberg, Austria, scoured California from Mexico to Napa Valley. They selected this site, finding it perfect.

We found an outstanding selection of wine and cookbooks, Jacques Pepin's pepper sauce, Sparrow Lane vinegars, Peju mustards and chocolate sauces, including Raspberry Cabernet and Merlot Fudge, and Scharffen Berger chocolate. Check out the elegantly sexy painted label on the $250 Cabernet bottle.

Fine points: If you are lucky, Alan Arnopole, who considers every visit to be an event, might yodel or perform impromptu rap for you in the barrel room. Claiming to have learned to yodel by jumping over cactus, he sings to the wine and claims it just may be what makes Peju's wines so exceptional. Tasting fee: $5.00. Featured wines: Cabernet Sauvignon, Merlot, Cabernet Franc, Syrah, Zinfandel, Provence table wine, Sauvignon Blanc, and Carnival (French Colombard). Owners: Anthony and Herta Peju. Winemaker: Sean Foster. Cases: 25,000. Acres: 30 planted.

Peju Province, *8466 St. Helena Highway, Rutherford 94573; phone (707) 963–3600, Web site www.peju.com. Open from 10:00 A.M. to 6:00 P.M. daily. Visa and MasterCard. Wheelchair accessible.*

Before you get into "downtown" Rutherford, Francis Ford Coppola's **Niebaum-Coppola Estate** is on your left. *Do not* turn west on Niebaum Lane. This is a road that does not lead to any wineries. Take the next left (west) off Highway 29 at the signs.

Flush with earnings from *The Godfather*, Eleanor and Francis Ford Coppola went to the Napa Valley to find a one-acre retreat, a place perfect for writing and creating. Instead they found this elegant estate, planted with vines in 1872 and acquired in the late 1870s by Finnish sea captain and Alaska fur trader Gustave Niebaum, who named the estate Inglenook. Niebaum's property was subdivided in 1969. Eventually, Heublein produced mass-market Inglenook wines in the winery facility. Coppola bought the Victorian estate home in 1975 and began to lust after the Inglenook Château to reunite the properties.

With *Bram Stoker's Dracula* profits, he paid most of the $10 million for the winery parcel in 1995, fulfilling his dream. The Coppolas turned the château into the Niebaum-Coppola Estate Winery and the Centennial Museum to showcase both the history of winemaking and Coppola's film career.

As you walk toward the château from the parking lot, you just know you have entered a movie set, complete with expansive walkways, decorative columns, and fountains. Once inside the heavy, cool building, notice the sweeping staircase made of exotic woods Coppola brought from Belize, where he owns a resort, Blancaneaux Lodge, in a remote rain forest. To the left facing the front of the building is a small shop, where you can buy a glass of wine, imported sodas, and apparel from both Neibaum-Coppola and Blancaneaux Lodge. The Coppola-conceived stained-glass window over the staircase depicts the historic estate's reunification.

As you turn right inside the main front doorway, a concierge can answer almost any question. Farther to the right are two large rooms full of wine tastes, excellent Coppola herbed olive oils and pastas, Italian ceramics, linens, candles, copperware, cigars and accessories, and the best selections of French and Italian food books we have seen. We were struck with the warm elegance of the Belize woods in these two vast rooms, as well as with the casual friendliness of the entire Niebaum-Coppola staff. You are welcome to sit at the long tables, sip wine, and enjoy the atmosphere and music, the latter of which comes from a player piano that sounds out songs written for *The Godfather* by Coppola's father, music publisher Carmine Coppola.

Wander through the entire building. Even the entrance lobby under the stairs has display cases full of Coppola family music and film awards, and an entertaining Coppola family tree. Be sure to pick up a copy of Coppola's *Zoetrope: All Story* magazine of short fiction, as well as a video or poster of Sofia Coppola's *The Virgin Suicides* movie.

Not incidental to all the movie jazz are some of America's finest vineyards and wines. Winemaker Scott McLeod (a well-known Italian name) received his B.S. in fermentation sciences at UC Davis and worked at Fattorie Isole e Olena in Tuscany's Chianti region and as winemaker at Fattorie Badia a Passignano in Tuscany, Robert Mondavi, Cain Cellars, and Charles Shaw and now Niebaum-Coppola.

Be sure to check out the many "all-natural" food products designed and developed by Eleanor Coppola. Her *Circle of Memory* is on display at the Oakland Art Gallery and travels to San Diego and Santa Fe in 2005.

Fine points: Academy Award statues for *Patton, The Godfather,* and *The Godfather, Part II,* Coppola's 1948 Tucker from the film *Tucker,* Don Corleone's desk and chair from *The Godfather,* and Oscar-winning costumes from *Bram Stoker's Dracula* are all on display. Tasting fee: $7.50, $20.00 for Reserves (you may keep the glass). Designated drivers receive nonalcoholic beverages. Featured wines: Niebaum-Coppola Estate wines, Blancaneaux Zinfandel, Cabernet Sauvignon, Merlot, Cabernet Franc, Rubicon (mostly Cabernet Sauvignon), and Dolcetto; Francis Ford Coppola Diamond Series including Bianco, Chardonnay, Merlot, Zinfandel, Claret, Syrah, Rosso, and Cask Cabernet; RC (Roman Coppola) Reserve Syrah; Edizione Pennino Zinfandel, named for Coppola's maternal grandfather, Francesco Pennino, with the label replicating the logo of Coppola's music publishing firm, Edizione Pennino; Francis Coppola Presents: Talia Rosé, Bianco, and Rosso; and Sofia Blanc de Blancs, also sold in a "mini" can, and named for daughter Sofia Coppola, now an Academy Award–winning screenwriter for *Lost in Translation.* Owners: Francis and Eleanor Coppola. Winemaker: Scott McLeod. Cases: 40,000. Acres: 195 planted of 1,654.

Niebaum-Coppola Estate, 1991 St. Helena Highway, Rutherford 94573; phone (707) 968–1100, toll free (800) 782–4266, Web site www.niebaum-coppola.com. Open from 10:00 A.M. to 5:00 P.M. daily; tours at 10:30 A.M. and 2:30 P.M. Visa, MasterCard, American Express, and Discover. Wheelchair accessible.

Cross Highway 29 very carefully when you leave, turning left to go north only when it is clearly safe. Almost immediately you come to the Rutherford Cross

Road, Rutherford Grill, St. Helena Olive Oil Co., and Beaulieu Vineyards on the right (east) side of the highway.

St. Helena Olive Oil Co. is on the east side of Highway 29 and next door to its own parking lot and Rutherford Grill. Owner Peggy O'Kelly dumped the hectic CPA's commute from St. Helena to San Francisco, partly to please her daughters and thus herself, and founded St. Helena Olive Oil Co. in this warehouse where current Congressman Mike Thompson once worked for Wilcox Tractor.

Peggy has fulfilled a brilliant dream, and she makes olive oils and fabulous vinegars right in the back of the shop. Her St. Helena Olive Oil Co.'s Extra Virgin Olive Oil won the Gold Medal and Best of Class awards at the 2001 Los Angeles County Fair. She now produces 2,000 cases of olive oil and 4,000 cases of vinegar per year.

Soft Polenta with Leeks

from Peggy O'Kelly, St. Helena Olive Oil Co., Rutherford

3 Tbs St. Helena extra virgin lemon olive oil
3 large leeks (white and green parts), thinly sliced
2 cups water
$1/4$ cup Cabernet Vinegar cuvee
2 cups chicken or vegetable stock
1 bay leaf
1 cup polenta
$1/3$ cup freshly grated Parmesan cheese
Star Sea Salt and freshly ground black pepper to taste

Heat 2 Tbs lemon olive oil in heavy large saucepan over medium heat. Add leeks, stir to coat. Cover and cook until leeks soften, stirring occasionally, about 10 minutes. Add water, Cabernet Vinegar, stock, and bay leaf. Bring to boil.

Gradually whisk in polenta. Reduce heat to medium-low and cook until mixture is thick and creamy, stirring often and thinning with more water or stock if necessary. Cook for about 35 minutes.

Remove pan from heat. Discard bay leaf. Stir in remaining olive oil and Parmesan cheese. Season with Star Sea Salt and freshly ground black pepper to taste. Serves 4. Serve with Chardonnay.

You can taste oils, vinegars, and local breads and watch the oils and vinegars being made. Just the smell of the place is enough to send a humble body to heaven. Bottling happens Tuesday through Friday from 8:30 A.M. to 4:30 P.M., so plan your travels accordingly. You will also find Amalfi collection of pottery (an Oakland product), Cabernet vinegar, French Provençal place mats, local organic lavender, soaps, and a variety of imported olive oils as well. Unlike many wine tasting rooms, Peggy's tasting room also offers refreshing Napa Valley Sodas, waters, Italian olives, and aioli (a sort of garlic mayonnaise).

Tasting is free, but Peggy charges $10 (and well worth it) for her Sensory Evaluation Classes to taste four exclusive all-organic, locally grown olive oils. Do not miss!

Check out the new boutique winery tasting bar in the back left corner of the cavernous store, which offers wines from Abiousness, Andrew Geoffrey, Anomaly, Arns, Chameleon, Chanticleer, Crawford, James Creek, Long Vineyards, Razi, Renard, Robert Foley Vineyards, Salexis, and Snowden Wineries.

St. Helena Olive Oil Co., 8576 St. Helena Highway, Rutherford 94573; phone (707) 967–1003, Web site www.sholiveoil.com. Open from 10:00 A.M. to 5:00 P.M. daily. MasterCard and American Express. Wheelchair accessible.

From the outside the **Rutherford Grill** looks like an ordinary roadside plastic-menu kind of place. It sits in front of Beaulieu Vineyards. Drive in Beaulieu's driveway and park either in its parking lot or behind the restaurant in a small lot shared with the tiny U.S. Post Office. Walk between the buildings to the patio and a bar (a poolside feeling without the pool), and on the right you will come to the dining-room entrance. Are you in for a surprise!

Dark wood, comfy leather booths, leather-covered counter stools, and beamed ceilings with skylights set the tone. Opened linen napkins serve as "tablecloths" at the counter, where many singles drop in and enjoy a hearty, adventurous lunch or dinner. Expect lots of noise and action, with waiters and cooks shouting and repeating orders. Refresh with the milk bottles of chilled water.

The food is California hearty with a twist, and they "take rotisserie cooking very seriously." Try the roasted chicken with mashed potatoes ($14) or sliced leg of lamb ($19). You can get the same chicken as a chicken sandwich with Jack cheese and marinated arugula ($11) with cole slaw or in a "very wild rice" salad,

Toni's Marinated Olives

from Rutherford Grill, Rutherford

$^1/_2$ cup fresh tarragon leaves

$^1/_4$ cup fresh thyme leaves

5 flat anchovy fillets

2 cups drained brine-cured black olives such as Kalamata or Niçoise

2 cups drained brine-cured green olives such as picholine

1 cup extra virgin olive oil

$^1/_2$ cup thinly sliced fennel bulb (anise)

$^1/_4$ cup fresh lemon juice

2 Tbs minced onion

2 Tbs minced garlic

1 Tbs anise seeds

2 tsp fennel seeds

2 tsp dried basil, crumbled

1 tsp freshly ground black pepper

2–4 Tbs balsamic vinegar

Chop tarragon and thyme, and mince anchovies. In a deep bowl stir together all ingredients except vinegar. Marinate olive mixture, covered and chilled, stirring occasionally, at least 6 hours and up to 3 days. Bring olive mixture to room temperature before proceeding.

To serve olives, transfer to a bowl with a slotted spoon and drizzle with vinegar to taste. Makes about 4$^1/_2$ cups.

or ask for a little of both for a unique salad orgy. Knife and Fork Barbecue Ribs are grilled over hardwood and basted with Texas Hill Country BBQ sauce and served with cole slaw and chips ($24). Rare tuna fans should try the Sashimi Tuna Salad ($15). Anglophiles will enjoy (we hope) the bangers and mash ($13), and adventurers might try the grilled ostrich ($22).

"This and Thats" include Chicago Style Spinach and Artichoke Dip ($12.00), iron skillet corn bread ($3.00), a "nice little house salad" ($6.00), a whole rotisserie chicken to go ($14.00), and Tony's marinated olives ($2.00). The menu warns that "the California legislature has determined that eating is a dangerous endeavor. At Rutherford Grill we serve rare tuna, use raw eggs in our Caesar salad and grind chuck roast in house for all burgers. Upon request, we will be happy to change what we feel is a safe and delicious presentation and serve your food consistent with California Codes 113995, 113996, and 113998."

Vegetarians also enjoy the Napa Valley Vegetable Platter or club sandwich. The Caesar Salad (with raw egg) comes with homemade corn bread croutons. The Grill has a good Napa and Sonoma wine list.

> **Rutherford Grill,** *1180 Rutherford Road, Rutherford 94573; phone (707) 963–1792, Web site www.rutherfordgrill.com. No corkage fee. Open from 11:30 A.M. to 9:30 P.M. daily summer, 11:30 A.M. to 9:00 P.M. daily winter. No reservations accepted. No corkage fee. Visa, MasterCard, and American Express. Wheelchair accessible.*

Seemingly behind the Rutherford Grill is the original champion of California Cabernet Sauvignon, **Beaulieu Vineyards,** known in the local vernacular as "B.V.," which, to some people, confuses it with Sonoma's Buena Vista Winery. Beaulieu is the oldest continuously producing winery in the Napa Valley.

The tasting room is in the newish, peaked-roof octagon building at the southeast corner of the Beaulieu complex. To the left of the entrance is a tree donated and planted by *Wine Spectator* in memory of Beaulieu's longtime winemaker and Napa wine guru, Andre Tchelistcheff.

Beaulieu Vineyards

Georges de Latour immigrated from Bordeaux, France, in the late 1800s to San Francisco, where he developed a successful cream of tartar business. After he and his bride, Fernande Romer, began their four-acre vineyard and named it Beaulieu ("beautiful place"), the dreaded phylloxera lice invaded, sending Georges back to France to find resistant rootstock. He brought some back to the Napa Valley, establishing a nursery and selling healthy vines to other vintners.

Surviving Prohibition by selling sacramental wines to the Catholic church in San Francisco, Georges switched from hard-to-get French oak barrels to American oak for his Cabernet Sauvignon, and he recruited Russian-born enologist Andre Tchelistcheff from Paris's Pasteur Institute in 1938. Two years later, Georges de Latour died, having won a gold medal and Grand Sweepstakes Award at the 1939 Golden Gate International Exposition for his 1936 Cabernet Sauvignon.

Having worked side by side with her husband, Madame de Latour took over management of the winery and named the Cabernet "Georges de Latour Private Reserve" in his honor. Relying on Tchelistcheff's expertise, she ran the winery until her death in 1952, expanding its prominence to the tables of Franklin D. Roosevelt and Winston Churchill.

Tchelistcheff gained worldwide fame and taught many prominent Napa winemakers, including Joseph Heitz, Miljenko Grgich, and Tom Selfridge. In 1963 he planted B.V.'s original Carneros vineyard, one of the first to realize the Carneros region's potential for fine grapes.

Beaulieu was sold to giant Heublein in 1969, which sold it in 1998 to United Distillers & Vintners (UDV Wines), which also owns Glen Ellen Winery in Sonoma Valley. In 2002 UDV sold Beaulieu to Diagio, as winery musical chairs continues.

Fine points: You can see Madame de Latour's influence in winemaking through the photos of Beaulieu Vintners' women and the placard honoring the "Women of Beaulieu." Tasting fee: $5.00 in Visitor Center for five wines; $25.00 for five Reserve wines. Featured wines: Georges de Latour Private Reserve Cabernet Sauvignon, Carneros Reserve Chardonnay, and Pinot Noir; the Signet Collection of Zinfandel, Ensemble (Rhone blend of Mourvedre, Grenache, Carignan, and Syrah); Coastal Series of Cabernet Sauvignon, Merlot, Chardonnay, Pinot Noir, and Sauvignon Blanc; and Coastal Cabernet Sauvignon, Merlot, Zinfandel, Sauvignon Blanc, Chardonnay, and Pinot Noir. Many older vintages available. Owner: Diagio. Winemaker: Joel Aiken. Cases: 1,500,000. Acres: 1,100 Napa Valley.

Beaulieu Vineyards, 1960 St. Helena Highway South, Rutherford 94573; phone (707) 967–5200, Web site www.bvwine.com. Open from 10:00 A.M. to 5:00 P.M. daily. Tours only during harvests. Visa, Master-Card, American Express, and Discover. Wheelchair accessible.

Just behind Beaulieu on Rutherford Road are nestled The Rancho Caymus Inn and La Toque.

Absolutely the most brilliant addition to the Napa Valley is Ken Frank's **La Toque** in the Rancho Caymas Inn, one of the valley's most lovely, and across Rutherford Road from La Luna Market.

Ken left his toque in Los Angeles to "take it easy" in the Napa Valley, but as creative people do, he couldn't help getting his juices going again. The cozy and calming decor in the dining rooms includes Spanish tile and fireplaces with candles burning in summer, and an elegant homelike deck that partly faces the inn's luxurious courtyard.

La Toque's menu changes weekly and frames a prix fixe ($98) six-course dinner with coffee and San Pellegrino and Evian waters included. The seasonal menu might include courses such as chestnut bisque with Chanterelles; seared foie gras; Dungeness crab croquette; Nantucket Bay Scallops; Niman Ranch shortribs braised all day in Rutherford red wine; salt-cured Muscovy duck foie gras; Hawaiian onega seared with orzo and lobster Merlot sauce; lamb saddle with cannellini beans; cheese with toasted walnut bread; and for dessert, pot de crème with a pumpkin donut and German chocolate terrine with white chocolate coconut ice cream, or Meyer lemon and huckleberry tart with crème fraîche sorbet. La Toque also offers a menu of wines paired with each course ($56 per person).

La Toque, 1140 Rutherford Road, Rutherford 94573; phone (707) 963–9770, Web site www.latoque.com. Beer and wine. Corkage fee: $18; 18 percent service charge added; no other tipping. Open from 5:30 P.M. for dinner Wednesday–Sunday. Visa, MasterCard, and American Express. Wheelchair accessible.

For a guide trip to Mexico, check **La Luna Market and Tacqueria** right across the street from La Toque for cheap Mexican foods, fabulous burritos, Mexican music, and a generally enlightening experience.

La Luna Market and Tacqueria, 1153 Rutherford Road, Rutherford 94573; phone (707) 963–3211. Open from 8:00 A.M. to 7:30 P.M. daily.

Grgich Hills Cellar

On the west side of the highway is **Grgich Hills Cellar,** the baby of Miljenko (Mike) Grgich, a native of Croatia and champion of its independence from the former Yugoslavia, and Austin Hills of San Francisco's Hills Brothers Coffee family and fortune. As you turn across the railroad tracks, notice the Croatian flag flying. You will also see the Croatian shield on Grgich Hills wine labels.

Mike Grgich brought to this 1977 wine marriage a degree in viticulture and enology from the University of Zagreb, as well as long stints as chemist at Beaulieu Vineyards; chief enologist at Robert Mondavi Winery; and limited partner, winemaker, and vineyardist at Chateau Montelena, where he created the Chardonnay that won "Best Chardonnay" at the 1976 Paris Tasting and put Grgich firmly on the world wine-celebrity map. As a result of this triumph, his Chardonnay has been served to President Bill Clinton at the California Cafe in Los Gatos, Queen Elizabeth II, King Juan Carlos of Spain, and President Jose Sarney of Brazil. President Ronald Reagan took four cases to Paris for French President François Mitterrand.

For his contribution to the wine marriage, Austin Hills brought money, a fine coffee taster's palate, a refined sense of business management, and a reserved manner that allows Grgich to create and promote great wines. Hills's wife, Erika, owns Erika Hills Antiques, just south of St. Helena.

Together, Grgich and Hills agreed on the European tradition of concentrating on quality instead of quantity of their wines, and it has paid off. Their Chardonnay is often called the best in the world, the Cabernet Sauvignon consistently receives high ratings, and the Fumé Blanc has won several gold and silver medals. The Violetta, named for Grgich's daughter and manager, Violet, is a late-harvest dessert wine of Riesling and Chardonnay that received a 95 from *Wine Spectator* in 1997.

Fine points: Tasting fee: $5.00, tour fee $10.00 per person. Enjoy the Old World feeling in the tasting room, with its dark wood, and take time to peruse the vast literature reprints and Croatian travel posters. You can also buy wooden boxes here for just $6.00 that are ideal for storing CDs. Grgich Hills now offers rare free barrel tastings; call for information. Featured wines: Chardonnay, Fume Blanc, Cabernet Sauvignon, Zinfandel, Merlot, and Violetta Late Harvest. Owners: Mike Grgich and Austin Hills. Winemaker: Mike Grgich. Cases: 80,000. Acres: 368 planted of 413 owned.

Grgich Hills Cellar, 1829 St. Helena Highway, Rutherford 94573; phone (707) 963–2784 or (800) 532–3057, Web site www.grgich.com. Open from 9:30 A.M. to 4:30 P.M.; tours 11:00 A.M. and 2:00 P.M., weekends, 11:00 A.M. and 1:30 P.M. Visa, MasterCard, and American Express. Wheelchair accessible.

Recognizable by its bright pink, white, and purple petunias visible from Highway 29, **Rutherford Gardens'** "Chateau Tomato" is a classically elegant vegetable stand featuring herb, flowers and veggie plants, snowball cauliflower, bok choy, cabbage, fennel, cut flowers, and whatever else is in season. The shade is pulled down when the outdoor stand is closed, and you pay your money in the honor box.

Rutherford Gardens, 1796 South St. Helena Highway, Rutherford 94573; phone (707) 967–8122. Open when they're open. No credit cards. Wheelchair accessible.

Provenance Vineyards took over the bold industrial-looking building that had housed Beaucanon Napa Valley, set back from Highway 29 and previously missed by many visitors. Part of the highly reputable Chalone Wine Group, Provenance repainted the building to give it depth, enhanced the gardens, redecorated the tasting room, and hired some fun locals to pour and explain their wines.

Winemaker Tom Rinaldi served as Duckhorn Wine Company's founding winemaker (where he stayed for twenty-two years), as he now does for Provenance. Rinaldi's goal is to use "top Napa grapes and making wine that is not only in the traditional Bordeaux style but also takes advantage of the latest research and technology."

Provenance's Rutherford Cabernet Sauvignon derives from the old Caymus Ranchero, once the ranch of one of Napa Valley's first nonnative settlers, George Yount, who arrived in 1838. Thomas Rutherford received part of the ranch when he married one of Yount's granddaughters, Elizabeth.

Eventually, the Catholic Diocese of San Francisco acquired the property and sold it to French immigrant Georges de Latour, founder of Beaulieu Vineyard, who called the vineyard BV number 3. Andy Beckstoffer purchased the vineyard in 1988, renamed it Vineyard Georges III, and replanted it with more appropriate rootstock. Provenance means "the study of the source of the materials that make up an area's sediment" in geology.

Domaines Barons de Rothschild purchased all Chalone holdings, including Provenance in 2004.

Fine points: Featured wines: Sauvignon Blanc, Merlot, and Cabernet Sauvignon. Owner: Domaines Barons de Rothschild. Winemaker and General Manager: Tom Rinaldi. Cases: 40,000. Acres: 43.

Provenance Vineyards, 1695 St. Helena Highway (Highway 29), St. Helena 94574; phone (707) 968–3633, Web site www .ProvenanceVineyards.com. Open 10:00 A.M. to 4:30 P.M. daily. Tasting fee: $10. Visa, MasterCard, and American Express. Wheelchair accessible.

To get to **Franciscan Vineyards,** just north of Quail Ridge, turn east onto Galleron Road. Turn left immediately into Franciscan's driveway and parking lot. (Galleron Road will also take you to Sullivan Vineyards, the next stop after Franciscan.) Enjoy the elegant visitor center with a view looking up the Napa Valley.

The real story of Franciscan is far greater than just this winery, which has never had any relationship to Franciscan orders of the Catholic church. Until recently, Franciscan was owned by Germany's Eckes Family and its vintner/president, Chilean Agustin Huneeus. (Huneeus owns other impressive properties, including the Quintessa Estate in Rutherford, huge Veramonte in

Franciscan Vineyards

Chile's Casablanca Valley, Mount Veeder Winery on the western slopes of Napa Valley, and Estancia Alexander Valley in Sonoma and Monterey Counties.)

In 1998 Huneeus sold Franciscan to the huge Canandaigua Brands, which also owns Simi Vineyards in Asti. Jon Moramarco was named CEO in 2004.

As you approach the winery's entrance, enjoy the humor of the cement "Rutherford Bench," a pun on the Rutherford bench (land section) where the winery is located; the purple, lavender, and mustard banners; and a gigantic fountain, along with an eighteenth-century wine press in front. A peaceful, enclosed patio planted with roses, off the tasting room, provides a relaxing place to sample Franciscan wines and your picnic lunch.

Fine points: Be sure to notice prize-winning artist David Lance Goins's designs for the Mount Veeder Winery labels. He also did graphics for Ravenswood Winery in Sonoma. Tasting fee: $5.00 classics regular wines, $10.00 Reserves. Featured wines: Franciscan Chardonnay, Zinfandel, Merlot, Cabernet Sauvignon, Cuvée Sauvage Chardonnay, Magnificat; Quintessa; Veramonte Casablanca Estate Chardonnay,

Sauvignon Blanc, Cabernet Sauvignon, Merlot, and Primus Merlot; Mount Veeder Winery Cabernet Sauvignon; Estancia Alexander Valley Estate Meritage, Cabernet Sauvignon, Merlot, and Simi; Estancia Monterey County Estate Bottled Chardonnay, Pinot Noir, Reserve Chardonnay, and Reserve Pinot Noir; and Simi Sauvignon Blanc, Chardonnay, Zinfandel, Cabernet Sauvignon, and Shiraz. Owners: Constellation Brands. Winemaker: Larry Levin. Cases: Franciscan 120,000; Mount Veeder 10,000. Acres: nearly 4,000 worldwide.

Franciscan Vineyards, 1178 Galleron Road, St. Helena 94574; phone (707) 963–7111, Web site www.franciscan.com. Open from 10:00 A.M. to 5:00 P.M. daily. Visa, MasterCard, American Express, and Discover. Wheelchair accessible.

If you leave the Franciscan parking lot by the southern exit onto Galleron Road, turn left (east) to **Sullivan Vineyards.** Turn left into Sullivan's gravel driveway. On your right will be the family's interesting two-story home with rolling lawns and a refreshing duck pond. The winery is to your left. Drive around to the south side of the winery and park. Both Boe, a labrador-retriever mix, and Zsa Zsa, the blonde Lab, will greet you, with a green tennis ball firmly planted in Zsa Zsa's mouth.

You taste Sullivan's estate-grown wines with Sean Sullivan, winemaker and son of the founder, right in the middle of the winery with the inventory and barrels. Sean's sister, Kelleen, is obviously a talented painter, as her winery poster demonstrates. The Sullivans have been growing grapes here since 1978, and founder Jim Sullivan (who died in June 2004) had been making wine since Sean was born in 1962. You can picnic at the table in the vegetable garden by appointment.

Fine points: Check out the elegant etched-crystal glasses ($32) as well as the tasteful shirts and well-priced hats ($20). Custom etched bottles are also available. Sullivan's special wines are all in the Bordeaux style and are promoted solely by word of mouth. The prized Coeur de Vigne is aged thirty-two months in oak. Tasting fee: $10, which can be credited to purchase. Featured wines: Cabernet Sauvignon, Coeur de Vigne (an estate blend), and Merlot. Owner: JoAnna Sullivan. Winemaker: Sean Sullivan. Cases: 3,700. Acres: 26.

*Sullivan Vineyards, 1090 Galleron Road, Rutherford 94573; phone
(707) 963–9646 or (877) 244–7337, Web site www.sullivanwine.com.
Open from 10:00 A.M. to 5:00 P.M. daily. Visa, MasterCard, and American Express. Wheelchair accessible.*

As you leave Sullivan, turn right (west) onto Galleron to Highway 29. Turn right
(north) to continue our tour.

The next three wineries moving north are on the west side of Highway 29.

Rutherford Grove Winery and Napa Valley Grapeseed Oil Company is
tucked back in a grove of century-old eucalyptus trees that envelop a lush expanse
of lawns and gardens, protected from highway traffic and noise. This is just part
of the reason it is the home of the Napa Valley Shakespeare Festival. Walking
into Rutherford Grove is a cool, peace-
ful experience, thanks to its dark redwood walls, cement floors, rattan chairs,
fireplace, and wrought-iron foot rail at
the tasting bar. Vaulted ceilings and
large windows showcase rotating art
shows.

Rutherford Grove is worth a visit if
only as a lesson in total-use recycling. In
back of the winery, they make naturally
cold-pressed grapeseed oil and compost
residue from fifty vineyards, which they
sell back to vineyards for organic fertilizer. You can taste the grapeseed oils in
the tasting room (but not the compost)
and purchase Merlot Coffee chocolate
sauce and Napa Valley Cabernet Salsa.

Founded by German-born Bernard
Skoda, Rutherford Grove was eventually purchased by the Pestonis, originally a Swiss-Italian family from Monte
Carasso. They have been in the Napa
Valley since Albino Pestoni arrived four
generations ago. Monte Carasso's
thirteenth-century monastery appears

Multigrain Rice with Wild Mushrooms

from Rutherford Grove Winery and Napa
Valley Grapeseed Oil Co., Rutherford

½ lb Chanterelle mushrooms
(or substitute of your choice)
Oil
¼ cup Napa Valley Grapeseed
2 cloves garlic, minced
fresh thyme
salt and pepper to taste
1 pkg multigrain rice

Cut mushrooms into ½-inch slices.
Sauté mushrooms in grapeseed oil
over medium heat for about 7 minutes. Add minced garlic, thyme, salt,
and pepper to taste and continue to
sauté, about 3 minutes more. Remove
from heat and set aside.

Follow cooking directions for
package of multigrain rice. Either stir
in mushroom mixture or spoon over
each serving of rice. Serves 6 to 8.

on some of the red table wine labels. Bob and Marvin Pestoni carry on the family tradition at Rutherford Grove.

Fine points: Available only in fine restaurants and wine shops, Rutherford Grove's wines can be found at Domaine Chandon's restaurant, Dean & DeLuca, and Mustards, Viognier in Palo Alto, and Chasen's in Beverly Hills. The tasting fee of $3.00 ($5.00 for Reserves) is refundable with purchase. Featured wines: Sauvignon Blanc, Chardonnay, Petite Sirah, Merlot, Sangiovese, and Cabernet Sauvignon. Owners: Bob and Marvin Pestoni. Winemakers: Andy Pestoni and Bob Pepi. Cases: 7,000. Acres: 30+.

Rutherford Grove Winery and Napa Valley Grapeseed Oil Company, 1673 St. Helena Highway, Rutherford 94573; phone (707) 963–0544, Web site www.Rutherfordgrove.com or www.napavalleygrapeseedoil.com. Open from 10:00 A.M. to 4:30 P.M. daily. Visa, MasterCard, American Express, and Discover. Wheelchair accessible.

Caramelized Onion and Goat Cheese Tarts

from Rutherford Grove Winery and Napa Valley Grapeseed Oil Co., Rutherford

3 medium-size yellow onions, chopped
¼ cup Napa Valley Grapeseed Oil
salt and pepper to taste
1 pkg Pepperidge Farm frozen puff pastry
flour
8 oz goat cheese
fresh herbs, such as thyme or tarragon

Sauté onions in grapeseed oil, adding salt and pepper to taste until onions are caramelized. Roll puff pastry on floured board. Using a 2-inch tart cutter (or jar top), cut the dough into circles or flower designs. Place on an ungreased baking sheet.

Place a generous teaspoon of caramelized onion in the center of each tart. Place ½ teaspoon or less of goat cheese on top of the onions. Add fresh chopped herbs of your choice and salt and pepper on each to taste. Bake in preheated 350° F oven for about 15 minutes, or until tarts are lightly colored and puffed, and cheese has melted. Makes about 24.

Whole Roasted Pork Loin Wrapped with Pancetta and Stuffed with Dried Fruit

from Rutherford Grove Winery and Napa Valley Grapeseed Oil Company, Rutherford

20 dried apricots

1/4 lb golden raisins

1 750-ml bottle dry red wine

4–5 lb pork loin, center cut, trimmed of fat

1 small bunch sage, finely chopped

1 small bunch thyme, finely chopped

salt and pepper to taste

1/2 lb pancetta, sliced thinly

Macerate until soft (approximately 1 hour) the apricots and golden raisins in separate bowls in enough of the red wine to cover. Preheat oven to 325°F.

Lay the pork loin onto a cutting board. Keeping the knife parallel to the board, slice lengthwise, leaving a 1/2-inch thickness unsliced on the other side (don't slice all the way through). Open up the pork loin like a book.

Place a layer of apricots down the center of the butterflied loin, then cover with a layer of raisins. Close the loin back to its original shape, tie in 3 or 4 places with string, and season thoroughly with sage, thyme, salt, and pepper. Wrap the strips of pancetta around the width of the entire loin until it is completely covered.

Roast in a 325°F oven, turning once while cooking to brown both sides, until medium doneness (about 40 minutes). Remove from oven and let rest in a warm spot. Serves 8.

Whitehall Lane Winery has created a state-of-the art tasting and winemaking facility with adventurous angles and gift and logo-wear merchandise.

The Leonardini family of San Francisco bought the estate in 1993 and have been at work updating the wine and facilities ever since, first with winemaker Gary Galleron and now with Dean Sylvester. Sylvester comes to Whitehall Lane from Newton Vineyard, Chimney Rock Winery, and Mario Perelli-Minetti Winery. Besides being readily accessible at the winery, you might catch Sylvester playing guitar as his therapy "outlet" on the nightclub circuit with musician Gary Yoder. Their olive oil and balsamic vinegar are excellent.

Fine points: Don't miss the barrel tasting tours at 1:00 and 4:00 P.M. Tasting fee: $5.00, $10.00 on weekends, and you can keep the glass or apply the fee to a purchase. Featured wines: Sauvignon Blanc, Chardonnay, Merlot, Cabernet Sauvignon, and Belmuscato. Owner: Thomas Leonardini. Winemaker: Dean Sylvester. Cases: 45,000. Acres: 110.

Whitehall Lane Winery, 1563 St. Helena Highway, St. Helena 94574; phone (707) 963–9454, Web site whitehalllane.com. Open from 11:00 A.M. to 5:45 P.M. daily. Visa, MasterCard, and American Express. Wheelchair accessible.

Whitehall Lane Napa Cabernet Red Risotto

from Whitehall Lane Winery, St. Helena

$\frac{1}{4}$ cup butter
1$\frac{1}{2}$ cups red onion, chopped
2 Tbs chopped fresh thyme
4 cups thinly sliced radicchio
1$\frac{1}{2}$ cups arborio rice (risotto)
3 cups canned vegetable broth
1 14-oz can cannellini beans, rinsed and drained (any white bean will work)
1$\frac{3}{4}$ cups Whitehall Lane Napa Cabernet
1 cup toasted walnuts, chopped
$\frac{1}{4}$ cup grated Parmesan cheese
salt and pepper to taste

Uncork a fresh bottle of the Cabernet, pour a glass for taste approval and for yourself! Remember, do not get too carried away in the enjoyment of the wine—you need 1$\frac{3}{4}$ cups for the recipe itself, leaving approximately 2 glasses for dinner.

Melt the butter in a large saucepan over medium heat. Add onion and sauté until soft and just beginning to brown, about 5 minutes. Mix in 1$\frac{1}{2}$ Tbs thyme. Add the sliced radicchio and the rice. Sauté until the radicchio wilts, about 3 minutes.

Meanwhile, begin to simmer the vegetable broth in a separate pot. Slightly increase heat and add the beans and 1 cup of wine to the rice mixture. Simmer until the wine is absorbed and stir. Add remaining $\frac{3}{4}$ cup of wine, while continuing to simmer, for about 3 more minutes.

When all of the wine is absorbed in the risotto, add the vegetable broth to the mixture. Stir to combine, then cover and simmer until all the liquid is absorbed and the rice is tender but firm in the center. Stir in the remaining $\frac{1}{2}$ Tbs thyme and the cup of walnuts, and add the $\frac{1}{4}$ cup Parmesan cheese. Season with salt and pepper and stir to combine. Transfer to a bowl, ready to serve with additional Parmesan at the table. Serves 4.

For a little side trip, turn right (east) onto Zinfandel Lane to **Raymond Vineyard & Cellar.** At 0.6 mile east of Highway 29, turn right (south) at Raymond's signs, go through the gates, and go another 0.2 mile.

On the outside, Raymond looks like a large California ranch house with gray vertical wood siding and stone walls and gorgeous renunculas in the garden. Inside, the tasting room, with its carpeting and dining table, makes you feel as if you're in someone's home. You will find green-and-burgundy aprons, pastas, Vin-Tea, Vintners Kitchen food products, Vine Village and French Press oils, and a Raymond Vineyard 550-piece puzzle.

Roy Raymond Sr. began working in the barrel room of Beringer Winery in 1933, married winemaker Otto Beringer's daughter, Jane, worked his way to manager, and left Beringer when Nestlé Corporation bought it. Raymond bought ninety acres here on Zinfandel Lane in 1971, with the first grapes harvested in 1974, developing highly revered Cabernet Sauvignons. Even though the late Roy Sr. had sold the winery to Kirin Brewery of Japan, he was often seen on his tractor mowing the winery's lush lawns, right up until his death in 1998. Roy Jr., Walter, and Craig Raymond, great-grandsons and great-great-grandson of Beringer, continue to manage Raymond.

Fine points: Tastings $5.00 to $10.00 for limited-production or hard-to-find wines. Featured wines: Sauvignon Blanc, Chardonnay, Cabernet Sauvignon, Merlot, Amber Hill Chardonnay, and Generations Cabernet Sauvignon. Owner: Kirin Brewery. Winemakers: Walter Raymond, Kenn Vigoda. Cases: 300,000. Acres: 600.

Raymond Vineyard & Cellar, 849 Zinfandel Lane, St. Helena 94574; phone (707) 963–3141 or (800) 525–2659, Web site www.raymond wine.com. Open from 10:00 A.M. to 4:00 P.M. daily. Visa, MasterCard, American Express, and JCB. Wheelchair accessible.

Milat Vineyards is one of the few remaining old wineries still run by the original owner family. Bob and Mike Milat and their wives, Joyce and Carolyn, and now David Duckhorn and Michelle Milat Duckhorn run the whole show, which is a family affair now including cousin Cliff Little. Bob and Mike grew up on the property where their family has been growing and selling grapes since 1949, eventually realizing that their high-demand grapes might just make good wine for them, too. They started making wine in 1986 and have since stopped selling grapes to others; they are keeping them all to make their own wines. You can buy

Milat Vineyards

these personal and reasonably priced vintages only here in the tasting room. Be sure to stop and enjoy stories about Croatian food and wine.

Fine points: The Milat family also offers three guest rooms in cottages in the vineyard and a converted loft in the barn, with queen beds, full baths and patios, coffeepots, and refrigerators from $125.00 to $150.00 per room per night. Tasting fee of $5.00 for logo glass. Featured wines: Chardonnay, Sweet Chenin Blanc, Zinfandel, Merlot, and Cabernet Sauvignon. Owners: The Milat family. Winemakers: Mike Milat and David Duckhorn. Cases: 3,600. Acres: 22.

Milat Vineyards, 1091 St. Helena Highway South, St. Helena 94574; phone (707) 963–0758 or (800) 546–4528, Web site www.milat.com. Open from 10:00 A.M. to 6:00 P.M. daily. Visa, MasterCard, American Express, and Discover. Wheelchair accessible.

Corison owner and winemaker Cathy Corison recently opened her small but fine winery to the public. Located just north of Milat, Corison's facility looks like a small barn, which it is. Upon any visit you may meet easily fifty percent of the staff, since there are only four people involved in the one-room winery. This is a fabulous chance to taste excellent Cabernet Sauvignon among the barrels at a "tasting" room in one corner.

With a degree in biology from Pomona College in Claremont and a graduate degree in enology from UC Davis, Cathy Corison made wine for others for more than twenty years. Corison began her Corison label in 1987 and worked for ten years as winemaker at Chappellet Vineyard.

Drive or walk around to the back of the building to enter.

Fine points: Featured wines: Cabernet Sauvignon, Syrah, Dry Gewürztraminer. Owner and winemaker: Cathy Corison. Cases: 4,000. Acres: 8.

Corison, 987 St. Helena Highway, St. Helena 94574; phone (707) 963–0826, Web site www.corison.com. Open 10:00 A.M. to 5:00 P.M. daily, with tours by appointment. Visa, MasterCard, and American Express. Wheelchair accessible.

As we approach the city of St. Helena, the winery and specialty food forests thicken. Winery buildings range from expensive cement blocks to expensive charming old Victorian homes and wood barns. Locals refer to this area as St. Helena Highway South, with St. Helena as the center of the universe, of course. To mapmakers, it is simply Highway 29.

But whatever it's called, it is an engrossing (interesting as well as fattening!) food-and-wine mecca that even the most casual food-and-wine fans will enjoy.

On the left (west) side of Highway 29, heading north, **Flora Springs Wine Company** has a relatively new tasting room. To get to the tasting room, turn west into the driveway just past Zinfandel Lane and Inglewood Avenue.

Owner John Komes commissioned Richmond, Virginia, artist Happy the Artist to paint the cartoonish murals depicting wine growing and the winemaking process on the tasting-room walls. Enjoy the exhibits of well-known artists' work in the tasting room.

If you want to visit the first Flora Springs vineyard and wineries, head to 1978 West Zinfandel Lane in St. Helena. The Komes purchased the "old ghost winery and vineyard in the western foothills of the Napa Valley" in 1977. Komes' children, John and Julie, got caught up in the venture. John used his skills as a contractor and businessman to renovate the historic buildings and begin the winery, and Julie's husband, Pat Garvey, left his job as a college administrator to tend the vineyards. After two vintages of learning and making the wine themselves, the family invited Ken Deis to become winemaker, with impressive results.

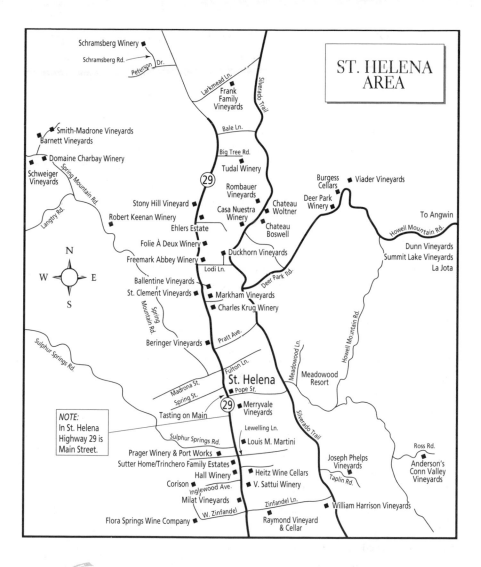

ST. HELENA AREA

Schramsberg Winery
Schramsberg Rd.
Peterson Dr.
Larkmead Ln.
Silverado Trail
Frank Family Vineyards
Bale Ln.
Smith-Madrone Vineyards
Barnett Vineyards
Big Tree Rd.
Domaine Charbay Winery
Tudal Winery
Schweiger Vineyards
Spring Mountain Rd.
29
Rombauer Vineyards
Burgess Cellars
Viader Vineyards
Stony Hill Vineyard
Deer Park Winery
Langtry Rd.
Robert Keenan Winery
Casa Nuestra Winery
Chateau Woltner
Ehlers Estate
Chateau Boswell
To Angwin
Howell Mountain Rd.
Folie À Deux Winery
Duckhorn Vineyards
Dunn Vineyards
Summit Lake Vineyards
La Jota
Freemark Abbey Winery
Lodi Ln.
Deer Park Rd.
Ballentine Vineyards
St. Clement Vineyards
Markham Vineyards
Charles Krug Winery
Spring Mountain Rd.
Howell Mountain Rd.
Beringer Vineyards
Pratt Ave.
Sulphur Springs Rd.
Fulton Ln.
Meadowood Ln.
Meadowood Resort
Madrona St.
St. Helena
Spring St.
29
Pope St.
Merryvale Vineyards
Silverado Trail
Tasting on Main
Lewelling Ln.
NOTE:
In St. Helena Highway 29 is Main Street.
Sulphur Springs Rd.
Louis M. Martini
Ross Rd.
Prager Winery & Port Works
Joseph Phelps Vineyards
Anderson's Conn Valley Vineyards
Sutter Home/Trinchero Family Estates
Hall Winery
Heitz Wine Cellars
Taplin Rd.
Corison
Inglewood Ave.
V. Sattui Winery
Milat Vineyards
Zinfandel Ln.
Flora Springs Wine Company
W. Zinfandel
Raymond Vineyard & Cellar
William Harrison Vineyards

N W E S

Fine points: Tasting fee: $5.00 regular wines, $12.00 Reserves. Flora Springs's 1991 Reserve Cabernet was selected number 3 wine in the world in *Wine Spectator's* "Top 100 Wines of the Year." Flora Springs's featured wines: Cabernet Sauvignon, Chardonnay, Sauvignon Blanc, Soliloquy, Merlot, Pinot Grigio, Sangiovese, and Trilogy. Owners: Jerome and Flora Komes. Winemaker: Ken Deis. Cases: 55,000. Acres: 650.

Flora Springs Wine Company, 677 St. Helena Highway, St. Helena 94574; phone (707) 967–8032, Web site www.florasprings.com. Open from 10:00 A.M. to 5:00 P.M. daily. Visa, MasterCard, and American Express. Wheelchair accessible.

Behind Flora Springs is **Coffee House,** which also joins Dean & DeLuca by parking lot. Enjoy the mosaics at the cafe's entrance. This spot features good coffee, coffee beans, Sweetie Pies cakes and pastries (the best!), sandwiches, salads, local art and music, checkers that you can pick up at the coffee bar and take to your table (chess is already set up), frozen drinks, and poetry readings. We particularly like the green chairs and tables right outside the cafe on the patio, on the non-parking-lot side. Use the drive-up window if you're in a hurry.

Coffee House, 677 St. Helena Highway, St. Helena 94574; phone (707) 967–0820. Open from 5:30 A.M. to 5:30 P.M. Monday–Friday, 6:30 A.M. to 3:30 P.M. Saturday, 7:30 A.M. to 3:30 P.M. Sunday. No credit cards. Wheelchair accessible.

Right next door, and in dramatic contrast to Coffee House, is famed **Dean & DeLuca,** the Manhattan "Purveyors of Fine Food and Kitchenware" founded on Prince Street in SoHo by former publishing executive Joel Dean and former history teacher and son of a food importer Giorgio DeLuca. Leslie Rudd owns a controlling interest in Dean & DeLuca and is responsible for its successful expansion, with Giorgio DeLuca continuing day-to-day management and his global search for the finest food products.

You can enter Dean & DeLuca from the parking lot to the store's south; or through the southern front door, which takes you into the fresh local produce, breads, and delicacies sections; or through the northern front door into the wine shop, where Hyde Park CIA graduate John Hardesty oversees 1,200 California wines, cognacs, armagnacs, mezcals, and cigars in a walk-in humidor, where his best customers have their own lockers.

In the produce department you might find black trumpet or hedgehog mushrooms, red and white Belgian endive, and Della Fattoria and Artisan breads. The deli is like no other and offers cherry peppers stuffed with provolone and prosciutto, Ozark and Serrano hams, salted capers, thirteen types of olives, duck confit, foie gras, and various herrings.

Forty of the world's best olive oils, mustards, and other delicacies lead you to the kitchenware section and finally to the cooked food case under the direction of executive chef Peter Halikas and his highly qualified crew. You might find rotisserie pork loin with stone-ground mustard and apricot preserves, chicken salad, yellow corn polenta with roasted mushrooms, or green-chile potato salad. You can even get elegant sandwiches to go for your picnic ($6.95). The take-home dinner menu changes weekly.

The espresso bar offers fresh fruit smoothies, shakes, and coffees, with stand-up cafe tables, and excellent restrooms down the hall.

Dean & DeLuca, 607 South St. Helena Highway, St. Helena 94574; phone (707) 967–9980, Web site www.deandeluca.com. Open from 9:00 A.M. to 7:00 P.M. daily, espresso bar open at 7:30 A.M. Monday–Saturday, 9:00 A.M. Sunday. MasterCard, American Express, and Discover. Wheelchair accessible.

On the east side of Highway 29 (here called St. Helena Highway South), you will find three great wineries right next door to one another. The first one you will come to going north is the venerable and fun **V. Sattui Winery.** Turn east onto White Lane and go over the railroad tracks to the winery's cool lawns and warm

V. Sattui Winery

welcomes. If the parking lot is too crowded, drive farther east on White Lane to additional parking.

Sattui is under-known for its fabulous delicatessen, pastries, and, of course, prize-winning wines, which are sold only here at the winery.

Vittorio Sattui came to California from Carsi, near Genoa, Italy, and eventually made wine in San Francisco's North Beach Italian neighborhood—but who wasn't making their own wine then? Purchasing grapes from the Napa Valley, Sattui moved his operation to Bryant Street, then closed down during Prohibition.

Vittorio's great-grandson, Daryl Sattui, began to reestablish the family winery, this time in the Napa Valley, in 1975, with the goal of making "wines my great-grandfather Vittorio would be supremely proud of." He even slept in a sleeping bag on the tasting room floor and took showers from the winery's hose, since he couldn't afford housing rent.

Opening the winery to the public on March 4, 1976, Daryl served wine tastes from a wooden plank bridging two barrels and kept the wine sales money in a wooden-box "cash register."

Daryl used a hand bottler and his great-grandfather's ninety-year-old corking machine to bottle his first wines and traded several cases of wine to a college friend to modify the original, historic label. Having no money to advertise, he hoped the wine would sell itself, and it has. And since all Sattui wines are sold here, a near-cult of devotees has developed of people who clamor to buy their wines directly from the winery.

In addition to the original winery building, where the delicatessen and tasting room are now, Sattui built a historically accurate, elegant stone winery building in 1985. It looks like one from the 1890s, with 3-foot-thick, hand-hewn stone walls and heavy rustic timbers. Be sure to take a self-guided tour of the stone building's underground cellars and small caves, where you will find a fascinatingly musty historical museum chronicling Sattui's and California's wine history.

Two acres of lawns, picnic tables, and century-old oak trees invite hundreds of picnickers to enjoy themselves daily. Kids run and scream, grandparents bask, and parents watch them all, eating and sipping wine all the way.

As you enter the old winery, the first thing you smell is cheese, not wine. And for good reason. An enormous Swiss Emmenthaler wheel and 200 varieties of imported and a few domestic cheeses greet you to the left of the door, along with Molinari salami, Sciambria and Acme breads, strawberries, apples, Dijon mustards, French cornichon pickles, Kalamata olives, Italian pepperoncini, and an entire wall of prepared-daily deli foods and Acme bread to go. Be sure to check out Sattui's own chocolate sauce and their Monastero Le Vallesi extra virgin olive oil from Tuscany. The charming staff offer you a choice of the day's cheese-tasting selections. Cheese shop manager Jean Varner came to Sattui from Oakville Grocery, where she served as assistant manager in charge of "charcuteries," specialty foods, and meats.

One of our most astounding food discoveries in the Napa Valley is Sattui's delicatessen. Feast your eyes upon fresh foods and reasonable prices of fresh artichokes, oven-roasted salmon with remoulade, smoked trout, Russian and American caviar, Gulf prawns with mustard sauce, steamed asparagus with olive oil, and prosciutto di Parma.

Watch for annual Tax Relief and Crush Parties, full of music, fine foods, fine Sattui wines, and added discounts on case purchases. This is one mailing list you must get on.

Fine points: No tasting fee. Sattui's Preston Vineyard Cabernet Sauvignons often win medals, including a "Best Cab in California" at the California State Fair. According to Sattui's brochure, *Wine Spectator* noted that V. Sattui has "garnered more gold medals in the big taste-offs than any other single winery in the Napa Valley." A must-stop! Sattui also is one winery that offers recycling bins! Featured wines: Chardonnay, Sauvignon Blanc, Johannisberg Riesling, White Zinfandel, Gamay Rouge, Suzanne's Vineyard Zinfandel, Merlot, Cabernet Sauvignon including three vineyard designates, Sattui Family Red and Cabernet Sauvignon, and dessert wines Muscat, Madeira, Colli del Trasimeno, Felicita, and Vin Santo. Owner: Daryl Sattui. Winemaker: Rick Rosenbrand. Cases: 45,000. Acres: 750.

V. Sattui Winery, 111 White Lane, St. Helena 94574; phone (707) 963–7774 or (800) 799–2337, Web site www.vsattui.com. Open from 9:00 A.M. to 6:00 P.M. daily, closes 5:00 P.M. November–February. Visa and MasterCard. Tasting room is wheelchair accessible, museum is not.

Right next door, to the north, is **Heitz Wine Cellars,** which is now just the winery's tasting room, with the actual winery currently located in a restored 1898 stone cellar originally built by Anton Rossi on a 160-acre property on Taplin Road, east of St. Helena. This is the original, where Alice and Joseph Heitz built a reputation and cult following for both Heitz's wines and his interesting personality.

Joe was from Illinois and Alice from South Dakota. They met in California in the 1940s. Joe earned two degrees in enology at UC Davis and spent seven years as understudy to the famed wine guru Andre Tchelistcheff at Beaulieu Vineyards. Joe and Alice purchased their first vineyard (eight acres) in 1961.

The three Heitz children grew up in the vineyards and business, and now David serves as winemaker, having made the 1974 commemorative bottling of Heitz Cellars' now famous Martha's Vineyard Cabernet Sauvignon as his first solo effort. Kathleen directs national and international sales and marketing, working with a biology degree from studies in Switzerland and at the University of Oregon. And Rollie oversees the company's finances and properties with his business degree from Santa Clara University.

The winery's redwood structure looks like a mountain cabin on the outside and an elegant parlor on the inside. The teensy, carpeted, and subdued tasting room, with interesting corkscrews and calming classical music, focuses on a glass-topped table, where you are served.

In the Heitzes' case, "Martha's Vineyard" refers to vineyards owned by Tom and Martha May near Oakville, while "Bella Oaks" refers to Barney and Belle Rhodes' vineyard abut 3 miles north of Martha's Vineyard, on the southwest side of Rutherford.

We are glad to have first visited this winery before the death of Joseph Heitz in December 2000. His passing was mourned by the entire Napa Valley. Since then, his wife and children have continued to carry on the family business.

Fine points: No tasting fee. Joe Heitz actually pioneered single vineyard designation wines in California. He was feted as one of the world's thirty top winemakers at La Tour d'Argent in Paris. Another must-stop. Featured wines: Chardonnay, Martha's Vineyard Cabernet Sauvignon, Napa Valley Cabernet Sauvignon, Trailside Vineyard Cab, Bella Oaks Cabernet Sauvignon, Zinfandel, Grignolino, Grignolino Rosé, Grignolino Port, and Ink Grade Port. Owner: Heitz family; Kathleen Heitz, president. Winemaker: David Heitz. Cases: 40,000. Acres: 350.

Heitz Wine Cellars, 436 St. Helena Highway South, St. Helena 94574; phone (707) 963–3542, Web site www.heitzcellars.com. Open from 11:00 A.M. to 4:30 P.M. daily. Visa, MasterCard, American Express, Diners Club, and JCB. Wheelchair accessible.

Just north of and next door to Heitz Cellars you will find **Louis M. Martini,** one of the oldest wineries in the Napa Valley. Three generations of colorful Martinis (men, that is) have dedicated themselves to finding the best land for growing grapes and matching soils and microclimates, following the old-country Italian traditions.

In 1906, the year of the San Francisco earthquake and great fire, Louis M. Martini and his father, Agostino, made their first wine in San Francisco. They eventually built a 60,000-gallon winery in the Bayview District. Louis M. took his wine on his market wagon when he was selling clams and mussels on Polk Street and sold his first gallon to the fish-shop owner, who gave a taste to the chicken-shop owner. Then *he* bought a gallon and gave a sample to the butcher next door, who also bought a gallon, and off to the wine races went Louis M. Martini. He opened the L. M. Martini Grape Products Company in Kingsburg, California, in 1922, to make sacramental and "medicinal" wines and grape concentrates.

Anticipating the repeal of Prohibition, the Martinis moved to the Napa Valley in 1933 to build their winery, one of the first to use cold fermentation. Five years later Louis M. purchased the Goldstein Ranch in Sonoma Valley and made it Italian-American by renaming it Monte Rosso. By 1942 Louis M. owned the Stanley Ranch in Carneros, foreseeing the potential of the now-famous wine-producing region that flops on both sides of the Napa–Sonoma County border.

In the early 1950s Louis M. introduced wind machines to protect vineyards from winter frosts and worked with UC Davis enologists to pioneer clonal research on Chardonnay, Pinot Noir, and Riesling grapes. By 1954 Louis P. Martini became the second-generation Louis Martini winemaker, introducing gondolas for grape harvesting in 1957. In the late 1960s he bottled the first Merlot in the United States. (Sadly, Louis P. Martini died in September 1998.)

Although the Martinis sold the winery to E. & J. Gallo in 2002 to improve distribution, Louis M.'s granddaughter, Carolyn Martini, is still involved, particularly in community relations.

While the winery building itself has a slightly industrial look, it's what's inside that counts. Just as you walk in the door, stop for a minute before the historic cases in the vestibule. Placards in the cases give a quick, succinct course in winemaking.

Fine points: Ask about the Los Ninos Series, dedicated to the births of Michael's and Carolyn's children with labels designed by the kids. Enjoy a picnic (bring with you) and Martini wines in Martini Park, the winery's garden courtyard. Tasting fees: $7.00 for most flights and $15.00 for a flight of single vineyard Cabernet Sauvignon. Featured wines: Zinfandel, Cabernet Sauvignon, Reserve Chardonnay, Barbera, Merlot, Gewürztraminer, and Moscato Amabile. Owners: E. & J. Gallo. Winemaker: Michael Martini. Cases: 180,000. Acres: 1,200.

Louis M. Martini, 254 St. Helena Highway South, St. Helena 94574; phone (707) 963–2736 or (800) 321–9463, Web site www .louismartini.com. Open from 11:00 A.M. to 5:00 P.M. daily. Visa, MasterCard, American Express, and Discover. Wheelchair accessible.

Hall Winery is the fabulous new boutique winery that replaced Edgewood south of St. Helena. Hall's motto is "It's the wines, silly." Sound a wee bit Clintonesque? For good reason. Co-owner Kathryn Hall is an attorney who served in the Clinton Administration as ambassador to Austria and moved to the Napa Valley from Texas with her husband, Craig Hall.

Kathryn's family had owned sixty-three acres of vineyards in Mendocino County, which she inherited and managed until 1992. In the process she studied vineyard management at UC Davis, raised two children, and met and married Texas financier Craig Hall. The Halls now own vineyards here and in the prized Alexander Valley.

The Hall family transformed a tomblike tasting room in an attractive stone building into an exciting, vivacious tasting experience filled with lots of laughter, with the knowledge and tone set by daughter Kristin. Everything, including the Halls' substantial art collection, is the finest. Tastes are presented in Riedel crystal stemware. Artwork shown in rotation includes that of Frank Stella, Jackson Pollack, Joel Shapiro, and Roy Lichtenstein. They also lured winemaker Mike Reynolds away from Schramsberg and are hoping to have world-renowned architect Frank Gehry design a new building for them.

Be sure to notice the red 7-foot-tall sculpture *Moebus Tower,* a horizontal figure eight that represents infinity, by Texas artist Michelle O'Michael. The redness of this work inspired the vibrant red color that has become Hall's signature. But remember, "It's the wines, silly."

Moebus Tower *by Michelle O'Michael at Hall Winery*

Fine points: Featured wines: Estate Sauvignon Blanc, Cabernet Sauvignon, Merlot, and Cabernet Franc. Owners: Kathryn and Craig Hall. Winemaker: Mike Reynolds. Cases: 20,000. Acres: 1,335.

Hall Winery, 401 Highway 29 South, St. Helena 94574; phone (866) 667–4255, Web site www.hallwines.com. Open 9:00 A.M. to 5:00 P.M. Monday–Friday, 9:00 A.M. to 5:30 P.M. Saturday, 11:00 A.M. to 5:00 P.M. Sunday. Tasting fee: $10, or $20 for tastes and tour at 11:00 A.M. or 2:00 P.M. Visa, MasterCard, and American Express. Wheelchair accessible.

Sutter Home/Trinchero Family Estates dates from 1874, and the name Sutter Home from 1900, when pioneer John Sutter's daughter named it for him, although Italian immigrants John and Mario Trinchero bought it in 1946 (still early by Napa standards) and majored in bulk wines until about 1970. They were well known for their mantra that if you could bring it through the front door, they would fill it with wine.

Wine industry innovator Bob Trinchero eked a rosé-style wine out of some Zinfandel grapes and called it White Zinfandel, which, as an almost "pop" wine, became the best-selling wine in the United States. Bob also developed the single-service bottles you get on airplanes and Amtrak.

While the company has three vineyards in the Napa Valley, most of the grapes come from the Sierra foothills, the flat Delta area near Sacramento, and the hot Sacramento Valley. All Trinchero Family Estates' vineyards are farmed organically or by sustainable farming practices.

When you drive up to the winery, you will be struck by the lovely Victorian home and gardens with their hundred varieties of roses, forty varieties of day lilies, and a camellia at the Victorian Inn's entrance that was planted in 1876. The large palm tree was brought from the Canary Islands in the 1940s. Our late, great friend, landscape architect Bob Ernest, designed the current gardens, using all-natural fertilizers and predatory insects to control pests.

The spacious, wood-walled tasting room is to your left. Here there are lots of serious wines—and humorous other stuff and staff. You can take a "Blend Your Own Wine" forty-five-minute seminar, discovering the differences among varietals and learning how to blend your own personalized wine, all for just $10.

Harvesting the Dream, a book about the Trinchero family by authors Kate Heyboe and Stanley Hock, was published in 2004.

Sutter Home/Trinchero Family Estates

Fine points: Sutter Home/Trinchero Family Estates is one of the few wineries that produces alcohol-free wine; it is available here under the Fre label. The winery also announces special sale deals on the blackboard daily, so you have to be here to know about them. The company also makes fruit-flavored wines. Tasting fee: "zip, zero, nada"; $5.00 for better wines. Featured wines: labels Sutter Home, Trinity Oaks, Reynolds, and Trinchero; various Zinfandels, Sauvignon Blanc, Chardonnay, Chenin Blanc, Cabernet Sauvignon, Merlot, Gewürztraminer, Barbera, Shiraz, Muscat Alexandria, and Triple Cream Sherry. Owner: The Trinchero family. Winemakers: Joe Shirley and Rick Oberschulte. Cases: 10,000,000. Acres: 5,500.

Sutter Home/Trinchero Family Estates*, 100 St. Helena Highway South, St. Helena 94574; phone (707) 963–3104, Web site www.tfe.com or www.sutterhome.com. Open from 9:30 A.M. to 5:00 P.M. daily. Visa, MasterCard, American Express, and Discover. Wheelchair accessible.*

One of our favorite discoveries is **Prager Winery & Port Works,** which is actually right behind Trinchero Family Estates' Victorian house off Lewelling Lane, a narrow little one-lane street.

Prager's tasting room is the downstairs of an old wooden barn at the rear of a small parking lot. Originally a carriage house and the John Thomann Winery and Distillery, built in 1865, the building must be very happy with its current tenant.

Jim Prager presides over his realm from a wooden bar stool and sees the cobwebs holding bottles on the windowsill as "the original web site." He sees the secondary "web site" as the one draping the picture of "my father's father's grandson." Hello? It's also fun to study the paper money wallpaper chipped in by Prager's visitors from all over the world. A huge musty Oriental rug, well-worn wooden captain's chairs, classic cigars, and a truly old corkscrew collection complete the stage setting.

In a stroke of genius, Jim and his wife, Imogene, left Orange County for Napa, developed a small shopping center (now the St. Helena Premium Outlets) north of St. Helena, and settled on his other true love, wine, and even more specially, port. Imogene runs a small B&B adjoining their lovely home next to the winery, and their children, John, Jeff, Peter, and Katie, are all involved in this down-home and highly personal effort.

Fine points: Here you can taste at least three of the six styles of port that Jim produces, all a blend of sweetness and brandy. Jim talks of evaporation as something "the angels love," and of his ten-year-old Noble Companion Ultra Premium Port as "smooth as a baby's bottom." We recommend all of his ports for an elegant taste experience, smooth even on a hot day. Don't miss the Chocolate Drizzle, Chocolate Mousse Balls, and interesting cigars. Tasting fee: $10, including 19 oz glass. Featured wines: Chardonnay, Cabernet Sauvignon, Aria White Port, Royal Escort Port, Madeline (late harvest Johannisberg Riesling), Noble Companion 10 Year Tawny Port, Alyssa, and Sweet Claire. Owner: James Prager. Wine and port maker: "God—we just tend the land," with the help of Pete Prager. Cellarmaster: Richard Lenney. Cases: 3,600. Acres: 15.

Prager Winery & Port Works, 1281 Lewelling Lane, St. Helena 94574; phone (707) 963–7678 or (800) 969–7678, Web site www
.pragerport.com. Open from 10:30 A.M. to 4:30 P.M. daily. Visa and MasterCard. Wheelchair accessible.

ST. HELENA

Almost a mile north of Trinchero Family Estates and Prager you will find what has become an interesting cluster of buildings, which include **Merryvale Vineyards,** the Real Foods group's Tra Vigne, Tra Vigne Pizzeria, and The Inn at Southbridge. (You are still on Highway 29, which, as you noticed, was called St. Helena Highway and St. Helena Highway South, and is now called Main Street in St. Helena proper. Confused enough? We are.)

The Mondavi family's first wine venture began here in the lovely stone structure that now houses Merryvale Vineyards. The first Napa Valley winery built after Prohibition, the Sunny St. Helena Winery was purchased and founded in 1983 as Merryvale by San Francisco developer Bill Harlan and friends, who renovated it and, in 1996, sold 60 percent to Jack Schlatter and his son Rene from Switzerland, who again renovated the winery while preserving its historic look. When Harlan first bought the winery, the wine was made at Rombauer Vineyards.

Fine points: Don't miss the Tank Room, with its 22,000-gallon wooden cask, and the Cask Room, lined with two stories of century-old 2,000 gallon casks, usually used for private and group parties. Book reservations to take the Wine Component Tasting Seminar, offered at 10:30 A.M. on Saturday and Sunday in the Cask Room ($15.00 per person). The tasting fee ranges from $5.00 to $12.00. Featured wines: Semillon, Chardonnay, Sauvignon Blanc, Merlot, Reserve Chardonnay, Reserve Merlot, Cabernet Sauvignon, and other limited production varietals. Owner: Jack Schlatter. Winemaker: Steve Test. Cases: 80,000. Acres: buy in Napa County.

Merryvale Vineyards, 1000 Main Street, St. Helena 94574; phone (707) 963–7777 or (800) 326–6069 outside California, Web site www.merryvale.com. Open from 10:00 A.M. to 6:30 P.M. daily. Visa, MasterCard, American Express, and Discover. Wheelchair accessible.

If you're famished, you're in Californian–Italian heaven, right within short-walking distance of Merryvale. Across Charter Oak Street you will find **Tra Vigne Pizzeria,** an upscale pizzeria that tries to fill the financial gap by offering reasonably priced food for both locals and visiting wine fans, including soups, salads, pastas, and desserts. You'll notice the place by the huge red-tomato metal sculpture on the front porch.

The yummy piadine are un-rolled-up roll-ups made from pizza dough, with Caesar salad, lettuce, tomatoes, and other veggies combined with skirt steak, grilled chicken, or gorgonzola piled high. Just try to eat this politely! They even bring you a diagram of eating directions. Pizzas and pizza crusts for the piadine are baked in a giant wood-burning brick oven.

Order with the computer host at the counter just as you walk in the door, then sit at a table and wait for your food and beverages to arrive. Enjoy your meal indoors or on the west-facing patio with black-and-white-striped umbrellas. Even the counter stools, shaped like screw-top tomato vines, keep the theme.

This is a great place for groups and kids. Cokes come with free refills if you go up to the bar/counter.

***Tra Vigne Pizzeria**, 1016 Main Street at The Inn at Southbridge, St. Helena 94574; phone (707) 967–9999. Open from 11:30 A.M. to 10:00 P.M. daily. Beer and wine. Visa and MasterCard. Wheelchair accessible.*

Just up Main Street at its intersection with Charter Oak Avenue is **Tra Vigne,** one of the Napa Valley's best-known restaurants. Real Foods group has succeeded in creating the feeling of a small Italian village with Tra Vigne, its courtyard, and the smaller Cantinetta Tra Vigne in an old sherry winery. Flowers brighten tables and spirits inside and out, even on rainy days.

Tra Vigne and Cantinetta Tra Vigne

Tra Vigne itself feels Italian the minute you walk in, with 30-foot ceilings, heavily draped entry, a hand-carved bar, and Italian beaded light fixtures. Helen Berggruen's colorful paintings and Cinzano red posters decorate the walls. Service is meticulous, while the feeling is elegantly casual. The restaurant makes its own mozzarella and prosciutto, presses its own olive oil, and grows its own table grapes.

Roasted Polenta and Balsamic Sauce

from Tra Vigne, St. Helena

POLENTA:

3 cups chicken stock	1 cup polenta meal
3 cups heavy cream	1 cup semolina
pinch nutmeg	½ cup grated Fontina
1 tsp salt	1 cup Parmesan
¼ tsp ground white pepper	

Combine stock, cream, grated nutmeg, salt, and pepper in a large, heavy-gauge pot. Bring liquid to a boil, then add the polenta and semolina gradually while stirring. Continue to cook over moderate heat while stirring constantly. Polenta is ready when it begins to pull away from the sides of the pot (approximately 10–15 minutes).

Remove from heat and stir in all the Fontina and ¾ cup Parmesan cheese until well incorporated. Spread polenta evenly on oiled sheet trays. Be sure to use trays that are not warped, and spread to a thickness of approximately ¾ inch.

Cool trays to room temperature, then cover with parchment and refrigerate. These may be prepared 48 hours in advance.

BALSAMIC SAUCE:

1 pint balsamic vinegar	2 bay leaves
1 chopped shallot	6 peppercorns
2 quarts stock (roasted chicken, veal, rabbit, or canned; if using a canned broth, do not salt any portion of the recipe)	1 stick sweet butter

Reduce the vinegar with the chopped shallots to a syrup consistency. Add the stock, bay leaves, and peppercorns. Reduce to a sauce consistency and strain.

TO ASSEMBLE:

Cut polenta into squares or triangles. Put on a buttered sheet pan, sprinkle generously with leftover Parmesan cheese, and put in a 500°F oven until golden brown. Remove from oven and finish sauce.

Bring reserved sauce to a simmer and whisk in butter, adjust salt and pepper to taste, and pour on plates before polenta. Serves 4.

Notes from Chef Michael Chiarello: "This is the very best recipe for polenta I have ever used. The ratio of liquid and dry ingredients is 3 to 1. For soft polenta, try a ratio of 5 or 6 to 1. I encourage you to change the recipe as you see fit."

Chef Michael Chiarello, creator of online shopping site www.napastyle.com (where you'll find everything you could ever want for your kitchen and more) and star of the PBS series *Michael Chiarello's Napa* (now in its third season), has added several cookbooks to his resume since leaving this charming Italian eatery. Chef Michael Reardon served as sous chef to Chiarello and now offers his own imprint on Tra Vigne's menu. His signature dishes include appetizers, such as grilled Monterey Bay calamari ($9.95), baked pecorino cheese pudding with rappini and cippolini onions ($9.95). Hungry travelers might try pasta with fresh squid, gulf prawns, mussels, borlotti beans and chard ($16.50), braised rabbit and wild mushroom ragu on pappardelle pasta ($16.95), roasted striped bass ($21.95), garlic roasted Dungeness crab (26.95), grilled Napa Valley lamb with potatoes au gratin ($20.95), or smoked and braised organic beef short ribs with garlic polenta ($21.95). All are exquisite. Lunch is slightly less expensive.

Passing of plates around the table and sharing are expected here. Do not leave without trying the Tiramisu do Cioccolata.

Although there is a full bar, be sure to check out Tra Vigne's exceptional Italian and California wine list, with an exclusive selection of 1987 Cabernet Sauvignons commemorating the restaurant's tenth anniversary. Take time to venture downstairs (under the guise of finding the restroom, if necessary) to see the interesting historic photos, including a locally famous train derailment.

If you're in the mood for a less formal and less expensive lunch or dinner, try **Cantinetta Tra Vigne** for excellent hot or cold panini (sandwiches), including a tasty roasted peppers with stracchino cheese and olives on a filone roll, grilled chicken breast with goat milk feta, and marinated roasted lamb loin ($8.95–$10.95); soups ($6.50); salads from Caesar to grilled wild king salmon; veggie lasagna; spring tarts; stuffed focaccia; or pastas, all under $15.00.

Pastries, from the Tra Vigne kitchen, are divine. You can also purchase Tra Vigne's fresh mozzarella ($8.00 per pound) as well as its fresh stocks, sauces, and dressings. What a treat!

Tra Vigne, Tra Vigne Wine Shop, and Cantinetta Tra Vigne, 1050 Charter Oak Avenue, St. Helena 94574; phone (707) 963–8888, Web site www.travignerestaurant.com. Open 11:00 A.M. to 10:00 P.M. Corkage: $18. Visa, MasterCard, Discover, Carte Blanche, and Diners Club. Wheelchair accessible from patio.

We want you to take the time to drive another block down Charter Oak behind Tra Vigne to Allison Street and the **Napa Valley Olive Oil Manufactory.** Leonora and Ray Particelli and Policarpo (Pol) Lucchesi are the current generation nurturing the family olive-oil business founded by Guillermo Guidi in 1930. As you might guess by their names, the owners are all from Lucca, Italy.

Surprisingly enough, when you walk into the old white-clapboard barn, you smell salami, seemingly tons of loose Molinari salami. Heaven! The two rooms' walls are covered with thousands of business cards, including ours on the door-frame. Wander through barrels and barrels of dried mushrooms, tubs of dried beans from French flageolet to Lupini and canellini, pickled everything, prosciutto bones for $10.00, bags of herbs, and containers of anchovies from small ($2.75) to major ($25.00). Check out the freezer in the front room full of delectable crab or lobster ravioli ($4.50), veggie or cheese tortellini or ravioli ($3.00), and lasagna ($6.75).

Be sure to notice the olive press brought from Lucca more than seventy years ago. The tracks in the wooden floor were caused by the cart (now filled with salami) that was used to move olives brought in from Napa fields by Carmelite nuns for pressing. The olive oil is now made in the Sacramento Valley and bottled here. It is available in regular or extra virgin, in sizes ranging from pints to generous gallons. The Extra Virgin (blue label) is quite potent, and Leonora recommends the regular Pure Olive Oil (white label) for most purposes.

Napa Valley Olive Oil Manufactory, 835 Charter Oak Avenue, St. Helena 94574; phone (707) 963–4173. Open from 8:00 A.M. to 5:30 P.M. daily. No credit cards. Wheelchair accessible.

Across Main Street (Highway 29) from Charter Oak Avenue and Tra Vigne is one of St. Helena's local favorites, **Taylor's Refresher.** Joel and Duncan Gott's version of Taylor's jazzed up the menu, as well as the prices, gardens, and general surroundings. The updated menu features ultimate burgers including the Western Bacon Blue Ring ($7.99); the California Chicken with Jack cheese, guacamole, and veggies ($8.99); an ahi burger seared rare with ginger wasabi mayo and Asian slaw ($11.99); fried calamari ($6.49); and classic Cobb salad ($12.99). Thick spoon-needed shakes may include Oreos or Snickers, and the tacos and onion rings still stand out. Joel Gott also makes excellent wines.

Taylor's Refresher, 933 Main Street, St. Helena 94574; phone (707) 963–3486. Open from 11:00 A.M. to 9:00 P.M. daily. Beer and wine. No credit cards. Wheelchair accessible.

We will walk you up the right (east) side of Main Street as far north as Pairs Restaurant and Tivoli. Then we will cross Main Street and walk back down the west side, guiding you into every shop, bakery, and restaurant along the way.

We highly recommend that you have a look at **Lolo's Second to None Consignment Shop.** Lolo's is funky, with used clothing, furniture, and eclectica.

Lolo's Second to None Consignment Shop, 1120 Main Street, St. Helena 94574; phone (707) 963–7972. Open from 10:30 A.M. to 5:30 P.M. Tuesday–Saturday, 10:30 A.M. to 4:00 P.M. Sunday–Monday. Visa, MasterCard, American Express, and Discover. Wheelchair accessible.

Villa Corona is a new and extremely clean Mexican restaurant run by the Villasenor family who come from Jalisco. House-made tortillas are actually made at their Napa store in the Bel-Aire Plaza Shopping Center, and they also have a restaurant in the Alamo-Peabody shopping center in Vacaville.

House specials include three versions of camarones or large prawns, including sautéed in garlic butter, sautéed in "very spicy sauce," or as a whole prawn cocktail with fresh avocado, cilantro, and onions (each $11.50). Choose from fifteen burritos from bean, rice, and cheese ($4.95) to one with prawns, chili pasilla, mushrooms, onions, rice, and cheese, topped with green sauce ($7.75). Platillos or combination plates are all $9.95, and breakfast includes huevos con chorizo, huevos rancheros, Chilaquiles, and eggs with burritos ($6.15–$7.25). Meat entrees range from a taco de carnitas (roasted pork, $3.50), to carne asada, chili verde (pork cooked in green sauce), or a carnitas plate (each $10.50). Chips and salsa are an extra $1.50.

Villa Corona, 1138 Main Street, St. Helena 94574; phone (707) 963–7812. Open 10:00 A.M. to 2:30 P.M. Monday, 10:00 A.M. to 9:00 P.M. Tuesday–Saturday, 11:00 A.M. to 5:00 P.M. Sunday. Beer and wine. Visa and MasterCard. Wheelchair accessible.

Tasting on Main is Robert Piziali's tasting room that replaced Ehlers Grove's "downtown" tasting room. Tasting on Main affords an artfully elegant opportunity to taste boutique wineries' products and nibble chocolates.

Wines poured here include those of Broman Cellars, Kelham Vineyards, Oakville Ranch, Richard Partridge, Miura, Saddleback Cellars, Venge Family Reserve, Robert Keenan, Reynolds Family Winery, and Ehlers Grove.

Tasting on Main, 1142 Main Street, St. Helena 94574; phone (707) 967–1042, Web site www.tastingonmain.com. Open 10:30 A.M. to 6:00 P.M. daily. Visa, MasterCard, and American Express. Wheelchair accessible.

St. Helena's few blocks of downtown are elegant yet homey, and the city is trying hard to keep it from becoming too touristy, while maintaining its usefulness to locals and allure to visitors. It feels like a step back several decades, with a gracious, relaxed ambience and elegant boutiques to suit most needs, mixed with a pharmacy and hardware store, important parts of a functioning downtown. Please note that some of these downtown businesses are closed on Tuesday; check the hours in the following listings carefully before visiting that day—we wouldn't want you to miss out on a place you particularly want to see.

Supreeya's Thai House adds some ethnic interest to St. Helena's dining scene in a small restaurant that transports one from Napa Valley to Thailand. Lunch specials include a choice of salad with peanut dressing or soup and range from mixed vegetables sautéed with tofu ($6.95) and Prik Khing with chicken, pork, beef, or tofu and red curry paste, bell pepper, and green beans ($7.95) to prawns with pineapple red curry and coconut milk ($9.50). Supreeya makes several noodle dishes including Pad Thai ($8.95), seven soups, salads such as Larb Gai and calamari salad ($7.95–$9.95), a wide variety of curries and seafood specialties, and twelve vegetarian entrees. They also state "no MSG in our cooking."

Supreeya's Thai House, 1146 Main Street, St. Helena 94574; phone (707) 967–0363. Open 11:00 A.M. to 9:00 P.M. Monday–Saturday, 11:00 A.M. to 8:00 P.M. Sunday. Beer and wine. Visa and MasterCard. Wheelchair accessible.

At **St. Helena Cyclery** you can rent tandem bikes, road, mountain, or hybrid bikes, as well as helmets and maps. Be sure to make a reservation for ten or more riders.

St. Helena Cyclery, 1156 Main Street, St. Helena 94574; phone (707) 963–7736. Open from 9:30 A.M. to 5:30 P.M. Monday–Saturday, 10:00 A.M. to 5:00 P.M. Sunday. Visa, MasterCard, and American Express. Wheelchair accessible.

The **Creative Needle** sells anything and everything you need for knitting, darning, and crocheting projects, including Adrienne Vittadini yarns.

Creative Needle, 1210 Main Street, St. Helena 94574; phone (707) 963–7533. Open Tuesday–Friday from 10:00 A.M. to 5:00 P.M., Saturday 10:00 A.M. to 1:00 P.M. Visa, MasterCard, and JCB. Wheelchair accessible.

Just two doors up, **Calla Lily** sells elegant fine linens and gifts.

Calla Lily, 1222 Main Street, St. Helena 94574; phone (707) 963–8188. Open Monday–Saturday from 10:00 A.M. to 5:00 P.M., Sunday 11:00 A.M. to 4:00 P.M. Visa, MasterCard, and American Express. Wheelchair accessible.

D. Champaign, "Where you can relax your style," purveys elegant casual men's resort wear, including designers such as Barry Bricken, Haupt, North 44, Java Lava, Columbian, Lazo, Tallia, Tommy Bahama, and Axis shirts, and Teva and H.S. Trask shoes.

D. Champaign, 1228 Main Street, St. Helena 94574; phone (707) 963–1782. Open from 10:00 A.M. to 6:00 P.M. daily. Visa, MasterCard, American Express, and Diners Club. Wheelchair accessible.

Next door, **Amelia Claire** offers elegant ladies' shoes, bags, and belts.

Amelia Claire, 1230 Main Street, St. Helena 94574; phone (707) 963–8502. Open from 10:00 A.M. to 6:00 P.M. daily. Visa and MasterCard. Wheelchair accessible.

Two doors farther on, **Cricket** sells playclothes versions of Reel, Avalon, Workshop, Citron, and Flax for luxuriating at resorts and San Francisco Hat Co. hats. Everything looks very comfortable.

Cricket, 1234 Main Street, St. Helena 94574; phone (707) 963–8400. Open from 10:00 A.M. to 5:30 P.M. daily. Visa, MasterCard, and American Express. Wheelchair accessible.

One of Kathleen's favorite shops in all of Napa County is **On the Vine,** a food-and-wine-lover's clothing and trinket boutique at the corner of Main and Hunt Streets. The shop's design alone is worth going in to see.

Don't miss the wine-and-food-inspired jewelry and "wearable art," including silver asparagus pins, whisk earrings, and silverware picture frames, and the lighthearted casual clothes perfect for traveling in the heat. Visitors from other countries have been known to come in, be astonished at the appropriateness of the clothing, and purchase whole racks of a style.

Hand-painted wearable art "Field of Grapes" silk jackets are $725, ties $100. Garnet Merlot grape earrings are $42. You can even find grape cluster cufflinks and tuxedo studs. Be sure to get on the mailing list to learn all the latest.

On the Vine, 1234 Main Street, St. Helena 94574; phone (707) 963–2209 or (800) 992–4339. Open from 10:00 A.M. to 5:30 P.M. daily. Visa, MasterCard, and American Express. Wheelchair accessible.

Continue northward on the right (east) side of Main Street. Once the **Wonderful Drug Store,** according to brass letters in the sidewalk, **Reed's** offers comfortable ladies' clothing from Calvin Klein, Harari, Loose Threads, Kevo, Kathleen Sommers, and Joan Vass, including loads of loose, white clothes for summer. This is a popular boutique both with locals and visitors.

Reed's, 1302 Main Street (at Hunt), St. Helena 94574; phone (707) 963–0400. Open from 10:00 A.M. to 5:30 P.M. daily. Visa, MasterCard, and American Express. Wheelchair accessible.

Next door to Reed's are two fun and wonderfully different (and differently wonderful) restaurants. The first one you come to is **Armadillo's,** serving fresh Californian-Mexican food. Fun primary colors permeate, with large murals, painted chairs and tables, and trademark mosaic-cornered tables. Copper palm trees greet you at the door.

Both Mexican and gringo food are served, including breakfast, with a special children's menu and crayons available. Locals come in here constantly on their lunch breaks, which tells you something about Armadillo's prices and consistency.

We particularly enjoy the Enchilada Pollo con Mole, fresh shredded chicken covered with house-made mole sauce. The best! Lots of vegetarian specialties grace the menu, popular with the large Seventh-Day Adventist community in the area. The chips are warm and the salsa fresh, served in a metal ice cream dish.

Armadillo's, 1304 Main Street, St. Helena 94574; phone (707) 963–8082. Open from 11:00 A.M. to 9:00 P.M. Sunday, Monday, Wednesday, and Thursday, 11:00 A.M. to 10:00 P.M. Friday–Saturday. Beer and wine. Visa and MasterCard. Wheelchair accessible.

COOK is a new restaurant that replaced one of our personal favorites, the Green Valley Trattoria, where locals and bocce teams hung out with opera music and posters and great casual Italian food.

COOK co-owner Jude Wilmoth saw one person's retirement as his opportunity. He and his brother Mike are "St. Helena kids" who grew up to like food. Jude cooked at Tra Vigne, Pere Jeanty, Piatti Sonoma, and the Napa Valley Grille.

COOK, 1310 Main Street, St. Helena 94574; phone (707) 963–7088. Beer and wine. Visa and MasterCard. Wheelchair accessible.

Fideaux has quickly become a destination "outfitter for cats and dogs" like no other, except for its sister store in Carmel. A former teacher, proprietor Jennifer Blevens certainly knows how to catch your eye and your passion for pets. You can spoil yours with bracelets, collars, Fideaux Futons washable beds, locally made pottery bowls, a wine barrel doghouse, dog clocks with tongues wagging, and guidebooks for traveling pets and the owners. Visiting dogs are welcome but must be on a leash.

Fideaux, 1312 Main Street, St. Helena 94574; phone (707) 967–9935, Web site www.fideaux-bestselections.com. Open from 9:30 A.M. to 5:30 P.M. daily. Visa, MasterCard, and American Express. Wheelchair accessible.

For an evening of cinema, the Cameo Theatre at 1340 Main Street (707–963–9779) is a classic theater playing slightly alternative first-run movies. Enjoy it for what it was and is. Advance tickets are available online at www.cameo cinema.com.

Marc Robbins and Wayne Bradshaw own and preside over both **Patina Fine Jewelry,** just north of the Cameo Theatre, and Palladium, between David's and Buchanan's on the west side of Main Street. Their personal delight and passion for their jewelry shows the minute you walk in the door. At Patina they sell estate jewelry, including platinum and diamonds, objets d'art, and antiques, ranging from the late 1700s through the 1960s and costing from $150 to $25,000.

Patina Fine Jewelry, 1342 Main Street, St. Helena 94574; phone (707) 963–5445. Open from 10:00 A.M. to 5:30 P.M. Monday–Saturday, 10:30 A.M. to 5:00 P.M. Sunday. Visa, MasterCard, American Express, and Discover. Wheelchair accessible.

One of the most professional and elegant galleries in the Napa Valley is **I. Wolk Gallery,** which features dramatic large paintings, works on paper, photography, and sculpture.

> *I. Wolk Gallery, 1235 Main Street, St. Helena 94594; phone (707) 963–8800, Web site www.iwolkgallery.com. Open from 10:00 A.M. to 5:30 P.M. Wednesday–Monday. Visa, MasterCard, and American Express. Partially wheelchair accessible.*

Steves' Hardware and Homeware, Inc. Since 1878, at the corner of Main Street and Adams, is a fine social and business institution whose existence reminds us all of what life was like in Napa and Sonoma Valleys before big wine came. If you are lucky, Carol Rutherford (yes, as in the town of Rutherford) or co-owner Louise Menegon will be presiding over the counter to the left of the entrance. They and the Steves family have the longevity and knowledge to tell you anything you could possibly want to know about the Napa Valley.

Steves' moved here in 1991 from next door, where they had been for 107 years in a store 2,000 feet smaller than this one. You will find Good Housekeeping's *Household Encyclopedia* on a James Graham stove with Le Creuset and Calphalon cookware. Rifles, guns, and ammo are sold along with Winchester sign replicas, paint, nails, sandpaper, copper cookware, ceramic animal salt-and-pepper shakers, tiles, canisters, pepper grinders, and wooden salad bowls. Well-selected cookbooks, toasters, tool belts, plumbing and garden supplies, glassware, and live fishing bait add to the good old hardware-store quality, disappearing at the hands of the chain stores but lovingly preserved at Steves'.

> **Steves' Hardware and Homeware, Inc. Since 1878,** *1370 Main Street, St. Helena 94574; phone (707) 963–3423. Open from 7:30 A.M. to 6:00 P.M. Monday–Friday, 7:30 A.M. to 5:30 P.M. Saturday, 9:30 A.M. to 4:00 P.M. Sunday. Visa, MasterCard, American Express, and Discover. Wheelchair accessible.*

Here we cross Main Street and, contrary to our nature, we suggest you walk the few steps back to the crosswalk and light. Traffic along Main Street is heavy, and crossing midblock creates confusion and infuriates local drivers.

It's worth it to drop into **Vanderbilt & Company–Napa Valley,** a shop and gallery of home and personal accessories, including Vietri Italian ceramic dishes and paintings, place settings, tablecloths and napkins, interesting cookbooks,

Phoebe Ellsworth's St. Helena paintings and white flower scene collection, and Vanderbilt's Napa Valley Collection of hand-painted platters, flower dinner plates (inspired by the rich colors and textures of the Napa Valley), all work of local artists such as Sherman Nobleman, John Nyquist, and Charles Gautreaux. The colors of the ceramics and the bed, bath, and table linens make us happy. Be sure to check out the closeout table in the back corner of the back room.

> *Vanderbilt & Company–Napa Valley, 1429 Main Street, St. Helena 94574; phone (707) 963–1010. Open from 9:30 A.M. to 5:30 P.M. daily. Visa, MasterCard, American Express, and Discover. Wheelchair accessible.*

One of our great surprise finds in St. Helena is **Sportago** for great outdoor clothes and emergency sports equipment. Forget your tennis racket? This is the place.

Christine Miller and Christina Stephens converted what had been an automobile dealership into the most appealingly abstract designed shop we have ever seen. Sportago is an authorized Patagonia dealer and also sells Prince and Wilson tennis rackets, balls, books, clogs, and jazzy Arnelle sunglasses.

> *Sportago, 1224 Adams Street, St. Helena 94574; phone (707) 963–9042. Open from 9:00 A.M. to 5:30 P.M. Monday–Saturday, 9:00 A.M. to 4:00 P.M. Sunday. Visa, MasterCard, and American Express. Partially wheelchair accessible.*

Local coffee lovers hang out at the **Napa Valley Coffee Roasting Company.** Since not too many visitors venture to the end of this single block off Main Street, this is a great place to find out what's happening locally. Sister to the store in Napa, it has the best coffee in town and is worth the extra steps. All your favorite espresso drinks, scones, and biscotti are here. Enjoy!

> *Napa Valley Coffee Roasting Company (with entrances on both Adams and Oak), 1400 Oak Avenue, St. Helena 94574; phone (707) 963–4491. Open from 7:30 A.M. to 6:00 P.M. Visa and MasterCard with $5.00 minimum purchase. Wheelchair accessible.*

Around the corner and half a block down Oak Street from the coffee roastery, dip into **The Big Dipper** ("Ice Cream Parlor with an Old-Fashioned Flavor"), across from St. Helena Elementary School. (Is this location or what?) More than an ice cream parlor, this place is an informal shrine and museum to ice cream parlor and Coca-Cola memorabilia. Be sure to look up at the stuff covering the walls, including huge ice cream cone displays and a 1908 ice cream dipper, a 1920 ice cream sandwich maker, and early milkshake blenders. Return to your childhood or earlier at the penny candy counter, games, and a jukebox you can play with all those oldie favorites.

The Big Dipper, 1336 Oak Avenue, St. Helena 94574; phone (707) 963–2616. Open from 11:30 A.M. to 8:00 P.M. Monday–Saturday, noon to 6:00 P.M. Sunday. Cash only. Wheelchair accessible.

We highly recommend that you return to Adams Street, follow it across Main Street for 2 blocks (or if you are on Main, turn east on Adams), and turn north on Library Lane to both the Silverado Museum and the George & Elsie Wood Public Library and Wine Library.

Silverado Museum is a near shrine to onetime Napa Valley resident Robert Louis Stevenson, established in 1969 by Charlotte A. Strouse and Norman H. Strouse, a former executive with J. Walter Thompson advertising.

The Silverado Museum is the largest of five museums dedicated to Stevenson (although Yale University has the largest collection of his manuscripts). In 2000 the museum acquired the Stevensons' marriage license issued in San Francisco on May 19, 1880, a diary written by Fanny Stevenson, and Stevenson's drawings between ages 6 and 18. There are loads of copies of various editions of his work for sale at the museum, which certainly heightened our interest in the author. Director Ed Reynolds and associate director Ann Kindred are treasures of knowledge about the author, his works, and his life.

Silverado Museum, 1490 Library Lane, St. Helena 94574; phone (707) 963–3757, Web site www.napanet.net/vi/silverado. Open from noon to 4:00 P.M. Tuesday–Sunday. Visa, MasterCard, and American Express. Wheelchair accessible.

Beside and behind the Silverado Museum is the **George & Elsie Wood Public Library** and the Napa Valley Wine Library, an unusual effort resulting from private and public funding.

Two things that make this library worth a trip are the Wine Library and its accompanying food-book collection. For visitors deeply interested in California wine-industry history and gossip, this is the place. The library attempts to collect every book worth its salt on wine, and it also has a substantial collection of food literature. A real treat to browse are the transcribed oral interviews done with all of the Napa Valley's prominent wine pioneers, from Maynard Amerine to Robert Mondavi, and many in between. To see these volumes, ask the librarian to unlock the glass doors. She might ask for your youngest child as a deposit, but it's only for a little while!

> *George & Elsie Wood Public Library, 1492 Library Lane, St. Helena 94574; phone (707) 963–5244 or call the Napa Valley Wine Library Association at (707) 963–5145. Open from noon to 9:00 P.M. Monday–Wednesday, 10:00 A.M. to 6:00 P.M. Thursday–Friday, 10:00 A.M. to 4:00 P.M. Saturday, 1:00 to 5:00 P.M. Sunday. Wheelchair accessible.*

Resuming our walk or roll down the west side of Main Street, at the corner of Adams you will find **Vasconi's Drugs,** a local Valu-Rite pharmacy, for all your emergency prescription and associated health needs, cards, trinkets, great postcards, and film and film processing. If you have the kids along, they can get crayons and other fun stuff to keep themselves occupied.

> *Vasconi's Drugs, 1381 Main Street, St. Helena 94574; phone (707) 963–1444. Open from 9:00 A.M. to 7:00 P.M. Monday–Saturday, from 10:00 A.M. to 5:00 P.M. Sunday. Visa and MasterCard. Wheelchair accessible.*

Olivier Napa Valley is a new olive oil retailer where you will find California olive and grapeseed oils bottled and in bulk vats. Tapenades, grilling sauces, mustards, balsamic vinegars, truffle oils, Asian peanut oil, and French place mats and tablecloths complete the picture, along with abundant tastes you pour yourself into tiny paper cups available throughout the shop. Owners Eric Klein and Kevin Buchholz also bottle oils for Williams-Sonoma and can do specialty labels on request.

> *Olivier Napa Valley, 1375 Main Street, St. Helena 94574; phone (707) 967–8777, Web site www.oliviernapavalley.com. Open from 10:00 A.M. to 6:00 P.M. Monday–Saturday, 11:00 A.M. to 5:00 P.M. Sunday. Visa, MasterCard, and American Express. Wheelchair accessible.*

At **Alan's Frames & Photography**, you can get film, picture frames, photos developed in one hour, and chat with the owner, who restored and recently sold his house, which had been M. F. K. Fisher's home for two decades here in St. Helena.

Alan's Frames & Photography, 1371 Main Street, St. Helena 94574; phone (707) 963–9294. Open from 9:00 A.M. to 6:00 P.M. Monday– Saturday. Visa and MasterCard. Wheelchair accessible.

Woodhouse Chocolate is a fabulous new addition to the Napa Valley food scene. After his family sold S. Anderson Winery, owner John Anderson and his wife, Tracy, followed their lifelong loves for chocolate and created this chocolate haven. Having graduated from Claremont McKenna College, Anderson went off to London, where he reveled in chocolates at Harrods', eventually worked in the candy department at Macy's, and tasted Caillebaut chocolates in Montreal. A graduate of the California Culinary Academy, Tracy Wood Anderson is choco-latier at Woodhouse, creating exquisite handmade Belgian-style morsels. She worked previously at the Calistoga Inn and Domaine Chandon. Three genera-tions are in the back practicing the art of chocolate making. A must visit!

Woodhouse Chocolate, 1367 Main Street, St. Helena 94574; phone (707) 963–8413, Web site www.woodhousechocolate.com. Open 10:30 A.M. to 6:00 P.M. daily. Visa, MasterCard, American Express, and Discover. Wheelchair accessible.

If you're thinking of taking home a colorful painting to remember your wine-country experience forever, be sure to stop at **Art on Main Street.** Bright and cheerful colors depict local vineyard scenes, painted primarily by local artists. We also like the classic French art posters. English wine-bottle stoppers cost only $9.50.

Art on Main Street, 1359 Main Street, St. Helena 94574; phone (707) 963–3350. Open from 10:00 A.M. to 5:00 P.M. daily. Visa, MasterCard, and American Express. Wheelchair accessible.

South just one door from the gallery is a local favorite, **The Model Bakery,** a wonderful bakery-cafe where you can get fabulous Old World–style scones, muffins, croissants, breakfast pastries, and breads to go or eat here with teas or Peet's Coffee espresso drinks. We love their oat bread. Light meals are also here to tempt, including daily specials such as fresh spinach soup ($3.75), meat or veg-gie brick-oven pizzas ($5.00), and a great sandwich special ($5.00).

Soft yellow walls, ceiling fans, and black-and-white-checked linoleum set the mood. If you're lucky, you can get a window table and alternate between peo-ple watching and newspaper reading.

St. Helena home of the late M. F. K. Fisher

The Model Bakery, *1357 Main Street, St. Helena 94574; phone (707) 963–8192. Open from 7:00 A.M. to 6:00 P.M. Tuesday–Saturday, 8:00 A.M. to 4:00 P.M. Sunday. Visa and MasterCard. Wheelchair accessible.*

Market is a popular new restaurant in an 1890 historic building that long housed Gayle's ice cream parlor and sandwich shop. Beau-Vine restaurant came and left quickly, leaving an old Brunswick bar supposedly used in the grand ballroom of the Palace Hotel in San Francisco.

Douglas Keane and Nick Peyton make a great combination to lure locals and visitors back time after time. Keane served as maitre d' and manager at Squire Restaurant at the Fairmont Hotel, Masa's, at the dining room of the Ritz-Carlton, and Farallon; he also co-created Restaurant Gary Danko. Peyton cooked at the Four Seasons Restaurant and Lespinasse in New York, was opening sous chef at Gary Danko, and served as executive chef at Traci des Jardin's Jardinière in San Francisco. The result is one of the best-priced best restaurants in the Napa Valley.

Lunch offers a three-course meal at $14.95 or a soup, sandwich 'n' treat at $9.95, plus great creative soups, Anchor Steam beer braised beef and bean chili ($7.50), chopped market salad with blue cheese and Hobb's bacon ($7.50–

$11.50), Thai marinated rock shrimp ($10.00), ahi tuna tartare ($11.00), a half-pound burger with Fiscalini cheddar cheese, grilled sweet onions, housemade pickles, and fries ($10.50), a portobello sandwich ($9.00), fish and chips, or buttermilk fried chicken ($13.50). Root beer floats with soft spun-to-order ice cream and housemade butterscotch pudding are $6.00 each, but try the "made at your table s'mores" for two ($10.00).

Dinner adds pastas with chanterelle mushrooms, chard, and squash or Prince Edward Island mussels ($14.50), pork chops, hanger steaks, and striped bass ($19.95 each). Market also features its American classics we mentioned on the lunch menu and a three-course dinner ($28.95).

Market only marks up wines by $15 over wholesale, which is a bargain.

Market, 1347 Main Street, St. Helena 94574; phone (707) 963–3799. Open 11:30 A.M. to 10:00 P.M. Sunday–Thursday, 11:30 A.M. to 11:00 P.M. Friday–Saturday. Full bar. Visa, MasterCard, and American Express. Wheelchair accessible.

David's is St. Helena's authorized Rolex and Cartier jewelry dealer since 1976.

David's, 1343 Main Street, St. Helena 94574; phone (707) 963–0239. Open from 10:00 A.M. to 5:30 P.M. Tuesday–Saturday. Visa, Master-Card, and American Express. Wheelchair accessible.

Bison is Main Street's newest high-fashion boutique featuring "American and European country life apparel" with a distinct Western flair. Owner Michelle Newman designs fabulous leather bags, Norwegian sweaters, and belts made in Italy, and also sells Double D Ranchwear, Bavarian blouses, silk scarves, and Austrian suede pants, as well as custom-made boots from the United States and Italy.

Bison, 1341 Main Street, St. Helena 94574; phone (707) 963–8883. Open from 10:00 A.M. to 5:30 P.M. Monday–Saturday, 10:30 A.M. to 4:00 P.M. Sunday. Visa, MasterCard, and American Express. Wheelchair accessible.

Wayne Armstrong and Marc Robbins, who own Patina across the street, have another fine boutique featuring contemporary jewelry. Stop in at **Palladium** just to soak up the ultracontemporary design—of both the store and its jewelry. Most of the latter is so beautiful that just viewing it is a peaceful experience.

Palladium, 1339 Main Street, St. Helena 94574; phone (707) 963–5900. Open from 10:00 A.M. to 5:30 P.M. daily. Visa, MasterCard, and American Express. Wheelchair accessible.

Buchanan's Stationery sells fine letter papers, artists' materials (in case you left sketch pads, pencils, watercolors, etc., at home), cards, gifts, and wrapping paper.

Buchanan's Stationery, 1337 Main Street, St. Helena 94574; phone (707) 963–3198. Open from 9:30 A.M. to 5:00 P.M. Monday–Saturday. Visa, MasterCard, and American Express. Wheelchair accessible.

Don't miss **Goodman's Since 1879,** just south of Buchanan's. The clothing is resort, the wine-country souvenir shirts resemble Hawaiian, the ceiling creaks, and the place is loaded with local history. Joking aside, those wannabe Hawaiian shirts are the best available in the Napa Valley.

Check out the historic-clothing display case toward the back of the store, the Abraham, Cecelia, Jacob, and Julius Goodman photos, the original articles of the 1906 incorporation of Goodman–Lauter Company, and the bargain balcony.

The women's clothing is natural fiber, loose and lovely, some in ample sizes, including Cut Loose dresses.

Goodman's Since 1879, 1331 Main Street, St. Helena 94574; phone (707) 963–1750. Open from 10:00 A.M. to 6:00 P.M. Monday–Saturday, 10:00 A.M. to 5:00 P.M. Sunday. Visa, MasterCard, and Discover. Wheelchair accessible.

One door down, **Nature Etc.** sells mood music, nature-learning toys and puzzles, and name bead bracelets in case you forget your name or your child's name.

Nature Etc., 1327 Main Street, St. Helena 94574; phone (707) 963–1706. Open from 10:00 A.M. to 5:30 P.M. Sunday–Thursday, 10:00 A.M. to 6:00 P.M. Friday–Saturday. Visa and MasterCard. Wheelchair accessible.

Wine fans should not miss the **St. Helena Wine Center,** where you can taste and purchase the finest and most rare wines made and sold in the Valley, often at discount prices. Many of the wines here are true collectibles.

Expanded into what was the sensuous Napa Valley Chocolates, the St. Helena Wine Center is primarily owned by the extremely knowledgeable and local Beringer family, founders of Beringer Vineyards. Recently the store began to offer high-end liquor, such as specialty tequilas, rums, vodkas, and single-malt scotches. Enjoy the partially enclosed tasting bar in the corner where you can chat with local winemakers and businesspeople.

> *St. Helena Wine Center, 1321 Main Street, St. Helena 94574; phone (707) 963–1313 or (800) 331–1311. Open from 10:00 A.M. to 6:00 P.M. Monday–Saturday, 10:00 A.M. to 5:00 P.M. Sunday. Visa, MasterCard, American Express, Diners Club, Discover, and JCB. Wheelchair accessible.*

Next door to St. Helena Wine Center, **Heaven & Earth** majors in aromatherapy, essences, and body, bath, and spirit goodies.

> *Heaven & Earth, 1313 Main Street, St. Helena 94574; (707) 963–1124. Open from 10:00 A.M. to 6:00 P.M. daily. Visa and MasterCard. Wheelchair accessible.*

Main Street Books is one of the smallest and most charmingly independent bookstores in the world. This is a real book-person's bookstore, featuring new and used books of literature, the classics, great children's books, and nice, warm people. Because of their space limitations, these folks have mastered the special-order process.

> *Main Street Books, 1315 Main Street, St. Helena 94574; phone (707) 963–1338. Open from 10:00 A.M. to 5:30 P.M. Monday–Saturday. Visa and MasterCard. Wheelchair accessible.*

One of St. Helena's landmarks is **Gillwood's Cafe,** a local institution and old-timey hangout for "homestyle cooking," even though it's only been here since 1990. Flowered vinyl tablecloths cover the tables, surprisingly comfortable wooden benches line the walls, and there's a "community table" down the middle of the dining room to "share with friends and neighbors." Locals sit reading books and newspapers as long as they want. Breakfast is better than standard and includes Dickinson's preserves to go with house-baked breads.

This is where you get those all-American reliables such as meat loaf with mashed potatoes, fresh vegetables, and mushroom gravy ($8.75), chicken fried steak with mashed potatoes and country gravy ($9.25), Yankee pot roast ($9.95), crispy boneless half chicken with creamed sweet Vidalia onions and country potatoes ($9.95), patty melts, BLTs, a good old tuna-salad sandwich ($6.40), and even a healthy apple, pecan, and Gorgonzola salad ($7.50). At lunch, all sandwiches come with green salad, french fries, or homemade soup. At dinner, salads are extra and come with a miniloaf of multigrain bread.

Gillwood's Cafe, 1313 Main Street, St. Helena 94574; phone (707) 963–1788. Open for breakfast, lunch, and dinner. Visa, MasterCard, American Express, Discover, and Diners Club. Wheelchair accessible.

Footcandy is Carolyn and Perry Butler's fabulous new shoe store that brings the big city to St. Helena, with Findings home furnishings and "cult designer shoes" by Manolo Blahnik, Jimmy Choo, Emma Hope, Giuseppe Zanotti, Marc Jacobs, Louella, and Bartley. The Butlers are British ex-patriots who came to California for high-tech businesses, eventually sold their computer company, and started Juslyn Vineyards.

Footcandy, 1239 Main Street, St. Helena 94574; phone: (707) 963–2040, Web site www.footcandyshoes.com. Visa, MasterCard, and American Express.

Eccola's women's resort clothing occupies the front of the St. Helena Hotel, a character of a small hotel whose lobby is packed with dolls, a pack-rat heaven. Once a flophouse, St. Helena Hotel is now a Victorian bed-and-breakfast. Walk down the short alleyway just to check out the lobby, complete with spittoons.

The next shop down the street is Sweet Pea, a great place for kids of all ages with Brio toys, trains, cars, and clothes. Its neighbor to the south is I-elle, which sells professional women's clothing both here and in Sonoma. My Favorite Things is a delightful shop with table settings, picture frames, and home accessories, perfect to take home as gifts.

Plan to spend some time wandering through **St. Helena Antiques & Other Fine Collectibles,** where you will find everything from old pots to huge and heavy statuary, a collector's treasure-hunt paradise.

St. Helena Antiques & Other Fine Collectibles, 1231 Main Street, St. Helena 94574; phone (707) 963–5878. Open from 11:00 A.M. to 5:00 P.M. Wednesday–Monday. Visa, MasterCard, and American Express. Wheelchair accessible.

Just south of the antiques heaven is **Giugni's Delicatessen,** an extremely local deli purveying everything from jawbreakers to great sandwiches. Papers tacked to the walls flap in the air conditioner's breeze, photos on the back wall are signed by Daryl Hannah and Joe Montana, and decades of old memories are collected and posted for all to enjoy. Attention British candy fans: Giugni's has Violet Crumbles and loose candy.

The sandwiches are huge and varied, with twelve bread and roll choices, plus twenty-three meats, from turkey pastrami to mild or hot coppa. Cheeses are just as abundant, and the service is cheerful and irreverent. Great pickups for picnics at the wineries, since very few of them are allowed to sell food.

> *Giugni's Delicatessen, 1227 Main Street, St. Helena 94574; phone (707) 963–3421. Open from 9:00 A.M. to 5:00 P.M. Beer and wine. No credit cards. Wheelchair accessible.*

South of the OK Barber Shop, where the barber snoops behind a screen in the back so that he can see you if you come in (reminiscent of a confessional), is **Mario's for Men,** a fashionable men's boutique with clothes from Jhane Barnes, Zanella, Nicole Miller, Mondo, and Cole-Haan, along with Caruso sport coats, Trafalgar Braces, Equilibrio shirts, leather shoes and belts, and other elegant resort and dining wear. (This is a brother store to D. Champaign on the east side of Main Street.)

> *Mario's for Men, 1223 Main Street, St. Helena 94574; phone (707) 963–1603. Open from 10:00 A.M. to 6:00 P.M. daily. Visa, MasterCard, American Express, Diners Club, Discover, and JCB. Wheelchair accessible.*

The next store down the street is San Francisco's splendiferous **Wilkes Sport,** a resort-wear child of Wilkes Bashford. Men and women will find the finest in fashion here from lots of Italian designers, including Zegna, Loro Piana, Biella, Piazza Sempione, and Industria, plus Yoshi Hishinuma. Wilkes Sport even provides treats for your dogs, who are most welcome here. How refreshing!

> *Wilkes Sport, 1219 Main Street, St. Helena 94574; phone (707) 963–4323. Open from 10:00 A.M. to 6:00 P.M. Visa, MasterCard, American Express, and Diners Club. Wheelchair accessible.*

Jan de Luz is an emporium of French Basque–origin household linens, based on traditional Basque cattle blankets once used by shepherds and farmers to protect their cattle against sun and insects. Seven stripes cross the original blankets and linens, signifying the seven Basque provinces, and colors identify native villages. Supposedly the wider the stripes, the wealthier the owner.

Originally the owners designed their fabrics and had them made in France, although now most are made in the United States but still of all-natural fibers. Here you will find elegant bathrobes, table linens, towels, aprons, curtain fabrics, furniture, and one of the best Basque cookbooks on Earth, by Gerald Hirigoyen. You can have linens embroidered by a machine right in the shop while you have lunch somewhere. Jan de Luz also has shops in Carmel and Carmel Valley.

Jan de Luz, 1219 Main Street, St. Helena 94574; phone (707) 963–1550. Open 9:30 A.M. to 5:30 P.M. daily. Visa, MasterCard, American Express, Discover, and Diners Club. Wheelchair accessible.

Now we come to **Ana's Cantina,** where El Salvador native Ana provides a unique hangout for bar regulars to spend their days and farm workers and winery owners to stop by for breakfast or come in after work to play pool, throw darts, listen to music from country to reggae, and dine on Ana's special food. Francis Ford Coppola drops in to sing karaoke in Spanish on Monday and Thursday nights under a huge canvas portrait of Frida Kahlo that hangs in "Ana's Gallery," which means the walls of the bar and restaurant. Coming partly from an Irish background, Kathleen was slightly alarmed by the regular "Black and Tan Night," but here it just means one night when they officially mix Guinness light and dark ales.

Music nights (Thursday, Friday, and Saturday) have featured Dana Hubbard and Philip Claypool, among others. The margaritas are famous, and the combination platillos range from only $5.95 to $7.95. Try the fajitas or Pollo Acapulco.

Ana's Cantina, 1205 Main Street, St. Helena 94574; phone (707) 963–4921. Open for breakfast and lunch daily, dinner 6:00 to 9:00 P.M. Thursday–Saturday. Visa, MasterCard, and Diners Club. Wheelchair accessible.

Some of the Napa Valley's best restaurants are on St. Helena's side streets, so now we will take you to them. Martini House is off Spring Street. Miramonte and Terra are next door to each other on Railroad Avenue, east of Main Street.

Pat Kuleto and Todd Humphries have rescued the wonderful craftsman home that opera singer Walter Martini and his wife, Dionisia, built here in 1923. **Martini House** would be worth a visit just for the interior design, even if the food weren't wonderful, which it is.

Local lore holds that Walter Martini often performed with Enrico Caruso at the Pacific Opera, and the Martinis moved to St. Helena from San Francisco after the 1906 earthquake. Eventually they bought the William Tell Hotel across the street, and he became a successful bootlegger during Prohibition, storing his stash in the wine cellar downstairs. Kuleto has created his version on Martini's wine cellar, and a walk downstairs is, in our view, mandatory to enjoy the ambience.

Kuleto has done his best to honor local Wappo Indian tradition and design, all the way from Native American patterned fabrics to papoose basket–shaped wall sconces. Todd Humphries, formerly of Campton Place, reigns as chef.

At lunch you may enjoy either a three-course prix fixe menu ($19.95) or order a la carte. A la carte favorites might include sweet corn chowder with Alaskan halibut ($9.00), watercress, endive, and Medjool date salad with Gorgonzola ($9.50), duck terrine with celeriac and apple salad ($10.00), a grilled Snake River Kobe beef burger with onion rings ($14.95), bay scallop salad with wild mushrooms and artichokes or sautéed lamb chops ($18.95), roast leg of rabbit ($15.95), grilled flatiron steak ($19.95), and spring navarin of lamb with stewed fava beans ($17.50).

Dinner affords a three-course prix fixe dinner ($39.50), an appetizer ahi tuna tartare ($13.50), and torchon of foie gras with white port gelée ($20.00). Entrees may include delectably light zucchini canneloni ($21.00), Alaskan halibut with chanterelle mushrooms ($25.50), sautéed venison loin ($29.00), Sonoma duck breast ($28.00), or roasted rack and loin of rabbit ($27.50). Market specials occasionally feature fettucini with white truffles from Umbria ($45.00), pan roasted sweetbreads ($14.00), or a roasted cauliflower mushroom with mushroom broth and truffle oil ($14.00). Desserts are outstanding, thanks to pastry chef Ethan Howard. Be sure to check out the ports, Madeiras, and sherries, with flights available, and more than forty wines by the glass.

Martini House, 1245 Spring Street, St. Helena 94574; phone (707) 963–2233, Web site martinihouse.com. Open from 5:30 to 10:00 P.M. Monday–Thursday, and 11:30 A.M. to 10:00 P.M. Friday–Sunday. Full bar. Corkage fee: $20 per bottle. Visa, MasterCard, American Express, and Discover. Ground-level dining room wheelchair accessible.

Cindy's Backstreet Kitchen is the newest creation of renowned chef and restaurant developer Cindy Pawlcyn, founder of Fog City Diner in San Francisco, Buckeye Roadhouse in Mill Valley, and now her Backstreet Kitchen.

For decades this location was home to Showley's Restaurant, and then to Pawlcyn's own Miramonte Restaurant, which didn't work. Now she has come up with a real winner! The space is complicated like a home, with hallways, niches, and funny corners, but it all works.

The food really works! Specialties include the house green salad with Cindy's spiced pecans and fresh pears ($6.50), a grilled rare ahi tuna soba noodle salad with Mizuna slaw and wasabi ($15.95), spice-rubbed quail with goat cheese polenta and double sherry sauce ("Cindy's favorite," $19.95), a grilled hanger steak with creamy butternut squash gratin ($18.95), slow braised short ribs ($19.95), and "happy chicken under a brick with garlic mashers and broccoli rabe" ($21.95). By the restaurant's definition, a "happy chicken" is one that is raised happy, free, and without chemicals, and goes to its death "happy."

Great Niman Ranch burgers, a crispy rock cod sandwich, grilled chicken BLTs, and a "Chinatown Duck Burger with Shiitaki mushroom ketchup" are available all day and all under $11 and super. A melt-in-your-mouth semolina batard from Panorama Bakery in San Francisco appears at your table, as does simple syrup for your ice tea. Cindy's hosts "Celebrity Bartender Nights" Thursday, featuring local winemakers as bartenders.

Cindy's Backstreet Kitchen, 1327 Railroad Avenue, St. Helena 94574; phone (707) 963–1200. Lunch 11:30 A.M. and on, Friday–Sunday, dinner nightly from 5:30 P.M. Full bar. Visa, MasterCard, American Express, Discover, and Diners Club. Dining room wheelchair accessible, restrooms are not.

Terra is one of California's finest and most creative restaurants, and one that gets lots of publicity. Hiro (Hiroyoshi) Sone and Lissa Doumani have created the perfect blend of history and culture in their restaurant in this historic 1884 Taylor, Duckworth & Company Foundry Building, dignifying the stone walls and large arched windows with a comfortable decor that immediately makes visitors feel at home.

Hiro developed and directed the kitchen at Wolfgang Puck's Spago in Los Angeles, and Lissa is earth mother and pastry chef, with deep roots in wine-country vineyards. The food they create speaks for itself in an unabashed California-Asian-French way, the definition of which you will experience by dining at Terra. The menu changes with the seasons.

Appetizers may include Dungeness crab salad with avocado and grapefruit ($14.50), "Duck, Duck, Duck" with duck rillettes, foie gras torchon, and giblets

Terra restaurant entrance

confit salad ($17.50), cream of Jerusalem artichoke soup ($10.00), lamb tongue tagine on chickpea puree ($12.50), or Panko-crusted Miyagi oysters with pork belly "kakuni" ($14.00). Main courses offered are sake-marinated Alaskan black cod and shrimp dumplings ($26.00), Maine lobster and Hokkaido scallops in wine butter sauce ($29.50), grilled quail with foie gras tortelloni with parsnip in forest mushroom game sauce ($29.00), and braised veal cheeks on Fontina cheese polenta with crispy sweetbreads ($27.50).

Desserts are equally wonderful, including a warm cheddar-cheese-crust apple pie with ginger ice cream ($8.00), chocolate bourbon cake with espresso ice cream and chocolate fudge sauce ($8.50), tiramisu ($7.50), or pistachio Burma with rose crème brûlée and seckel pear poached in pomegranate molasses ($8.00).

Terra's wine list is exceptional, which should be no surprise.

Terra, 1345 Railroad Avenue, St. Helena 94574; phone (707) 963–8931. Open for dinner Wednesday–Monday. Beer and wine. Visa, MasterCard, Diners Club, and Carte Blanche. Wheelchair access down the alleyway to the back.

Pinot Blanc, just south of St. Helena proper, is the northern exposure of famed restaurateur Joachim Splichal's Patina Restaurant in Los Angeles. Greg Stillman executes the orders as executive chef in this unusually good small chain. Other Patina restaurants include Pinot Bistro in Studio City, Cafe Pinot in downtown Los Angeles, Pinot Hollywood, Pinot Provence in the Westin South Coast Plaza in Costa Mesa, and Pinot Brasserie in the Venetian Resort in Las Vegas.

Pinot Blanc has one of the most soothing decors in the wine country, with its dignified dark wood walls, clublike bar, and private-feeling dining areas. Check out the great French magazine cartoons on the lounge walls and the wall-paper of actual wine labels on the walls down the hall to the restrooms.

Pinot Blanc serves lunch, late lunch, and dinner, with daily specials. Some of the most popular dishes are sweetwater oysters on the half shell from Hog Island ($2.00 each), Provencal fritto misto of fennel, onions, haricot vert, rock shrimp, and calamari ($11.25), and steamed black mussels with Pernod and fennel broth and garlic crostini ($11.50). Sandwiches include choices of salmon club, cheese-burger, or portobello ($9.25–$15.25), pasta with braised lamb ($17.75), ricotta gnocchi with butternut squash ($17.50), or Balsamic marinated flatiron steak with french fries ($20.95). Dinner adds a duck leg confit ($15.50), pomegranate marinated venison loin on honey braised endive with turnip cream ($25.95), pan roasted salmon with creamy leeks ($22.95), and Sonoma duck breast with spaet-zle and braised red cabbage ($23.95).

> *Pinot Blanc, 641 Main Street (Highway 29), St. Helena 94574; phone (707) 963–6191. Open for lunch and dinner. Corkage fee: $15. Visa, MasterCard, American Express, Discover, Diners Club, and JCB. Wheel-chair accessible.*

ST. HELENA TO CALISTOGA

As we head north on Highway 29 from St. Helena, the first two major stops are on your left (west). Beringer Vineyards comes up quickly on the left barely out-side St. Helena, and the Culinary Institute of America's western campus and its Wine Spectator Greystone Restaurant appears 0.4 mile farther.

Amidst what our children called "the tree tunnel" and Napans call the "Row of Elms," you enter **Beringer Vineyards,** "the oldest continuously operating win-ery in the Napa Valley." Beringer is the most spectacular winery setting in the Val-ley, with exquisitely cultivated gardens, vast lawns (no picnicking, please),

Caesar Salad with Garlic Oil

from Beringer Vineyards, St. Helena

DRESSING:

1 Tbs Dijon mustard	1 anchovy fillet
1 Tbs lemon juice	1 Tbs Parmesan cheese, grated
1 tsp salt	1 tsp ground black pepper
1 Tbs red wine vinegar	½ cup Beringer Infused Garlic
1 tsp garlic, minced	Grape Seed Oil

CROUTONS:

1 cup sourdough bread cut into ³/₄-inch cubes

1 Tbs Infused Garlic Grape Seed Oil

salt to taste

SALAD:

3 Tbs Parmesan cheese, grated

1 head romaine lettuce (washed and cut into 1-inch pieces)

Combine first 9 ingredients in a blender to make the Caesar dressing.

Toss the bread cubes with Garlic Grape Seed Oil and salt to taste. Bake croutons in an oven at 450°F for 4–5 minutes until lightly golden.

Toss the lettuce with the dressing. Add the croutons and the Parmesan cheese, and toss again. Serves 4.

preserved historic buildings, fun tours, and ample wine tasting in three places. But the wine is made across the road where you can't go, so enjoy showtime here.

In 1876 German immigrants Jacob and Frederick Beringer bought land and founded Beringer Winery. Chinese laborers returning to the San Francisco Bay Area, after completing the transcontinental railroad, hand-chiseled rock tunnels 250 feet into the hills. Wines are still aged and stored here.

After the winery was built, Jacob lived in an existing 1848 farmhouse on the property, now restored and expanded and called Hudson House, which serves as Beringer Vineyards' Culinary Arts Center and home of the School for American Chefs.

Frederick began construction of the seventeen-room mansion to re-create the family home on Germany's Rhine River. Frederick's Rhine House is now listed in the National Register of Historic Places and serves as Beringer's hospitality center. We recommend just walking into Rhine House to experience its opulence. An excellent collection of books on wine and food are available in what was Frederick Beringer's library. Notice the stained-glass windows.

Premium-wine tastings take place upstairs in the Private Reserve Room (regular tasting and souvenir purchasing is in the Old Bottling Room and the Rhine House toward the back of the property). Enjoy delicious tastes of breads, oils and sauces such as four dipping and marinade oils, olive and grapeseed oils, yummy mayonnaise, bread spreads (artichoke and garlic eggplant), and pasta sauces.

Fine points: In September 2000, the Nestlé Corporation sold Beringer Wine Estates to Foster's Brewing Group, Ltd., of Australia and its Midara Blass international wine division. The Beringer family has the St. Helena Wine Center in downtown St. Helena on Main Street. Tasting fee: three tastes for $5.00 in the Old Winery Gift Shop, or a flight of three Reserves or limited production at $16.00 in Rhine House, with credit against purchase. Featured wines: White Zinfandel, Johannisberg Riesling, Chenin Blanc, Gewürztraminer, Alluvium Blanc, Viognier, Chardonnay, Gamay Beaujolais, Pinot Noir, Zinfandel, Cabernet Sauvignon, and dessert wines. Recently inaugurated are White Merlot, and six "Founder's Estate" wines, which are lighter versions of Merlot, Syrah, Pinot Noir, Chardonnay, Cabernet Sauvignon, and Sauvignon Blanc, all at $10.00 or $11.00 a bottle. Owner: Foster's Brewing Group's Midara Blass. Winemaker: Ed Sbragia. Cases: Undefined. Acres: 600.

Beringer Vineyards, 2000 Main Street, St. Helena 94574; phone (707) 963–4812, Web site www.beringer.com. Open from 10:00 A.M. to 6:00 P.M. during daylight savings time, rest of year 10:00 A.M. to 5:00 P.M. daily except Thanksgiving, Christmas, and New Year's. Tours ($5.00) are every hour from 10:00 A.M. to 5:00 P.M. Visa, MasterCard, American Express, and Discover. Old Bottling Room is wheelchair accessible.

As you progress northward you absolutely must stop at the **Culinary Institute of America at Greystone,** the thirty-acre western campus for continuing education of the CIA–Hyde Park, New York, the foremost culinary educational institution in the United States.

While this campus welcomes professionals in a wide range of fields connected to food and wine (including writers), home chefs are welcome to indulge in watching cooking demonstrations held in Greystone's exquisite Ecolab Theatre ($5.00, and you get a hat to take home).

Built in the late 1880s for William Bourn and Everett Wise as a cooperative winery where Napa Valley growers could make wine and circumvent San Francisco's tightly controlled wine dealers, Greystone is built in the Richardsonian–Romanesque style with 22-inch-thick walls of locally quarried tufa stone. It is now listed in the National Register of Historic Places. Notice the cathedral ceilings, grand arches, tasteful antiques, and massive handcrafted furniture, combined with the latest state-of-the-art cooking equipment.

First known as the Bourn and Wise Cellar, Bourn sold the building in 1894 to Charles Carpy, a founder of the California Wine Association, which then became one of the largest wine producers in California. At its peak under the CWA, Greystone could make 1,349,000 gallons of wine with a marvelous gravity system. Eventually passing through several owners, the Christian Brothers bought the property in 1950, making brandy and wine here for many years.

Heublein bought Christian Brothers' wine line and eventually closed down the operation at Greystone. The Culinary Institute bought the building from Heublein, which, in turn, made a magnificent donation to the nonprofit CIA, enabling it to embark on a fabulous restoration project you can now enjoy.

Do not miss the De Baun Museum, where you can view Christian Brothers' famed winery leader's Brother Timothy's fabulous corkscrew collections, wine-making artifacts, a Tuscan olive press, and an extensive collection of oak cooperage. In front of the building and to the left, stroll through the organic Cannard herb garden on little terraces and wander among culinary herbs, onion and garlic beds, edible flowers and herbal teas, and the salad-greens plot. This garden provides the teaching and restaurant kitchens with more than 145 different types of vegetables, sixty varieties of culinary herbs, twenty-seven types of fruit, and eleven varieties of berries.

The fifteen acres of Merlot grapes on the grounds result in custom-crushed and custom-bottled Greystone Cellars wine, available at the Campus Store and in the *Wine Spectator* Greystone Restaurant. The newly expanded Spice Islands Marketplace has the best of every cooking utensil imaginable, 1,500 cookbook titles including children's cookbooks, the CIA videotape series, all prices and colors of chef's uniforms and aprons, and a world market of unusual spices and ingredients. Check out the big stove imported from the Hyde Park campus.

Be sure to take a pause to refresh at the De Baun Café, where you can sample pastry students' works of art and sip excellent Peets coffee inexpensively. Venture into the De Baun Theatre, where home cooks can watch masters cook up a storm ($25).

Now to experience the *Wine Spectator* Greystone Restaurant, where every Adam Tihany–designed table has a view of the restaurant's chefs (no students) at work. You can dine and sip in front of the roaring fireplace or bask in the sun on the terrace overlooking Charles Krug Winery and part of the Napa Valley.

An excellent eight-page wine list accompanies the creative menu, which may include duck confit salad ($10.00); oven-roasted sweetbreads ($14.00); licorice-braised beef shortribs ($27.00); or potoato gnocchi with a walnut sauce ($17.00). Don't miss the $7.50 desserts.

There's even a menu of fine and unique cigars. Servers provide cutters and matches so that you can indulge in the cigar in the terrace's designated smoking area.

> ***The Culinary Institute of America at Greystone,*** *2555 Main Street, St. Helena 94574; phones: main telephone (707) 967–1100, restaurant (707) 967–1010, continuing education (707) 967–0600, De Baun Theatre cooking demonstration reservations (707) 967–2320, Web site www.ciachef.edu and www.digitalchef.com. Restaurant open from 11:30 A.M. to 9:00 P.M. Sunday–Thursday, 11:30 A.M. to 10:00 P.M. Friday and Saturday; Spice Islands Marketplace open from 10:00 A.M. to 6:00 P.M. daily. Demonstrations and kitchen viewings at 10:30 A.M. and 1:30 and 3:30 P.M. Saturday and Sunday. Visa, MasterCard, American Express, Diners Club, and Discover. Wheelchair accessible via parking lot and terrace at north end of building.*

As you leave the Culinary Institute, turn left to continue north on Highway 29 to Charles Krug, Markham, St. Clement, Freemark Abbey, Folie à Deux, Ehlers Grove, Frank-Rombauer/Hanns Kornell Champagne, and Stonegate wineries, plus an entrance to Sterling—all before you get to Calistoga.

Turn right (east) just north of the Culinary Institute of America to **Charles Krug Winery,** the "oldest operating winery in the Napa Valley," founded by Prussian-bórn Charles Krug. Krug died in 1892, and San Francisco banker James Moffitt bought the winery from Krug's heirs. (Remember, Beringer claims to be the "oldest continuously operating winery," the key word being *continuously.*)

Rosa and Cesare Mondavi purchased the property from Moffitt in 1943. Their son, Peter Mondavi Sr., named one of twelve "Living Legends" by the Napa Valley Vintners' Association, took over the winery in 1966 and instilled cold fermentation and use of French oak barrels, then passed management duties on to his sons, Peter Jr. and Marc. They all live on the family estate.

Olive trees line the driveway to the historic buildings and the separate tasting room (be sure to try the Charles Krug Peter Mondavi Family Extra Virgin Olive Oil, based on Krug estate olives). Catch the fabulous view of Greystone, and take time to picnic in the vineyards.

If you had any previous misgivings about Krug wines, try them again. They are contenders, particularly the Cabernets and Pinot Noir. You will find Krug wines under both Charles Krug and C. K. Mondavi labels. Their Generations blend won gold medals in 1998 competitions at the National Orange Show, Monterey Wine Competition, and *Dallas Morning News* Wine Competition. Enjoy bread squares to dip into Tuscan Hills grapeseed or olive oils, excellent herbes de Provence, and Scharffen Berger chocolates.

Fine points: Featured wines: Chardonnay, Sauvignon Blanc, Cabernet Sauvignon, Merlot, Zinfandel, Pinot Noir, and Generations (blend of Cabernet Sauvignons). Tasting fee: $5.00 for regular wines, $8.00 for family Reserves. Owner: Peter Mondavi Sr. Winemakers: John Moynier and David Galzignato. Cases: Charles Krug 100,000, C. K. Mondavi 1,000,000. Acres: 800+.

Charles Krug Winery, 2800 North Main Street, St. Helena 94574; phone (707) 967–2200, Web sites www.charleskrug.com and www.ckmondavi.com. Open from 10:30 A.M. to 5:00 P.M. daily. Visa, MasterCard, American Express, and Discover. Wheelchair accessible.

Markham Vineyards will be on your right going north. Look for a rather industrial new building at the front with flagpoles, dramatic dripping fountains filled with floating lilies, and lovely marguerites in the entrance patio.

The historic building was built as La Ronde Winery in 1874 by prospector Jean Laurent, and it passed through various owners over the decades. Bruce Markham bought the winery in 1977 and sold it in 1988 to giant Mercian, Japan's largest wine importer.

The tasting-room entrance is to the left at the rear of the entrance patio, with the daily Tasting Menu posted on a tripod at the door. Mercian has put millions into elegant blonde-wood floors, ever-changing art shows, high ceilings, and jazz background music—obviously someone talented is in charge of display and color. Venture upstairs to the gallery for seasonal exhibitions. Watch for summer trunk shows and book signings on Saturday.

You might be interested in the Oaxacan pottery and posters, Napa Valley Wine Auction posters, olive oils, cookbooks, lead-free pewter flatware and corkscrews, jewelry, and wine bottles of doggie treats called Chateau Pooche.

Fine points: The Chardonnay, Sauvignon Blanc, and Merlot have all been rated tops in California by *Wine Spectator.* Tasting fee: $5.00 to $10.00. Featured wines: Chardonnay, Merlot, Zinfandel, Petit Syrah, Pinot Noir, and Cabernet Sauvignon. Owner: Mercian of Japan. Wine-maker: Kimberlee Nicholls. Cases: 150,000. Acres: 400.

Markham Vineyards, 2812 St. Helena Highway North, St. Helena 94574; phone (707) 963–5292. Open from 10:00 A.M. to 5:00 P.M. daily. Visa, MasterCard, American Express, and JCB. Wheelchair accessible.

The next winery going north is **St. Clement Vineyards** in a big yellow-and-white Victorian house up the hill to the left (west) of Highway 29. Leave Markham and turn right, ready to turn left almost immediately and carefully. Park in the lot below and hike up the path, climb the steps, and rest and recover at the patio's wrought-iron tables and chairs. If the hike didn't take your breath away, the view will. As you walk in the front door, turn right to the library and feast your eyes on a marvelous collection of wine books, which you are welcome to leaf through.

San Francisco glass merchant Fritz Rosenbaum built this elegant Gothic-Victorian in 1878 and lived in the house with his family while producing commercial wines in the stone cellar beneath the house, the eighth bonded winery in the Napa Valley.

Bill Robbins bought the property, restored the building, and started Spring Mountain Winery here. It was Robbins's Parrott Mansion, to which he moved Spring Mountain, that was the residence in the *Falcon Crest* nighttime soap. The name St. Clement refers to an island at the mouth of the Potomac River where interim owner Dr. Bill Casey, a Maryland ophthalmologist, loved to sail.

Japanese Sapporo beer company bought the property from Casey in 1987, and in September 1999, St. Clement was sold to Beringer Wine Estates. Both are now owned by Foster's Brewing Group Ltd. of Australia.

St. Clement Vineyards

Fine points: Tasting fee: $5.00. Featured wines: Chardonnay, Sauvignon Blanc, Merlot, Cabernet Sauvignon, and Oroppas, a Bordeaux-style blend. Owner: Foster's Brewing Group Ltd. of Australia. Winemaker: Aaron Pott. Cases: 25,000. Acres 3.

St. Clement Vineyards, *2867 St. Helena Highway North, St. Helena 94574; phone (707) 967–3033 or (800) 331–8266, e-mail info@ stclement.com, Web site www.stclement.com. Open from 10:00 A.M. to 4:00 P.M. daily. Visa, MasterCard, American Express, and Discover. Wheelchair accessible, although slightly precarious, by parking in lot at top of driveway.*

With bumper stickers asking "Where the Hell is Ballentine Vineyards?" Betty and Van Ballentine launched their own winery in 1998 after growing grapes and making wines for others for decades. Look for **Ballentine Vineyards** on the east side of Highway 29, north of Markham and south of Freemark Abbey. It has a new tasting room, well worth the stop for the fun and wine.

Ballentine's label is an interesting old survey map of Napa Valley showing the soil conditions exactly where their vineyards are. Give this one a chance.

Fine points: No tasting fee. Featured wines: Zinfandel, Merlot, Syrah, Meritage, red table wine. Owners: Van and Betty Ballentine. Wine-maker: Bruce Devlin. Cases: 12,000. Acres: 100.

Ballentine Vineyards, 2820 St. Helena Highway North, St. Helena 94574; phone (707) 963–3493 or 963–7919, Web site www .ballentinevineyards.com. Open from 8:00 A.M. to 4:30 P.M. by appointment Monday–Friday. Tasting room open 10:00 A.M. to 4:00 P.M. Visa and MasterCard. Wheelchair accessible.

A Dozen Vintners is a small, interesting tasting room that replaced a musty old antiques store that was rarely open. Owner Norm Alumbaugh owns the Eagle & Rose Hotel in downtown St. Helena, as well as a motel behind the tasting room and three others, and Eagle & Rose Vineyards & Winery in Pope Valley near Middletown.

A Dozen Vintners offers tastings of hard-to-get-to wines and wineries, such as Adams Ridge, Destino Wines, Domaine Charbay, Eagle & Rose, Fife Vineyards, Howell Mountain Vineyards, Lamborn Family Vineyards, Livingston Moffett Vineyards, Reverie Winery, Spelletich Cellars, and von Strasser Winery. Von Strasser discourages visitors to their winery who are not already familiar with their wines or ready to buy six to twelve bottles, so try it here.

A Dozen Vintners, 3000 Highway 29 North at Lodi Lane, St. Helena 94574; phone (707) 967–0666, Web site www.adozenvintners.com. Open 10:30 A.M. to 5:30 P.M. daily. Tasting fee: $5.00 for six wines, $10.00 for a flight of top Reserves. Visa, MasterCard, and American Express. Wheelchair accessible. Parking lot in back via Lodi Lane.

In the same building as A Dozen Vintners is **Café 29.** Rick Healy has opened a new practical restaurant with quick service perfect to put guests on the Napa Winery Shuttle located in the same little building.

All day breakfast is hearty, and all egg dishes are served with hash browns or Café 29 bleu cheese home country potatoes and a basket of toast. All of the preceding with two eggs and choice of chicken apple sausage, Applewood smoked bacon, or ham, are $8.00. You can create your own omelette, adding up to three items for $9.50 or up to six add-ons for $12.50. German pancakes come with lemon wedges, powdered sugar, and melting butter ($8.00), and there are several "plated breakfasts" with eggs, meats, fruits, coffee, and more than you can eat. Try the crepes, either for breakfast or for dessert with lunch.

Lunch includes several creative salads, crab cakes with chunky blue cheese vinaigrette ($10.50), sandwiches and burgers ($10.50), chicken potpies ($12.50), and steaks, salmon, pastas, and fish and chips, all under $15.00.

Café 29, 3000 Highway 29 North at Lodi Lane, St. Helena 94574; phone (707) 963–9919, Web site www.cafe29.com. Open 7:00 A.M. to 3:00 P.M. daily. Beer and wine. Visa and MasterCard. Wheelchair accessible. Parking lot in back via Lodi Lane.

To get back on our tour, head north on Highway 29. At your next stop, you can visit Freemark Abbey, Hurd's Bees Wax Candles and Gourmet, and the superb Brava Terrace restaurant.

Freemark Abbey Winery's name has nothing to do with the Catholic church, although many of us grew up believing there were monks wandering around in long brown robes. The name is actually a combo of Southern Californians Albert "Abbey" Ahern, Charles Freeman, and Markquand Foster, who bought Lombarda Cellars in 1939.

Founder Josephine Marlin Tychson in 1886 became the first woman to build and operate a winery in California, which she called Tychson Cellars. San Lorenzo, California, native Josephine and her Danish husband, John Tychson, moved here in 1881 to cure his tuberculosis. They bought 147 acres, known as Tychson Hill, on the west side of Highway 29, for $8,500. He died, and Josephine built a 50-square-foot redwood winery and hired Nils Larsen as foreman to make wine, producing Zinfandel, Riesling, and a Burgundy blend. When phylloxera attacked, she sold the winery to Larsen, who sold it to Antonio Forni, a friend of Josephine's, who renamed it Lombarda Cellars in 1898.

A thinking man, Forni made Chianti and other Italian-style wines to sell to Italian immigrants working Barre, Vermont's, marble and granite quarries. Using stones from nearby Glass Mountain, Forni expanded by building a new structure around the wooden one so he wouldn't have to move the tanks and later removed the redwood building. Prohibition shut Forni down, and along came the Freemark Abbey boys in 1939, who sold their wine primarily in San Francisco.

Freemark Abbey went through several owners, ending up with a group that included the late Chuck Carpy and Jim Warren, Dick Heggie, Brad Webb, and Laurie Wood. Carpy is generally credited with resurrecting the winery.

Enjoy the living-room feeling in the tasting room with large upholstered chairs, elegant wood furniture, and a roaring fire in the walk-in fireplace. Even-

Freemark Abbey's comfortably elegant tasting room

tually the tasting room will move into the original stone cellar out front that used to house Hurd Bees Wax Candles.

Fine points: Tasting fee: $5.00 (you keep the glass). Featured wines: Chardonnay, Cabernet Franc, Cabernet Sauvignon-Sycamore, Cabernet Sauvignon, Merlot, Sangiovese, Petite Sirah, Viognier, Johannisberg Riesling, Cabernet Franc, Merlot, and Edelwein gold late harvest Riesling. Owners: Legacy Estates, LLC. Director of Winemaking: Ted Edwards. Winemaker: Tim Bell. Cases: 50,000. Acres: 330.

Freemark Abbey Winery, 3022 St. Helena Highway North, St. Helena 94574; phone (707) 963–9694. Open from 10:00 A.M. to 6:00 P.M. (closes early in winter). Visa, MasterCard, and American Express. Wheelchair accessible.

Changes are brewing in Freemark Abbey's complex. Hurd Bees Wax Candles moved to Calistoga to make room for Freemark's new tasting room, the Brava Terrace restaurant closed, and the fun **Silverado Brewing Co.** opened in Freemark's streetside building.

There's a well-worked saying in the Napa and Sonoma wine regions: "It takes a lot of beer to make good wine." Silverado Brewing Co. caters to those lunch and after-work tastes and even provides some good grub if you want to stick around. Owner-brewer Ken Mee's beers include Amber Ale, Pale Ale, Oatmeal Stout, and Blond Ale. The long picnic tables outside are inviting but a bit noisy with traffic rushing by on Highway 29.

Enjoy excellent fried calamari ($7.00); Chinese chicken salad ($10.50); Bay shrimp and avocado salad ($8.00); fat Niman Ranch natural beef burgers ($7.50); New York hot pastrami with Gruyère cheese on rye ($11.00); Niman Ranch St. Louis ribs ($14.50–$22.00); steaks, pastas, lamb shanks, and, their favorite, beer-battered fish and chips ($9.50).

Silverado Brewing Co., 3020-A North St. Helena Highway, St. Helena 94574; phone (707) 967–9876. Open from 11:30 A.M. to 9:30 P.M. Sunday–Thursday, dining till 10:00 P.M. Friday–Saturday, bar till 2:00 A.M. Full bar. Visa and MasterCard. Wheelchair accessible.

On to more wineries and the St. Helena Premium Outlets. After you leave the Freemark Abbey complex, head north and over a little hill, at the bottom of which is the driveway to **Folie à Deux Winery.** Turn right (east) at the colored flags flying across from the St. Helena Premium Outlets, and right again at the oak tree. The little yellow century-old farm house and its new add-on serve as tasting room in this bucolic setting.

Enjoy your picnic at a table on the lawn under the old oak tree. You can even tour the new caves Friday and Saturday at 11:00 A.M. and 1:00 P.M. by appointment.

When the two psychiatrists who founded the winery told psychiatrist friends they were going to fulfill a mutual dream by starting a winery, their friends said the couple were showing classic symptoms of *folie à deux,* a term that refers to two "batty individuals [who] share the same delusional ideas or fantasies about the real world." In other words, they were both crazy. Indeed.

Folie à Deux began producing wine in 1981 with grapes from its twelve acres. In 1995 renowned winemaker Dr. Richard Peterson and friends bought the winery and hired winemaker Scott Harvey. Watch for the Amador Zinfandel from the 130-year-old Grandpère Vineyard. Be sure to taste St. Helena Olive Oil Company's flavored oils and their new Eggplant Marinara.

Fine points: Featured wines: Chardonnay, Cabernet Sauvignon, Merlot, Zinfandel, and Menage à Trois. Owner: Trinchero Estates (Sutter Home). Winemaker: Joe Shirley. Cases: 25,000. Acres: 13.

Folie à Deux Winery, 3070 North St. Helena Highway, St. Helena 94574; phone (707) 963–1160 or (800) 473–4454, Web site www.folieadeux.com. Open from 10:00 A.M. to 5:00 P.M. daily. Visa, MasterCard, and American Express. Wheelchair accessible via south side of house, with disabled parking close by.

To get to **Ehlers Estate,** turn right (east) on Ehlers Road off Highway 29, then left at the sign to the small pinkish beige stone building with planters full of colorful flowers and a black iron rocking chair near the tall sliding wooden door. Notice the gorgeous wildflowers growing beneath the grove of olive trees next to the winery. You are welcome to picnic here, reminiscent of some extremely romantic French scenes. If no one seems to be around, ring the bell by the door.

French entrepreneur Jean Leducq sought what he believed to be the best property in the United States to grow and produce exceptional Bordeaux-style

Ehlers Estate

Chicken Salad

from Ehlers Estate, St. Helena

1 tsp salt
$^1/_2$ tsp freshly ground pepper
olive oil cooking spray
1 lb boneless, skinless chicken breasts
$^3/_4$ cup plain nonfat yogurt
1 Tbs Dijon mustard
2 Tbs freshly chopped chives
1 Tbs freshly chopped tarragon
1 Granny Smith apple
juice of $^1/_2$ lemon
1 cup finely diced fennel
$^1/_2$ cup finely diced celery
2 cups red seedless grapes, cut in half
6 slices pumpernickel bread
1 bunch watercress, tough stems removed

Combine salt and pepper in a bowl. Coat bottom of a large sauté pan with cooking spray and then heat over medium-high heat.

Sprinkle chicken with some of the salt mixture and place chicken in sauté pan. Reduce heat to medium and cover. Cook until chicken is cooked through, about 12 minutes, flipping halfway through cooking time. Remove from pan and set aside.

In a bowl combine yogurt, mustard, chives, tarragon, and remaining salt mixture. Core the apple and cut into $^1/_4$-inch diced chunks, then place in a medium bowl with lemon juice and toss to combine. Add fennel, celery, and grapes. Cut reserved chicken into $^1/_2$-inch pieces. Add to salad with yogurt dressing, and stir to combine. Serve on pumpernickel bread, open-faced, with watercress. Serves 6.

wines, and here it is! Leducq bought the surrounding vineyards in the 1980s and more recently bought the historic 1886 "ghost" B. Ehlers building.

Leducq retained French enologist Jacques Boissenot to plan, design, and oversee farming practices in the vineyard, Nils Venge as a winemaking consultant, and Daniel O'Donnell, formerly a chef and winemaker for Ehlers Grove, as winemaker. After a period as Leducq Vineyards, in July 2003 the name went back to the winery's roots as Ehlers Estate. If you are lucky, staff member T'Anne Butcher, who comes from a highly respected Napa and Sonoma winemaking family, will be around to help you as tasting room and sales director.

Fine points: Featured wines: Napa Valley Merlot, Cabernet Sauvignon, Cabernet Franc, and Sauvignon Blanc. Owner: Leducq Foundation. Winemaker: Rudy Zuidema. Cases: 8,000. Acres: 41.

Ehlers Estate, 3222 Ehlers Lane, St. Helena 94574; phone (707) 963–5972, Web site www.ehlersestate.com. Open from 10:00 A.M. to 5:00 P.M. daily. Visa, MasterCard, and American Express. Wheelchair accessible.

Three miles north of the Freemark Abbey complex and half a mile north of Ehlers Estate is **Bale Grist Mill State Historic Park,** a wonderful place to take kids of all ages. Follow signs up the hill and park in the designated lot. Then walk down an asphalt path (no dogs, please) through thick, luxuriant green growth. You can hear the water in Mill Creek as soon as you get out of the car.

The mill was built in 1846 by Dr. E. T. Bale, grantee of Carne Humana Rancho. When settlers arrived in the Napa Valley in the 1830s and 1840s, they planted corn and wheat to replace the oats they found growing wild. To convert these grains to usable flour, they needed a mill, which also became the local social center and gathering place. The miller was the local big shot, someone to whom everyone spoke, a collector of gossip, and an adviser on banking and business.

A real character, Bale shot at Salvador Vallejo twice on a Sonoma street during an argument. Bale barely escaped lynching and went to jail; partly due to untrue rumors that settlers were going to storm the jail and get him out, the governor ordered him released. Somewhat sobered by the experience,

Old Bale Mill Cheese Spoon Bread

from Bale Grist Mill State Historic Park, St. Helena

You can purchase a whole booklet of recipes from Bale Grist Mill State Historic Park, but we include here one of the miller's recipes that is not in that cookbook.

2 cups milk or buttermilk (buttermilk makes it even better)
2 Tbs butter
1$\frac{1}{2}$ cup cornmeal
2 eggs, separated
1$\frac{1}{2}$ cups grated cheddar cheese
$\frac{1}{2}$ tsp salt

Preheat oven to 375°F. Grease baking dish. Bring milk to just below boiling. Add butter. Gradually stir in cornmeal. Cook over medium heat, stirring constantly 2 minutes or until thick. Remove from heat, stir in egg yolks, cheese, and salt. Beat egg whites until stiff. Fold into mix.

Place dish in oven and bake 35 minutes.

Bale settled down on his rancho and sold off some land to finance building this mill. A subsequent owner of the mill and land, Mrs. Sara Lyman, deeded it all to the Native Sons of the Golden West in 1923.

Now George Stratton is the miller, and he does his thing four times a day on the weekends at unspecified times. Sometimes he even makes bread on the wood stove in the granary. You can buy (and we did) all sorts of ground-here rye, whole wheat, cornmeal, and pastry flour, and polenta by the half or whole pound, as well as an excellent historic cookbook ($5.00). You can also follow a 1.02-mile trail from Bale Mill State Historic Park to Bothe Napa Valley State Park. The Culinary Institute of America at Greystone in St. Helena brings students here to learn the elementary process of making flour and bread.

> **Bale Grist Mill State Historic Park**, *3369 Highway 29, St. Helena 94574; phone (707) 942–4575. Open from 10:00 A.M. to 5:00 P.M. daily. Admission fee: $2.00 adults, $1.00 children (under 17), which is also good to get into Bothe Napa Valley State Park up the road and state historic buildings on Sonoma Plaza the same day. Wheelchair accessible on paths to the park. The historic mill is not wheelchair accessible.*

Bale Mill Pine Furniture on your left (west) going north is in a two-story old white structure that was actually an inn but feels more like a whorehouse, with little rooms upstairs, escape routes, and creaky floors. Here you will find fabulous framed and large French posters, pine furniture made locally, wrought iron, iron canopy beds upstairs, and the world's best straw sun hats. Owner Tom Scheibal also has Tivoli on the north end of St. Helena proper, and Dottie Richolson is design consultant and elegant hostess. Be sure to stop in.

> **Bale Mill Pine Furniture** *(also known as Bale Mill Classic Country Furniture), 3431 St. Helena Highway North, St. Helena 94574; phone (707) 963–4595. Open from 10:00 A.M. to 5:00 P.M. Wednesday–Monday. MasterCard and Visa. Not wheelchair accessible.*

Bothe Napa Valley State Park entrance is just a mile north of Bale Mill, and you can walk between the two parks on a trail. Bothe is nearly 2,000 acres of lush laurel, madrone, and oak trees that afford quiet campsites and nonvineyard views from the top of Coyote Peak. You can swim in the natural spring pool ($3.00) near the visitor center or ride horseback with Napa Valley Trail Rides ($50.00 for one and a half hours, $55.00 for two hours). Be sure to visit the Native American Plant Garden, Wappo People next to the visitor center. Enjoy Redwood Trail along Ritchey Creek Canyon and picnics under the towering Douglas firs.

Bothe Napa Valley State Park, 3801 St. Helena Highway North, Calistoga 94515; phone (707) 942–4575. Open from 8:00 A.M. to sunset. Admission fee: $2.00 per vehicle, $1.00 senior's car. Parts of the park are wheelchair accessible.

Benessere means "well-being" or "prosperity," according to John and Ellen Benish of Chicago, who purchased a dilapidated winery in bankruptcy court in 1994 from Charles Shaw, now famous for "Two Buck Chuck" wines sold originally through Trader Joe's for $1.99. Using their fortune gained from a large Midwestern schoolbus company, the Benishes uprooted all the vines and replanted. Enjoy the elegance, creek, and picnic facilities at this pleasant location.

Fine points: Featured wines: Pinot Grigio, Sangiovese, Zinfandel, Syrah, Merlot, Cabernet Sauvignon, and Port. Owners: John and Ellen Benish. Winemaker: Chris Deardon. Cases: 5,000. Acres: 36 planted of 42, and buy fruit from Carneros.

Benessere Vineyards, Inc., 1010 Big Tree Road, St. Helena 94574; phone (707) 963–5853, Web site www.benesserevineyards.com. Open 10:00 A.M. to 4:00 P.M. daily, 11:00 A.M. to 5:00 P.M. daily in summer. Visa, MasterCard, and American Express. Wheelchair accessible.

Practically across the road is Larkmead Lane, which leads to **Frank Family Vineyards,** formerly Hanns Kornell Champagne Cellars, one of Marilyn Monroe's wine-country hangouts. It was originally Larkmead Cellars from 1884–1938, when Hanns Kornell bought it. In the meantime, Treasury Department villains came in with sledgehammers during Prohibition and destroyed the wine tanks, sending a "river" of red wine flowing down the road. It is now owned by grape grower Richard Frank and managed by Koerner Rombauer of Rombauer Vineyards. Rombauer brings their crushing pad to this partnership, and Richard Frank is a former president of the Academy of Television Arts and Sciences.

Marilyn Monroe was a very close friend of Hanns Kornell. When she used to visit the Calistoga baths when hubby Joe DiMaggio was off playing baseball, she would plant herself on a couch in what is now the outer tasting room and spend the afternoon sipping Champagne and listening to Kornell's stories. Hence, the life-size portrait and Andy Warholesque series over the reserve wine bar in the back room. On June 15, 2000, the winery suffered a horrible fire in its warehouse. Much of the stock was lost, but the winery has totally recovered and is back better than ever with a new, even bigger warehouse.

Frank Family Vineyards tasting room entrance

Fine points: Featured wines: Chardonnay, Merlot, Zinfandel, Brut, Blanc de Blancs, Blanc de Noirs, Rouge, Extra Dry, and Alexander Valley Cabernet. Owner: Richard Frank. No tasting fee. Winemaker: Todd Graff. Cases: 20,000.

Frank Family Vineyards, 1091 Larkmead Lane, Calistoga 94515; phone (707) 942–0859 or (800) 574–9463. Open from 10:00 A.M. to 5:00 P.M. daily. Visa, MasterCard, and American Express. Tours are wheelchair accessible, but the historic tasting room is not. The staff, however, is happy to help anyone needing assistance.

To visit prized **Schramsberg Vineyards,** you must make an appointment ahead of time, according to Napa County regulations. It is well worth making the call ahead of time to experience its highly regarded sparkling wines. Turn left (west) off Highway 29 at Peterson Drive and wander through lush woods, turning onto Schramsberg Road and taking care around curves for about a mile, and watching for deer. Schramsberg's Blanc de Blancs was the first non-French champagne served in the White House.

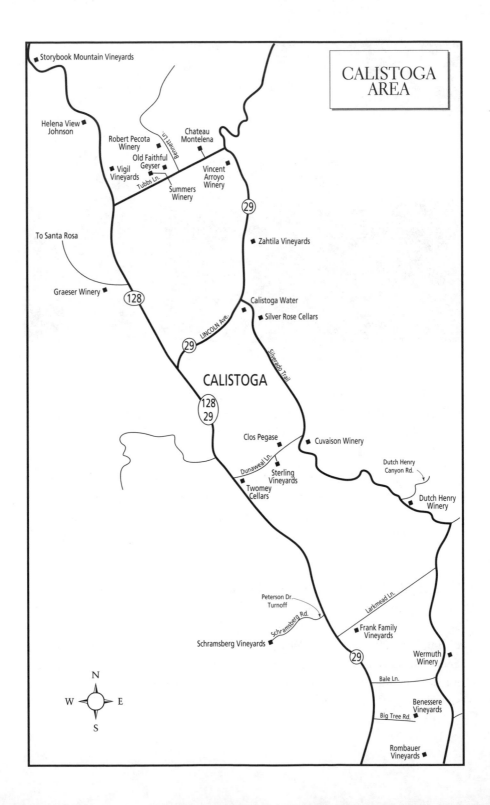

German immigrants Annie and Jacob Schram founded the winery in 1862 as the first winery on the hillsides of the Napa Valley. Chinese laborers cleared the scrub oak and replaced them with vineyards, along with a network of 2 miles of tunnels and caves in the soft volcanic rock.

The Schrams built the large Victorian house as they prospered, and they hosted Robert Louis Stevenson here in 1880. He later devoted a whole chapter to Schramsberg in his *Silverado Squatters*. The entire 200-acre Schram estate became a California Historical Landmark in 1957. Until his death in 1998, owner Jack Davies and his wife, Jamie Davies, with the influence of the Davies's friend and environmentalist Dorothy Erskine showing everywhere, dedicated themselves and Schramsberg to drawing on the best of the past to create premier sparkling wines in the *méthode champenoise*. Jamie continues that tradition today.

As you arrive at the sloped parking lot, you are greeted by handsome and huge Dalmatians and Irish setters, who lazily get up to welcome you to their home. The cozy tasting room is to the left of the parking lot, just beyond the elegant pond with its statue of a frog wearing a tuxedo and holding a champagne bottle and glass. Plan a little time to look at the fascinating photos and letters on the walls, and enjoy the high quality of shirts, ice buckets, hats, champagne stoppers, and even a flashlight and a copy of Stevenson's *Silverado Squatters* ($6.00).

Schramsberg pond and tasting room entrance

Schramsberg certainly takes the sweepstakes for prestigious pourings of their wines, including dinners at the White House for Presidents Reagan and the first Bush, for Queen Noor of Jordan, for Princess Grace of Monaco, for Prince Charles and Princess Diana, for Mikhail Gorbachev, for President Richard Nixon and Chou En-lai, and at the North Pole. Proceeds from sales of Quernica go to the Jack Davies Fund of The Community Foundation of Napa Valley for land preservation.

Fine points: Tasting fees: $7.50 to $15.00 for Reserve Library wines. Featured wines: Blanc de Blancs, Blanc de Noirs, Brut Rosé, Quernica Brut Rosé, Cremant, and J. Schram. Owner: Jamie Davies. Winemaker and General Manager: Hugh Davies. Cases: 50,000. Acres: 200.

Schramsberg Vineyards, 1400 Schramsberg Road, Calistoga 94515; phone (707) 942–4558, Web site www.schramsberg.com. Open from 10:00 A.M. to 4:00 P.M. daily by appointment only. Visa, MasterCard, and American Express. Wheelchair accessible.

Go back to Highway 29 and turn left (north) to go to Sterling Vineyards and **Twomey Cellars.**

Twomey Cellars is a definite must-visit in the Napa Valley. Twomey was founded by Silver Oak partner Raymond Duncan, who is also a Denver oilman and cattle rancher. Duncan purchased the former Stonegate Winery location in June 2004, and quickly invested and improved the visitor facilities and winery to a thing of beauty, turning management over to his four sons. Ramona Behrens manages the tasting room and creates the perfect calming ambience.

All Twomey Merlots originate in a single Napa Valley vineyard, Soda Canyon Ranch. Winemaker Daniel Baron has worked with some of the greatest winemakers and cellar workers in the world at Pomerol and St. Emilion.

Fine points: Featured wines: Merlot. Owners: Raymond Duncan and family. Winemaker: Dan Baron. Cases: 7,000. Acres: 148.

Twomey Cellars, 1183 Dunaweal Lane, Calistoga 94515; phone (800) 505-4850, Web site www.twomeycellars.com. Open 9:00 A.M. to 4:00 P.M. Monday–Saturday. Tasting fee: $5.00. Visa, MasterCard, and American Express. Wheelchair accessible.

The enormous white Moorish-looking edifice you see on a hill to the east of Highway 29 is **Sterling Vineyards,** a remarkably striking structure built in 1973. It is not a monastery, as many of us have grown up believing. To find your way there, turn right on Dunaweal Lane for 0.4 mile, then turn right (south) at the white mausoleum-style arches. Even the divided driveway hints that something interesting is ahead.

Park in the parking lot and get in line to pay your tram fee ($6.00 adults). You cannot drive up to the winery, so you have to take the tram, except for visitors with disabilities, who can ride in a van. The Disneyesque experience again contributes to the mood.

Brace yourself for a spectacular view, relaxed tasting, and glorious balcony seating where servers bring the wine to you, truly unusual in this stand-up-to-the-bar-and-have-a-sip wine country. Take yourself on an excellent self-guided tour and enjoy the Three Palms Art Gallery. This is a must-stop experience like no other.

Peter Newton, an English paper broker, started the winery in 1964 and sold it to Coca-Cola in 1977, which later sold it to the Joseph E. Seagram & Sons group in 1983. Tremendous investment is obvious, but you can't miss the Old St. Dunstan's Church bells Newton brought to chime every half hour to remind him of his English origins. This is one winery where you can also purchase film and Calistoga mineral water. Kids are served juices in the tasting room.

Fine points: Admission fee: $15, with tasting of three vintages, $10 for minors, more for Reserves; includes tram fee, with children given juice and "coloring packet" to keep them entertained. Featured wines: Chardonnay, Sauvignon Blanc, Cabernet Sauvignon, Merlot, Pinot Gris, Pinot Noir, Viognier, Sangiovese, Syrah, Muscat Canelli, and Malvasia Blanc. Owner: Diageo Chateau and Estate Wines (purchased Seagram in 2004). Winemaker: Rob Hunter. Cases: 360,000. Acres: 1,200.

Sterling Vineyards, 1111 Dunaweal Lane, Calistoga 94515; phone (707) 942–3344, Web site www.sterlingvineyards.com or www .aboutwines.com. Open from 10:30 A.M. to 4:30 P.M. daily. Guided tours on the hour from 11:00 A.M. to 2:00 P.M. Visa, MasterCard, American Express, and JCB. Winery is wheelchair accessible, tram is not, and restrooms at tram station are. A wheelchair-accessible van is available.

One of the many first impressions at Clos Pegase

For a nearby wildly different art and wine experience, visit **Clos Pegase** across Dunaweal Lane and eastward from Sterling. You can also get to Clos Pegase easily by turning west from Silverado Trail.

Jan and Mitsuko Shrem's shrine to art and wine is a must-see on the Napa wine trail. Here several senses will be pleased. Just driving into the parking lot is a pleasure, so be alert to large abstract sculptures in the fields and vineyards surrounding the winery.

The whole place celebrates Pegasus, the winged horse who brought us art and wine by releasing the Spring of the Muses. Water flowing from the spring gave new life to the vines, inspiring the gift of poetry in those who drank the wine.

A native of Colombia with Jewish heritage, Shrem made his first fortune importing technical books to Japan and then translating and publishing them there. He hired famed Princeton architect Michael Graves to design his wine and art gallery in 1984 and acquired outstanding works, including some by Jean Dubuffet, Francis Bacon, Max Ernst, Tanguy, Miro, Kandinsky, Oscar Dominguez, Jacques Lipschitz, Matta, Auguste Herbin, and Appel. Many of the paintings in Shrem's collection, including his prized *Pegasus,* painted circa 1890 by French artist Redon, grace the winery and its wine labels. The sculpture gardens include important works of Dubuffet, Richard Serra, Mark di Suvero,

Mitsuko Shrem's Grilled Quail with Herb Sauce

from Mitsuko Shrem of Clos Pegase, Calistoga

6 to 8 quail
7 Tbs olive oil
2 tsp cumin, ground
2 tsp coriander, ground
1 Tbs lemon juice
2 shallots, diced
1 lemon, sliced thin

Cut quail in half. Wash halves.

Quail marinade: Mix 4 Tbs olive oil, 1 tsp ground cumin, and 1 tsp ground coriander in a bowl, and marinate washed quail halves for one hour.

Grill quail to your specifications.

Herb sauce: Mix together 1 Tbs lemon juice, 3 Tbs olive oil, 1 tsp ground cumin, 1 tsp ground coriander, and shallots in a bowl.

Prepare serving plates by drizzling herb sauce directly on the plate. Place grilled quail on top of sauce, then drizzle more sauce on top of quail. Garnish with fresh lemon and serve warm. Serves 6. Serve with Clos Pegase Cabernet Sauvignon or wine of your choice.

Robert Morris, Anthony Caro, Tony Smith, Henry Moore, Cardenas, Tony Cragg, Sandro Chia, and Elyn Zimmerman.

Having broken out of a few accepted ruts himself, Shrem advocates that you break out of your wine rut and not allow yourself to be intimidated by wines or winemakers. Freeze good wine if you want to—Shrem does.

Fabulous sculptures greet you throughout the winery, including a sculpture at the end of the cave of Dionysus depicting his decision between wine and love. There's a free presentation on 4,000 years of art a couple of times a year. Don't be so distracted by the art that you miss the fine wines, and they are. Be sure to venture into the 21,000-square-foot volcanic cave complex, appointed with rare artifacts and sculpture nestled in wall alcoves. We hope you will be lucky enough to attend an event in the Cave Theater. All of Clos Pegase's dramatic spaces are available for use, even the Cask Room.

Fine points: Tasting fee: $5.00 whites, $10.00 reds, $25.00 Reserves. Free tours 11:00 A.M. and 2:00 P.M. Featured wines: Chardonnay, Pinot Noir, Merlot, Cabernet Sauvignon, Claret, Hommage series blends, Zinfandel, and Zin blends. Owners: Jan and Mitsuko Shrem. Winemaker: Shaun Richardson. Cases: 45,000. Acres: 420.

Clos Pegase, 1060 Dunaweal Lane, Calistoga 94515; phone (707) 942–4981, Web site www.clospegase.com. Open from 10:30 A.M. to 5:00 P.M. daily. Visa, MasterCard, American Express, and Discover. Wheelchair accessible.

Let's head back west on Dunaweal Lane (turn right coming out of Clos Pegase and left out of Sterling) and turn right (north) on Highway 29 to Calistoga.

As you drive into Calistoga, you can choose. You can pass the intersection of Highway 29 and Lincoln Avenue, Calistoga's main street, and continue northward as Highway 29 turns onto Lincoln, goes through Calistoga, and turns left (north) to Clear Lake. Highway 128 (straight ahead) takes us to the Petrified Forest, Vigil Vineyards, and Tubbs Lane, where you will find Summers Winery, Old Faithful Geyser, and Chateau Montelena. If you take this route, you can easily continue 0.2 mile eastward to Highway 29 and turn right (south) back toward Vincent Arroyo Winery, Zahtila Vineyards, Calistoga, and the Silverado Trail. Or you can turn right (east) onto Lincoln Avenue at the flashing red light and enjoy downtown before continuing on to wineries and the Silverado Trail.

We will visit the wineries before strolling through town, taking you first to Vigil Vineyards, the farthest one north. At the flashing red light, continue straight ahead on Highway 128 instead of turning right (east) on Lincoln and Highway 29. You may want to stop 0.8 mile north of Lincoln at the Calistoga Pioneer Cemetery to learn a little local history.

If you want to take a 4-mile detour to the **Petrified Forest,** go ahead, following the signs west from Highway 128 1 mile north of Lincoln. "Petrified Charlie" Evans happened upon a petrified tree stump while wandering with his cows and thus discovered the petrified forest covered with volcanic ash. Now you can drive in, take a tour of the important biggest and oldest trees, and visit the museum and store in the Ollie Bickee House for souvenirs

Petrified Forest, 4100 Petrified Forest Road, Calistoga 94515; phone (707) 942–6667. Admission fee $5.00 for adults, $4.00 for children 12–17 and seniors 60 and over, $2.00 for children 6–11; under 6 free. Visa, MasterCard, American Express, and Discover. Partially wheelchair accessible.

In 0.8 mile north of Highway 128's intersection with Petrified Forest Road, you come to Tubbs Lane, with the light green Mitchell's Drive-In on the right (southeast corner). To get to Summers Winery, Old Faithful Geyser, and Chateau Montelena, turn right at Tubbs Lane.

The first winery you come to going east from Highway 128 on Tubbs Lane north of Calistoga is the **Summers Winery,** also just west of Old Faithful Geyser. Jim and Beth Summers bought the old San Pietro Vara Winery in 1996, renamed the vineyard Villa Andriana after their young daughter, and began to make Merlot with their grapes that had previously produced acclaimed Merlots for other wineries.

Enjoy the intimate tasting room with a photography exhibit and paintings, a small labeled vineyard just off the tasting room patio, and the new bocce court. You can even join Summers' Bacchus and Bocce Club, a guaranteed fun adventure.

Fine points: Tasting fee: $5.00 (refundable with purchase). Featured wines: Merlot, Charbono, Cabernet Rosé, Zinfandel, Viognier, Chevalier Noir, Bianco, Rosso, Cabernet Cuvee, Petit Syrah, Muscat Caneli, and Chardonnay. Owners: Beth and Jim Summers. Winemaker: Ignacio Blancas. Cases: 7,000. Acres: 28.

Smoked Duck Breast with Cabernet/Blackberry Glaze

from Summers Winery, Calistoga

2 baskets fresh blackberries
$\frac{1}{2}$ bottle Summers Cabernet Sauvignon
Wonton wrappers, cut into quarters
1 lb smoked duck, sliced thin and fat removed (1 lb feeds about 10–15 people)

Remove seeds from blackberries with a food mill. Process the blackberries and Cabernet until smooth. Simmer blackberries and Cabernet over low heat until like gelatin. This can be prepared in advance and refrigerated for 1–2 weeks. Reheat before serving to make into a spooning consistency.

Spray cookie sheet with Pam. Bake wonton pieces for 4–6 minutes until lightly golden. Layer wonton cracker with slice of smoked duck breast and drizzle with blackberry/Cabernet glaze (light on the glaze). Serve with Summers Winery Cabernet Sauvignon.

Summers Winery, 1171 Tubbs Lane, Calistoga 94515; phone (707) 942–5508, Web site sumwines.com. Open from 10:30 A.M. to 4:30 P.M. daily. Visa, MasterCard, and American Express. Wheelchair accessible.

Old Faithful Geyser brings us a spectacle of nature every forty minutes right here on Tubbs Lane. Enter the parking lot and walk into the building to pay for your right to see the phenomenon. Now a private enterprise, free viewings are blocked by tall bamboo and pampas grass. This geyser is one of three legitimately called "Old Faithful"; the others are in New Zealand and Yellowstone National Park. This Old Faithful is also an official U.S. Weather Station.

Some parts of the year, somewhat unpredictably, the geyser spouts every ten minutes, varying by the weather, tides, earth stresses, and season. The water is always 350°F and shoots about 60 feet into the air. When the water erupts more frequently than every forty minutes, owner Olga Kolbek begins to be alert for earthquakes, since it has acted up before almost all of the major nearby earthquakes.

The little ticket and convenience store stocks film, postcards, drinks, microwave sandwiches, snacks, excellent brochures and information pamphlets in twenty-three languages, and lots of local lore and conversation from the family. You are welcome to bring picnics and use their tables near the geyser, just so you pay the admission price.

Old Faithful Geyser, 1299 Tubbs Lane, Calistoga 94515; phone (707) 942–6463. Open from 9:00 A.M. to 6:00 P.M. daily in summer, 9:00 A.M. to 5:00 P.M. in winter. Admission: $6.00 adults, $5.00 seniors, $2.00 children 6–12. Visa and MasterCard. Wheelchair accessible.

As you leave Old Faithful, turn left (east) onto Tubbs Lane to **Chateau Montelena,** one of the Napa Valley's most majestic and respected wineries. It is an absolute must-stop on your personal wine tour. Six-tenths of a mile east of Old Faithful turn left (north) up Chateau Montelena's narrow paved driveway. Cyclists love the ride up here, but picnicking is by reservation only. The stone fountain rocks were cut out of the cliff now covered with moss, ivy, and ferns to the left of the winery entrance. To see the old château, go down the stairs to the right of the tasting room.

Along with Stag's Leap, Chateau Montelena was one of two Napa wineries to defeat the French in a blind Paris wine tasting in 1976. Chateau Montelena's 1973 Chardonnay beat the best from Burgundy. Upon winning the tasting, owner

Chateau Montelena's tasting room entrance

Jim Barrett said, "Not bad for kids from the sticks." It was only his second vintage since resurrecting the winery, which had stopped bottling fifty years earlier.

Humor pervades this elegant establishment, including a life-size chessboard painted on the barrel room floor, where players walk around to move their men. Three generations of Barretts work at every level of production.

Alfred Tubbs began Chateau Montelena in 1882 by planting 254 acres of vines. By 1896 the winery was the seventh largest in the Napa Valley. The winery itself is carved into the north side of a hill, forming its own cave, with walls 3 to 12 feet thick. In 1960 Chinese immigrant Yort Franks built a "moat" called Jade Lake around the winery, which is now a beautiful fish and wildlife sanctuary inhabited by swans and geese and lucky picnickers. In 1972 James Barrett bought the chateau, brought in the latest winemaking equipment, and replanted the vineyard. You are welcome to explore the grounds and visit Jade Lake.

Be sure to indulge in this elegant experience. Robert M. Parker Jr., in *The Wine Advocate*, said, "This is a splendid winery at the top of its game."

Fine points: Tasting fee: $10. Featured wines: Estate Cabernet Sauvignon, Chardonnay, Riesling, Cabernet Sauvignon, and Zinfandel. Owner: James Barrett. Winemaker: Bo Barrett. Cases: 35,000. Acres: 120.

Chateau Montelena Winery, 1429 Tubbs Lane, Calistoga 94515; phone (707) 942–5105, Web site www.montelena.com. Open from 9:30 A.M. to 4:00 P.M. daily. Visa, MasterCard, and American Express. Tasting room is wheelchair accessible.

Now you can either return to Highway 128 the way you came and turn left on 128 to Lincoln Avenue and downtown Calistoga, or you can complete the winery loop by turning left (east) as you leave Chateau Montelena, go 0.2 mile to Highway 29, and turn right (south) toward Calistoga. In 0.4 mile you cross the 1902 Garnett Creek Bridge, and in another 0.5 mile turn right at Greenwood Avenue to **Vincent Arroyo Winery.** Turn right at the sign and go down the gravel driveway past the house to the beige barn winery. Notice the beautiful roses, lawns, and picnic tables, all for your pleasure.

Vincent Arroyo is the owner's name, not the Spanish name of the Vincent Riverbed. Vince is a warm, earthy fellow who, fortunately, gave up life as a mechanical engineer in Silicon Valley to make wine here in the far north of the Napa Valley. He learned to make wine hands-on from his Spanish father, who was a home winemaker. Always accessible to tasters, Vince teaches visitors about wine and loves to talk with young couples who are just venturing into the wine field. The entire winery is in one little room, so visitors can learn a lot from the source.

Vincent Arroyo wines are sold only here at the winery, so get them while you can. The winery hosts an annual open house featuring vintage wines, food, and winemakers' dinners for $80. The event is held the first weekend in May. Be sure to get on the mailing list, because tickets usually sell out to loyal fans within five days. Enjoy barrel tastings the last weekend in February. Because 80 percent of the wine is sold before it's bottled, you can now buy wine futures here.

Fine points: Featured wines: Chardonnay, Melange (red blend), Cabernet Sauvignon, Merlot, Zinfandel, Sangiovese, Petite Sirah, Petit Sirah Port, and J.J.'s blend. Owner: Vincent Arroyo. Winemaker: Vincent Arroyo. Cases: 7,000. Acres: 80.

Vincent Arroyo Winery, 2361 Greenwood Avenue, Calistoga 94515; phone (707) 942–6995 and (800) 690–1173, Web site www .vincentarroyowinery.com. Open from 10:00 A.M. to 4:30 P.M. daily by appointment only. Call ahead. Visa, MasterCard, American Express, and Discover. Wheelchair accessible.

John and Sandy and Tony and Laura Zahtila needed to try something beyond roofing contracting and tech industries and purchased what used to be Traulsen Vineyards, now named **Zahtila Vineyards.** Be sure to notice the 300 rosebushes and paths winding through them. This is one of the smallest, most intimate wineries you will find, with its tasting room at a table just outside the barrel room and winery door. Now Laura is sole owner of the winery and snatched energetic Catahoula restaurant manager Sal Maffetone away to manage the winery. Sal cooked at Tribeca in Los Angeles, so watch for cozy food and wine events.

Winemaker Corey Beck, assistant winemaker at Niebaum-Coppola Estate for years, concentrates on making a truly fine Zinfandel, which was served to Francis Ford Coppola at his own restaurant for his birthday dinner. Be sure to try Zahtila's venture into Cabernet Sauvignon.

Fine points: Tasting fee: $2.00 (refunded with purchase). Featured wines: Zinfandel, both Zahtila and Traulsen, and Cabernet Sauvignon. Owner: Laura Zahtila. Winemaker: Corey Beck. Cases: 3,000. Acres: 4.

Zahtila Vineyards, 2250 Lake County Highway, Calistoga 94515; phone (707) 942–9251, Web site www.zahtilavineyards.com. Open from 10:00 A.M. to 5:00 P.M. daily. Visa, MasterCard, and American Express. Not wheelchair accessible.

CALISTOGA

Calistoga tops off the Napa Valley 75 miles from San Francisco. Founded more than 130 years ago as a hot springs resort, Calistoga still feels like a small western town where you might expect to see horses tied at the sidewalk's edge and guys swaggering up to the saloon's swinging door. Calistoga generously provides a parking lot for residents and visitors that runs behind all the shops on the south side of Lincoln Avenue.

We begin our walking tour of Calistoga at the western end of Lincoln Avenue, where Highway 29 turns east and Highway 128 goes north. (*NOTE:* In downtown Calistoga, Lincoln Avenue is Highway 29.) We will first take you up the south side of the street, then back down the north side of Lincoln Avenue, with a 1-block sidetrack on Washington Street to Wappo Bar Bistro and the Sharpsteen Museum.

Coming from Chateau Montelena, Summers Winery, or Vincent Arroyo Winery, begin the walking tour by starting with the south side of Lincoln.

LINCOLN AVENUE, SOUTH SIDE

The first notable building you come to on your right is the venerable **Calistoga Inn and Restaurant,** whose dining room is every local's favorite birthday celebration place, because "everyone knows and loves Rosie." Owner/chef/hotelier Rosie Dunsford is a member of the Calistoga City Council and hosts clusters of unofficial gatherings.

The 1882 hotel has eighteen reasonably priced upstairs rooms ($75 midweek and $100 weekends) with shared baths, a restaurant, and "one small brewery," and its office is around the corner on Cedar Street, between window boxes draped with bright red geraniums.

In the summer you can dine on the old, comfortable patio overlooking the river in front of the Napa Valley Brewing Company in the former pump house. The restaurant offers live music every night except Monday. Check out the collection of turkey platters rimming the dining room and dish towels hanging all over the place, along with Christmas lights that "go outside in summer." Try Napa Valley Brewing Company's Calistoga Pilsner, Wheat Ale, Red Ale, and Porter, priced from $1.00 for a 4-ounce taster to $13.00 for a pitcher.

Calistoga Inn's revamped menu is truly interesting and varied. Salads are meals. We like the Dungeness crab cakes with celery root–apple remoulade ($13.25), the nostalgic iceberg lettuce wedge with Oregon bay shrimp and thousand island dressing ($10.75), the "mac and squeeze" ($10.50), the flatiron pot roast ($16.00), Tillamook cheeseburger ($9.75), pepper-crusted duck breast ($12.95), and garlic-crusted calamari ($8.75). Dinner may include excellent steaks; a mixed grill of Australian lamb chop, semiboneless quail, and smoked duck sausage ($21.95); or vegetarian casserole ($14.50).

Calistoga Inn and Restaurant, 1250 Lincoln Avenue, Calistoga 94515; phone (707) 942–4101, Web site www.calistogainn.com. Open for

Napa Valley Brewing Company patio at the Calistoga Inn

lunch and dinner. Full bar. Corkage fee: $10.00 per 750 ml bottle; "cakeage" (if you bring your own birthday cake) $2.25 per person. Visa, MasterCard, and American Express. Restaurant is wheelchair accessible; the hotel is not.

As you progress eastward on Lincoln Avenue, the next interesting stop is the **Lee Youngman Galleries,** featuring works by national and Napa Valley artists, including Gene Zesch bronze sculpture, Neil Boyl and Paul Youngman works, local vineyard scenes, handmade paper, Navajo turquoise and silver jewelry, Betty Carr and Howard Carr works, Joe Beeler bronze sculpture, and early California paintings. Youngman also has a frame shop just beyond the auto parts store next door.

Lee Youngman Galleries, 1316 Lincoln Avenue, Calistoga 94515; phone (707) 942–0585. Open from 10:00 A.M. to 5:00 P.M. daily. Visa, MasterCard, Discover, and American Express. Wheelchair accessible through the parking lot and back door.

In this land of spas and mineral and mud baths, you will find many body care possibilities, including **Free Time,** which offers toys, lotions, soaps, walk-in massages and facials, and seasonal specials.

Free Time, 1348 Lincoln Avenue, Calistoga 94515; phone (707) 942–0210. Open from 10:00 A.M. to 6:00 P.M. Sunday–Thursday, to 9:00 P.M. Friday–Saturday. Visa, MasterCard, and Discover. Wheelchair accessible.

Copperfield's Books, a small, independent bookstore exchange, opened here recently and offers used and new books.

Copperfield's Books, 1330 Lincoln Avenue, Calistoga 94515; phone (707) 942–1616. Visa and MasterCard. Wheelchair accessible.

Margaux Singleton moved her **Enoteca Wine Shop** "downstairs" and across the street, and now more visitors can find her fabulous collection of hard-to-find wines. Many of the wineries she represents make fewer than 200 cases of each wine and do not have tasting rooms. She also carries some real collectors' bottles from Chateau d'Yquem, La Mondotte, and Chateau Mouton Rothschild, as well as Screaming Eagle and Jack Russell, and those of "garagistes," the home winemakers with licenses. Calistoga artist Carlo Marchiori painted the interior murals to look like an Italian wine cave.

Enoteca Wine Shop, 1348-B Lincoln Avenue, Calistoga 94515; phone (707) 942–1117. Open 11:30 A.M. to 5:30 P.M. daily. Visa, MasterCard, and American Express. Wheelchair accessible.

Fisherman's Valley is a new fried fish shop that reeks of yummy unhealthy grease, fish, and french fries. (Charbroiled alternatives are available.) Coleslaw is excellent. Brothers Joe and Ernie Nuñez share cooking duties.

Fisherman's Valley, 1350 Lincoln Avenue, Calistoga 94515; phone (707) 942–6468. Open from 11:00 A.M. to 9:00 P.M. Sunday–Thursday, until 10:00 P.M. Friday–Saturday. Beer and wine. No credit cards. Wheelchair accessible.

Next door is one of our favorites, and one voted Napa residents' favorites, too, **Soo Yuan Chinese Food,** serving Mandarin and Szechuan specialties. The owner had restaurants in Taiwan and Vallejo before moving here a few years ago and now boasts a "Best Asian Restaurant in the Napa Valley" award (1999). Lunch at under $6.00 is a healthful bargain, with no MSG, and includes a light soup and several selections from the menu of fresh entrees. Portions are so large, two can almost share one lunch. Ironically, the narrow room and Chinese decor make us feel as if we are in a small restaurant in an Asian country. Napa residents drive for miles for the food, and Soo Yuan will deliver to your hotel room.

Soo Yuan Chinese Food, 1354 Lincoln Avenue, Calistoga 94515; phone (707) 942–9404. Open from 11:00 A.M. to 9:30 P.M., serving continuously. Beer and wine. Visa, MasterCard, American Express, and Discover. Wheelchair accessible.

Boskos Ristorante is definitely here, serving cafeteria style with windows open onto the sidewalk and a wheelchair ramp entry. A sign commands you to ORDER WITH CASHIER BEFORE TAKING A SEAT. Choices include pizza from a wood-burning oven in the back ($9.95–$12.95), loads of fresh pastas, roasted garlic chicken and other salads ($5.75–$10.50), and their own garlic bread ($2.50–$4.75). It's a good informal place to go with the kids and still have some creative food. There are lots of wines by the glass, or select a bottle from the rack across from the cashier and then pay for it at the register. Don't miss the historic photos in the hallway to the restrooms.

Boskos Ristorante, 1364 Lincoln Avenue, Calistoga 94515; phone (707) 942–9088. Open from 11:00 A.M. to 10:00 P.M. daily. Beer and wine. Visa and MasterCard. Wheelchair accessible.

At the corner of Lincoln and Washington Streets, **Brannan's Grill** is named for Calistoga historical bigwig Sam Brannan, but it's owned by Ron Goldin and Mark Young, who also own Checkers up the street and in Santa Rosa. When Ron and Mark took on the building, which last housed the Silverado Restaurant and Tavern, they discovered huge beams beyond a false ceiling and created a meticulously restored American Craftsman interior and a new terraced dining space with windows opening onto Lincoln Avenue. The nineteenth-century Brunswick bar was discovered under layers of cigarette smoke and tar. Calistoga artist Carlo Marchiori created a trompe l'oeil mural as a backdrop for the dining room. Ron and Mark have also planted the Young–Goldin Truck Farm on their ranch to provide fresh produce for Brannan's year-round. Goldin and Young recently opened the Flat Iron Grill up the street, expanding their Napa-Sonoma empire.

Chef Joel Erlich came to Brannan's from Martini House in St. Helena and loves to mix regional specialties, as Brannan's menu reflects. You might try grilled yellowfin tuna ($23), or roasted Sonoma chicken ($17). Carnivores will love the porterhouse pork chop with morel mushrooms ($19). Several excellent local wines are available by the glass. Goldin and Young and partner/winemaker Rudy Zeduma now make an excellent Syrah available at the restaurant. You can also enjoy an excellent bar menu and fabulous desserts at $5.50.

Brannan's Grill, 1374 Lincoln Avenue, Calistoga 94515; phone (707) 942–2233, Web site www.brannansgrill.com. Open from 11:30 A.M. to 10:00 P.M. daily. Visa and MasterCard. Wheelchair accessible.

One of our secret favorites we almost hate to tell people about is the under-heralded **All Seasons Bistro,** also on Lincoln right across Washington from Brannan's. Located in the Del Mar Building, the All Seasons seems hidden right on Calistoga's prime corner. The interior feels like an old, unpretentious big-city bistro, with black-and-white linoleum floors, wooden benches with restful cushions for your back, and views of the community's comings and goings. The lively paintings on the walls come from I. Wolk Gallery in St. Helena. Feel free to have fun sitting at the counter.

Owned by Alex Dierkhising, who also has Hydro Bar & Grill across the street, All Seasons has the mother of all wine lists in quality if not in quantity.

Small plates tempt with a trio of caviars with saffron beet, truffle, and ginger with dilled crème fraîche and fried capers ($18.75), wild king salmon roll wrapped in Nori with Shiitake-ginger duxelle ($8.00), or wild mushroom ravioli ($8.50).

Or try Robert Redford's favorite warm spinach salad with smoked chicken and bacon ($9.00), pastas, and special sandwiches.

Dinner offers grilled quail stuffed with foie gras and morels ($17), roast sirloin of Colorado lamb ($26), braised beef short ribs ($22), and "Everything from the Rabbit" with thyme gnocchi and braised Swiss chard ($24).

What is truly unusual about All Seasons is its wine shop to the left at the back of the restaurant. This is the finest restaurant wine shop anywhere, as we discovered by looking for a few obscure bottles that happened to be here. The wine shop sponsors "Wine Basics–A Down to Earth Tasting and Discussion" that includes family-style All Seasons lunch and tasting and primarily features Napa Valley and French wines.

> *All Seasons Bistro, 1400 Lincoln Avenue, Calistoga 94515; phone (707) 942–9111, Web site www.allseasonswineshop.com. Open for lunch from 11:30 A.M. to 2:30 P.M. Thursday–Sunday, dinner from 6:00 to 9:00 P.M. nightly; wine shop open from 11:00 A.M. to 6:00 P.M. Thursday–Monday. Beer and wine. Corkage fee: $15. Visa and MasterCard. Wheelchair accessible.*

The Surfwood Bar is exactly what it says for lots of locals, with good weekend music from the likes of Philip Claypool.

Beyond the Surfwood is **Checkers Pizza & Pasta** restaurant, which is a great informal place for pizzas, wonderful salads, huge calzones, and vegetarian and carnivore sandwiches served on focaccia bread with soup or salad. Pizza add-ons of goat cheese, sun-dried tomatoes, and others are only $1.00. Chef Douglas Wattson has added some protein to the menu in the form of seafood, such as scallops and mussels. Yes, this Checkers is related to the one in Santa Rosa.

Enjoy Chico sculptor Daniel Parks's flying monsters hanging from the ceiling and the Pasta Piper airplane hanging over the wine bar. Lots of humor and color keeps you going while you wait for your food. Checkers is owned by the same great team as Brannan's, Mark Young and Ron Goldin.

Try the roasted leg of lamb sandwich ($8.25), a great Caesar salad, or the butternut squash ravioli ($10.95).

Checkers Pizza & Pasta, 1414 Lincoln Avenue, Calistoga 94515; phone (707) 942–9300. Open from 11:00 A.M. to 10:00 P.M. daily. Beer and wine. Visa and MasterCard. Wheelchair accessible.

Next to Checkers, Calistoga Natural Foods sells sandwiches, wheat grass smoothies, health books, lotions, and vitamin supplements. Moreno's offers quickie burritos, tostadas, hot dogs, and shaved ice, while the Smoke Shop and Liquor Store provides the obvious and emergency corkscrews.

Flat Iron Grill is the newest creation of Brannan's owners, Ron Goldin and Mark Young. Replacing short-lived CinCin at this location, Flat Iron Grill offers great basic American carnivore comfort foods, plus macaroni and cheese and grilled salmon. Go for the chopped wedge salad with blue cheese ($5.95), a flat-iron steak with potatoes au gratin ($15.95), beef brisket ($13.95), baby back ribs with coleslaw ($14.95–$18.95), and an ample steak burger ($10.95).

Flat Iron Grill, 1440 Lincoln Avenue, Calistoga 94515; phone (707) 942–1220. Open from 11:30 A.M. to 3:00 P.M. and 4:30 to 9:30 or 10:00 P.M. daily. Full bar. Corkage fee: $10. Visa and MasterCard. Wheelchair accessible.

A favorite coffee destination for both Calistoga locals and *The New York Times* is the **Calistoga Coffee Roastery** coffee clinic. Clive Richardson and Terry Rich roast thirty-five kinds of coffee beans, six of which are decaf, and sell beans (whole or ground) as well as espresso drinks, poached eggs, sandwiches, bagels, and—surprise—Calistoga waters bottled right around the corner. They also make blends for the Culinary Institute of America's *Wine Spectator* Greystone Restaurant.

A sign on the wall quotes Clive: DRINK MORE COFFEE, YOU SLEEP WHEN YOU ARE DEAD. New customers ask if there's a charge for the entertainment (Clive). In a cozy side room facing the street, kids can sit at their own table and play with a plastic toy espresso machine. Enjoy the shaded deck on the east side of the coffee clinic.

Calistoga Coffee Roastery, 1631 Lincoln Avenue, Calistoga 94515; phone (707) 942–5757 or (800) 879–5282. Open from 6:30 A.M. to 6:00 P.M. daily (closed Christmas). No credit cards. Wheelchair accessible.

Keep walking to the old Calistoga Depot built in 1886 by Sam Brannan, who brought the steam train and people to Calistoga. From 1912 to 1937 electric trains also came to Calistoga and terminated at what is currently the Calistoga Fire Station. The Calistoga Depot was converted to historic exhibits and small specialty shops in 1976, and Greyhound Bus purchased the Napa InterUrban in 1936, took out the tracks, and started running diesel-spouting buses up Napa Valley. You might also enjoy Tin Barn Antiques and Calistoga Gardens next to Nance's Hot Springs.

LINCOLN AVENUE, NORTH SIDE

Heading back west on Lincoln Avenue, Calistoga Photography will develop your film in one hour. Then we come to the wonderfully elegant **Mount View Spa and Mount View Hotel,** home of Stomp. In an attempt to bring the outside in, artists have painted ivy on the hotel's art deco lobby walls, surrounding thick, soft sofas and soothing music.

Once called the European Hotel, the Mount View was built in 1919 and now has a swimming pool and thirty-three rooms, suites, and cottages with hot tubs, all extremely pleasant and ranging from $130 to $250.

> *Mount View Spa and Mount View Hotel, 1457 Lincoln Avenue, Calistoga 94515; phone (707) 942–6877. Visa, MasterCard, and American Express. Wheelchair accessible.*

Stomp replaced Jan Birnbaum's Catahoula Restaurant & Saloon in the Mount View Hotel in 2004. Executive chef Chris Aken and sous chef Brian Treitman worked here when it was Catahoula and create a true Napa Valley fusion cuisine.

Seasonal salads might include grilled local figs and endive with toasted hazelnuts and Wisconsin buttermilk blue cheese ($10) and an all-natural Angus beef tartare with shallots, caper berries, and quail egg ($13). Small plates offer all-natural veal sweetbreads with crispy turnip palatte and spiced pears ($13), prosciutto di Parma with Black Mission figs and camembert ($10), or crispy fish bits with Tunisian-style chili paste ($12).

Entrees range from a spice bouillabaisse with saffron rice, house-made chorizo, and a toasted baguette ($26) and striped bass with spaghetti squash and micro mirepoix ($27) to seared maple leaf duck breast with lee-potato tian ($26) and pork and veal chops and steak ($29–$37). An alternative "Neither" seafood nor meat entree offers vegetables ($15).

Stomp offers an extensive cheese list, as well as forty Napa Valley wines by the glass. Chocolate fans will enjoy the "chocolate soup," a soft baked chocolate soufflé with whipped crème fraîche ($8.50).

Stomp, 1457 Lincoln Avenue, Calistoga 94515; phone (707) 942–8272. Open 6:00 to 9:00 P.M. Tuesday–Thursday and Sunday, 5:30 to 10:00 P.M. Saturday. Full bar. Visa, MasterCard, and American Express. Wheelchair accessible.

South of Mount View and Catahoula are Calistoga Jewelers (every town has one) and North Star, with T-shirts, bracelets, and trinkets. The Evans Designs Gallery & Studio Outlet branch sells ceramics at a discount, and Casa Design has interesting home furnishings.

L. Funke & Son Department Store has been a great emporium of comfortable clothes serving Calistogans since 1904 and is located in the stone Fisher Building. Funke features New Options dresses, Blue Cactus, Caribe, and Jan Michaels designs for women, and Pendleton shirts, Levis, Dockers, Reyn Spooner, Paradise Found wild shirts, Back East, Johnny Cotton, and Tommy Bahama for men.

L. Funke & Son Department Store, 1417 Lincoln Avenue, Calistoga 94515; phone (707) 942–6235. Open from 9:30 A.M. to 6:00 P.M. Monday–Saturday, 11:00 A.M. to 4:00 P.M. Sunday. Visa and Master-Card. Wheelchair accessible.

Right next to L. Funke is fun **Cafe Sarafornia,** a name made of the leftovers of Sam Brannan's combination of Saratoga and California to get Calistoga. The oldest continuously operating restaurant in Calistoga, Cafe Sarafornia is a very informal restaurant that opens onto the sidewalk and features champagne mimosas, oatbran pancakes ($4.75–$5.75), healthy omelettes ($9.25), salmon and eggs ($9.95), famous huevos rancheros ($8.95), a good Mandarin Chicken or Thai vegetable salad ($9.95), a great salmon Caesar salad with extra anchovies ($9.95), blue cheese pasta with grilled chicken ($10.95), or the fabulous Special Blue Burger ($7.50) (which you can also enjoy as turkey), and Jalisco Club sandwiches ($8.95). (Owner Drake Dierkhising is the brother of Alex, who owns Hydro Bar & Grill three doors down and All Seasons Bistro and Wine Shop across Lincoln Avenue.) Be prepared to wait in line on the sidewalk on weekends for breakfast. Great kids menu ($4.50). Locals love this place, as do we.

Blue Cheese Pasta

from Drake Dierkhising, Cafe Sarafornia, Calistoga

(*NOTE:* I love Drake's recipes because they are so easy!—Kathleen Hill)

1 oz olive oil

½ onion, or large chunk, chopped

2 oz mushrooms, sliced

6 oz whipping cream

1–2 oz blue cheese, any type, amount depends on how much you love blue cheese

8 oz chicken breast or thigh meat cut ¾ -inch thick

Pinch of fresh thyme or sage, chopped

Salt and Tabasco sauce to taste

6-8 oz Penne or fettuccine pasta, or any variety

Dash of paprika

In an at least 1-quart sauté pan, sauté the onions in 1 oz olive oil. When done add mushrooms and whipping cream. Allow cream to reduce by about a quarter, then add blue cheese. About 2 minutes later add the chicken and herbs. Add salt to taste, and then Tabasco sauce. Finally add the pasta until well coated and serve in a bowl. Garnish with a dash of paprika. Serves 2. Serve with Sauvignon Blanc.

Cafe Sarafornia, 1413 Lincoln Avenue, Calistoga 94515; phone (707) 942–0555. Open from 7:00 A.M. to 3:00 P.M. daily. Beer and wine. Visa and MasterCard. Wheelchair accessible.

Thomas Kinkade presents his inevitable tourist gallery between the Dierkhisings' restaurants. Alex Dierkhising's **Hydro Bar & Grill** at the corner of Lincoln and Washington is a locally popular pub and casual restaurant where you can enjoy hummus and veggies, steak sandwiches, half-pound burgers, pastas, salads such as a classic shrimp Louie ($10.95), and crispy-crust pizzas. Try the housemade spicy beer sausage with garlic aioli or the fabulously different lasagna with goat's milk cheese, tomatoes, spinach, and roasted peppers. Dinner also offers a pound of dry-rub slow-cooked pork ribs with fries ($17.95). Hydro is handy because it serves a late-night menu until 11 o'clock after everyone else has closed, and its prices are reasonable, from $4.50 to $17.95. Those of you who need a beer break from all that wine can select from more than twenty microbrews. Hydro bills itself as "the place to party in Calistoga." So be warned. Big breakfasts with "customized" omelettes, pancakes, and French toast.

Hydro Bar & Grill, 1403 Lincoln Avenue, Calistoga 94515; phone (707) 942–9777. Open from 7:30 A.M. to 11:30 P.M. daily. Full bar. Visa and MasterCard. Wheelchair accessible.

Take the time to walk west 1 block on Washington Street for a few minutes to the Wappo Bar Bistro and the Sharpsteen Museum.

The **Wappo Bar Bistro** is one of Calistoga's most interesting and widely publicized restaurants, with an exquisite patio gathering place and a simple but elegant narrow dining room. Wappo is the anglicized version of *Guapo*, meaning "brave," the name given by early Spanish-speaking settlers to local American Indians.

Flavors come from Latin America, Africa, and the Mediterranean, so be sure to wear your adventure hat when you try Wappo. There are also plenty of standards with a twist, such as roasted pork sandwich with sweet-and-sour cabbage ($13.00) or grilled eggplant sandwich on focaccia with baked goat cheese ($11.00), but try the seafood chowder ($10.00), duck carnitas ($12.00), Ecuadorian braised pork ($17.50), osso bucco with creamy polenta ($18.50), or the sensational Vatapa stew, with scallops, shrimp, snapper, black beans, and feta topped with peanut sauce and sautéed bananas ($13.50).

At dinner roasted vegetables with polenta and persillade ($12.50), Ugandan peanut chicken with roasted yams, banana, and coconut ($15.50), and Hornada Ecuadoran braised pork with chile and beer with stuffed potato pancake and hominy ($17.75) are marvelous experiences, as is the osso bucco gremolata veal shanks with white wine and porcini mushroom sauce with risotto Milanese ($17.00). Caesar and local greens salads are also available for a little familiarity.

Wappo Bar Bistro, 1226B Washington Street, Calistoga 94515; phone (707) 942–4712. Open from 11:30 A.M. to 2:30 P.M. and 6:00 to 9:30 P.M. Wednesday–Monday. Full bar. Corkage fee: $10. Visa, MasterCard, and American Express. Wheelchair accessible.

The city of Calistoga has done some very smart things. It moved one of Sam Brannan's cottages downtown and graciously allowed Bernice and Ben Sharpsteen, the latter a major creator for Walt Disney, to build a museum of Calistoga and wine country history—the **Sharpsteen Museum**—and threw in a senior center and police station to form an efficient and attractive small civic complex.

Ben Sharpsteen was an Academy Award–winning animator, producer, and director for Walt Disney Studios, who retired with his wife to their ranch in Calistoga, which his grandmother had acquired in the 1800s. The ultimate fan of Sam Brannan—resort builder, promoter, pioneer, publisher, entrepreneur, soldier of fortune, and the person who brought the railroad to Calistoga and put it on the map—Sharpsteen dedicated his creative energies in "retirement" to designing and building the Sharpsteen Museum.

A side benefit to the public is that we get to view Sharpsteen's Academy Awards and loads of memorabilia from the early Disney studios, as well as Sharpsteen's collections of California automobile license plates and hubcaps dating from wooden-spoke carriages. In a well-planned compact space, you will also see dioramas of Sam Brannan's original resort, which he called "The Saratoga of the Pacific," and which he built in 1859 when he bought a square mile of land containing the hot springs at the foot of Mount St. Helena, beginning the fad of "taking the waters in Calistoga." California + Saratoga = Calistoga. At one time his resort had a hotel and thirteen cottages, a stable and racetrack, telegraph, bathhouse and pool, an observatory, a skating rink, riding trails, a distillery and winery, and a cooperage shop.

You can also learn from a Napa Valley Timeline, a beautifully restored stagecoach, and a simulated barn interior with a collection of period farming tools, then walk into the Brannan cottage to see what life was like and experience the simulated interior of a general store, kitchen, and blacksmith shop from the 1800s. The little shop at the entrance also stocks the best collection of Napa Valley history books and pamphlets available anywhere.

Sharpsteen Museum, 1311 Washington Street, Calistoga 94515; phone (707) 942–5911. Open from 11:00 A.M. to 4:00 P.M. daily. Admission fee: donation. No credit cards. Wheelchair accessible.

Walk back the short block to Lincoln Avenue and turn right (west) to continue your exploration of Calistoga's shops. Bella Tootsie sells Bass, Sam & Libby, and kids' shoes, sunglasses, and rain boots in what was a glorious bank building. Nature Etc. purveys its educational nature toys and books as it does in Sonoma and St. Helena. The Candy Cellar sells not-made-here saltwater taffy, Jelly Bellies, and fudge from barrels, and Mr. Moon's offers a good kids' stop, or a stop for good kids, with Beanie Babies, souvenirs, shirts, and body lotions.

For a little local color, you might want to follow the in-ground train tracks and saunter back to **Susie's Bar,** truly a working men's and women's bar with "no beer on draught" and Napa Fairgrounds (in Calistoga) Sprint Car Races posters and fans. Pool tables and pinball machines complete the picture. The old tracks used to bring flour bins from the street back to the ovens when Susie's was a bakery fifty years and more ago.

Susie's Bar, 1365 Lincoln Avenue, Calistoga 94515; phone (707) 942–6710. Open from 9:00 P.M. to 2:00 A.M. Full bar. No credit cards. Wheelchair accessible.

At **Schat's Bakkery,** Jan Schat, former director of baking at Il Fornaio, follows his Dutch great-grandfather Peter Schat into the very independent baking business. Baked goods are excellent, but we had to struggle with the staff to put all the listed ingredients in our smoothie, and we lost the argument to get what was left in the canister. The server claimed, "I always sample that part." Still good.

Schat's Bakkery, 1353 Lincoln Avenue, Calistoga 94515; phone (707) 942–0777. Open from 6:00 A.M. to 10:00 P.M. Wednesday–Monday. No credit cards. Wheelchair accessible.

Up some narrow stairs between Wexford & Woods and the Calistoga Bookstore, a wooden butler beckons you to Upstairs Enoteca, Margaux Singleton's Wine Shop, and Lone Dog Fine Art & Antiques.

We especially enjoy the **Calistoga Bookstore,** where you find great vacation reading and travel material, as well as school and art supplies, crayons, pads, and mood music.

Calistoga Bookstore, 1343 Lincoln Avenue, Calistoga 94515; phone (707) 942–4123. Open from 10:00 A.M. to 6:00 P.M. Sunday–Thursday, 10:00 A.M. to 9:00 P.M. Friday–Saturday. Visa, MasterCard, and American Express. Wheelchair accessible.

Heading west, next comes the Lincoln Avenue Spa, Tammy's New Leaf ladies' clothes, and an extraordinary local art gallery, **The Artful Eye.** We loved the blown glass, hand-painted platters, Steven Dixon jewelry, salt and pepper chess sets, books, wearable art clothing, wild-looking home accessories, and hand-carved lamps. Don't miss it.

The Artful Eye, 1333A Lincoln Avenue, Calistoga 94515; phone (707) 942–4743. Open from 10:00 A.M. to 6:00 P.M. daily. Visa, MasterCard, and American Express. Wheelchair accessible.

Detour north on Cedar Street to **Ca'toga Galleria D'Arte.** Carlo Marchiori, self-proclaimed maestro d'arte, has built an unusual art gallery on Cedar Street, which exclusively shows his work created at his Palladian villa north of Calistoga. He opens his house and workshop for tours at 11:00 A.M. Saturday, May–October ($20). Tickets are available at the gallery.

His gallery exemplifies his style, with a mural painted on the barrel-vaulted ceiling showing the Ptolemic constellations and a terrazzo floor that is a chart of the pre-Copernicus universe. Marchiori produces plates, cups, vases, and all sorts of collectibles.

Born in Italy, Marchiori studied classic art and academic design in Padua and Venice, left Italy for Canada, where he worked as an illustrator and film animator for CBC Television and the National Film Board of Canada, was nominated for a 1967 Academy Award for an animated short, and abandoned filmmaking and advertising for mural painting. Since 1978 he has lived and worked in San Francisco.

Ca'toga Galleria d'Arte, 1206 Cedar Street, Calistoga 94515; phone (707) 942–3900, Web site www.catoga.com. Open from 11:00 A.M. to 6:00 P.M. Thursday–Monday. Visa, MasterCard, and American Express. Wheelchair accessible.

Just across Cedar Street is **Pacifico Restaurante Mexicano,** a refreshingly popular local Mexican restaurant that's best known for its signature fish dishes, particularly the grilled snapper or prawns sautéed several ways, and shrimp and fish ceviche ($8.75). You will find Oaxacan cheeses, grilled chicken tacos, red snapper tacos ($7.95), and even tamales stuffed with mushrooms, roasted poblanos, tomatoes, and tomato chile salsa ($7.25). And for the less adventurous, Salvador Gomez cooks good hamburgers served with a Caesar salad ($4.50) and carne asada burritos ($8.75).

The rooms are wide open and decorated with primary colors, with lots of Mexican masks; a fountain cools on hot days. The margaritas and Fiesta Hour (4:40–6:00 P.M. Monday–Friday) are famously good in this up-to-date spot owned by John Seeger of Boskos Italian restaurant down Lincoln.

Pacifico Restaurante Mexicano, 1237 Lincoln Avenue, Calistoga 94515; phone (707) 942–4400. Open from 11:00 A.M. to 10:00 P.M. Monday–Friday, 10:00 A.M. to 10:00 P.M. Saturday–Sunday. Full bar. Visa and MasterCard. Wheelchair accessible.

4

The Silverado Trail

As you turn down the Silverado Trail from Calistoga's Lincoln Avenue, don't miss the old, overflowing water truck on a mound "announcing" the Calistoga Mineral Water Company. Luella Ackerman founded the company in 1916 and sold it to Enrichetta and Giuseppe Musante in 1920.

Giuseppe had a soda fountain and candy store called The Railway Exchange, where he sold ice cream, phosphates, and other soda-fountain goodies. One day in 1920 he was drilling for a well at his Railway Exchange and tapped into a geyser that blew him off his scaffold and burned him so badly that he had to be hospitalized. Giuseppe had discovered the Calistoga geyser, and he soon began to sell the mineral water from the geyser in his fountain. In 1924 he set up a bottling line and began selling Calistoga Sparkling Mineral Water.

The company passed through many owners, and in 1971 a Pepsi Cola truck driver named Elwood Sprenger bought the company when it was in one of its sad-shape phases. Soon thereafter Perrier started advertising the glories of mineral waters in the United States; Perrier bought the company from Sprenger in 1980. In 1991 the Nestlé Corporation bought the Perrier Group, and Calistoga Mineral Water is now the top-selling water in the western United States.

The old truck is as close as you can get to the plant, and there are no tastings or tours—just an interesting story.

The Silverado Trail vintners and resorts refer to themselves as being along "The Road Less Traveled" on "the quiet side" of the Napa Valley. And they are right—although there is more and more much-aligned traffic in the Napa Valley generally. The Silverado Trail feels more like the Sonoma Valley than busy Napa Valley. The Trail feels less commercial, or at least less hustle-bustle, more rural, and more peaceful. Cyclists will enjoy the generous marked bike lanes on both sides of the road as well as the fewer cars and seemingly more polite drivers than on Highway 29. We love it.

Most of the attractions on the Silverado Trail are highly reputed wineries and resorts, so prepare to enjoy. All of the crossroads go all the way across Napa Valley to Highway 29. Many of the wineries featured in this chapter can be found on maps in earlier chapters.

Silver Rose Cellars is "the only resort winery" in the Napa Valley, offering a day spa, putting green, Jacuzzis for at least two people, resort rooms, and much more. Combine the facilities with rare and free barrel tastings every morning at 11:00, and you can go straight to wine lovers' heaven! J-Paul and Sally Dumont bought the neighboring bed-and-breakfast in 1985 along with twenty-two acres, rebuilt it in 1989, and eventually added eleven rooms and a conference center. They've now opened a multisided visitor center with restaurant space upstairs with spectacular views, including the Inn & Spa and its putting hole complete with sand trap. Unlike most Napa County wineries, Silver Rose is within the Calistoga city limits and is not governed by county regulations prohibiting wineries with restaurants. So watch for great things to happen here. You will enjoy the knowledge and grace with which Michael Chramko manages the visitor center.

The Dumonts put in the lake you see outside the tasting room, which performs several functions, including running hot air through the water to create air conditioning. Sally Dumont designed the unusual interior, including the restrooms whose lights are motion sensitive and go on when you enter and off when you leave. Calistoga architect Bev Moore designed the building with radiant heating in the floor. We appreciate the extra roomy parking places in the lot, so that your car doesn't get dinged while visiting.

Check out J-Paul's twenty years' worth of bidding paddles from his community donations through the Napa Valley Wine Auction.

Fine points: Tasting fee: $5.00, barrel tasting $10.00 (call ahead). Featured wines: Chardonnay, D'Argent Chardonnay, Merlot, Jupilles Merlot, Cabernet Sauvignon, and Dentelle (Bordeaux blend). Owners: J-Paul, Sally, and Derrick Dumont. Winemaker: Cary Gott. Cases: 3,000. Acres: 20.

Silver Rose Cellars, 400 Silverado Trail, Calistoga 94515; phone (707) 942–9581 or (800) 995–9381, Web site www.silverrose.com. Open from 10:00 A.M. to 5:00 P.M. daily. Visa, MasterCard, American Express, and Discover. Wheelchair accessible.

Half a mile south of the Calistoga Mineral Water Company, you come to Dunaweal Lane to your right, taking you to the Clos Pegase, Sterling, and Stonegate wineries discussed in the previous chapter.

Just 0.2 mile past Dunaweal Lane (1.8 miles from Silverado Trail and Lincoln Avenue in Calistoga), don't miss **Cuvaison Winery** on your left (east) side. Park and enter the homelike white-stucco building with a tile roof and Dutch door. The large parking lot and lush lawns—and gardens with plenty of picnic tables—encourage visitors to stay awhile.

Founded in 1969 by two Silicon Valley engineers, Thomas Parkhill and Thomas Cottrell, Cuvaison is now owned by one of Switzerland's wealthiest men, Thomas Schmidheiny of Holderbank (supposedly the world's largest cement company). Money and good taste show throughout. Schmidheiny wisely bought acreage in Carneros, and most of the winery's grapes come from his vineyards in that prime growing region straddling the Sonoma–Napa County line. Cuvaison's wines were served in the White House to residents of the Republic of China and Russia. The '97 Chardonnay was served on the papal jet. You might want to indulge in Cuvaison's lovely pastel color-coordinated shirts and hats.

Fine points: Cuvaison's cozy and elegant tasting room features a wine bar and shop with excellent selections of silver jewelry and corkscrews, books, and shirts. Membership in Club Cuvaison brings extraordinary discounts. Tasting fee: $8.00–$10.00; you keep the glass. Featured wines: Chardonnay, Pinot Noir, Merlot, Cabernet Sauvignon, Port, and Zinfandel. Owner: Thomas Schmidheiny. Winemaker: Steve Rogstad. Cases: 63,000. Acres: 400.

Cuvaison Winery, 4550 Silverado Trail, Calistoga 94515; phone (707) 942–6266, Web site www.cuvaison.com. Open from 10:00 A.M. to 5:00 P.M. daily April–November, 11:00 A.M to 4:00 P.M. Sunday–Thursday, 10:00 A.M. to 5:00 P.M. Friday–Saturday, December–March. Tours at 10:30 A.M. by appointment. Visa, MasterCard, and American Express. Wheelchair accessible.

Cuvaison on the Silverado Trail

As you leave Cuvaison, turn left onto the road very carefully and go south on the Silverado Trail, to **Dutch Henry Winery,** a true family operation started by Kendall Phelps and Scott Chafen. Dutch Henry is an almost two-story building, nestled against the hillside on the east side of the road.

A former administrator of San Francisco's late French Hospital (now Kaiser), Kendall Phelps said they had to make up a name for the winery because he was not related to either of the prominent Kendall or Phelps wine families. Recently Scott and Les Chafen bought out Phelps's interest, so it is now all theirs.

Two pantingly friendly Airedale terriers greet you, followed by Spike the cat. While there's a small tasting room at the northern end of the building, the real action is in the large winery room, where you may enjoy barrel tastings with one of the owners. Try the new bocce-ball court, as well as their certified virgin olive oil; 2,000 pounds of the winery's olives from 700 trees yield two cases of the delicacy.

Fine points: Tours consist of standing in the middle of the tank room and spinning yourself around, hopefully with a bit of local wry humor. If you like the wine, buy it here because it's your only chance. Tasting fee: $5.00. Featured wines: Chardonnay, Pinot Noir, Merlot, Syrah, Meritage, Cabernet Sauvignon, and Zinfandel. Owners: Les Chafen and Scott Chafen. Winemaker: Scott Chafen. Cases: 5,000. Acres: 16 and buy locally.

Dutch Henry Winery, 4310 Silverado Trail, Calistoga 94515; phone (707) 942–5771, Web site www.dutchhenry.com. Dogs friendly. Open from 10:00 A.M. to 5:00 P.M. daily. Visa, MasterCard, American Express, and Discover. Wheelchair accessible.

Larkmead Lane comes in to your right 0.5 mile south of Dutch Henry. It will take you west to the Frank Family Vineyards mentioned in the previous chapter. For now, continue another 0.7 mile to one of the two smallest wineries in the Napa Valley, **Wermuth Winery.**

When we visited Wermuth, owner/winemaker Ralph Wermuth came out to our car and apologized because there were so many cars (four) parked at his winery's entrance. His wife, Smitty, who designed their label and poster, had "a few of the ladies over to lunch today." Believe the sign that says IF I'M NOT HERE, HONK HORN, I'M AROUND. —RALPH.

A Canadian doctor with a few intriguing eccentricities and interests, Ralph uses an eighteenth-century wood basket press. He "can't stand automatic things" and likens his winemaking methods versus more modern ones to rowing across a pond instead of using a motorboat.

Wermuth's tiny tasting room has a slanting wood ceiling and windows facing west, yellow walls, a green cement floor, and a worn wooden counter—all resembling a sauna in the summertime. It's well worth a stop for this slightly eccentric and different winemaking experience. Ralph will gladly show you around with a little notice. Smitty paints and offers note cards featuring painting reproductions in the tasting room.

Fine points: Tasting fee: $2.00, refundable with purchase. Featured wines: Gamay, Cabernet Sauvignon, and various whites. Owner and winemaker: Ralph Wermuth. Cases: 400. Acres: 2.

Wermuth Winery, 3942 Silverado Trail, Calistoga 94515; phone (707) 942–5924. Open "loosely" from 11:00 A.M. to 5:00 P.M. daily. If OPEN sign is up, Ralph is in. Visa and MasterCard. Wheelchair accessible.

Next, you might like to visit **Rombauer Vineyards,** 1.6 miles south of Wermuth and 1.1 miles south of the intersection of Bale Lane, on the right (west) side of Silverado Trail. Turn right at Rombauer's sign and the big American flag. Be sure to stay to the right as you wind up the steep and beautiful driveway to Rombauer's pink cement-block building in a small forest—a 0.3-mile drive well worth the trip just to see the view, even if you aren't interested in Rombauer's limited-production wines. Notice the "R" metal gate leading down a flowered path to the winery's caves, gorgeous pink and orange impatiens, and the brown Rolls-Royce in the parking lot. Photos of Senator John McCain and singer Barbra Streisand line the walls, along with a Braniff poster, of particular interest if you're old enough to remember that now-defunct airline.

Koerner Rombauer is a former Braniff International pilot who, with his wife, Joan, bought this property in 1972. The grand-nephew of Irma Rombauer of *The Joy of Cooking* fame, Koerner spreads his "Joy of Wine" message through his wines, brochures, and T-shirts. The Rombauers' children, Koerner (K. R.) Rombauer III and Sheana, are both active in the winery. (Koerner Rombauer is owner and has an interest in Napa Cellars.)

Fine points: Rombauer's retail sales room is cozy, and Jim Kozier and Harvey Posert are among the most informative hosts in Napa Valley. No tasting fee. Featured wines: Chardonnay, Cabernet Sauvignon, Merlot, Zinfandel, Cabernet Franc, Le Meilleur du Chai ("The Best of the Cellar") Bordeaux blend, and Zinfandel Port. Owners: Koerner and Joan Rombauer. Winemaker: Gregory Graham. Cases and acres: Undefined.

Rombauer Vineyards, 3522 Silverado Trail, St. Helena 94574; phone (707) 963–5170, Web site www.rombauervineyards.com. Open from 10:00 A.M. to 5:00 P.M. daily. Visa, MasterCard, and American Express. The tasting room is wheelchair accessible.

As you leave Rombauer, turn right (south) onto the Silverado Trail. On your left will be Chateau Boswell, a curious Elizabethan structure that is never open to the public.

Just 0.3 mile south of Rombauer's driveway and slightly past Chateau Boswell, turn right (west) into **Casa Nuestra Winery**. In this sublime setting the winery blends in with the oak trees' leaves, as if you are sitting in someone's picturesque yard.

Casa Nuestra Winery, St. Helena

Gene Kirkham is an amusing and committed civil-rights lawyer who mostly left the hustle and bustle in the mid-1970s for this once "remote" part of the Napa Valley. He works to keep the county from paving his gravel road and practices sustainable agriculture without fertilizers, pesticides, or herbicides. He uses cover crops and hand labor and is a leader in the Save the Wild Habitat movement. Go for the wines and to pick up the humorous and informative newsletter. After you read it once, you will want to be on the mailing list.

Fine points: Tasting fee: $5.00, refundable with purchase. Featured wines: Chenin Blanc, Riesling, Cabernet Sauvignon, Cabernet Franc, Merlot, Meritage, and Tinto Classico. Owners: Gene and Cody Kirkham. Winemaker: Allen Price. Cases: 1,500. Acres: 20.

Casa Nuestra Winery, 3451 Silverado Trail, St. Helena 94574; phone (707) 963–5783, Web site casanuestra.com. Open from 10:00 A.M. to 5:00 P.M. daily. Visa, MasterCard, and American Express. Not wheelchair accessible without staff assistance.

A mile south of Casa Nuestra, **Duckhorn Vineyards** is just off the west side of the Silverado Trail, on Lodi Lane. Only open for the sale of wine, Duckhorn's superb Merlot alone is worth many fans' whole trip to the Napa Valley, as are the Cabernets and the fun, bargain Decoy label line. Enjoy the gray-and-white two-story Victorian-style farmhouse tasting room, with its shaded, wrap-around porch.

Fine points: Tasting fee: $10. Seated educational tasting with food pairings and other programs: $20. Featured wines under Paraduxx, Decoy, and Duckhorn labels: Merlot, Cabernet Sauvignon, and King Eider Vermouth. Owners: Margaret and Dan Duckhorn. Winemaker: Mark Beringer. Cases: 60,000. Acres: 200+.

Duckhorn Vineyards, 1000 Lodi Lane, St. Helena 94574; phone (707) 963–7108. Open for retail sales only from 10:00 A.M. to 4:00 P.M. daily. Tours available Saturday by appointment. Visa, MasterCard, and American Express. Wheelchair accessible.

As you leave Duckhorn, come back to the Silverado Trail and turn right (south). Cross the intersection with a stoplight at Deer Park Road, which to the east leads to Angwin. If you would like to try extremely fresh local fruit and vegetables, stop at the two little fair-weather produce stands on the western corners of the crossroads.

Along with Auberge du Soleil, just south of here, **Meadowood Resort** is one of the two most elegant places to stay in the Napa Valley, and even the whole of Northern California. To get there, turn left (east) onto Howell Mountain Road and then left onto Meadowood Lane. The resort's excellent signage is extremely helpful to first-time visitors. Follow the well-kept road past tennis courts, swimming pools, the golf course, and the perfectly manicured croquet courts. New England–style cottages and lodges dot the 250-acre wooded property, located at the foot of Howell Mountain. The resort's whole ambience feels like understated, elegant New England.

The Restaurant at Meadowood and the Grill facing the golf course are legendary for the ultimate in sophisticated service, dining, and prices. The open-beamed cathedral ceilings and bucolic views will enhance your dining experience. Most diners are guests at the resort, but the public is also welcome for Chef Vincent Nattress's Sunday brunch ($39). Prix fixe dinner choices always include an

Meadowood Resort

excellent vegetarian dinner ($65–$125). Regulars usually indulge in the daily soufflé. Breakfast by the pool is especially exhilarating. The Grill is open for breakfast and lunch for more inexpensive but equally good meals, from burgers ($12) to veal scaloppini ($19) and spa cuisine.

Fine points: All rooms have air conditioning, ceiling fans, private decks facing greenery, and every amenity imaginable, with the most expensive four-bedroom suites running about $2,000 per night. The spa and health facilities alone could keep you occupied for days.

Meadowood Resort and The Restaurant at Meadowood, 900 Meadowood Lane, St. Helena 94574; phone (707) 963–3646 or (800) 458–8080, Web site www.meadowood.com. Visa, MasterCard, American Express, and Diners Club. Wheelchair accessible, but call ahead for details.

Don't miss **Joseph Phelps Vineyards,** which is on the east side of the Silverado Trail. If you have visited Meadowood, turn left (south) onto Silverado Trail, then turn left (east) onto Taplin Road and drive for 0.3 mile. If you didn't visit Meadowood, just go east on Taplin for 0.3 mile. Turn left through the wooden gate and

take the paved road uphill for 0.5 mile. You have to make an advance appointment to tour and taste, but it's worth the effort to see the redwood barn and
sophisticated wine production systems.

As you walk into the winery's courtyard, turn left to the barn and retail
room. Take a whiff of the blooms from the wisteria covering the overhead trellis,
which is made from century-old recycled bridge timbers. Just inside the door
look to the left at the gorgeous Great Hall dining room. In good weather, tastings are held out on the deck overlooking the Napa Valley; in bad weather, you
get to taste in the dining room. Knowledgeable and friendly hosts make the
whole experience attractive. The entire place exudes Joseph Phelps's and his
staff's love of what they are doing.

Fine points: Joseph Phelps's winemaker, Craig Williams, is biodynami-
cally farming a Pinot Noir vineyard in tiny Freestone in Sonoma
County. Biodynamic farming relies mainly on the lunar calendar. Featured wines: Chardonnay, Sauvignon Blanc, Cabernet Sauvignon, Merlot, "Insignia" Bordeaux blends, "Vin du Mistral" Rhone Valley–style
Syrah, Viognier, and Le Mistral. Owner: Joseph Phelps. Winemaker:
Craig Williams. Cases: 100,000. Acres: 600.

*Joseph Phelps Vineyards, 200 Taplin Road, St. Helena 94574; phone
(707) 963–2745 or (800) 707–5789, Web site www.jpvwines.com. Open
for sales from 9:00 A.M. to 5:00 P.M. Monday–Saturday, 10:00 A.M. to
4:00 P.M. Sunday. Tasting and tours by appointment. Visa, MasterCard,
and American Express. Wheelchair accessible.*

Leaving Joseph Phelps, go back down Taplin Road to the Silverado Trail, turn
left very carefully, and head south past Zinfandel Lane.

For a Wild West Italian experience, try **William Harrison Vineyards.**
Turn right off the Silverado Trail at the sign and pass the family home, sometimes with kids riding their bikes through puddles, to the two-story stone building. Patio tables and chairs invite you to the deck, and geraniums in window
boxes set the cheerful tone.

The Perelli and Minetti families have been making wine since 1250 in Italy,
and they have been making wine in this country since 1902 "without a computer, so who needs one?" Notice the accordion and piano (go ahead!), and the
Perelli-Minetti family tree of four generations in the United States (and proud
of it) on the door. William Harrison is Mario's nephew and has been making
wine since 1992.

William Harrison Vineyards

Fine points: When the tasting room is full of tasters, this place almost sounds like an Old West bar. The tasting fee of $5.00 is waived with purchase. Featured wines: All estate William Harrison Cabernet Sauvignon, Rutherford Red Meritage, Cabernet Franc, and nonestate Chardonnay. Owner: William Harrison. Winemaker: Rob Gilson. Cases: 2,000. Acres: 10.

William Harrison Vineyards, *1443 Silverado Trail, St. Helena 94574; phone (707) 963–8310. Open from 11:00 A.M. to 5:00 P.M. daily. Visa and MasterCard. Wheelchair accessible.*

When you leave the winery, turn right (south) onto Silverado Trail and continue for about a mile to Rutherford Hill Road. Turn left (east) to visit Auberge du Soleil and Rutherford Hill Winery & Picnic Grounds.

Voted by *Gourmet* magazine readers in 1998 to be the ninth top hotel in the world, **Auberge du Soleil** attracts the wealthy and famous from around the world. This is a modestly elegant resort where you can hide away in your cabin or mingle in the bar overlooking Napa Valley.

The atmosphere is Southern France/Mediterranean, and no wonder. Owner Claude Rouas, once of L'Etoile in San Francisco's Huntington Hotel and later of

Sautéed Diver Scallops with Cauliflower, Capers, and Almonds

from Auberge du Soleil, Rutherford

½ cup Balsamic vinegar, reduced
2 quarts water
2 cups cauliflower florets
¼ cup cream
1 Tbs extra virgin olive oil
8 fresh scallops (dayboat if available, 2–3 oz each)
1½ Tbs unsalted butter
2 Tbs capers
2 Tbs slivered almonds, toasted
2 Tbs golden raisins
1 Tbs chopped parsley

In a small saucepan, bring vinegar to a boil, reduce by half, and reserve.

Bring 2 quarts of water to a boil and season with salt to taste. Break apart one head of cauliflower into equal pieces, reserving 1 cup of the better florets for garnish. Add the first cup of cauliflower florets and cook until tender, about 60 seconds. Drain and plunge florets in ice bath to stop the cooking process. In a saucepan, cover the other cup of florets with cream and cook for 8 minutes. Puree and put through a fine mesh sieve. Keep warm.

Warm two 7-inch sauté pans. Add olive oil to one pan. Season the scallops with salt and pepper. When the pan just starts to smoke, add the scallops. Cook for about 1 minute on each side, depending on the thickness of the scallops. When scallops show a little color, turn them over. In the other pan, add butter and cook the butter until it begins to brown. Add the second cup of florets and cook for 1 minute. Season with salt and pepper. Add the capers, almonds, raisins, and parsley.

On warmed plates, put a small circle of the cauliflower puree in the middle. Add the raisin caper ragout to the middle. Top with the scallops, cooked to medium rare. Drizzle the Balsamic reduction around the plate with extra virgin olive oil to garnish. Serves 2. Serve with Sauvignon Blanc or Chardonnay.

the successful Piatti Ristorante chain, hails from French Algeria. One brother, Maurice, co-owns Fleur de Lys in San Francisco; his other brother, Albert, created the late, great Le Beaujolais and now works at the Yountville (original) Piatti.

Check out the Auberge Boutique and the Gayle Houston Salon (by appointment). Tennis, swimming, massage, a new gym, and full spa treatments are yours for the asking—and, of course, paying.

No detail is overlooked, and it's as if the staff spend all their time trying to anticipate new human or culinary needs. While meals here are expensive, Executive Chef Andrew Sutton offers both healthy and not-so-healthy foods. Meals are available morning, noon, and nighttime, too. Asterisks on the menu indicate vegetarian dishes. Two asterisks signal spa cuisine.

At breakfast Valencia orange juice is a mere $8.00, while the continental breakfast is $16.00. The All American, with eggs, meats, potatoes, and toast, is $18.00. Try the brioche French toast ($17.00); the Napa ham, Gruyère, and spinach omelette ($18.00); or housemade popovers ($17.50). Chocolate waffles, pancakes, huevos rancheros, lox and bagels, and Starbuck's coffee are also on the menu.

Lunch gets interesting, with a chilled pea soup with Maine crab ($13), a beautiful white and green asparagus salad ($12), Wolfe Ranch quail ($15), or a foie gras and roast duck club with bleu cheese and apple-smoked bacon ($23). Great risottos, salmon, steak, and ahi tuna make lunch choices difficult.

For dinner you can indulge in the Prix Fixe "Sharing of the Senses" menu: $75–$105 per guest for five courses; paired with wine the price is $187 per guest. Varying by season, dinner may include Peeky Toe crab salad, Hamachi sashimi, sautéed foie gras, Wolfe Ranch quail with crushed fava beans, Liberty Farms duck with pea tendrils, roasted saddle of lamb with eggplant puree and chickpea frites, and, for dessert, caramelized strawberries and almond financier with marscapone ice cream. For a more casual bistro menu of soups, salads, sandwiches, and pizzetta, try The Bar.

Auberge du Soleil, 180 Rutherford Hill Road, Rutherford 94573; phone (707) 963–1211, Web site www.aubergedusoleil.com. Open for breakfast from 7:00 to 11:00 A.M. daily, for lunch 11:30 A.M. to 2:30 P.M. daily; for dinner 6:00 to 9:30 P.M. Monday–Friday, 5:30–9:30 P.M. Saturday–Sunday. The Bar is open from 11:00 A.M. to 11:00 P.M. (no reservations). Visa, MasterCard, American Express, and Diners Club. The restaurant is wheelchair accessible, as are some of the rooms in the resort.

Just up the hill from Auberge du Soleil, enjoy **Rutherford Hill Winery,** set in what looks like a sophisticated, well-designed barn with rough wood walls. The windows frame perfect white clouds, and a century-old olive grove covers the hillside below to create the most romantic picnic grounds in Northern California. We once heard a young woman coming out the door of Rutherford Hill's tasting room remark, "I'm in heaven now" (to which her male companion responded, "You are?").

No wonder she felt so good. The tasting room is full of excellent wines (be sure to try the Merlot), Calistoga waters, iced tea, fudge and garlic sauces, chocolates, wine and food books, cigars, elegant leather cigar cases and cigar books, French Laguiole wine openers ($119.95), and marble ashtrays. Try to visit the largest man-made wine-aging caves in California, which go nearly a mile into the rock—the best part of Rutherford Hill's frequent tours.

Fine points: Founded by William P. Jaeger Jr., Charles Carpy, and Thomas Witter, Rutherford Hill was purchased in 1996 by the Terlato family of Chicago. The $10 tasting fee includes logo glass, tour, and tastes of regular wines; $15 includes logo glass, tour, and Reserve tastes. Featured wines: Chardonnay, Gewürztraminer, Sangiovese, Merlot, Cabernet Sauvignon, and Zinfandel Port. Owners: The Terlato family. Winemaker: Dave Dobson. Cases: 125,000. Acres: Undefined.

Rutherford Hill Winery, 200 Rutherford Hill Road, Rutherford 94573; phone (707) 963–7194 or (800) 726–5226, Web site www.rutherford hill.com. Open from 10:00 A.M. to 5:00 P.M. daily; free tours at 11:30 A.M. and 1:30 and 3:30 P.M. daily; no reservations. Visa, MasterCard, American Express, Diners Club, and Discover. Wheelchair accessible.

In case you've been enjoying yourself just a little too much in the tasting room, drive carefully back down Rutherford Hill Road. Pay special caution to guests leaving Auberge du Soleil; they sometimes forget to look up the hill for oncoming cars.

Back down at the Silverado Trail, turn left (south) and proceed to **Round Hill Vineyards & Cellars,** which has one of the most interesting family stories in the Napa Valley. Turn into Round Hill's driveway and take the left side of the fork toward the retail-sales section. Check out the terra-cotta pot sculptures in the trees to the right of the parking lot.

A successful and popular buyer at Joseph Magnin's clothing stores in San Francisco, Virginia McInnis married Ernie Van Asperen and honeymooned at the Roundhill Resort in Jamaica. (Guess where the winery's name came from?)

Terra-cotta pot sculptures welcome visitors to Round Hill Vineyards & Cellars

A protégé of master marketeer and creative genius Cyril Magnin, Virginia applied her substantial skills to developing Round Hill Family of Wines, including Van Asperen and Rutherford Ranch wines. With the help of industry veteran Mike Hardy, Virginia is following her vision to cease production and sale of Round Hill's generic wines, so there are some real bargains available here. Virginia is developing the Van Asperen Signature wines, with the first release in 1997 of its 400-case Cabernet Sauvignon, in addition to selling Round Hill and Rutherford Ranch wines. Be sure to enjoy Bill Hamilton's cartoons on the walls. The Van Asperens recently sold Round Hill to Marco and Theo Zaninovich, who produce bulk wines near Bakersfield in the San Joaquin Valley. Ernie and Virginia Van Asperen remain president and CEO of Round Hill.

Fine points: No wine tastings here. Featured wines: Chardonnay, Cabernet Sauvignon, Merlot, Signature Reserve, Rutherford Ranch Chardonnay, Sauvignon Blanc, Cabernet Sauvignon; Roundhill Chardonnay, Cabernet Sauvignon, Merlot, and White Zinfandel. Owners: Marco and Theo Zaninovich. Winemaker: Bob Broman. Cases: 400,000. Acres: 210.

Round Hill Vineyards & Cellars, 1680 Silverado Trail, Rutherford 94574; phone (707) 968–3200, Web site www.roundhillwines.com. Open from 10:00 A.M. to 4:30 P.M., sales only. Visa, MasterCard, American Express, and Discover. Wheelchair accessible.

If you're ready for a 10-mile round-trip detour adventure to the Rustridge Ranch & Winery, Bed & Breakfast, & Thoroughbred Ranch, with the Nichelini Winery thrown in, turn east up Conn Creek Road, which becomes Sage Canyon Road (Highway 128) opposite Villa Mt. Eden Winery.

If you want to continue on our tour without the long side trip, we offer a much shorter one here to Frog's Leap Winery and Caymus Vineyards on Conn Creek Road, which runs west along the side of Villa Mt. Eden Winery. Should you choose this alternative to the 10-mile trip, just skip the following paragraphs on Nichelini and Rustridge wineries.

If you want to go the long, exquisite, and winding way, after you pass Lake Hennessy on your left, take Chiles Valley Road (Pope Valley Road) northeastward, then turn back on Lower Chiles Valley Road (Highway 128) to **Rustridge Ranch & Winery, Bed & Breakfast, & Thoroughbred Ranch.** (The easier but less scenic way is to go straight up Sage Canyon to Highway 128 and turn left to Nichelini Winery and Rustridge.)

You truly feel as if you have arrived at someone's home when you drive into Rustridge's wandering, bumpy road, and you have. As you pass the home and B&B, tennis court and swimming pool—going slowly of necessity—owners Susan and Jim or marketing manager Mark Serrano will jump into their cars and tail you as you follow the signs through the horse paddocks to the winery. This is a very personal winery, with wine prizes and wines displayed on tables.

Winemaker Susan Meyer and her husband, thoroughbred racehorse trainer Jim Fresquez, combine their interests and talents most successfully on Susan's family ranch to raise racehorses and make good wine. Old horse equipment decorates the rails around the winery in this heavenly meadow high in the Chiles Valley. Picnics are encouraged on the lawns and at tables under a huge, shady oak tree. Try not to miss this experience!

Fine points: The ranch has been breeding and training horses since the 1950s, with an occasional winner at Santa Anita. The winery has had several winners, too, especially its Cabernet Sauvignon. Tasting fee: $5.00, refundable with wine purchase. Featured wines: Chardonnay,

Savory Winter Quiche with Leeks and Brie

from Susan Meyer, Rustridge Ranch & Winery, St. Helena

(*NOTE*: Susan Meyer uses this quiche as an appetizer, but it also makes a good breakfast main course.—Kathleen Hill)

$\frac{1}{2}$ cup flour
3 Tbs unsalted butter
1 Tbs cold vegetable shortening
$\frac{1}{4}$ cup ice water
2 cups thinly sliced leeks, only the white and green parts (chopped shallots or thinly sliced yellow onion may be substituted for the leeks)
Optional fillings: 5 slices bacon, cooked crispy and crumbled, or 6–8 mushrooms thinly sliced
1 small clove garlic, minced
2 Tbs olive oil
3 eggs
$\frac{1}{2}$ cup milk or cream
$\frac{1}{4}$ tsp each of dried thyme and sage, more if fresh
$\frac{1}{2}$ cup brie cheese, cut into chunks

Preheat oven to 450 degrees.

For the crust: In a medium bowl, mix flour with butter and shortening, using a pastry blender or fork. Slowly add water until mixture begins to bond. Form a ball with hands, handling as little as possible. Add only enough water to keep mixture together. Roll out and place in 9-inch pie tin or quiche pan. Bake about 5–10 minutes in hot oven until crust browns slightly.

For the filling: While crust is baking, rinse leeks in sieve, removing any mud. Shake dry and sauté leeks, onions, or shallots, and mushrooms or bacon if you choose, with garlic in olive oil over medium heat until soft and tender (about 8 minutes). Remove from heat. In a small bowl, mix eggs, milk, and herbs, and season with salt and pepper to taste.

Into the partially cooked crust, spread cooked leeks and garlic (and mushrooms or bacon), and sprinkle evenly with chunks of brie. Pour egg mixture over top and bake at 425 degrees for 15 minutes. Reduce heat to 350 degrees and bake another 10 minutes until quiche is set and top is slightly brown. Let cool slightly before serving. Total preparation time: 1 hour. Serves 4 as main course, 8 as an appetizer. Serve with Rustridge Chardonnay.

Cabernet Sauvignon, Zinfandel, and Sauvignon Blanc. Owners: Susan Meyer and Jim Fresquez. Winemaker: Susan Meyer, Kent Rosenblum, consulting. Cases: 2,000. Acres: 442 (50 in grapes).

Rustridge Ranch & Winery, Bed & Breakfast & Thoroughbred Ranch, 2910 Lower Chiles Valley Road, St. Helena 94574; phone (707) 965–2871 for winery, (707) 965–9353 for B&B, or (800) 788–0263. Open from 10:00 A.M. to 4:00 P.M. daily. Visa, MasterCard, American Express, and Discover. Wheelchair accessible.

As you leave Rustridge, which you may not want to, turn left on Lower Chiles Valley Road to reach **Nichelini Winery,** one of the oldest in the Napa Valley. Founded in 1890, Nichelini is Bonded Winery No. 843, and the old Nichelini family home hangs over the edge of the hillside with the winery. Park in the gravel pullouts along the road (don't knock on the door of the white house—it's a private home). Walk down the steep driveway between the original dark,

Nichelini Winery

weathered wood winery and the house to the cellar level, where you will find a bar made of barrel wood and picnic tables on the grass near the creek. There's also a bocce-ball court for family and guests.

Fine points: Nichelini is famous for its Old Vine Zinfandel from eighty-year-old vines and is now owned by the grandchildren of Anton Nichelini, who say that Nichelini "is the oldest winery owned by the same family in the Napa Valley." No tasting fee. Featured wines: Old Vine Zinfandel, Cabernet Sauvignon, Merlot, and Petite Syrah. Owners: Greg Boeger, Susan Boeger, Toni Nichelini, and Dick Wainright. Winemaker: Greg Boeger. Cases: 3,000. Acres: 100.

Nichelini Winery, 2950 Sage Canyon Road, St. Helena 94574; phone (707) 963–0717. Open from 10:00 A.M. to 6:00 P.M. Saturday, Sunday, and holidays, 10:00 A.M. to 5:00 P.M. during daylight savings time, and by appointment Monday–Friday. Visa and MasterCard. Not wheelchair accessible.

After enjoying the Nichelini Winery, go back down to the Silverado Trail to resume your tour. Carefully cross the Silverado Trail to **Villa Mt. Eden Winery and Conn Creek Winery,** a remodeled, pink-stucco, state-of-the-art edifice and winery just south of the Conn Creek Road/Rutherford Cross Road.

(Or you can cross Silverado Trail to Conn Creek Road, which becomes Rutherford Cross Road, and visit Frog's Leap and Caymus Wineries, which are open by appointment.)

Villa Mt. Eden's origins date to the 1880s, when John Bateman planted the original eighty acres. Some of Bateman's original property was expanded by its next owner, George S. Meyer of Oakland, who began to make wine. California Wineries owned the No. 11 Bonded Winery in the early 1940s, and Jim and Ann McWilliams bought it in 1969 from Baron Constantine Ramsay. In 1995 Washington State winery giant Stimson Lane bought and moved Villa Mt. Eden here, to sister winery Conn Creek's facility, and completed the ultimate renovation in 1998. Unfortunately, Jim McWilliams passed away in June 2002.

The elegant tasting room and winery, with the property lined by olive trees, looks across the Silverado Trail toward Auberge du Soleil, up the hill. You will find a pleasant tasting bar to the right as you enter and an attractive gift shop to the back. Colorful grapevine pottery and dishes rest on heavy wood furniture along with books and wining and dining accessories.

Fine points: Be sure to sample the Orange Muscat, only 4 percent alcohol and a great topping on ice cream or cheesecake or dribbled into champagne. We enjoy just sipping it. No tasting fee Monday–Thursday, $10 Friday–Sunday. Featured wines: Villa Mt. Eden: Chardonnay, Syrah, Cabernet Franc, Pinot Noir, Zinfandel, Merlot, Cabernet Sauvignon, and Orange Muscat. Conn Creek: Cabernet Franc, Cabernet Sauvignon, and Merlot. Owners: Stimson Lane (U.S. Tobacco). Winemakers: Mike McGrath for Villa Mt. Eden, Jeff McBride for Conn Creek. Cases: 60,000 Villa Mt. Eden, 8,000 Conn Creek. Acres: 1,168 and buy from others.

Villa Mt. Eden Winery and Conn Creek Winery, 8711 Silverado Trail, St. Helena 94574; phone (707) 944–2414 or (800) 793–7960, Web site www.villamteden.com. Open from 11:00 A.M. to 4:00 P.M. Monday–Friday, 10:00 A.M. to 4:00 P.M. Saturday. Visa, MasterCard, American Express, and Discover. Wheelchair accessible.

For a quick and delightful distraction, follow Conn Creek Road (also called Highway 128 and Rutherford Cross Road) down beside Villa Mt. Eden to the Napa Valley Grapevine Wreath Company, Frog's Leap, and Caymus wineries.

You come to brown-shingled **Napa Valley Grapevine Wreath Company** on the first turn of Conn Creek Road off the Silverado Trail. The Wood family turns their Cabernet Sauvignon vines into other people's treasures, including baskets, hearts, crosses, wine holders, magic wands, and, by golly, wreaths. This is a wonderful recycling project, making the most of every part of the vine.

Napa Valley Grapevine Wreath Company, 8901 Conn Creek Road (Highway 128), Rutherford 94573; phone (707) 963–8893. Open from 10:30 A.M. to 5:30 P.M. Thursday–Monday. Visa and MasterCard. Wheelchair accessible.

Just around the bend west of the wreath company is **Frog's Leap Winery,** in a big old barn built by C. T. Adamson in the late 1800s. Frog's Leap purposely doesn't have a sign on the road to make it a wee bit difficult to visit. Just turn off Conn Creek Road when you see the biggest barn around.

Adamson made and sold bulk wine here, and for ninety-six years the building served as a farming center to store and dry cherries and prunes. In 1994 Frog's Leap moved here from the "frog farm" where they started by leaps and bounds.

Frog's Leap Winery's leaping frog checks which way the wind blows

The leaping frog on top of the winery's roof doubles as a weather vane. Park in the lot and walk to the back of the property on the right side of the barn (facing it) to the Vineyard House retail room. If no one is there, venture through the raised organic vegetable and herb beds. Frog's Leap has the funniest winery voice mail and Web site.

Fine points: No tasting fee, except $5.00 per person for groups of eight or more. Featured wines: Sauvignon Blanc, Chardonnay, Zinfandel, Merlot, and Cabernet Sauvignon. Owners: Julie and John Williams. Winemaker: John Williams. Cases: 47,000. Acres: 40.

Frog's Leap Winery, 8815 Conn Creek Road (Highway 128), Rutherford 94573; phone (707) 963–4704, Web site www.frogsleap.com. Open from 10:00 A.M. to 4:00 P.M. Monday–Saturday, tours and tasting by appointment. Visa, MasterCard, and American Express. Wheelchair accessible.

Farther down Conn Creek Road is **Caymus Vineyards,** the world renowned producers of Special Selection Cabernet Sauvignons, which *Wine Spectator* rates in its "Top 10" as often as it does Chateau Margaux's. To get there, drive south on Conn Creek from where the Rutherford Cross Road (Highway 128) intersects with it. Caymus is on the left (east) side of the street.

To enter, you must approach the gate, buzz, and inquire whether appointments are available. Or you can call ahead. Caymus schedules its appointments carefully so that all guests can be treated privately. Wines are served in the cream-colored dining room with brick floors to the right of the entrance.

The Charles Wagner family began farming here in 1906, and Chuck Wagner was born and raised on the property, the son of Charlie and Lorna Wagner. Founder Charlie Wagner, a grand character with whom visitors loved to chat, died in February 2002 at the ripe age of eighty-nine. The Wagners named their winery in honor of the Caymus Indians and from the original land grant known as Rancho Caymus, given to George Yount in 1836. They show their respect for the land by allowing their wines to develop primarily on their own. Besides good wine you can purchase great logo hats ($13), corkscrews, shirts, and the *Wine Spectator's Buying Guide and California Wine Book.*

Fine points: No tasting fee. Featured wine: Cabernet Sauvignon. Owner: Chuck Wagner. Winemaker: Chuck Wagner. Cases: 54,000. Acres: 65.

Caymus Vineyards, 8700 Conn Creek Road, Rutherford 94573; phone (707) 967–3010, Web site www.caymus.com. Open from 10:00 A.M. to 4:00 P.M. daily, wine tasting by appointment. Visa, MasterCard, and American Express. Wheelchair accessible.

If you're famished, rush west on the Rutherford Cross Road to Rutherford Grill at Highway 29. Otherwise, we recommend that you retrace your tracks back to Silverado Trail by turning right when you leave Caymus and continuing back northeastward. When you get to the Silverado Trail, turn right (south) to continue.

Quintessa is the fabulous crescent-shaped image against the hill on the west side of Silverado Trail. Designed by Walker Warner Architects of San Francisco, Quintessa presents one of the most interesting man-made visual images in the Napa Valley, completing the goals of the late previous owner of the property, San Francisco restaurateur George Mardikian.

Quintessa's dramatically elegant yet comfy tasting room sits on top of the crescent-shaped cave entrance, and the architecture is worth the trip on its own.

Owners Agustin and Valeria Huneeus are both natives of Chile. Agustin started in the wine business in 1960 as principal stockholder and CEO of Concha y Toro, which grew to be Chile's largest winery under his leadership. In the early 1970s, Chile's difficult political climate led Agustin to New York to head Seagram's worldwide operations, including wineries in Germany, France, Spain, Italy, Argentina, Brazil, New Zealand, and California, where he served as president of Paul Masson. In 1985 he became partner and acting president of Franciscan Estates, which he expanded to include Franciscan Oakville Estate, Simi, Mount Veeder, Estancia, and Veramonte in Chile. Agustin remains chairman of the board of Franciscan Estates, even after selling it to Constellation Brands, and Franciscan handles sales and marketing for Quintessa.

Valeria Huneeus started out to study medicine but wandered into viticulture and enology, earning a Ph.D. in biochemistry from Columbia University after she and her husband moved to New York. We thank her for spending ten years researching cholesterol and cell metabolism with the Veterans Administration at the University of California Medical Center in San Francisco. Saying she "…wanted to see the sun again," Valeria launched into developing the Mistral vineyard in Santa Clara County with her husband.

Winemaker Aaron Pott came to Quintessa from St. Clement in June 2004, while winemaker Sarah Gott worked for eight years at Joseph Phelps Vineyards. Following the birth of her child in June 2004, Sarah now serves as consulting winemaker. Call ahead.

Tastes are $25 and include a plate of artisinal cheese served at a table and a tour.

Fine points: Featured wines: One Bordeaux-style blend per year. Owners: Agustin and Valeria Huneeus. Winemaker: Aaron Pott, with Sarah Gott consulting. Cases: Unavailable. Acres: 280.

Quintessa, 1601 Silverado Trail, Rutherford 94573; phone (707) 967–1601, Web site www.quintessa.com. Open 10:00 A.M. to 4:00 P.M. daily, tours at 10:30 A.M., 12:30 P.M., and 2:30 P.M. Tasting fee: $25, waived with purchase of a bottle or two half bottles. Visa, MasterCard, and American Express. Wheelchair accessible.

Don't miss **Mumm Napa Valley,** about a mile south of Villa Mt. Eden Winery on the right (west) side of the Silverado Trail. Red flags hint that you have arrived at the winery, which was modeled after an early 1900s barn with screened porches. Cyclists enjoy the bike rack. When you enter the winery, a gift shop is on the right. The tasting porch lies beyond, facing south and west and overlooking sumptuous vineyards and the Mayacamas Mountains. Sit at a table, and the champagne will be brought to you. Heaven!

The French Champagne maker Mumm gave original Mumm Napa Valley winemaker Guy Deveaux, a native of Epernay in the heart of France's Champagne district, carte blanche to develop this estate's sparkling wine works, and Mumm's vineyard along Highway 12 in Carneros between Sonoma and Napa is named for him. Joseph E. Seagram & Sons owns the French Mumm company as well as Mumm Napa Valley and Sterling Vineyards.

Mumm provides a whole cultural and educational experience, with tours through its demonstration vineyards and video monitors, as well as the fabulous Ansel Adams "The Story of a Winery" permanent photo exhibit in the Art Gallery. Adams's photo series resulted from his friendship with Otto E. Meyer, president of the wine division of Joseph E. Seagram & Sons. Mumm Napa Valley sparklings have been served in the White House to British Prime Minister Tony Blair and French Prime Minister Jacques Chirac. You can buy it in all quantities, from splits to Balthazars (12 liters).

The gift shop is a delight, with everything from books and maps to film and aspirin. The staff encourage individuality and fun. We found them to be the most friendly and helpful around. In the late 1990s and early 2000s, Mumm was center stage in winery ownership musical chairs. Diagio bought both Sterling and Mumm and then sold Mumm to Allied Domecq.

Fine points: Tasting fee: $5.00–$12.50. Private tastings: $10.00–$20.00. Featured wines: Blanc de Blancs, DVX, Brut Prestige, Blanc de Noirs, Sparkling Pinot Noir, Demi Sec, and Extra Dry dessert wine. Owner: Allied Domecq. Winemaker: Ludovic Dervin; General Manager, former winemaker: Rob NcNeil. Cases: 200,000+. Acres: 1,200.

Mumm Napa Valley, 8445 Silverado Trail, Rutherford 94573; phone (707) 942–3434, Web site www.mumm.com. Open from 10:00 A.M. to 5:00 P.M. daily. Free tours hourly from 10:00 A.M. to 3:00 P.M. Visa, MasterCard, American Express, and JCB. Wheelchair accessible.

When you leave Mumm, turn right (south) onto the Silverado Trail. Watch carefully for **ZD Wines** just 0.3 mile south. ZD's tile roof is what you see from the road. Turn right (west) at the sign and park in the lot. Follow the path beside the winery by the lawns and tree roses in the patio to the large wood doors and the tasting room. White walls highlight the many soft-colored woods in the room and its Mexican-tile floor.

ZD was founded in the Carneros District in 1968 by aerospace engineers Norman de Leuze and Gino Zepponi, with $3,000 each. They obtained the first Sonoma County winery permit issued in twenty years and purchased grapes from Rene di Rosa to make wine "in Sonoma from grapes grown in the Carneros region of Napa." Ten years later they moved the winery here. Since Zepponi's tragic death in an automobile accident, the de Leuze family has developed ZD alone, with mother Rosa Lee and son Brett handling marketing. Robert serves as winemaker, and Julie is administrative director—and a fabulous cook. In 2000 ZD poured its thirtieth release of Carreros Pinot Noir.

We encourage you to visit this happy and quietly elegant winery. Check out the tasteful and high-quality shirts and hats, ZD-logo cork pullers, and aprons. If you visit on the weekend, be sure to try the wine-and-cheese seminars at 11:00 A.M.

Fine points: Tasting fee: $5.00 for current wines, $10.00 for Reserves or older wines. ZD provides small baskets of sliced bread to cleanse your palate between wines. ZD wines have been served at state dinners in the White House by three presidents. Featured wines: Chardonnay, Cabernet Sauvignon, and Pinot Noir. Owners: The de Leuze Family. Winemaker: Chris Pisani. Winemaster: Robert de Leuze. Cases: 30,000. Acres: 35.

ZD Wines, 8383 Silverado Trail, Napa 94558; phone (707) 963–5188, Web site www.zdwines.com. Open from 10:00 A.M. to 4:30 P.M. daily. Visa, MasterCard, and Discover. Wheelchair accessible.

Almost 1½ miles south of ZD and on the left (east) side of Silverado Trail, you might want to visit **Miner Family Winery** (formerly Oakville Ranch Winery). Bob Miner, founder of the Oracle Corporation, and his wife, Mary, bought the initial acreage for this winery in 1989 and began making wines. In 1996 they purchased the adjacent property, the brand-new but never used Stratford Winery. After Bob Miner's death, Mary ran it for a while, then sold it to nephew David Miner, his wife, Emily, and his parents, Ed and Norma. The winery's Cabernets have received ratings of 90 or higher consistently since 1989.

Set slightly up the slope from the road, the winery has a towering, vanilla facade. The pleasant tasting room (on the second floor—an elevator is available)

Asian Crab Cakes with Lime-Ginger Sauce

from Miner Family Winery, Oakville

CRAB MIXTURE:

1 small yellow onion, finely minced

8 oz fresh crabmeat

2 slices white bread, broken into pieces

1 egg, beaten

1 Tbs gingerroot, grated

2 tsp fresh lemongrass, minced

6 Tbs butter, melted

mixed baby greens

salt and pepper to taste

SAUCE:

3 Tbs lime juice

1 tsp lime rind

3 Tbs soy sauce

1 Tbs gingerroot, grated

⅓ cup peanut oil

Sauté the onion in 3 Tbs butter until soft and just golden on edges. Remove from pan and mix with crab, bread pieces, egg, gingerroot, and lemongrass.

Form crab mixture into small patties on a cookie sheet. Cover with plastic wrap and chill for at least an hour. In small skillet, brown cakes in melted butter until golden brown.

Arrange one cake just to one side on bed of greens and drizzle with the following sauce.

In a small bowl, whisk lime juice, lime rind, soy sauce, gingerroot, and peanut oil. Serve with Miner Family Vineyards Viognier. Serves 4.

is beige with light hardwood floors covered with Oriental rugs. There is an excellent selection of books on a large dining table and a glassed-in humidor to keep cigars at the perfect temperature. Walk down the hall toward the restrooms and look through the windows to the barrel room with pinkish-beige walls. Relax on the patio furniture and take in the spectacular Napa Valley view.

Fine points: Tasting fee: Ranch wines $5.00–$10.00. Featured wines: Oakville Ranch and Miner Family Vineyards Chardonnay, Sauvignon Blanc, Pinot Noir, Merlot, Cabernet Franc, Sangiovese, Viognier, Zinfandel, Cabernet Sauvignon, Petit Syrah, and Dry Rosé of Sangiovese. Owners: Dave and Emily Miner, Ed and Norma Miner. Winemaker: Gary Brookman. Cases: 4,000 Oakville Ranch, 20,000 Miner Family. Acres: 80 of 300 in use.

Miner Family Winery, 7850 Silverado Trail, Oakville 94562; phone (707) 944–9500, Web site www.minerwines.com. Open from 11:00 A.M. to 5:00 P.M. daily; tours by appointment only. Visa, MasterCard, and American Express. Wheelchair accessible.

We highly recommend a slight detour west on Oakville Cross Road to Plumpjack, Groth, and the prized Silver Oak wineries. If you prefer to continue southward on the Silverado Trail instead, turn left very carefully out of Miner Family Winery and then left again to Vine Cliff's driveway.

The first of the three wineries on Oakville Cross Road that you come to from the Silverado Trail is **Plumpjack Winery**, a venture of San Francisco's Plumpjack Cafe owners and thirty-something movers and shakers: Plumpjack managing director and San Francisco Mayor Gavin Newsom and Bill and Gordon Getty. Plumpjack made news in 2000 by breaking with tradition and introducing a screw-top bottle (instead of cork), formerly thought of as a sacrilege by wine snobs.

Three-tenths of a mile from the Silverado Trail, turn north at the sign, take a sharp left in front of the winery building, then turn right into Plumpjack's parking lot. Walk on rose-colored gravel through herb gardens and olive trees to the tasting room on the left of the tank house. Admire the shiny copper "chandelier" in the middle of the room.

Located in what used to be Jim and Ann McWilliams' Villa Mt. Eden Winery (now Stimson Lane's Villa Mt. Eden), Plumpjack has great picnic tables, Henry IV Shakespearean decor, and a youthful irreverence unusual in these parts. The sign opposite the tasting room reads: IMPRESS YOUR DATE, IMPRESS YOUR FRIENDS. WHAT THE HECK—IMPRESS SNOOTY WAITERS NAMED MAURICE.

Fine points: The logo shirts and hats are highest quality, as are the emerging wines. Tasting fee: $5.00. Featured wines: Chardonnay, Merlot, Syrah, Cabernet Sauvignon, and Cabernet Cuvee. Owners: Gavin Newsom, Bill and Gordon Getty. Winemakers: Anthony Biagi and Nils Venge (consultant). Cases: 8,000–10,000. Acres: 50.

Plumpjack Winery, 620 Oakville Cross Road, Oakville 94562; phone (707) 945–1220, Web site www.plumpjack.com. Open from 10:00 A.M. to 4:00 P.M. daily. No picnics and no tours. Visa, MasterCard, and American Express. Gravel makes wheelchair access difficult.

Groth Vineyards & Winery's impressive edifice

Practically adjoining Plumpjack is **Groth Vineyards & Winery,** the baby of Judy and Dennis Groth, the latter a former CPA with Ernst Young & Co., former executive vice president of Atari and president of Atari's International Division, and one of the wine industry's truly nice guys. You can't miss the enormous rose-stucco Mission-style structure with its blue tile fountain and sweeping steps, designed by Napa architect Bob Gianelli. The monumental building northeast of the winery is the Groths' new home.

When you enter the lovely cavernous rooms, the first thing you see are daughter Suzanne Groth's bold, colorful, and fun paintings, which also adorn the winery's posters and wine labels. Walk through the large dining room with its dramatic fireplace, Nino Barrucca serving platters and bowls, and seating for crowds. (Unfortunately, the dining room is used only for house and trade events.) Through the arched windows you can see the barrel aging room. Walk out onto the patio to enjoy the view of vineyards to the north.

Judy and Dennis met in the first grade in Sunnyvale and are still together. They introduced the concept of winemakers getting equity (10 percent) in the winery instead of just being employees. With great success they hired Villa Mt. Eden's winemaker, Nils Venge, to create the wines, since they knew nothing about the process. They now release their Reserve Cabernet Sauvignon the last Saturday before February 1, the same day Silver Oak releases theirs.

Fine points: In 1988 Robert Parker called Groth "one of California's hottest wineries" and gave Groth's 1985 Cabernet Sauvignon a rare "perfect" score, immediately spiking the demand for Groth's 400 cases. The winery makes more than ten times as many cases now. Tasting fee: $10, refundable with purchase. Featured wines: Chardonnay, Sauvignon Blanc, Cabernet Sauvignon, and Merlot. Owners: Dennis and Judy Groth. Winemaker: Michael Weis. Cases: 45,000. Acres: 165.

Groth Vineyards & Winery, 750 Oakville Cross Road, Oakville 94562; phone (707) 944–0290, Web site www.grothwines.com. Open from 10:00 A.M. to 4:00 P.M. Monday–Saturday, closed Sunday; tours 11:00 A.M. and 2:00 P.M. Monday–Friday, 11:00 A.M. Saturday. Visa, MasterCard, and American Express. Wheelchair accessible by entrance to left of stairs and elevator to second floor.

Leaving Groth, turn right (west) onto Oakville Cross Road. Go about half a mile to the superb **Silver Oak Cellars.** Turn left (south) into Silver Oak's double driveway, lined with olive trees and silver oaks, to what was once the Oakville Dairy. Silver Oak makes only Cabernet Sauvignon—and makes only the best Cabernet Sauvignon in the Napa Valley and possibly anywhere. Try to sneak a taste of its Meyer Family Port.

Original partner, president, and winemaster Justin Meyer was once a teacher-coach member of the Christian Brothers religious order. He was "drafted" to work at Christian Brothers Winery instead of teaching. Experiencing every job in the winery, adding B.S. and M.S. degrees in viticulture and enology in addition to his M.S. in economics, Justin left the order after fifteen years to create his own winery, with the intent of making the best Cabernet in the world. He did. Having taught "Wine Appreciation" at Napa Valley College, he also wrote *Plain Talk about Wine,* a fun and user-friendly book about viticulture, enology, and wine appreciation. It is available in Silver Oak's tasting room.

Partner Raymond Duncan is an investor, Denver oilman, buffalo rancher, and co-owner of an art gallery. Ray and Justin began their endeavor in 1972 to plant and manage 750 acres that Ray owned in the Napa and Alexander Valleys. In 1975 they bought Franciscan Winery from bankruptcy. There they crushed

Silver Oak Cellars

and bottled Silver Oak's grapes from 1975 to 1981. They sold Franciscan to the Eckes Company of Germany in 1979.

You can see the result of their efforts in this elegant, stone monastery–looking winery. As you enter the dark tasting room, it might take your eyes a few moments to adjust from the sunlight outside. Tasters may sit on stone benches or upholstered black wrought-iron furniture.

Silver Oak also has a winery in Sonoma County's Alexander Valley in what was once the old Lyeth Winery facility. At both wineries Justin made a masterful effort of creating a family among staff members. Ray Duncan bought out Justin Meyer's Silver Oak interest in 2001. He hired Daniel Baron as winemaker. Justin Meyer passed away in August 2002.

Fine points: Be sure to look into the glassed-in Library Room, where Silver Oak's finest bottlings are stored. Sliding glass doors lead to the barrel and tank rooms, where the Cabernets are aged at least thirty months in American oak barrels. Tasting fee: $10 including souvenir glass. Featured wines: Cabernet Sauvignon and Port. Owner: Raymond Duncan and family. Winemaker: Daniel Baron. Cases: 50,000. Acres: 220.

Silver Oak Cellars, 915 Oakville Cross Road, Oakville 94562; phone (707) 944–8808, Web site www.SilverOak.com. Open from 9:00 A.M. to 4:00 P.M. Monday–Saturday. Free tours at 1:30 P.M. Monday–Friday. Visa, MasterCard, and American Express. Wheelchair accessible.

As you leave Silver Oak, we suggest that you turn right (east) onto Oakville Cross Road and go back to the Silverado Trail. Turn right (south) onto Silverado Trail and turn left (east) to visit Vine Cliff Winery.

Vine Cliff Winery has finally opened its doors to the public, and what a treat! You can enjoy a lovely pond, honking bullfrogs, a tour of the caves, and wine tasting right in the small ghost winery. Built for locals George Burrage and Thomas Tucker in 1871, mostly by Chinese laborers, what's left of the original stone cellar and processing area are right behind the current winery. Phylloxera invaded and basically killed the vines and the owners. After Burrage and Tucker died, San Franciscan John Fry bought the property and, with a fortune made in Nevada silver, sat on boards of several companies, including the Napa Wine Company. During its original life, Vine Cliff served as the wine cellar for the original Napa Wine Company, a group of allied wine producers. You can still see remnants of the four-story gravity-flow winery, whose upper three wooden stories burned down in 1900. (For information on the current Napa Wine Company, see chapter 3.)

Part of the original Rancho Caymus land grant that General Mariano Vallejo gave to George Yount in 1836, the land and winery sat dormant for eighty-four years. Chuck and Nell Sweeney bought the property in 1985, planted vines, and enjoyed their first vintage in 1990. We have Nell to thank for the lovely landscaping, and a visitor center is in the planning stages.

But for now, try tasting Vine Cliff's elegant wines at a heavy old baking table in the tasting room, and a tour of the 15,000-square-foot cave dug 100 yards deep into the hill.

Fine points: Tasting fee: $15. Featured wines: Chardonnay, Cabernet Sauvignon, and Merlot. Owners: Charles and Nell Sweeney. General manager and director of winemaking operations: Robert Sweeney. Winemaker: Rex Smith. Cases: 8,000. Acres: 100.

Vine Cliff Winery, 7400 Silverado Trail, Napa 94558; phone: (707) 944–2399, Web site www.vinecliff.com. Open from 10:00 A.M. to 5:00 P.M. daily by appointment only. Visa, MasterCard, and American Express. Tasting room is not wheelchair accessible, but cave is, and staff will bring tastes to cave.

"Wild" boar guarding the pond at Vine Cliff Winery

Robert Sinskey Vineyards

As you leave Vine Cliff to go south to Robert Sinskey Vineyards, turn left out of Vine Cliff's driveway, very carefully. **Robert Sinskey Vineyards** is up the hill to the left (east). Nestled in soft hills, the winery has ivy-covered stone walls, rose gardens, interesting half-circle benches, a half-circle fish pond (no coins, please), and great views. Enjoy the vegetable and herb gardens in the summer.

Robert Sinskey is a graduate of the Parsons School of Design in New York. He designed the winery and does all the graphics. His father, Dr. Robert Sinskey, was a partner in Acacia Winery in Carneros when the Chalone group bought it.

As you enter the cavernous tasting room and kitchen, hosts greet you as if you have just arrived in their home. Because Robert Sinskey believes so strongly in the importance of food and wine, he has a gorgeous professional kitchen right in the tasting room—and a house chef. You will see both a historic wood stove and ultramodern ovens, wood-burning ovens, a television/video screen, a full range of professional pots and pans, and a magnificent view of Silverado Vineyards across the road.

Robert brings in restaurant chefs from all over the country to conduct cooking classes, including Joseph Keller, Craig Stoll, Mark Sullivan, James Ormsby, and Maria Helm Sinskey, author of the recently published cookbook,

The Vineyard Kitchen. Get on the mailing list if you might be interested in the dinner series. Tours include a culinary tour, a cave and cellar tour, and a wine library tour (for eight or more).

Every year Robert Sinskey stages his fun Pinot Release Party so you can "hear the gospel according to Pinot," feast on "life-sustaining creations," listen to "down-home music," and "take The Pinot cure." It all takes place close to May 1.

Robert Sinskey Vineyards became Certified Organic in 2001.

Fine points: You can purchase the best olive oils and books here. Tasting fee: $20, with $10 refundable with purchase of two or more bottles. Featured wines: Chardonnay, Pinot Noir, Merlot, Cabernet Sauvignon, Cabernet Franc, and Pinot Blanc. Owner: Robert Sinskey. Winemaker: Jeff Vimig. Culinary Director: Maria Helm Sinskey. Cases: 25,000. Acres: 205.

Robert Sinskey Vineyards, 6320 Silverado Trail, Yountville 94558; phone (707) 944–9090 or (800) 869–2030, Web site www. robertsinskey.com. Open from 10:00 A.M. to 4:30 P.M. daily. Tasting and tours by appointment only. Visa, MasterCard, American Express, and Discover. Wheelchair accessible.

As you leave the winery, turn left (south) onto the Silverado Trail, and then turn right (west) on Yountville Cross Road, where you will find S. Anderson and Goosecross Cellars. If you choose not to make this detour, just continue southward to Shafer and Silverado vineyards.

Head down the slight hill on Yountville Cross Road, then left into **Cliff Lede Vineyards,** a small family winery of great taste and flower-bedecked ambience. The exquisite lawns, rose-covered arbors, and gazebo with gravel patio made us want to move right in.

Previous owner Carol Anderson graduated from UC Davis's School of Viticulture and Enology and created S. Anderson Champagnes and Chardonnays. Her late husband, Stanley, supervised planting of the noble vinifera Chardonnay and Pinot Noir vineyards in the Stag's Leap and Carneros districts, as well as creation of the caves and winery. In early 2002, Canadians Cliff and Cheryl Lede (pronounced LAY-DEE) bought S. Anderson, having developed an international construction business from Alberta. Longtime fans of S. Anderson's cult-wine, Richard Chambers Cabernet Sauvignon, the Ledes found the opportunity to purchase the winery through friend Ray Signorello.

Smoked Trout and Lemon Crème Fraîche in Endive Spears

from Kim Whistler for Cliff Lede Vineyards (formerly S. Anderson), Yountville

NOTE: If you want to prepare some of the components in advance so you just have to assemble before serving, I recommend dicing the beets and onions ahead of time and refrigerating them in Ziplock bags. Also, preparing the crème fraîche in advance and letting it refrigerate for a few hours gives the flavors time to meld. —Kim Whistler

1 beet (optional)
½ cup crème fraîche
½ tsp fresh lemon juice
1 tsp lemon zest
1 tsp fresh dill, snipped
Pinch salt
2 small heads endive
4 oz pack smoked trout (may substitute smoked salmon)
1 red onion, finely chopped
Small quantity lemon zest and dill fronds for garnish

If you choose to use the beet, allow plenty of time to cook and cool it. Boil until very tender (about 45–50 minutes), cool in water, peel, and then finely dice.

To prepare the lemon crème fraiche, mix the crème fraîche, lemon juice, lemon zest, dill, and salt in a small bowl. Cover and refrigerate until ready for use.

Pull off, wash, and dry individual endive leaves. On each leaf, spoon about ½ tsp diced beet. Place a small chunk of trout on top of the beet. Spoon about 1 tsp of lemon crème fraîche on the trout. Sprinkle a bit of chopped red onion on the crème fraiche.

Garnish with one or two pieces of lemon zest and a small dill frond. Serve with S. Anderson 1998 Blanc de Blanc from Cliff Lede Vineyards.

The Ledes have redone the tasting room, added sculptures, and divided the wine varietals into three groups: Cliff Lede for still wines, S. Anderson for sparkling wines, and Poetry for proprietary Cabernet Sauvignon.

The caves hold 400,000 bottles of Champagne, Chardonnay, and Cabernet aging in the barrel. These are great places for candlelit parties and chamber-music concerts.

Fine points: Get on their mailing list for the Cliff Lede Newsletter." Tasting fee: $10. Featured wines: Chardonnay, Merlot, Cabernet Sauvignon, Blanc de Noirs, sparkling wines, Claret, Syrah. Owners: Cliff and Cheryl Lede. Winemaker: Marco DiGiulio. Cases: 12,000. Acres: 66.

Cliff Lede Vineyards, 1473 Yountville Cross Road, Yountville 94599; phone (707) 944–8642 or (800) 428–2259, Web site www .cliffledevineyards.com. Open from 10:00 A.M. to 5:00 P.M. daily, tours at 10:30 A.M. and 2:30 P.M. Visa, MasterCard, and American Express. Wheelchair accessible.

As you leave Cliff Lede, turn left onto Yountville Cross Road, then turn right on State Lane to visit **Goosecross Cellars,** a fun, informal, and homey winery behind the old Gorsuch home. Goosecross is a rough translation of *Gorsuch,* an Old English name meaning "where the goose crosses the stream." Canada geese cross the Napa Valley here in their migration north and south.

Two wooden geese in front of the house suggest that you go to the right and park beside the winery's tanks in back of the house. Ring the bell if you don't see anyone, and walk between the tanks to the tasting-room door, where Tyrone, a black Lab, used to greet visitors until the coyotes got him. Now you can meet Maidchen, another black Lab, and Humdinger, the winery cat. The tasting room, gift shop, and winery are all one, which makes this stop especially fun.

Patt and Rey Gorsuch founded the winery and passed it on to their son and winemaker, Geoff, whose business partner is David Topper. As director of hospitality, Colleen Tatarian Topper oversees the retail center as well as the popular "Wine Basics" classes. Colleen and David met "on the job" and got married right here at the winery.

Fine points: You can purchase minor snacks such as Wisecrackers, chocolate turtles, and tapevades, and sample cheeses, pretzels, mustards, and a generous supply of Hershey's kisses. Check out the triple chocolate-dipped bottles of wine. Tasting fee: $5.00 for five wines. Goosecross rarely submits its wines to review by magazines or contests. Be sure to ask about the elegant Aeros Merlot. Featured wines: Chardonnay, Sauvignon Blanc, Syrah, Merlot, Cabernet Sauvignon, and Zinfandel. Owners: Geoff Gorsuch and David Topper. Winemaker: Geoff Gorsuch. Cases: 10,000. Acres: 15.

Mediterranean Pork Tenderloin

from Colleen Topper of Goosecross Cellars, Yountville

2 Tbs chili powder
2 Tbs cumin
¼ tsp garlic salt
2 pork tenderloins (1½ lbs each)
8 oz plain yogurt
2 Tbs mayonnaise
½ cup cilantro leaves, loosely packed
½ small red chili pepper, minced
½ lime, juiced
6 basil leaves, chopped
¼ tsp ground coriander
½ tsp fennel seed

In a small bowl, combine chili powder, cumin, and garlic salt. Spread seasoning in baking pan. Roll pork tenderloin in the spices and refrigerate for 3 hours.

To make the sauce, combine yogurt, mayonnaise, cilantro, minced chili pepper, lime juice, basil leaves, coriander, and fennel in a food processor and process until smooth. Refrigerate until ready to serve.

Prepare barbecue and heat grill to low fire. Caramelize the outside of the pork tenderloin by turning meat on all sides, about 1 minute per side. Cover the grill and cook through over low fire for approximately 28 minutes, turning every 7 minutes. Remove meat from grill, cover with foil, and let cook 10 minutes.

Slice pork tenderloin into ½-inch slices. Arrange on plates and spoon sauce over the top. Serves 4. Serve with rice pilaf, Greek salad, and Goosecross Syrah.

Goosecross Cellars, 1119 State Lane, Yountville 94599; phone (707) 944–1986 or (800) 276–9210, Web site www.goosecross.com. Open from 10:00 A.M. to 4:00 P.M. daily. Visa, MasterCard, and American Express. Wheelchair accessible.

Back to the Silverado Trail to a series of interesting and excellent wineries. Turn right (south) from Yountville Cross Road onto the Silverado Trail. To get to **Shafer Vineyards,** turn left (east) at the Shafer sign and turn left again in 0.2 mile, keeping to the right side so that you will be on the upper part of the divided road. Continue for 1 mile, passing sensuous rolling hills, a valley, and vines circling knolls all around. You arrive at what looks like a two-story ranch home with a large oak tree in front. The working part of the winery is on your left. Just looking at the earth-colored stucco, stone, and natural wood relaxes visitors.

John Shafer left the publishing business in Chicago in 1972 and moved his family to this rocky, hilly vineyard in the Napa Valley. He discovered that what looked like lousy soil and water conditions turned out to stress vines and produce prized intense flavors in his wines. John's son Doug studied at UC Davis, graduating in enology and viticulture, and became Shafer winemaker in 1983. He was soon joined by Elias Fernandez as assistant winemaker. Now Elias is winemaker. Doug became president in 1994, when John became chairman of the board.

Their dog Tucker will welcome you. Be sure to collect the vast selections of printed information and recipes that Shafer makes available for free to visitors.

Roasted Garlic Mashed Potatoes

from Shafer Vineyards, Napa

1 medium head garlic
½ Tbs olive oil
4–6 potatoes
2 Tbs butter
½ cup milk
salt and white pepper to taste

Slice off top of garlic head. Pour olive oil into opening and wrap in foil. Place garlic into 350°F oven for 30–45 minutes until soft. Remove from oven and allow to cool. Squeeze out garlic cloves. Remove any skins and mash into a smooth paste.

Bring 2–4 quarts of salted water to a boil. Peel potatoes and cut into ½-inch cubes. Add potatoes to boiling water and cook until soft (approximately 10 minutes). Drain and place in bowl with garlic and remaining ingredients. Mash until well incorporated and smooth. Serves 4.

Fine points: Shafer wines have been served at the White House to Queen Elizabeth II and Prince Philip of Britain and to President Hosni Mubarak of Egypt. No tasting fee. Featured wines: Red Shoulder Ranch, Chardonnay, Merlot, Hillside Select, Cabernet Sauvignon, Firebreak, Sangiovese, Syrah, and Port. Owner and CEO: John Shafer. President: Doug Shafer. Winemaker: Elias Fernandez. Cases: 32,000. Acres: 200.

Shafer Vineyards, 6154 Silverado Trail, Napa 94558; phone (707) 944–2877, Web site www.shafervineyards.com. Open from 9:00 A.M. to

4:00 P.M. Monday–Friday for retail sales. Tours and tasting by appointment only, so call ahead. Visa and MasterCard. Wheelchair accessible by driving up behind the winery to the back.

Back on the west side of Silverado Trail, **Baldacci Family Vineyards** is located just south of the Yountville Crossroad, culminating a dream of owner Thomas Baldacci. Known for his Castle Construction company that builds primarily in East Bay redevelopment areas, Baldacci, his wife, Brenda, and family bought this property and 1916 vineyard at the southern end of the Stags Leap District in 1997. The Baldaccis have replanted the old vineyard block by block.

The tiny tasting room belies the fun, information, and wines at Baldacci. A patio filled with umbrellaed tables offers a welcome respite from the rigors of stand-up wine tasting. Brenda spends most of her time taking care of four red-headed sons and has earned her own vineyard designated wine, Brenda's Vineyard Cabernet Sauvignon. Check out the 7,000-square-foot cave dug into the knoll under the Baldacci's house.

Fine points: Tasting fee: $5.00, refundable with purchase. Featured wines: Cabernet Sauvignon, Pinot Noir, and Syrah. Owners: Thomas and Brenda Baldacci and family. Winemaker: Rolando Herrera. Cases: 2,000. Acres: 22.

Chocolate-Caramel Oat Squares

From Brenda Baldacci,
Baldacci Family Vineyards, Napa

1¹/₂ cups flour
1¹/₂ cups Quaker Oats
1¹/₂ cups firmly packed brown sugar
¹/₂ tsp baking soda
¹/₄ tsp salt
³/₄ cup chilled unsalted butter
12 oz chocolate chips
¹/₂ cup whipping cream
14 oz caramels

Preheat oven to 350 degrees.

Place first six ingredients in food processor and mix until crumbly. Press mixture, reserving 2 cups, into bottom of a 9" x 13" ungreased baking dish. Sprinkle chocolate chips over mixture and set aside.

Bring cream to a simmer over low heat and add caramels until melted. Pour over chocolate chips and then carefully sprinkle remaining crumble mixture on top. Bake for approximately 15 minutes; cool completely. Cut and serve at room temperature or chilled. Serve with Baldacci Cabernet Sauvignon.

Baldacci Family Vineyards, 6236 Silverado Trail, Napa 94558; phone (707) 944–9261, Web site www.baldaccivineyards.com. Open by appointment 11:00 A.M. to 4:00 P.M. Friday–Sunday. Visa, MasterCard, American Express, and Discover. Wheelchair accessible.

Silverado Vineyards is 2 miles south of the Yountville Cross Road and just south of the road to Shafer Vineyards. Turn right (west) up Silverado's driveway to its gorgeous Italian gardens and courtyard, fountain, flowers, benches, and Old World ambience. There are glorious views from the private knoll above the Napa Valley.

Long ago Lillian Disney, Diane Disney Miller, and Ron Miller set out to grow some of the best grapes in the Napa Valley and to "deliver the best wine the Napa Valley could produce at a fair price." Named for an abandoned silver mine, Silverado symbolizes the Disney family's commitment to Napa wine. They see themselves as "prospecting," as Robert Louis Stevenson suggested winemakers do, seeking viticultural paydirt.

Silverado Vineyards' courtyard entrance

Toward that goal, the Disneys brought in John Stuart before construction to take charge of technical design and vineyard development. Highly regarded by colleagues and wine reviewers, Jack is a fifth-generation Californian with a literature degree from Stanford and graduate training in viticulture and enology from UC Davis.

Do not miss this informally elegant experience in the new visitor center and its phenomenal view of the Napa Valley and Mt. St. Helena. You can even sign in on the electronic guest list computer. Enjoy Merlot-filled chocolates ($11 per box).

Join the club so you can attend Silverado Vineyards' fun Quicksilver Wine Club Grilling Festival and Contest.

Fine points: Tasting fee: $10–$20. Featured wines: Sauvignon Blanc, Chardonnay, Sangiovese Rosato, Sangiovese, Merlot, and Cabernet Sauvignon. Owners: Diane Disney Miller and Ron Miller. Winemaker: Jon Emmerich. Cases: 90,000. Acres: 400.

Silverado Vineyards, 6121 Silverado Trail, Napa 94558; phone (707) 257–1770, Web site www.silveradovineyards.com. Open from 10:30 A.M. to 5:00 P.M. daily May 15–September 15, 11:00 A.M. to 4:30 P.M. daily the rest of the year; tours at 10:30 A.M. and 2:30 P.M. daily, by appointment only. Visa, MasterCard, and American Express. Wheelchair accessible.

As you come back down Silverado's driveway, turn right (south) again onto the Silverado Trail to **Pine Ridge Winery,** 0.4 mile down the road. Turn right (west) at Pine Ridge's sign. As you approach the winery, you get a feel of the place from the adult tire swings hanging from pine trees, among which you are welcome to stroll, swing, or picnic. There are even barbecue grills for your use.

Be sure to walk through Pine Ridge's demonstration vineyard adjoining the south side of the parking lot and at the foot of the ridge covered with pines, and call ahead to make an appointment to tour the vast caves dug half a mile into the volcanic rock hillside, housing 4,400 French oak barrels of wine.

Founded by Gary and Nancy Andrus, Pine Ridge is now operated by Pine Ridge Winery, LLC, with George Scheppler serving as president and CEO of this winery and Archery Summit in the Red Hills of Dundee, Oregon. The Andruses built Archery Summit Winery and actually made Archery Summit's first Pinot Noir vintages here before the winery was completed. Scheppler

Morel Mushroom and Asparagus Tart with Black Peppercorn Cream

from Chef Eric C. Maczko, Pine Ridge Winery, Napa

2 sheets puff pastry dough (8" x 10")

1 bunch asparagus

1 pint heavy cream

2 Tbs black peppercorns, whole

6 oz fresh morel mushrooms (or 2 oz dried morels)

2 Tbs unsalted butter

Kosher salt, as needed

Black pepper, freshly cracked as needed

1 Tbs thyme, chopped

1 tsp tarragon, chopped

1 Tbs parsley (whole leaves) to garnish

1 egg yolk, beaten with 1 Tbs water

4 oz grated Gruyère cheese

Preheat oven to 375 degrees. Allow pastry dough to come up to room temperature for 20 minutes prior to rolling out. On a lightly floured work surface, roll dough lightly to form approximately 8" x 10" sheets. Cut into 5-inch circles, reserving remaining dough for another purpose. Puncture each tart 3–4 times with a fork. Double over outside edge to form a raised $^1/_2$-inch crust. Chill on parchment-lined sheet tray.

Blanch asparagus in a 4-quart sauce pot of boiling salted water until tender (3 minutes). Shock immediately in ice water. Dry on paper towels. Cut off the tips and reserve. Dice remaining stems and reserve separately.

Steep heavy cream and whole black peppercorns for 10 minutes. Do not boil.

Lightly brush away any dirt from morel mushrooms. (If using dried mushrooms, soak in hot water or hot mushroom stock for 15–30 minutes. Remove, and reserve soaking liquid for another purpose.) Sauté mushrooms lightly in butter until tender. Season with salt and pepper and half of the thyme and tarragon. Strain the heavy cream through a fine-mesh strainer over the mushrooms. Simmer and reduce by one-quarter.

Meanwhile, brush puff pastry rounds with egg wash. Bake in preheated oven for 15–20 minutes until lightly browned and gently raised. If undercooked, bake an additional 5 minutes.

Spoon mushrooms and cream into centers of tarts. Arrange asparagus tips up in circle around mushrooms. Place diced stems in middle and sprinkle with Gruyère. Bake for an additional 8 minutes until cheese is melted and golden. Remove from oven and garnish with remaining herbs. Serve immediately. Makes 4 tarts. Serve with Chardonnay or Sauvignon Blanc.

Pine Ridge Winery

began his wine career working for Baron Philippe de Rothschild as U.S. château director and served as president of this California company and as co-CEO of Opus One, a joint venture of Rothschild and Robert Mondavi (as described in chapter 3).

Fine points: Pine Ridge uses olive trees as active participants in organic farming, since they attract blue-green sharpshooters (like grasshoppers) and keep them busy so they don't attack the vines. Tasting fee: $20, with $30 for Reserve tasting in the Hillside Room, at 11:00 A.M., 1:00 P.M., and 3:00 P.M. Featured wines: Chardonnay, Cabernet Sauvignon, and other Bordeaux. Owner: Pine Ridge Winery LLC. Winemaker: Stacy Clark. Chef: Eric Maczko. Cases: 60,000. Acres: 225 in Napa Valley.

Pine Ridge Winery, 5901 Silverado Trail, Napa 94558; phone (707) 252–9777, Web site www.pineridgewinery.com. Open from 10:30 A.M. to 4:30 P.M. daily. Tours by appointment at 10:00 A.M., noon, and 2:00 P.M. Visa, MasterCard, American Express, and Discover. Wheelchair accessible.

Just 0.2 mile south on the east side of Silverado Trail is **Steltzner Vineyards.** The winery is set in a new California/ Mediterranean stucco structure, in a flat valley within view of the road. Turn left at the sign. The tasting room is the long, narrow entrance to Steltzner's caves, which are dug into the hillside. The winery office building is topped with a three-story observation tower, offering a bird's-eye view of the surrounding Stag's Leap region.

Steltzner Vineyards tower and cave entrance

Rick Steltzner is a third-generation Californian who grew up in Livermore working part time for Wente Brothers Winery. He earned an MFA degree at Sacramento State College. Soon his life as an artist on St. Helena's Lodi Lane forced a change of career in order to stay in the Napa Valley.

Rick bought some land in the Stag's Leap District in 1964 (smart move) and began to grow grapes, drawing on his childhood memories of his mentor, Ernest Wente. Since he turned out to be good at caring for vineyards, Rick established and managed vineyards for other growers and wineries. He then started his own winemaking operation in a converted prune-dehydrating shed. He now enjoys high ratings from many reviewers.

Fine points: Tasting fee: $5.00, tour $12.00 per person. Featured wines: Sauvignon Blanc, Chardonnay, Claret, Merlot, Cabernet Sauvignon, Sangiovese, Merlot Grappa, Merlot Port, and Pinotage (a South African cross). Owners: Richard and Christine Steltzner. Winemaker: Tim Dolven. Cases: 15,000. Acres: 100.

Steltzner Vineyards, 5998 Silverado Trail, Napa 94558; phone (707) 252–7272, Web site www.steltzner.com. Open from 10:30 A.M. to 4:30 P.M. Monday–Saturday, 11:00 A.M. to 4:30 P.M. Sunday. Visa, Master-Card, and American Express. Wheelchair accessible.

As you leave Steltzner, turn left (south) and head south on the Silverado Trail for 0.5 mile to **Stag's Leap Wine Cellars,** whose sign comes up quickly down a hill on the left (east). Stag's Leap's world-class Cabernet Sauvignon won the Paris Bicentennial Tasting in 1976, causing French judges at the blind tasting to proclaim, "At last a good French wine!"

Stag's Leap is actually an old Indian name given to a rock formation on the hillside and later applied to the local wine appellation. Be sure to notice co-owner Barbara Winiarski's artistic sandstone floors in the reception hall, as well as her gardens and comfortable design concepts.

Founder Warren Winiarski was born in Chicago of Polish parents. His last name means "from the vine" or "winemaker's son." Warren should have known that, since his father made dandelion wine and fruit cordials in their home basement, he was fated to make elegant wines someday instead of following his liberal arts degree or the political history and theory he studied in Italy. While a liberal arts lecturer at the University of Chicago, he and his wife, Barbara, began to think of farming as an alternative to big-city life.

The Winiarskis moved to California in 1964. Warren first worked as an apprentice for Lee Stewart at Souverain Winery, then as assistant winemaker for Robert Mondavi in 1966, while looking for land similar to Nathan Fay's, whose wines he admired greatly. He found forty-four acres next to Fay Vineyard. Partly planted by Barbara and their children, it is now Stag's Leap Wine Cellars.

Fine points: In 2000 the Smithsonian Institution completed a yearlong project of recording life at Stag's Leap. Tasting fee: $10. Featured wines: Chardonnay, Sauvignon Blanc, White Riesling, Cabernet Sauvignon, Merlot, and Hawk Crest Merlot. Owners: Warren and Barbara Winiarski. Winemaker: Warren Winiarski. Associate Winemaker: Nicki Pruss. Cases: 75,000. Acres: 205.

Stag's Leap Wine Cellars, 5766 Silverado Trail, Napa 94558; phone (707) 944–2020, Web site www.cask23.com. Open from 10:00 A.M. to 4:30 P.M. daily. Visa, MasterCard, and American Express. Wheelchair accessible.

Be sure to go up the driveway to one of Napa's "ghost wineries," **Regusci Winery,** to experience truly old Napa family vinting. Regusci's building is known as the Grigsby Building Occidental Winery because pioneers Terrill and Charles Grigsby had it constructed here in 1878 by Caucasians, partly in response to the *St. Helena Star*'s anti-Chinese call to oust Chinese laborers.

Regusci Winery's Grigsby Building

The building features 2-foot-thick hand-cut lava stone walls, which provide natural cooling. The original winery operated on a gravity system, with crushing on the third floor; the juice was gravity fed to the second floor for settling and fermentation, then down to the bottom floor for barrel storage and aging. During Prohibition, the third floor became a distillery for bootleg wine, and the second floor became a dairy.

Gaetano Regusci bought the property in 1932 and made his own wines, while farming corn, hay, prunes, and walnuts and raising cattle and hogs. Eventually, Gaetano's son Angelo took over, and after the family grew grapes for others for years. Angelo's son Jim and Jim's wife, Diana, reestablished the winery, with their first vintage crush in 1996.

Enjoy the cool, historical tasting room, with olive oil tastes and fun historic posters.

Fine points: Tasting fee: $5.00. Featured wines: Estate-grown Zinfandel, Merlot, and Cabernet Sauvignon. Owners: Jim and Diana Regusci. Winemakers: Angelo Regusci and Charles Hendricks. Cases: 5,000. Acres: 300.

Regusci Winery, 5584 Silverado Trail, Napa 94558; phone (707) 254–0403. Open from 10:00 A.M. to 5:00 P.M. daily. Visa, MasterCard, and American Express. Wheelchair accessible.

Next in our progression southward on the Silverado Trail is **Chimney Rock Winery,** located in a large, white, monastic-looking building, a replica of a South African winery with the Dutch Huguenot architectural influence of Capetown. Drive 0.8 mile south of Stag's Leap Wine Cellars and turn left when you see the signs.

Poplar trees line the buildings. You can sip in the beautiful courtyard, but no picnicking is allowed.

Co-owner Sheldon (Hack) Wilson developed the Pepsi market throughout Africa as the founding bottler on the African continent. He also served as president of Pepsi United Bottlers for Los Angeles, Mexico, and Puerto Rico. Hack explored vineyard property in Bordeaux but directed his attention to the Napa Valley with the encouragement of his friend, the late Alexis Lichine.

Hack purchased the Chimney Rock Golf Course and the adjacent mountain in 1980, bulldozed nine holes (seventy-five acres), and planted his vineyard estate. The Wilson family and their partners, the Terlato Wine Group, replaced the remaining nine holes of the golf course with new vineyards in 2000.

Fine points: Behind the counter in the tasting room, you can get up close and personal with special-label Chimney Rock bottles made for the final cast party of *Cheers;* parties for television shows *Wings* and *Empty Nest;* the movie *Victor-Victoria;* the Long Beach Grand Prix; and NBC's *Today* show. Tasting fee: $7.00 per glass, including souvenir glass, for current vintages, $12.00 for Reserves. Featured wines: Fumé Blanc, Arneis, Rosé of Franc, Cabernet Sauvignon, and Elevage. Owners: Stella and Sheldon Wilson family, the Paterno Group, and the Terlato Wine Group. Winemaker: Douglas Fletcher. Cases: 20,000. Acres: 65.

Chimney Rock Winery, 5350 Silverado Trail, Napa 94558; phone (707) 257–2641 or (800) 257–2641, Web site www.chimneyrock.com. Open from 10:00 A.M. to 5:00 P.M. daily. Visa, MasterCard, and American Express. Wheelchair accessible.

Cajun Beef Skewers with Rouille

from Craig Linowski, Executive Chef for the Terlato Wine Group, Napa

SKEWERS:

1 lb tri-tip beef

16 skewers

¼ cup Chimney Rock Elevage

2 Tbs garlic, minced

2 tsp fresh thyme, minced

juice of 1 lemon

salt and pepper to taste

ROUILLE:

1 red bell pepper, roasted and peeled

1 small hot red chili pepper

2 cloves garlic

1 egg yolk

½ tsp salt

black pepper, freshly ground, to taste

¾ cup olive oil

1 tsp lemon juice

FOR THE SKEWERS (THE DAY BEFORE):

Mix all "skewers" ingredients except beef, salt, and pepper together in a bowl and set aside to marry for 2 hours. Slice beef in strips and add to marinade. Let sit overnight.

On serving day: Season beef with salt and pepper, place on skewers, and grill.

FOR THE ROUILLE:

Place roasted peppers in food processor. Add chili pepper, garlic, egg yolk, salt, and pepper. Puree until smooth. While the machine is running, slowly drizzle in the oil. Process until mixture is thick and smooth. Transfer to a bowl, add lemon juice, and season to taste.

Serve rouille with grilled beef skewers. Serves 4. Serve with Chimney Rock Elevage.

Clos du Val

Right next door, to the south of Chimney Rock, is **Clos du Val,** which means "a small vineyard estate in the valley"—appropriate for a family whose roots are in France. As you approach the winery, notice the American and French flags, loads of California poppies, magnolia trees, a little lake, roses along the paths, and an herb garden of lavender, rosemary, and thyme.

Owner John Goelet descends from a distinguished French wine family. His mother, Anne Marie Guestier, was a descendant of François Guestier, who worked for the Marquis de Segur, owner of Chateaux Lafite and Latour. His son, Pierre François Guestier, owned Chateau Beychevelle and was a partner in the Barton & Guestier wine firm.

Goelet was introduced to Bernard Portet, a native of the Médoc region of Bordeaux and then a recent graduate in agronomy, viticulture, and enology from the renowned University of Montpellier in France. Portet came from a family involved in winemaking in Cognac and Bordeaux for generations. The two men searched the world and decided that this was the perfect site for their winery.

The interesting Clos du Val wine labels introduce you to the Three Graces— Aglaia (Splendor), Euphrosyne (Mirth), and Thalia (Good Cheer)—daughters of Zeus and Eurynome, and thought to be the loveliest figures of Greek mythology. When the Greek gods planned a banquet, the Three Graces were the first to be invited. They subsequently enchanted the gods, and no banquet was complete without them. Clos du Val hopes you will feel the same way about their wines.

Don't miss the Ronald Searle whimsical wine illustrations commissioned by John Goelet in 1977, which you can purchase for a bargain $9.00 in the fun and elegant tasting room. Check out the specially etched wine bottles.

Fine points: Clos du Val is a sponsor of the Aspen Music Festival. Tasting fee: $5.00. Featured wines: Sémillon, Ariadne, Chardonnay, Zinfandel, Sangiovese, Pinot Noir, Merlot, and Cabernet Sauvignon. Owner: John Goelet. Winemaker and president: Bernard Portet. Cases: 70,000. Acres: 300.

Clos du Val, 5330 Silverado Trail, Napa 94558; phone (707) 259–2225, Web site www.closduval.com. Open from 10:00 A.M. to 5:00 P.M. daily. Visa, MasterCard, American Express, and Discover. Wheelchair accessible.

A mile and a half south of Clos du Val, also on the east side of Silverado Trail, you will find the elegant **Signorello Vineyards.** Its driveway is lined with plum trees and Italian junipers as you climb through vineyards. The modest, tasteful Italian decor includes painted arches and a glass desk in the cozy vestibule.

The tasting bar is right in the tank and aging room. Tasting is hosted by Chris Carmichael. You will enjoy the scale of everything here.

Fine points: You can't miss the Dan Marino football jersey personally signed to owner Ray Signorello. Signorello's wines receive high ratings from *Wine Spectator.* Tasting fee: $10. Featured wines: Chardonnay, Seta, Merlot, Cabernet Sauvignon, Pinot Noir, Zinfandel, and Syrah. Owner: Ray Signorello Jr. Winemakers: Pierre Birebent and Ray Signorello Jr. Cases: 8,000. Acres: 52 planted of 100.

Signorello Vineyards, 4500 Silverado Trail, Napa 94558; phone (707) 255–5990, Web site www.signorellovineyards.com. Open from 10:00 A.M. to 5:00 P.M. daily, by appointment. Visa, MasterCard, and American Express. Wheelchair accessible.

One of the most intriguing wineries growing on the east side of Silverado Trail promises to be **Darioush Winery,** the passion of Darioush Khaledi, owner of Value Plus Marts and KV Markets in Los Angeles and a 1970s immigrant from Iran.

Darioush Winery's new "Persepolis" design

For years we tasted Darioush wines in an elegant trailer. Now you can visit his magnificent monument to Iran's ancient city of Persepolis, designed by Persian classicists Ardeshir and Roshan Nozari. Jessica Richarson offers a full concierge service in the tasting room to make reservations of all kinds for visitors. Enjoy many fountains, indoors and out, an amphitheatre, and many more elegant features.

When all the building is completed, Darioush Winery will feature formal Mediterranean gardens with plants native to the Middle East, stone from the same source as that used for Persepolis, and an elegant architectural and cultural experience unparalleled in the Napa Valley. You can peruse Persian cookbooks, history books, and substantial cultural brochures. Complimentary fruit juices, pistachios, and Voss Norwejian water are available on request—what a gracious idea!

Darioush smartly hired Bernard La Borie as president and Steve Devitt, formerly winemaker at neighbor Signorello Vineyards.

Fine points: Tasting fee: $10. Featured wines: Chardonnay, Cabernet Sauvignon, Merlot, Viognier, and Shiraz. Owner: Darioush Khaledi. Winemaker: Steve Devitt. Cases: 10,000. Acres: 53.

Darioush Winery, 4240 Silverado Trail, Napa 94558; phone (707) 257–2345, Web site www.darioush.com. Open from 10:30 A.M. to 5:00 P.M. daily Visa, MasterCard, American Express, and Discover. Wheelchair accessible.

Just south of Darioush is **Hagafen Cellars, Inc.** Hagafen originally got its grapes from Rene Di Rosa's Winery Lake Vineyard and now have their own producing vineyard. Be sure to stop here and feel the comfy contrast with the majestic Iranian monument at Darioush. "Hagafen" means "the vine" in Hebrew.

Originally a sociology major at UCLA, owner and winemaker Ernie Weir got interested in viticulture and enrolled in the viticulture program at UC Davis after he traveled to the Napa Valley, and then founded Hagafen Wine Cellars in 1979.

Ernie decided to make premium wines that could also be designated "kosher" by following strict rabbinic requirements, which makes making excellent wines more difficult but pure. Rated as some of the best kosher wines in the world, Hagafen wines are highly sought after, have received loads of gold medals, and have been served at the White House for many elegant events. Hagafen is a must-visit! Closed on Saturday for the Sabbath.

Fine points: Featured wines: Brut Cuvee Sparkling Wine, Chardonnay, Johannisberg Riesling, Sauvignon Blanc, Cabernet Sauvignon, Merlot, Pinot Noir, and Syrah. Owner and winemaker: Ernie Weir. Cases: 8,000. Acres: 20.

Hagafen Cellars, Inc., 4160 Silverado Trail, Napa 94558; phone (707) 252–0781, Web site www.hagafen.com. Open 11:00 A.M. to 4:00 P.M. Sunday–Friday. Tours at 11:00 A.M. by appointment only. Visa, MasterCard, American Express, and Discover. Wheelchair accessible.

Reynolds Family Winery is located south of Darioush Winery and brings together several active participants in the wine business. The Reynolds family shows its respect for natural beauty and the fruits of the land in several ways, including using the incandescent yellow mustard flower on their labels. Every year Napa Valley vineyards are blanketed with mustard used as a form of fertilizer, which has led to the annual Mustard Festival (see p. 323).

Reynolds makes only artisan-handcrafted premium Cabernet Sauvignon at the "foot of the Stags Leap District" in the proposed Silverado Bench appellation.

Fine points: Featured wines: Chardonnay, Pinot Noir, Cabernet Sauvignon, and a blend. Owners: Steve and Suzie Reynolds. Winemaker: Steve Reynolds. Cases: 5,000. Acres: 10.

Reynolds Family Winery, 3266 Silverado Trail, Napa 94558; phone (707) 258–2558, Web site www.reynoldsfamilywinery.com. Open 10:00 A.M. to 4:30 P.M. daily by appointment. Tasting fee: $10. Visa, Master-Card, and American Express. Wheelchair accessible.

To get to **Monticello Corley Family Vineyards,** take Oak Knoll Lane west from the Silverado Trail or east from Highway 29. It is closer to Silverado Trail. Turn south on Big Ranch Road, then east into Monticello's driveway.

You will be amazed at the resemblance of Jay Corley's "Jefferson House" to Thomas Jefferson's estate in Virginia. One-third the size of the original, Corley's is decorated in colonial furnishings and incorporates Jefferson's own designs throughout, since local architect Lou Gerhardt used actual plans from Jefferson's Monticello. Even the vast gardens are planted on Jefferson's principle of having

Monticello Corley Family Vineyards

Honey Glazed Shallots with Monticello Estate Pinot Noir

David Lawson, former chef at Monticello, Napa

4 Tbs butter
2 Tbs vegetable oil
20 whole, peeled shallots
¼ cup Monticello Estate Grown Pinot Noir
¼ cup honey
salt and fresh cracked black pepper

Place butter and oil in large sauté pan. Heat until very hot. Sauté shallots in oil until browned. Add Pinot Noir and simmer 5 minutes. Add honey and salt and pepper to taste. Cover, reduce heat, and simmer 15 to 20 minutes or until shallots are tender. Serve as a side dish with grilled pork or chicken. Serves 6. Serve with Monticello Estate Grown Pinot Noir.

something in bloom at all times. The Corleys honor Jefferson as "the first American viticulturist," among his many other accomplishments.

Monticello wines have been served at White House dinners honoring Thomas Jefferson. Enjoy the relaxing historic atmosphere. The tasting room staff is lively and lots of fun.

Fine points: Tasting fee: $7.50. Featured wines: Chardonnay, Cuvée Cabernet Sauvignon, Pinot Noir, Merlot, Zinfandel, Merlot Chateau M (Sauvignon Blanc/Sémillon blend), and Domaine Montreaux Vintage Brut. Owner: Jay Corley. Winemaker: Chris Corley. Cases: 15,000. Acres: 80.

Monticello Corley Family Vineyards, 4242 Big Ranch Road, Napa 94558; phone (707) 253–2802 or (800) 743–6668, Web site www .corleyfamilynapavalley.com. Open from 10:00 A.M. to 4:30 P.M. daily. Visa, MasterCard, American Express, and Discover. Wheelchair accessible.

Just south of Monticello Corley Family Vineyards, don't miss **Andretti Winery,** of, yes, that Mario Andretti. Andretti has built a lovely Tuscan villa with all the feeling of his native Italy, complete with piazza, bubbling fountain, handworked iron balustrades on the residence, display kitchen for parties and cooking

Andretti Winery's Tuscan villa courtyard

demonstrations, bocce-ball court, and demonstration vineyard. You can buy exquisite rare Andretti race car driving books, shirts, and hats, to say nothing of the great wine.

Bob Pepi, who began Pepi Winery with his father, Robert Pepi, has been with Andretti from its founding in 1995. Indianapolis 500 and Daytona 500 winner Andretti partnered with longtime pal and former Kmart president and CEO Joe Antonini to start the winery.

Fine points: Tasting fee: $5.00; $8.00 with logo glass; estate wines $10.00. Featured wines: Chardonnay, Sauvignon Blanc, Cabernet Sauvignon, Pinot Noir, Pinot Gris, Montona, Merlot, and Sangiovese. Owners: Andretti Wine Group. Winemaker: Bob Pepi. Cases: 30,000. Acres: 50.

Andretti Winery, 4162 Big Ranch Road, Napa 94558; phone (707) 255–3524 or (888) 460–8463. Open from 10:00 A.M. to 5:00 P.M. daily. Visa, MasterCard, and American Express. Wheelchair accessible.

Luna Vineyards, one of Napa Valley's newer wineries, was started in 1995 by George Vare and Mike Moone, neither of whom was new to the wine business. Vare had organized Geyser Peak, and Moone had been in sales with Beringer for years. Combine those talents with those of winemaker John Kongsgaard, a thirteen-year veteran of Newton Vineyards, and you have a full set of "Lunatics."

Vare and Moone bought St. Andrews winery at this location and re-planted the old Chardonnay vineyard to Pinot Grigio, now the largest planting of Pinot Grigio in Napa Valley. The "Lunatic" partners even play classical music for their vines, and the vines respond in kind.

The newly remodeled tasting room offers a quiet respite from downtown Napa or the bustle of the rest of the Valley, with a large tasting bar, cool tile, and enough space to breathe. For now, the "Lunatics" are making only a few Italian varietals and making them very well.

Scallops and Mushrooms in Cream Sauce

from Jim Elder, Vice President of Sales, Luna Vineyards, Napa

2 Tbs butter	2 Tbs cognac
2 Tbs finely chopped shallots	1 tomato, peeled, seeded, and diced
1/4 lb fresh mushrooms, thinly sliced	1/4 cup orange juice
1 lb scallops	1/4 tsp orange zest
salt and pepper to taste	1 cup heavy cream

In a sauté pan melt butter over medium heat; add shallots, stirring for about 30 seconds. Add mushrooms and cook, stirring for about 2 minutes. Add scallops, salt, and pepper, and cook, stirring about 1½ minutes. Add cognac and cook briefly.

Transfer scallops and mushrooms to a sieve placed in a bowl to collect the juice. Add diced tomato, orange juice, and orange zest to sauté pan and cook, stirring about 1 minute. Add cream and any liquid that has accumulated from the scallops. Bring to a boil and cook over high heat for 2 minutes. Add scallops and mushrooms to sauce and heat briefly.

Serve with steamed rice. Serves 4.

Fine points: Tasting fee: $5.00. Featured wines: Pinot Grigio, Sangiovese, and Merlot. Owners: George Vare and Mike Moone. Founding winemaker: John Kongsgaard. Winemaker: Kelly Wheat. Cases: 40,000. Acres: 22 estate vineyards.

Luna Vineyards, 2921 Silverado Trail, Napa 94558; phone (707) 255–5862, Web site www.lunavineyards.com. Open from 10:00 A.M. to 5:00 P.M. daily; tours by appointment. Visa, MasterCard, American Express, and Discover. Wheelchair accessible.

The most southern winery on the Silverado Trail is homey **Van der Heyden,** the pride and joy of Andre and Sande Van der Heyden and their family. Van der Heyden claims to be the only winery in the world that produces a Late Harvest Cabernet Sauvignon. It, like all their wines, is sold only here in the tasting room.

To get here, turn right (west) at the multicolored flags to the Van der Heyden home. There are lots of RVs near the vineyard. The small, homemade, slightly funky tasting room is in the rear. Wooden cutouts of Dutch people hold signs directing you to the tasting room. If the American flag is out, the winery is open.

House cats sit on needlepoint chairs and Oriental rugs, and the ceiling is taped together here and there, but who's looking? A football signed by the whole San Francisco '49ers football team sits in a glass case, alongside Dutch porcelain figurines.

A former furniture-business owner, Van der Heyden first made wine in his basement and gave winemaking classes in a Piedmont, California, lawyer's basement. He used to sell lots of his wine in the Netherlands, a result of the Dutch ambassador to the United States taking some of these wines home, but his wines have become so popular that he now sells it all right here at the winery. He also does wine-tasting cruises and tastings in conjunction with Holland America Line.

Fine points: This place is a don't-miss, once-in-a-lifetime experience. Andre sells chocolate truffles for $2.50 to accompany sips of his rare Late Harvest Cabernet Sauvignon. Tasting fee: $5.00. Featured wines: Chardonnay, White Table Wine, Cabernet Sauvignon, Late Harvest Cabernet Sauvignon, Late Harvest Zinfandel, and Late Harvest Semillion. Owner, winemaker, "and janitor and everything in between": Andre Van der Heyden. Cases: 2,500. Acres: 20.

Van der Heyden, 4057 Silverado Trail, Napa 94558; phone (707) 259–9473. Open from 10:00 A.M. to 6:00 P.M. daily. Visa, MasterCard, American Express, Discover, and JCB. Wheelchair accessible.

Barely south and across the Silverado Trail from Van der Heyden, you might want to stop into the **Soda Canyon Store,** which was recently spiffed up with a new interior design and inviting umbrella tables on the lawn next to the river. Here you'll find excellent sandwiches and salads; Seattle's Best Coffee espresso drinks; last-minute supplies; rare and special local wines from family wineries; hot foods ranging from crab cakes to macaroni and cheese, tri-tip, and rotisserie chickens; juicy gooey stuffed eggs; and lots of local color.

Soda Canyon Store, 4006 Silverado Trail, Napa 94558; phone (707) 252–0285. Open from 6:00 A.M. to 7:00 P.M. Monday–Friday, 6:30 A.M. to 7:00 P.M. Saturday, 7:00 A.M.–7:00 P.M. Sunday. Visa and MasterCard. Wheelchair accessible.

Hardman Avenue, which leads to Silverado Golf Course and Resort and William Hill Winery, is off to the left (east) from Silverado Trail, 1 mile south of the Soda Canyon Store. Hardman follows the ups and downs of the local landscape and runs right into the **Silverado Country Club,** a vast resort focused on golf at two courses. If you're a golf devotee, this is it in Northern California.

Individuals own the cottages here and rent them to guests through the club. The restaurant is elegant, and locals like the Sunday brunch.

Silverado Country Club, 1600 Atlas Peak Road, Napa 94558; phone (707) 257–0200. Visa, MasterCard, American Express, Discover, Diners Club, and Carte Blanche. Wheelchair accessible.

Turn left onto Atlas Peak Road when you reach Silverado Country Club and follow **William Hill Winery**'s signs up the hill. Here you can inhale the most spectacular view in the southern Napa Valley.

William Hill began his winery in 1976, developing prize vineyards on the Silverado bench, and produced excellent Chardonnay and Cabernet Sauvignon. He built this newer winery in 1990. It was so impressive that the Wine Alliance of William Hill, Atlas Peak, Clos du Bois, and Callaway near Temecula in Southern California were bought by Hiram Walker and Allied Domecq in 1991.

Try to visit Friday through Sunday, when the staff offer food and wine pairings, which might include tapenades and fresh local strawberries. Enjoy relaxing,

Wild Mushroom Pâté

from William Hill Winery, Napa

2 cups chicken broth
2 oz dried porcini mushrooms
8 Tbs unsalted butter
1½ cups chopped shallots
3 lbs mixed wild and white mushrooms
1–2 tsp fresh thyme, chopped
4 oz softened cream cheese
2 Tbs fresh chives, chopped
salt and pepper to taste

Heat chicken broth to simmer and add porcini mushrooms. Let soak 20–30 minutes. Strain mushrooms through cheesecloth or paper towels and reserve liquid. Wash porcinis to remove any extra sand.

In a large skillet, heat butter and shallots for 5+ minutes, until golden. Add wild and white mushrooms and thyme and continue to simmer until mushrooms are golden. Add porcinis and strained soaking liquid and simmer until most of the liquid has evaporated. Stir in cream cheese, chives, salt, and pepper. Cook until cheese has melted.

Transfer mixture into food processor and blend until smooth. Serve with sourdough bread or melba toast.

NOTE: Use only those wild mushrooms you can identify.

tasting the wines, and soaking in the view from wrought-iron tables and chairs on the patio.

Fine points: William Hill's wine labels all feature biologically accurate representations of the Chardonnay, Cabernet Sauvignon, and Merlot vine leaf appropriate to the wine in the bottle, with interesting explanations of the leaf's qualities. Tasting fee: $5.00, or $10.00 for six samples. Featured wines: Chardonnay, Merlot, Cabernet Sauvignon. Owner: Allied Domecq. Associate Winemaker: Alejandro Waner. Cases: 90,000. Acres: 130.

Napa Valley view from William Hill Winery

William Hill Winery, *1761 Atlas Peak Road, Napa 94558; phone (707) 224–4477, Web site www.williamhillwinery.com. Open from 10:30 A.M. to 4:00 P.M. daily. Visa, MasterCard, and American Express. Wheelchair accessible.*

As you leave William Hill Winery or Silverado Country Club, continue south on Atlas Peak Road to the historic **Del Dotto Caves** in the old Hedgeside Distillery, one of Napa Valley's "ghost wineries." Farther down Atlas Peak is the Jessel Gallery at the corner of Trancas Boulevard.

The ivy-covered Hedgeside winery building was built in 1885 by Morris M. Estee from Pennsylvania, who became a lawyer, a member of the California legislature, a law book author, and an organizer of the Napa Vinicultural Society. Closed by Prohibition, Hedgeside reopened right after repeal as a new distillery and produced alcohol for the government during World War II. Notice the old local stone exterior, marble floors, and mahogany cabinets.

David and Yolanda Del Dotto have lovingly restored the Hedgeside building and offer their own superb wines in their 200-foot natural limestone caves,

Sauce for Beef or Veal Parmesan

from Delores (Dee) Del Dotto, Del Dotto Caves, Napa

¼ cup olive oil

½ cup chopped garlic

¼ cup chopped parsley

1 yellow onion, chopped

1 cup chopped celery

1 cup chopped bell pepper

1 small can tomato sauce

1 large can whole tomatoes or 10 fresh tomatoes

2 cups chicken broth

1 cup water

½ cup cooking sherry

1 Tbs Italian seasoning

1 bay leaf

1 tsp oregano

1 lb mushrooms, sliced

1–2 lbs round steak or veal (8 oz per person)

4 eggs, beaten

1 cup cracker meal

Parmesan cheese, to taste

Preheat oven to 350° F. Sauté chopped vegetables in olive oil until tender. Add tomato sauce, tomatoes, chicken broth, water, and sherry. Add Italian seasoning, bay leaf, and oregano. Then add mushrooms and cook down for about 10 minutes until sauce thickens and flavors cook together.

Pound and tenderize round steak or pound veal and cut into 4-oz pieces or larger. Dip each piece in beaten egg, then cracker meal. Sauté in olive oil just until crisp. Put meat in large glass or metal baking pan, cover with sauce, and bake at 350° F for 45 minutes. Serve hot with Parmesan cheese sprinkled over the top. Serves 4.

as well as tasting opportunities of rare boutique wines from Del Dotto, and Saddleback as well as David's favorite wines from France and Italy.

Fine points: Tasting fee: $10, including one-hour tour and barrel tasting, or $30 for tour and tasting including paired cheeses with every wine Del Dotto bottles and winemaking secrets. Featured wineries and wines: Del Dotto's estate-grown Cabernet Sauvignon, Cabernet-Sangiovese blend, Merlot, and Cabernet Franc. Owners: David and Yolanda Del Dotto. Winemaker: Nils Venge. Cases: 6,000. Acres: 14.

Del Dotto Caves, 1055 Atlas Peak Road, Napa 94558; phone (707) 256–3332 (Hedgeside), (707) 253–5087, Web site www.deldottovine yards.com. Open from 11:00 A.M. to 5:00 P.M. daily. Visa, MasterCard, American Express, and Discover. Wheelchair accessible.

Now head south to Trancas Boulevard, turn right (west), and you're on your way back to Highway 29.

Salud!

5
Where to Stay in the Napa Valley

Here we list each establishment's price range, most valid from late spring into fall; prices are typically lower the rest of the year. The prices also vary between weekdays and weekends and are subject to change without notice. Often there are discounts for AAA, AARP, or other organizations. Many places require a two-day minimum. Under California law no indoor smoking is allowed.

NAPA

Hotels, Motels, and Inns

The hostelries in the city of Napa are all of good quality and are listed here in order, based on the distance from Highway 29.

Carneros Inn, 4048 Sonoma Highway (#12 and #121), Napa 94559; phone (707) 299–4900; $325–$1,200. Completed in 2004, 90 cottages, 500 to 1,200 square feet, spa, unusual design.

River Terrace Inn, 1600 Soscol Avenue, Napa 94559; phone (707) 866–NAPAFUN, Web site www.riverterraceinn.com.

Embassy Suites—Napa Valley, 1075 California Boulevard, Napa 94558; phone (707) 253–9540, Web site www.embassy suites.com; 205 suites in three Mediterranean style stories; $335–$480 Friday–Saturday. Restaurant in atrium, giant fireplace in lobby, indoor and outdoor pools; pets OK.

Best Western Elm House Inn, 800 California Boulevard, Napa 94558; phone (707) 255–1831, Web site www.bestwestern.com; 17 large units in three stories; $188–$209. Some fireplaces, whirlpool, spa, large hot tub, continental breakfast; no pets.

Wine Valley Lodge, 200 South Coombs Street, Napa 94559; phone (707) 224–7911, Web site www.winevalleylodge.com; $59–$165. Continental breakfast.

Napa Valley Travelodge, 853 Coombs Street, Napa 94558; phone (707) 226–1871; 44 units; $90–$200. Small outdoor pool; no pets.

Napa River Inn, 500 Main Street, Napa 94558; phone (707) 251–8500, Web site www.napariverinn.com; 66 rooms, including 8 deluxe historic rooms; opened June 2000, part of Hatt Building restoration; all rooms have river-boat theme; $179–$349 Sunday–Thursday, $199–$499 Friday–Saturday, breakfast included at Sweetie Pies in complex; pets OK with fee.

The Chablis Inn, 3360 Solano Avenue, Napa 94558; phone (707) 257–1944, Web site www.chablisinn.com; 34 units, some efficiencies; $90–$195. Outdoor pool, spa, and whirlpool.

Napa Valley Marriott, 3425 Solano Avenue, Napa 94558; phone (707) 253–7433, Web site www.vpnational.com/tours/sfonp; 272 units; $109–$279 ("concierge" breakfast). New wing, new furniture, feather beds, Harvest Cafe Restaurant, heated outdoor pool, and spa.

The Chateau, 4195 Solano Avenue, Napa 94558; phone (707) 253–9300, Web site www.napavalleychateauhotel.com; 115 units; remodeled in 2000; some quite large rooms; $89–$239. Outdoor pool, spa, meeting facilities, free movies.

John Muir Inn, 1998 Trower Avenue, Napa 94558; phone (707) 257–7220, Web site www.johnmuirnapa.com; 59 units in three stories, some efficiencies; $125–$210. Outdoor pool, continental breakfast; no pets.

Best Western Inn at the Vines, 100 Soscol Avenue, Napa 94558; phone (707) 257–1930, Web site www.innatthevines.com; 68 units, including deluxe; $99–$259. Outdoor pool, whirlpool. No pets.

Milliken Creek Inn and Spa, 1815 Silverado Trail, Napa 94558; phone (707) 225–1197, Web site www.millikencreekinn.com; new outdoor spa facility, tubs, massage, facials.

Bed-and-Breakfasts

These entries are listed from downtown Napa to farther out in the countryside. They are an architectural historian's delight. Almost all require a two-night minimum stay on weekends.

The Beazley House, 1910 First Street, Napa 94558; phone (707) 257–1649, Web site www.beazleyhouse.com; 11 individualized darkly romantic rooms; $180–$295. This 1902 Colonial Revival was Napa's first B&B (in 1981).

Daughter's Inn, 1938 First Street, Napa 94558; phone (707) 253–1331, Web site www.daughtersinn.com (sister of Beazley House).

The 1801 Inn, 1801 First Street, Napa 94558; phone (707) 224–3739, Web site www.the1801inn.com; 8 rooms, all with fireplaces; $219–$275. A 1903 Queen Anne Victorian.

The Old World Inn, 1301 Jefferson Street, Napa 94558; phone (707) 257–0112, Web site www.oldworldinn.com; 8 rooms in 2 historic houses, cottage; $179–$335. One room with whirlpool, some canopied beds.

Cedar Gables Inn, 486 Coombs Street, Napa 94558; phone (707) 224–7969, Web site www.cedargablesinn.com; 6 rooms; $189–$309. Sixteenth-century–style shingled English 1892 manor house included in *Best Places to Kiss* series of travel guides.

Hennessey House B&B Inn, 1727 Main Street, phone (707) 226–3774, Web site www.hennesseyhouse.com; 10 rooms; $129–$299. An 1889 Queen Anne Victorian and carriage house listed in the National Register of Historic Places.

The Blue Velvet Mansion, 443 Brown Street, Napa 94558; phone (707) 253–2583; 14 rooms, 1 2-room suite; $159–$359. An 1886 Queen Anne Victorian.

Churchill Manor, 485 Brown Street, Napa 94558; phone (707) 253–7733, Web site www.churchillmanor.com; 10 rooms; $155–$275. This 1889 Second Empire mansion is in the National Register of Historic Places.

McClelland-Priest B&B, 569 Randolph Street, Napa 94559; phone (707) 224–6875 or (800) 290–6881, Web site www.historicinnstravel.com; 5 rooms; $189–$269. An 1879 house, elegantly decorated. Large suites, Jacuzzis.

La Belle Epoque, 1386 Calistoga Avenue, Napa 94558; phone (707) 257–2161 or (800) 238–8070, Web site www.labelleepoque.com; 6 rooms; $199–$285. An 1893 Queen Anne Victorian.

Arbor Guest House, 1436 G Street, Napa 94558; phone (707) 252–8144, Web site www.arborguesthouse.com; 5 rooms; December–March 15: $120–$175; remainder of year: $145–$210; some specials. A 1906 Colonial-style home, with choice of fireplace or spa in carriage house or garden.

The Napa Inn, 1137 Warren Street, Napa 94558; phone (707) 257–1444 or (800) 435–1144, Web site www.napainn.com; 14 rooms; $120–$220. An 1899 Victorian on residential street, stained-glass windows. Inn recently acquired the 1877 Bedford House next door, which is in the National Register of Historic Places.

Stahlecker House, 1042 Easum Drive, Napa 94558; phone (707) 257–1588 or (800) 799–1588, Web site www.stahleckerhouse.com; 4 rooms with spas; $152–$232, possible discounts. Country inn beside running creek.

Candlelight Inn, 1045 Easum Drive, Napa 94558; phone (707) 257–3717, Web site www.candlelight.com; 9 rooms with varied classic decor; $139– $299. A 1929 English Tudor with modern amenities including pool, in park on the bank of Napa Creek.

Oak Knoll Inn, 2200 East Oak Knoll Avenue, Napa 94558; phone (707) 255–2200; 3 large rooms; April–Thanksgiving: $285–$550, remainder of year: $285–$395. French-style country inn built in 1984, surrounded by vineyards. Given 4 kisses by *Best Places to Kiss in Northern California.*

Inn on Randolph, 411 Randolph Street, Napa 94558; phone (707) 257–2886, Web site www.innonrandolph.com; 5 rooms; $169–$219; cottages: $299–$319. Lovingly restored 1860 landmark Gothic Revival Victorian.

La Residence Country Inn, 4066 Highway 29, Napa 94558; phone (707) 253–0337 or (800) 253–9203, Web site www.laresidence.com; 20 rooms (including 4 suites); $200–$350. An 1870 Gothic Revival mansion and "French Barn."

Country Garden Inn, 1815 Silverado Trail, Napa 94558; phone (707) 255–1197; 8 rooms; $135–$155. English style inn in an 1860 carriage house beside river.

Resorts

Silverado Country Club Resort, 1600 Atlas Peak Road, Napa 94558; phone (707) 257–0200, Web site www.silveradoresort.com; 280 units; $195–$600. New full-service spa; no pets.

YOUNTVILLE

Hotels, Motels, and Inns

Vintage Inn, 6541 Washington Street, Yountville 94599; phone (707) 944–1112, Web site www.vintageinn.com; 80 rooms; $310–$550. Built in 1970s, several buildings designed by Kipp Stewart. All units have fireplace, balcony or patio, whirlpool tub, handcrafted furniture.

Napa Valley Lodge, 2230 Madison Street, Yountville 94599; phone (707) 944–2468, Web site www.woodsidehotels.com; 55 rooms; by court $302, with deluxe fireplace $332, deluxe suites $445. Renovated in 2001 in Tuscan style, elegant lobby with large fireplace, conference facilities; no pets.

Napa Valley Railway Inn, 6503 Washington Street, Yountville 94599; phone (707) 944–2000; November–April: $75 Sunday–Thursday, $95 Friday–Saturday; May–October: $95 Sunday–Thursday, $125 Friday–Saturday. An unusual inn constructed of 9 old railroad cars (including 3 cabooses).

Villagio Inn & Spa, on Washington Street, Yountville 94599; phone (707) 944–8877 or (800) 351–1133, Web site www.villagio.com; 112 rooms; $310–$1,090 (less December–February); Tuscan design, conference center, spa, AAA rating, 4 diamonds.

Bed-and-Breakfasts

Oleander House, 7433 St. Helena Highway (Highway 29), Yountville 94599; phone (707) 944–8315, Web site www.oleander.com; 5 rooms; December–April: $145–$180; May–November: $160–$195. Two-story French Country home built in 1982.

Maison Fleurie, 6529 Yount Street, Yountville 94599; phone (707) 944– 2056, Web site www.foursisters.com; 13 rooms; $125–$260. If you're looking for a colorful past, this is the place. Built of fieldstone and brick in 1873 as an inn, it became a bordello, then a speakeasy; owned by Four Sisters Company, specializing in historic West Coast inns.

Petit Logis Inn and B&B, 6527 Yount Street, Yountville 94599; phone (707) 944–2332 or (877) 944–2332, Web site www.petitlogis.com; 5 rooms; $125–$149 Sunday–Thursday, $205 Friday–Saturday. Breakfast $20.

Bordeaux House, 6600 Washington Street, Yountville 94599; phone (707) 944–2855 or (800) 677–6370, Web site www.bordeauxhouse.com; 7 rooms; $145–$185. Air conditioning, some fireplaces and balconies, full breakfast. No pets.

Burgundy House, 6711 Washington Street, Yountville 94599; phone (707) 944–0889, Web site www.burgundyhouse.com; 5 rooms; $125–$175. An 1893 French-style stone inn originally built as a brandy distillery, in National Register of Historic Places; full breakfast.

Hillview Country Inn, Yountville 94599; phone (707) 224–5004, Web site www.hillviewinnnapa.com; 3 rooms; $175–$200. A century-old farmhouse in the middle of vineyards, with farm furniture, including four-poster; full breakfast.

RUTHERFORD

Hotels, Motels, and Inns

Rancho Caymus Inn, 1140 Rutherford Cross Road, Rutherford 94573; phone (707) 963–1777, Web site www.ranchocaymus.com; 26 rooms; $150–$430. Beautifully designed Spanish-style, with tiled roof, open-beamed ceilings, courtyard, gardens, handcrafted furniture from Mexico and Ecuador; no pets.

Resorts

Auberge du Soleil, 180 Rutherford Hill Road, Rutherford 94573; phone (707) 963–1211, Web site www.aubergedusoleil.com; 50 rooms (19 are suites); January–March: $450–$2,500; April–July: $525–$3,200; August–November: $550–$3,500; December: $500–$2,800. Southern France country style with wooden shutters. Private entries, terraces, refrigerators, wet bars, elegance throughout. This resort is set on thirty-three hillside acres among olive trees and grew from the world-famous Auberge du Soleil restaurant. If price is no object, then this is the tops in Napa Valley luxury. Three tennis courts, outdoor pool, spa, exercise room, whirlpool. Not recommended for children under 16. No pets.

ST. HELENA

Hotels, Motels, and Inns

Harvest Inn, One Main Street (Highway 29), St. Helena 94574; phone (707) 963–9463, Web site www.harvestinn.com; 54 rooms; $240–$675 (honeymoon suite). Tudor-style stone building situated in vineyard. Two outdoor pools, Jacuzzis, many fireplaces, wet bars, balconies, continental breakfast; no pets.

El Bonita Motel, 195 Main Street (Highway 29), St. Helena 94574; phone (707) 963–3216, Web site www.elbonita.com; 42 rooms, some efficiencies; $129–$269, off season less; pool.

Vineyard Country Inn, 201 Main Street (Highway 29), St. Helena 94574; phone (707) 963–1000; 21 two-room suites, $240. All rooms in this beautifully appointed French country inn have wood-burning fireplaces, wet bar, and fridge; most have balconies.

The Inn at Southbridge, 1020 Main Street (Highway 29), St. Helena 94574; phone (707) 967–9400; 21 large rooms; $275–$450 Sunday–Thursday, $395–$535 Friday–Saturday. Designed by architect William Turnbull Jr., with a winery theme, and completed in 1995.

Hotel St. Helena, 1309 Main Street (Highway 29), St. Helena 94574; phone (707) 963–4388 or (888) 478–4355; 18 rooms; $125–$185 Sunday–Thursday, $165–$175 Friday–Saturday; suite $375. This 1881 historic hotel had deteriorated into a fleabag before it was rebuilt and lovingly restored with its original nineteenth-century feeling.

Wine Country Inn, 1152 Lodi Lane, St. Helena 94574; phone (707) 963–7077, Web site www.winecountryinn.com; 25 rooms; $185–$380. Most rooms in this New England–style inn have antiques, balconies, or decks. Facility has tennis courts, outdoor pool, spa, fitness center, 9-hole golf course, 2 world-class croquet courts (pro Jerry Stark), dining room, and wine center run by "wine tutor" John Thoreen.

Resorts and Spas

St. Helena has two resorts, which are also spas providing mineral and mud baths and a variety of healthy "treatments" to bring pleasure and tone up your system.

Meadowood Napa Valley, 900 Meadowood Lane, St. Helena 94574; phone (707) 963–3646, Web site www.meadowood.com; 85 cottages (50 rooms, 35 suites), and lodges nestled in forest; rooms: $400–$800; suites: $750–$1,215; lodges: $760–$3,585, lower in winter and early spring.

White Sulphur Springs, 3100 Sulphur Springs Road, St. Helena 94574; phone (707) 963–8588, Web site www.whitesulphursprings.com; 28 rooms and 9 creekside cottages; $110–$205 Friday–Saturday, $85–$175 Sunday–Thursday. The oldest resort in Napa County, established in 1852. Set in a canyon, surrounded by redwood and fir trees on 330 acres.

Bed-and-Breakfasts

The Ink House, 1575 St. Helena Highway South (Highway 29), St. Helena 94574; phone (707) 963–3890, Web site www.inkhouse.com; 7 rooms;

$117–$225, full breakfast; no pets. An 1884 Italianate Victorian, in National Register of Historic Places.

Rose Garden Inn, 1277 St. Helena Highway South (Highway 29), St. Helena 94574; phone (707) 963–4417, Web site www.rosegardeninn.net; 4 rooms; $135–$180. Century-old farmhouse set among vineyards.

Shady Oaks Country Inn, 399 Zinfandel Lane, St. Helena 94574; phone (707) 963–1190, Web site www.shadyoaksinn.com; 4 rooms, 2 in 1920s Craftsman house and 2 in 1880s-era stone winery; $189–$249, less off-season. Antiques, patio with pillars entwined by century-old wisteria.

Zinfandel Inn, 800 Zinfandel Lane, St. Helena 94574; phone (707) 963–3512, Web site zinfandelinn.com; 3 rooms; $175–$330 (with lower off-season rates). English Tudor–style house with beautiful landscaping.

La Fleur B&B, 1475 Inglewood Avenue, St. Helena 94574; phone (707) 963–0233; 3 rooms; $195. An 1882 Queen Anne Victorian in the midst of a working vineyard and winery.

Sunny Acres B&B, 397 Main Street (Highway 29), St. Helena 94574; phone (707) 963–2826; 2 rooms; $125–$150. Restored 1879 Victorian originally built for Dr. George Belden Crane, one of the valley's first grape growers, in midst of 20 acres of vineyard.

Ambrose Bierce House, 1515 Main Street (Highway 29), St. Helena 94574; phone (707) 963–3003, Web site www.ambrosebiercehouse.com; 2 rooms, 1 suite; $199–$269 (less off-season). An 1872 Victorian where acerbic journalist Ambrose Bierce once lived.

Adagio Inn, 1417 Kearney Street, St. Helena 94574; phone (707) 963–2238, Web site www.adagioinn.com; 3 rooms; $250–$290 (less off-season). New owners Betsy and Scott Buckwald in 1999 completely redecorated, added new furnishings, VCRs, and complimentary videos to this early 1900s Edwardian home.

Cinnamon Bear B&B, 1407 Kearney Street, St. Helena 94574; phone (707) 963–4653; 3 rooms; $125–$225. A 1904 Craftsman house. Veranda around house.

Bylund House, 2000 Howell Mountain Road, St. Helena 94574; phone (707) 963–9073, Web site www.bylundhouse.com; 2 rooms; $95–$200. Modern Italian villa with sweeping valley views, balconies; children and pets "discouraged."

Hilltop B&B, 9550 St. Helena Road, St. Helena 94574; phone (707) 944–0880; 4 rooms; $145–$225. Modern ranch house in the Mayacamas Mountains 6 miles west of town.

Oliver House Country Inn, 2970 Silverado Trail North, St. Helena 94574; phone (707) 963–4089 or (800) 682–7888, Web site www.oliverhouse.com; 4 rooms; $165–$295. Swiss Bavarian chalet.

Glass Mountain Inn, 3100 Silverado Trail North, St. Helena 94574; phone (707) 968–9400 or (877) 968–9400, Web site www.glassmountaininn.net; 3 rooms; $270–$290; full breakfast. Shingled house with steeple roof. Old wine cave on premises.

Spanish Villa, 474 Glass Mountain Road, St. Helena 94574; phone (707) 963–7483, Web site www.napavalleyspanishvilla.com; 3 rooms; $155–$275. Spanish-style country inn in a wooded valley.

Bartels Ranch and B&B Country Inn, 1200 Conn Valley Road, St. Helena 94574; phone (707) 963–4001, Web site www.bartelsranch.com; 4 rooms; $265–$425. Jami Bartels originally designed this large rock-and-redwood ranch house for a household of children (including a succession of exchange students) in the middle of sixty acres. For honeymooners and lovers there is the "Heart of the Valley Suite," with heart-shaped whirlpool and steam shower for 2.

Elsie's Conn Valley Inn, 726 Rossi Road, St. Helena 94574; phone (707) 963–4614, Web site www.elsiesinn.com; 3 rooms; $185–$275 (call for off-season rates). Rose garden, views from several terraces.

Erika's Hillside, 285 Fawn Park Road, St. Helena 94574; phone (707) 963–2887; 3 suites; $125–$275. Swiss chalet on three-acre hillside garden, terraced rock walls, shaded by oak trees.

Wine Country Victorian and Cottages, 400 Meadowood Lane, St. Helena 94574; phone (707) 963–0852, Web site www.anotherplanet.to; Queen Anne Suite in classic Victorian and 2 cottages on woodland estate; $215–$255, 2 couples in cottage $420. Decorator furnishings.

Rustridge Ranch and Winery, 2910 Lower Chiles Valley Road, St. Helena 94574; phone (707) 965–2871, Web site www.rustridge.com; 3 rooms; $165–$250. Tennis, full breakfast.

CALISTOGA

Spas, Resorts, and Baths

Nowadays the spas and baths are the centerpieces of the resorts in Calistoga, long famed for natural hot springs and mud and mineral baths. In most cases you do not have to stay at the resort to enjoy spa privileges. Here we list only those places with lodging.

Dr. Wilkinson's Hot Springs Resort, 1507 Lincoln Avenue, Calistoga 94515; phone (707) 942–4102, Web site www.drwilkinson.com; 42 rooms, recently renovated, many with kitchenettes; $109–$159; $139–$189 for the Victorian rooms. Sadly, the venerated Dr. John Wilkinson died in March 2004, but his children carry on his resort and spa and mud baths.

Indian Springs Resort and Spa, 1712 Lincoln Avenue, Calistoga 94515; phone (707) 942–4913, Web site www.indianspringscalistoga.com; 16 newly renovated cottages; $185–$500 (3 bedrooms). Calistoga's oldest continuing resort. Site of centuries-old Indian sweathouse called *Ta Latta Lu Si* (oven place in the Mayacamas language).

Calistoga Village Inn and Spa, 1880 Lincoln Avenue, Calistoga 94515; phone (707) 942–0991, Web site www.greatspa.com; 41 rooms; $79–$159. Mineral water spa and pool with views of hills; conference rooms.

Calistoga Spa Hot Springs, 1006 Washington Avenue, Calistoga 94515; phone (707) 942–6269, Web site www.calistogaspa.com; 57 units, all with kitchenettes; $100–$150. Four mineral pools; children OK. Three nights required June 15–September 15.

Eurospa and Inn, 1202 Pine Street, Calistoga 94515; phone (707) 942–6829, Web site www.eurospa.com; 16 rooms; packages include room for 2, spa treatment, and meal. Spa packages, $189–$229, available for both in-house and day guests; lodging only $119–$159. Outdoor pool, Jacuzzi, continental breakfast.

Golden Haven Hot Springs and Resort, 1713 Lake Street, Calistoga 94515; phone (707) 942–6793, Web site www.goldenhaven.com; 30 rooms, many with kitchenettes; $65–$175. Set in oaks with gardens. Spa packages including day guests available.

Silver Rose Inn and Spa, 351 Rosedale Road, Calistoga 94515; phone (707) 942–9581, Web site www.silverroseinn.com; 20 rooms; $165–$250 Monday–Thursday, $195–$295 Friday–Sunday. Spa packages available. Rooms split between 2 lodges, on knoll and in vineyard. Individually decorated rooms.

Hotels, Motels, and Inns

Calistoga Inn and Brewery, 1250 Lincoln Avenue, Calistoga 94515; phone (707) 942–4101, Web site www.napabeer.com; 18 rooms; $75 Sunday–Thursday, $110–$125 Friday–Saturday. This 1882 classic hotel in the heart of town was reconstructed in 1987. It rests above a restaurant and brewpub, which produces beers such as Calistoga Wheat Ale and Calistoga Red Ale. Outdoor dining. Shared bathrooms and showers.

Roman Spa Hot Springs Resort, 1300 Washington Street, Calistoga 94515; phone (707) 942–4441; 60 rooms, 26 with kitchens, 1 with 2 bedrooms; June 15–Labor Day: $106–$200, remainder of year: $86–$168. Various packages.

Mount View Hotel, 1457 Lincoln Avenue, Calistoga 94515; phone (707) 942–6877, Web site www.mountview.com; 34 rooms; $175–$325. Restored 1919 Mission Revival hotel with some cottages. Once Calistoga's prestigious European Hotel, it is listed in the National Register of Historic Places. It now has 9 elegant suites with period furniture, redecorated art deco lobby, outdoor pool, and Jacuzzi; no pets.

Hideaway Cottages, 1412 Fairway, Calistoga 94515; phone (707) 942–4108, Web site www.hideawaycottages.com; 17 cottages, some with kitchenettes; $109–$550 (2 bedrooms). Next to Dr. Wilkinson's Hot Springs Resort.

Cottage Grove Inn, 1711 Lincoln Avenue, Calistoga 94515; phone (707) 942–8400, Web site www.cottagegrove.com; 16 cottages with unique interiors; $235 Sunday–Thursday, $295 Friday–Saturday (lower in off-season). Historically on promenade of Sam Brannan's resort of mid-1880s.

Best Western Stevenson Manor Inn, 1830 Lincoln Avenue, Calistoga 94515; phone (707) 942–1112; 34 rooms; $80–$189. Renovated in fall 2000 after fire. Outdoor pool, sauna, continental breakfast.

Comfort Inn Napa Valley North, 1865 Lincoln Avenue, Calistoga 94515; phone (707) 942–9400, Web site www.callodging.com; 54 rooms, many with views; $70–$199. Sauna, small outdoor pool, whirlpool. Free breakfast. Pre-registration urged to get scenic rooms. No pets.

Carlin Country Cottages, 1623 Lake Street, Calistoga 94515; phone (707) 942–9102, Web site www.carlincottages.com; 15 rooms, 8 with kitchens; $89–$150 Monday–Thursday, $125–$205 Friday–Sunday.

Bed-and-Breakfasts

Larkmead Country Inn, 1103 Larkmead Lane, Calistoga 94515; phone (707) 942–5360, Web site www.larkmeadinn.com; 4 rooms; $150. Early 1900s Palladian-style house. One room with king-size brass bed, antiques; continental breakfast; no pets.

The Elms, 1300 Cedar Street, Calistoga 94515; phone (707) 942–9476 or (888) 399–3567, Web site www.theelms.com; 7 rooms; $135–$245. An 1871

French Second Empire–style house; in the National Register of Historic Places.

La Chaumiere, 1301 Cedar Street, Calistoga 94515; phone (707) 942–5139 or (800) 474–6800, Web site www.lachaumiere.com; 2 rooms, plus a log cabin; $165–$195. A Cotswold cottage with lush garden, patio, $195–$250.

Garnett Creek Inn, 1139 Lincoln, Calistoga 94515; phone (707) 942–9757, Web site www.garnettcreek.com; 5 rooms; $165–$295. Recently remodeled nineteenth-century Victorian; garden, private decks, continental breakfast.

Hotel d'Amici, 1436 Lincoln, Calistoga 94515; phone (707) 942–1007; 4 suites; $150–$225. Formerly Brannan's Loft. In 1998 the Pestoni family—longtime owners of the hotel and Rutherford Grove Winery—completely remodeled this venerable inn and changed its name.

Brannan Cottage Inn, 109 Wapoo Avenue, Calistoga 94515; (707) 942–4200, Web site www.brannancottageinn.com; 6 rooms, including 2 suites; $125–$165. An 1860 Greek Revival inn, the only survivor from Sam Brannan's Hot Springs Resort. The oldest building in Calistoga, fully renovated in 1990s, listed in National Register of Historic Places. No pets.

Sleepy Hollow B&B, 911 Foothill Boulevard, Calistoga 94515; phone (707) 942–4760; $100–$125. Country-style inn.

Christopher's Inn, 1010 Foothill Boulevard, Calistoga 94515; phone (707) 942–5755, Web site www.christophersinn.com; 22 rooms, including 9 suites; $175–$425. Country Georgian–style inn.

Calistoga's Wine Way Inn, 1019 Foothill Boulevard, Calistoga 94515; phone (707) 942–0680, Web site www.napavalley.com/wineway; 6 rooms; $90–$180; mudbath for couples, $69. A 1915 Craftsman home.

The Pink Mansion, 1415 Foothill Boulevard, Calistoga 94515; phone (707) 942–0558, Web site www.pinkmansion.com; 6 rooms; $165–$345. An 1875 Victorian house included in *Best Places to Kiss* series of travel guides.

Calistoga Wayside Inn, 1523 Foothill Boulevard, Calistoga 94515; phone (707) 942–0645, Web site www.calistogawaysideinn.com; 3 rooms; $140 Monday–Thursday, $165 Friday–Sunday. A 1926 Spanish-style home with waterfall into pond, gardens for meditation.

Culver Mansion, 1805 Foothill Boulevard, Calistoga 94515; phone (707) 942–4535, Web site www.culvermansion.com; 6 rooms; $180–$200. An 1875 Victorian and Registered Historical Landmark; outdoor pool.

Calistoga Country Lodge, 2883 Foothill Boulevard, Calistoga 94515; phone (707) 942–5555, Web site www.countrylodge.com; 6 rooms; $130–$195. A 1910 Southwest-style lodge; outdoor pool, Jacuzzi.

Foothill House, 3037 Foothill Boulevard, Calistoga 94515; phone (707) 942–6933, Web site www.foothillhouse.com; 4 suites; $175–$325. An 1897 renovated farmhouse and cottage, recommended in *Best Places to Kiss* series of travel guides.

Scarlett's Country Inn, 3918 Silverado Trail, Calistoga 94515; phone (707) 942–6669; 3 suites; $125–$185. Lawns, pines, vineyards, outdoor pool, fireplace, air-conditioning.

Trailside Inn, 4201 Silverado Trail North, Calistoga 94515; phone (707) 942–4106, Web site www.trailsideinn.com; 3 suites; $165–$185. A 1930s farmhouse with fireplaces, vineyard, air-conditioned, outdoor pool.

Quail Mountain B&B, 4455 North St. Helena Highway, Calistoga 94515; phone (707) 942–0316; 3 rooms; $100–$130, depending on season. Set about 300 feet above highway, on twenty-six acres; full breakfast.

Ranches

Mountain Home Ranch, 3400 Mountain Home Ranch Road, Calistoga 94515; phone (707) 942–6616, Web site www.mtnhomeranch.com; 7 cabins, 7 hotel rooms, 8 cabanas; $72–$142 high season, $52–$120 rest of year. Hiking trails, 2 outdoor pools.

Triple-S Ranch, 4600 Mountain Ranch Road, Calistoga 94515; phone (707) 942–6730, Web site www.triplesranch.com; 7 cabins; $50 for single, $70 for 2, $10 for each additional person; reasonable dinners, particularly steaks, April–December. Hiking, bocce-ball.

ANGWIN

Angwin is a predominantly Seventh Day Adventist town east of St. Helena in the hills up Deer Park Road.

Bed-and-Breakfast

Forest Manor, 415 Cold Springs Road, Angwin 94508; phone (707) 965–3538, Web site www.forestmanor.com; 3 rooms; May–October: $175–$395; November–April: $145–$355. In English Tudor inn on twenty acres, vaulted ceilings.

6

Beyond Wine Tasting

Wining and dining and general gastro-touring are primary activities in the Napa Valley, but there are many other wonderful things to do in this heaven on Earth. Here we tell you about where to find some of the favorites, including ballooning, biking, horseback riding, gliding, and golfing. We also describe less active pursuits, such as getting spa treatments, meandering through farmers' markets, and taking river cruises. So here we go—up, up, and away.

BALLOONING

Ballooning is best and most peaceful in the early morning, when winds are calm and the air is cool. Most balloon flights in the Napa Valley end with brunch in a restaurant, and some include champagne. Most flights cost $115–$185 for adults and $150 for children ages 1 to 16. Here's an alphabetical list of balloon-flying companies. All of them encourage you to bring cameras and personal video equipment.

Above the West, P.O. Box 2290, Yountville, CA 94599; phone (707) 944–8638.

Balloon Aviation of Napa Valley, 6525 Washington, Yountville 94559; phone (707) 944–4400 or (800) 367–6272. Sunrise launches in vintage 1870 balloon; champagne lunch.

Balloons above the Valley, 5091 Solano Avenue, Napa 94558; phone (707) 253–2222.

Bonaventura Balloon Company, 133 Wall Road, Napa 94558; phone (707) 944–2822 or (800) 359–6272; Web site www

.bonaventuraballoons.com. Has been used and recommended by *Forbes* magazine, Universal Studios/ABC-TV, and *Gourmet* magazine. Includes champagne.

Napa Valley Aloft, 6525 Washington Street, Yountville 94599; phone (707) 944–8638.

Napa Valley Balloons, P.O. Box 2860, Yountville 94599; phone (707) 944–0228 or (800) 253–2224. The hour-long flight with Napa's oldest ballooning company culminates with a catered sparkling-wine brunch.

BICYCLE RIDING AND BIKE RENTALS

Napa Valley is an ideal locale for biking because, except for a few slight climbs, it's pretty flat. The heavy traffic makes cycling on Highway 29 hazardous, but bike lanes run the full length of the Silverado Trail. The Trail also has fewer cars and a generally quieter ride and ambience than Highway 29.

Here's an alphabetical list of bike rental (and repair) shops. Most charge about $25.00 a day, or about $7.00 an hour for rentals.

Bicycle Trax, 796 Soscol Avenue at the corner of Third Street, Napa 94559; phone (707) 258–8729. Voted "Best Bike Shop in the Napa Valley."

Getaway Bicycle Tours, P.O. Box 273, Calistoga, CA 94515; phone (800) 499–2453

Napa Valley Bike Tours, 68 Coombs Street, Suite #11, Napa 94559; phone (707) 251–8687. Can pick up at bus terminal.

Palisades Mountain Sport, 1330B Gerard, Calistoga 94515; phone (707) 942–9687. Mountain and hybrid bike rentals and expert mechanics available.

St. Helena Cyclery, 1156 Main Street, St. Helena 94574; phone (707) 963–7736. Rentals of hybrid bicycles for touring; the rental fee includes helmet, lock, water-bottle cage, and rear rack.

Yountville Bike Rentals, P.O. Box 2472, Yountville, CA 94599; phone (707) 944–9080. Includes helmet and a map of Napa Valley.

BOCCE

When was the last time you played bocce? Give it a try. Public bocce courts are located right in downtown Yountville, south of new hotels on the west side of Washington Street. Take the Yountville exit off Highway 29, turn right (east) to Washington Street, and turn right (south) again. The bocce-ball courts will be on your right. Bocce-balls are available at a small rental fee. Call Brent Randol, (707) 483–3630, to schedule free games.

HANG GLIDING

Crazy Creek Soaring, 18896 Grange Road, Middletown 95461; phone (707) 987–9112, Web site www.crazycreekgliders.com. Founded in 1968 as Calistoga Soaring Center, the business moved north up Highway 29 to Middletown in 1991. The glider port is in the center of a 600-acre ranch in the eastern foothills of the Mayacamus Mountains. Your affable glider pilots recommend that you "surf the invisible waves of air breaking over the mountains as your glider swoops and soars on silent wings." Go ahead! Open every day, weather permitting, from 9:00 A.M. to sunset. You may ride solo or as a couple. Maximum combined weight is 340 pounds. The cost ranges from $140 for one person for twenty minutes to $290 for two people for forty minutes.

GOLFING

Not surprisingly, Napa Valley has lovely golf courses. Most of the courses are open to the public; two are not.

Courses Open to the Public

Aetna Springs Golf Course, 1600 Aetna Springs Road, Pope Valley 94567; phone (800) 675–2115. Nine holes, driving range, picnic and barbecue facilities, forty-five minutes north of Napa. Greens fees: $15 weekdays, $20 weekends.

Chardonnay Golf Club, 2555 Jamieson Canyon Road (Highway 12 between American Canyon and Highway 80), Napa 94558; phone (707) 257–8950. Two eighteen-hole courses, lovely setting, restaurant. Greens fees: $50 weekdays, $79 weekends.

Mount St. Helena Golf, Napa Valley Fairgrounds, Calistoga 94515; phone (707) 942–9966. Flat nine holes, barbecue area, RV park, seniors' programs, snack bar. Greens fees: $12.00 weekdays, $18.00 weekends; seniors $9.00 weekdays, $12.00 weekends.

Napa Municipal Golf Course at John F. Kennedy Park, 2295 Streblow Drive, Napa 94558; phone (707) 255–4333. Eighteen holes, cocktail lounge, restaurant, outside deck. Greens fees: $20–$49.

Yountville Golf Course, 7801 Solano Avenue, Yountville 94599; phone (707) 944–1992. Nine holes, restaurant, beer and wine bar, new management, increased length to 3,000 yards, par 34. Greens fees: $14, $10 early bird before 8:00 A.M.

Private Courses

Meadowood Resort, 900 Meadowood Lane, St. Helena 94574; phone (800) 458–8080. Open to members and resort guests only. Members of other clubs may play. Nine holes. Greens fees: $20–$49.

Silverado Country Club, 1600 Atlas Peak Road, Napa 94558; phone (707) 257–0200. Open to members and resort guests only. Greens fees: resort guests $125 and up, members of reciprocal clubs $135, including cart.

TENNIS

The climate in Napa Valley makes for some fantastic tennis. Try out these courts on your visit. They are open to the public and are available on a first-come, first-serve basis.

Public Courts

Calistoga Public Tennis Courts, Stevenson and Grant Streets; phone (707) 942–2838. Four courts, lighted at night.

Napa Public Courts, Napa Valley College (Highway 12 south of Napa); phone (707) 257–9529; and at Vintage High School, 1275 Trower Avenue; Napa High School, 2475 Jefferson Street; and Silverado Middle School, 1133 Coombsville Road, all in Napa.

St. Helena Public Tennis Courts, Robert Louis Stevenson School, 1316 Hill View Place; St. Helena High School, 1401 Grayson Avenue; Crane Park off Crane Avenue; phone (707) 963–5706.

Private Courts

Meadowood Resort, 900 Meadowood Lane, St. Helena 94574; phone (707) 963–3646. Courts open to members and guests only.

Silverado Country Club and Resort, 1600 Atlas Peak Road, Napa 94558; phone (707) 257–0200. Courts open to members and guests only.

TOURS

Every entrepreneur in the Napa Valley is some sort of tour guide, some more reputable than others. Here we identify a few—but perhaps our book will help you be your own best guide.

Antique Tours Limousine Service, phone (707) 226–9227. Tour in elegantly restored, 1947 convertible Packard limousines for an unforgettable Gatsby-esque experience. The cars are equipped with stereo, electronic bar, champagne bucket, gourmet picnic lunch, and privacy window. These limos accommodate up to six passengers in the rear, and two more up front. Rates: $60 per hour weekdays, $80 per hour weekends, both with three-hour minimums. Let your guides select the wineries to visit, or go to those of your choice.

Beau Limousine Napa Wine Tours, phone (800) 387–2328, Web site www.beaulimousine.com. Choose from a variety of packages, from a $49 five-hour wine tour to a $168 dinner on the Wine Train and a five-hour wine tour. Prices are based per person ($168 per person, with a minimum of six people) and include champagne. Stretch limousine or "limousine party bus."

Bridgeford Flying Service (Napa Valley Airport; 707–224–0887 or 707–644–1658) offers sensational tours by air in its Cessna Skyhawk or Cessna Centurion, for groups of any size. Fly over the Napa Valley, Lake Berryessa, Golden Gate Bridge and San Francisco Bay, and along the Pacific Coast and the Russian River in Sonoma County. Make up your own tour—they'll fly you.

Destination: Napa Valley Historical Tours, phone or fax (707) 965–1808. Covers history and historical wineries, native cultures and pioneer settlers, St. Helena's nineteenth-century architecture, Calistoga spas and silver mines, enology, stone bridges, water towers, Victorian homes, landmarks, and ranchos; $39 for a half-day tour.

Napa Valley Wine Train, 1275 McKinstry at Soscol Avenue, Napa 94559; phone (707) 253–2111 or (800) 522–4142. The Wine Train is a more than three-hour, 36-mile ride up the spine of the Napa Valley along the tracks built by Samuel Brannan for the Napa Valley Railroad Company in 1864 and last owned by the Southern Pacific. It is also an elegant gourmand trip into the past, with plush railroad cars and the best Napa Valley wines and excellent food served in a 1917 Pullman Dining Car.

Golden Grain (Rice-a-Roni) Macaroni Company and Ghirardelli Chocolate president Vincent de Domenico perseveres with his Wine Train.

(Mrs. de Domenico told Kathleen, "He never had a model train as a child.") It runs at 11:30 A.M. and 6:30 P.M. weekdays, 8:55 A.M. and 12:30 and 6:00 P.M. weekends. The food is excellent and reasonably priced. Executive Chef: Kelly Macdonald. Reservations are necessary—and mandatory for the winemakers' lunches on Friday. Jackets suggested on dinner train. Prices range from $40 to $140; a children's menu is available.

Royal Coach Limousine Service, Inc., phone (800) 995–7692, has basically the same features as Antique Tours, but without lunch. Royal coach features more traditional cars. Executive Limousine, (707) 257–2949, offers sedans, stretches, and super-stretches for transportation and wine tours, as do Napa Valley Crown Limousine, (707) 257–0879, (707) 226–9500, and (800) 286–8228; Classic Limousine, (707) 253–0999; Odyssey Limousine, (800) 544–1929; Premier Limousine, (707) 226–2106; and Napa Valley Limousine Services, (707) 258–0689, which also has "licensed bodyguards."

Villa Ca 'Toga House Tour, from Sharpsteen Museum, 1311 Washington Street, Calistoga 94515; phone (707) 963–4171. Artist Carlo Marchiori conducts a tour once each May. Shuttle buses from the Sharpsteen Museum; $20 donation to the museum. The museum also sells detailed books for self-guided auto or foot tours.

Walking Historical Tour of Yountville, pick up map at Yountville Chamber of Commerce.

SPAS

Calistoga majors in spas, mud baths, massages, and mineral baths from the natural wells located in the area. Spas abound in Napa Valley; some provide lodging, while others are day spas. Here we tell you about a few of the best. They all take major credit cards and reservations.

Calistoga Spa Hot Springs, 1006 Washington Street, Calistoga 94515; phone (707) 942–6269.

Dr. Wilkinson's Hot Springs, 1507 Lincoln Avenue, Calistoga 94515; phone (707) 942–4102.

Indian Springs, 1712 Lincoln Avenue, Calistoga 94515; phone (707) 942–4913.

Lavender Hill Spa, 1015 Foothill Boulevard, Calistoga 94515; phone (707) 942–4495 or (800) 528–4772. No lodging.

Mount View Spa at the Mount View Hotel, 1457 Lincoln Avenue, Calistoga 94515; phone (707) 942–5789 or (800) 772–8838.

Nance's Hot Springs, 1614 Lincoln Avenue, Calistoga 94515; phone (707) 942–6211.

FARMERS' MARKETS

Every week three farmers' markets attract locals and visitors alike to the freshest of fresh vegetables and flowers from the Napa Valley and other prime California agricultural sources.

Napa Chef's Market, at the Napa Town Center, on and off First Street, Napa 94558; phone (707) 255–8073; Friday 4:00–9:00 P.M., May–September. Good family fun in this downtown mall atmosphere. Many vendors set up on First Street, in the walkways within the open-air mall. Napa Valley chefs give cooking demonstrations at 6:00 P.M., and local bands play live music.

Napa Downtown Farmers' Market, in the parking lot on West Street between First and Pearl Streets, Napa 94558; phone (707) 252–7142; Tuesday 7:30 A.M.–noon, May–October. This market features some local produce in a neighborhood atmosphere. If you time it right, you can stay on for lunch at nearby restaurants.

To get to the **St. Helena Farmers' Market,** in Crane Park, turn west off Highway 29 onto Grayson Avenue between the A&W root-beer restaurant and St. Helena High School, St. Helena, 94574; phone (707) 252–2105, Friday 7:30–11:30 A.M. May–October. This market has the most gourmet atmosphere and delicacies; a must for food lovers visiting the Napa Valley.

7

History of the Napa Valley

Once upon a time there were no grapevines, no wineries, and no wine in Napa Valley. There was just a long, narrow valley—no more than 5 miles wide at any point—with a river meandering southward down to a gigantic bay sheltered from the ocean. At the head of the valley was a dark mountain, which, at 4,343 feet, was the highest for a hundred miles in any direction.

Within the shadow of that mountain, along the shores of the river, beneath the canopy of thousands of oak, fir, and redwood trees, and in the hills that bordered the valley lived more than 5,000 Native Americans. Their ancestors had first migrated to the valley more than 7,000 years earlier.

By the time Europeans discovered the valley, it was home to several peoples, including a Coast Miwok tribe (which the Mexicans named Wappos, a corruption of the Spanish *guapos,* meaning "brave ones"). These people called themselves Mayacamas. They lived northwest of the Pomo and Wintun groups, who had come across the hills from the Sacramento Valley. Tribelets included the Callajomans, near St. Helena and Oakville; the Caymus, around Yountville; the Napa (spelled *Nappa* by the first white settlers), between the river and present-day Napa city; the Ulcas, east of the Napa River; and the Suscol, south toward the bay. A Miwok band, the Huichica, spilled over from Sonoma Valley in the southwest, in what is now called the Carneros District. To the southeast, at the present-day city of Vallejo and beyond, lived the brave and combative Suisun.

Hunters and gatherers, these peoples lived on game, fish, roots, berries, and a rough bread made from acorns ground with a mortar and pestle. There was no agriculture. Simple thatched huts provided shelter from late autumn to early spring; then they set up outdoor camps for hunting and fishing closer to the shores of rivers, streams, and the bay.

Like most Natives of northern California, these first denizens of the Napa Valley were far more hygienic than the white invaders, bathing every day. The men and boys regularly and purposely perspired in a sweathouse, waiting until the heat was nearly unbearable before rinsing off in a cold stream. These buildings doubled as a meeting place for the elders. It was an existence lived in harmony with nature.

FATHER ALTIMIRA "DISCOVERS" THE VALLEY

San Francisco Bay was "discovered" in 1769 by a company of Spanish soldiers led by Gaspar de Portola, who sent Sergeant Jose Ortega circling the bay to find a route to Drake's Bay to the north. Ortega stopped at Carquinez Strait, across the bay from the delta of the Napa River, and turned back. Thus Napa Valley remained little more than a rumor to the outside world for another fifty years. In 1817 a small mission was built in San Rafael as a sanitarium for sick Indians.

When the Mexicans gained independence from Spain in 1822, their government was anxious to counter possible Russian movement from Fort Ross at Bodega Bay, and the Franciscan friars wanted to found a northern mission where food could be produced. A young Spanish priest, Father Jose Altimira, was sent from Mission San Francisco de Assisi (Mission Dolores) in Yerba Buena with a troop of mounted soldiers to locate a likely site. Altimira passed through San Rafael on June 16, 1823, and headed over the first range of hills to the Petaluma plain. He then led his party over the next range of hills eastward and for two days explored Sonoma Valley.

Altimira and his military escort turned east again and rode over the hills more or less along the route of current Highway 121—they were the first non-natives to see the Napa Valley. It was July 1, 1823. After crossing the Napa River, they climbed a hill east of the present-day site of Napa State Hospital, from which they could see the sweep of the southern valley. After another day of exploration, they returned to the Sonoma Valley. There he started construction of Mission San Francisco Solano. It was dedicated on April 4, 1824.

The Napa Valley was just too distant from the mission in San Rafael to be considered for a new mission location. However, this verdant valley and its "pagan natives" easily came within the expanding control of the Sonoma mission.

Some 1,300 Natives were baptized between 1823 and 1834, and as many as 700 lived under serflike conditions in or around the Sonoma mission. The whip was used to enforce rules and punish runaways. Most of the Indians in the Napa Valley avoided living at the mission.

VALLEJO AND THE MEXICAN LAND GRANTS

In 1834 the Mexican government decreed that the missions be "secularized" and their lands and buildings taken over by the government. Sent north from Monterey was twenty-nine-year-old Lieutenant Mariano G. Vallejo, who assumed control of the mission lands covering the region from present-day Petaluma, through Sonoma Valley, and all of Napa Valley.

The first American to settle in the Napa Valley was George C. Yount, guided there in 1831 by twenty-four-year-old frontiersman Guy Freeman Fling, who had "gone native," living with Indians around Monterey and adopting their ways. As he stood on the cusp of Mount St. Helena (not yet so named), Yount reputedly announced to the wind that "in such a place I would like to live…." A North Carolinian with a wandering foot, he had left his wife, Eliza, and their three children in Missouri one day in 1826 to lead a pack train to New Mexico—and never returned. He hunted everything from elk to otters, for a time made shingles, and in 1833 became sort of a jack-of-all-trades for both the San Rafael and Sonoma missions.

When Mariano Vallejo took command of Sonoma, he contracted with Yount to make shingles for the roofs of the mission building he was having restored, and for his own palatial adobe facing the Sonoma eight-acre plaza. Yount told Vallejo that his one desire was to have land of his own, and he knew just the place. With Vallejo's endorsement, on March 23, 1836, Yount received a grant of 11,814 acres in the heart of the Valley, called Rancho Caymus after the Caymus tribe. With the labor of Natives from the Sonoma mission, he built a two-story blockhouse that served as both a home and a bastion from which Indian attacks could be repelled.

In May 1836 Vallejo gave two grants to Nicolas Higuerra: one where Napa City now stands and another in the Carneros—a total of 2,638 acres. Higuerra built an adobe house and planted beans.

A native Californio, born in Monterey like General Vallejo, was Cayetano Juarez, who had come to Sonoma as a seventeen-year-old soldier in 1827. He received a two-square league (8,865 acre) grant called Tulucay, on the east shore of the Napa River, southeast of present-day Napa city. Juarez built an adobe house. Today it is the oldest building still standing.

The next beneficiary of the largesse of General Vallejo was brother Salvador Vallejo. Salvador was granted the traditional two square leagues, which comprised two tracts, called the Trancas and the Jolopa. He built a good-size adobe home for himself off what is now called the Silverado Trail, and two more for ranch workers. Later he received an additional 6,652 acres.

The Berryessa family was given two large grants in 1836 totaling more than 17,000 acres. This land was called the Mallocomas (or Mayacamas), which covered the northern end of the Valley, including today's Calistoga. In 1843 they acquired an even bigger grant, more than 35,000 acres, much of which was then Berryessa Valley and is now under the artificially created Lake Berryessa. This grant was, oddly, named Las Putas Rancho (*puta* is Spanish for "whore"). The name survives as Putah Creek.

Edward Bale was an eccentric, twenty-nine-year-old English physician when he landed in Monterey from a ship out of Boston. For a couple of years, he practiced medicine in Monterey. He wooed and wed the young niece of General Vallejo, Maria Soberanes, converted to Catholicism, and became a naturalized Mexican citizen. While in Monterey he obtained a permit to open a drugstore but began selling liquor, which was against the law. For this he was arrested and fined. Despite Bale's indiscretion, Vallejo appointed him "Surgeon of the California Forces," since he was the only doctor around. Bale and his wife moved to Vallejo's headquarters in Sonoma.

But Bale soon ran afoul of brother-in-law Salvador, accusing him of making a pass at Bale's wife, who was also Salvador's niece. Salvador administered a whipping to Bale. A battered and humiliated Bale responded with two shots at Salvador, missed, and was thrown into what passed for a jail in Sonoma. Through the intervention of the British consul in Monterey, no punishment was meted out.

Despite all this discord, in 1841 General Vallejo arranged a two-square league grant for Bale in Napa Valley—perhaps to get him out of town—between the grants to Yount and the Berryessas, and including the future site of St. Helena. It was officially given the unusual name of Carne Humana—literally "human flesh" (and you thought Whore's Ranch was bad)—which was apparently a corruption of an Indian name for the area. The Spanish and English ears for native tongues were notoriously weak, and the newcomers seemed to care little for the names the Natives gave to land that was being stolen from them.

In the area where Highway 121 links Napa and Sonoma Counties today, another expatriate American, Jacob Leese, who happened to be married to Vallejo's sister Rosalie, received the Huichica grant in exchange for property in Yerba Buena (San Francisco), where he was a trader, and moved to Sonoma.

Two Americans settled and received grants beyond the eastern hills. William Pope, a former trapper and hunter in the southwest who had been living in the Los Angeles pueblo with his Mexican wife and children, was given Pope Valley. Pope had only six months to enjoy his land, for he suffered a near-amputation of his leg when an ax slipped, and he bled to death. The other to receive a land grant was Colonel John Chiles, an old Indian fighter and guide across the plains as early as 1841, who brought Yount's children from Missouri in 1843. The following year he received the Chiles Valley grant. He continued his guiding work, settled permanently with his family in 1852, and built a flour mill.

THE DEHUMANIZATION OF THE INDIANS

But what of the original residents: the Wappo, Pomo, Coast Miwok and all their subnations, the Mayacamas, Caymus, Suscol, Huichica, and Nappa?

Many of the Indians had become restless under mission life. They often ran away, only to be hunted down by the Mexican soldiers assigned to the Sonoma mission. Between 1837 and 1839 a smallpox epidemic killed hundreds of Natives, who lacked immunity to the European malady. Other diseases, such as cholera, and the overconsumption of hard liquor (unknown to the Indians before the Europeans came) reduced the population.

Fearful of Indian attacks, Mariano Vallejo put the problem in the hands of his brother Salvador, who used his small troop of soldiers to show force. In the one outright battle fought in the Soscol (a Spanish spelling of Suscal) area between Mexican soldiers and a large band of rebelling Indians who had invaded from the southeast, the Natives lost more than 200, against the deaths of only two Mexicans.

However, General Vallejo soon entered into peace treaties or alliances with several of the chiefs of neighboring tribes. The most valuable of these arrangements was a long-term pact with Chief Solano (a name given when he was baptized at the mission) of the Suisun. The imposing Solano stood 6 feet 7 inches and was probably the tallest Native in Northern California. He was smart and loyal to Vallejo. The Suisun were willing to fight off any tribes that had any ideas of threatening the Mexican settlement. It was Solano who arrested Dr. Bale when he ran off after shooting at Salvador Vallejo.

George Yount

Nevertheless, the Natives had become dehumanized in the eyes of Salvador and his squad, as well as some of the early settlers. In 1841, responding to reports of cattle being stolen by Natives in the upper Napa Valley, a group of soldiers and settlers under the direction of Salvador Vallejo surrounded a sweat house near Mount St. Helena. As the Indian men and boys stepped out, one by one they were shot and killed—more than a hundred in all. An entire village lost its menfolk.

George Yount, on the other hand, was friendly with the Indians. He hired them to build his blockhouse and an adobe home. Only once were shots fired at Yount's blockhouse. Most settlers found that the Indians were good workers and trustworthy if treated fairly and given respect.

Eventually, some of the Native survivors were induced to move to a reservation in Mendocino County, established in 1856.

In 1841 the Russians at Bodega Bay sent an exploring party eastward to Mount St. Helena, where they planted a copper tablet memorializing the visit on the mountain's western peak and raised a Russian flag. That symbolic effort was the last Russian move to enlarge their influence in California, and they soon sold Fort Ross to John Sutter.

The origin of the name St. Helena has several versions. In 1823 Father Altimira declared that it looked like "Saint Helena on her bier," referring to the sculptured tomb of the saint at the abbey in Rheims. Some suggest that it was named for Saint Helena, patron saint of Russian royalty. Others theorize that the name honored the wife of the governor-general of Siberia and Fort Ross or for a ship of that name that brought supplies to Fort Ross. Take your pick, but Altimira was there first.

THE BEAR FLAG REVOLT

Meanwhile, by 1840 wagon trains were beginning to wend their way west, mostly to Oregon. The Kelsey family train (including Ben Kelsey's wife, Nancy, the first white woman to cross the plains) came down from the Columbia River in 1844 to the Napa Valley. Those who trekked over the Sierra Nevadas stopped at Sutter's Fort and then dispersed from there.

By 1846 about 10 percent of the population of Alta California were transplanted Americans. In Napa Valley there were maybe a dozen houses and a non-Native population of less than fifty.

U.S. President James K. Polk had an acquisitive eye on California and the Southwest. Captain John C. Fremont ("The Pathfinder") was sent roaming about southern Oregon beyond the reach of Mexican authorities, with a crew of "topographical engineers," including scout Kit Carson, with secret orders. In early June 1846 Fremont rode south to Sutter's Fort, where he encountered an irregular company of twenty-two American settlers desirous of throwing off Mexican rule. Fremont urged them to intercept a herd of horses being sent by General Vallejo to General Jose Castro in Santa Clara, and they did so.

Now with first-class mounts, the Americans decided they would capture Sonoma, the frontier capital of Mexican authority. Led by Ezekiel Merritt, a Fremont man, they set out for Sonoma and on June 13 stopped at the Bale rancho in Napa Valley, where they met a group of Napa Valley settlers, whose spokesman was John Grigsby. Eleven of the Napa Valley men, including Grigsby, three Kelsey brothers (Ben, Sam, and Andy), and teenager Nathan Coombs, agreed to become part of the force. Late at night the thirty-three riders headed westward over the hills.

They galloped into the Sonoma plaza shortly after dawn on June 14. General Vallejo was asleep. Awakened by the whoops and hollers of a rowdy-looking band of armed riders, Vallejo invited in the leaders. He offered them brandy and wine and spoke of having a discussion on a "friendly" basis until interrupted by Merritt, who announced that they "meant business" and intended to set up an independent California government. Merritt also placed under arrest General

Vallejo, his brother Salvador, brother-in-law Jacob Leese, and his secretary Victor Prudon.

Nevertheless, General Vallejo ordered wine for all the men under Merritt's command. Some of the men drank too much and began talking about looting, until William Ide, the co-leader of the Grigsby-Ide wagon train, made a stirring speech reminding the invaders that their goal was to form a republic free of Mexico. His oratory caused them to elect Ide the first and only president of the Republic of California.

President Ide prepared a proclamation printed in English and Spanish, while William Todd (nephew of Mary Todd Lincoln) made a flag out of a petticoat and a chemise, drew a red star in the corner, ran a strip of red flannel along the bottom, and drew a bear, which looked for all the world like a misshapen pig. With "poke juice" he printed in the words CALIFORNIA REPUBLC, but then had to blot out the last syllable to insert the missing *I*. The concept of a bear flag was apparently the idea of Napa Valley's Peter Storm, who in later years would display his version with a bear standing on its hind legs. Vallejo and his aides were taken to Sutter's Fort and put in jail, where they languished for two months.

The California Republic lasted just twenty-five days. Before June was over Fremont showed up in Sonoma and incorporated the Bear Flaggers into what he called the California Battalion, making Grigsby commander of one of three companies. On May 13, 1846, the United States had declared war on Mexico, supposedly over a border dispute along the Rio Grande. However, official news of the war did not reach Monterey until the second week in August.

When the Mexican War ended with the Treaty of Guadalupe Hidalgo in 1848, California became American land. All Californios were granted full benefits of American citizenship; and the vast majority of former Mexican citizens, including the Vallejos and the Napa Valley Californios, swore loyalty to the United States.

NATHAN COOMBS LAYS OUT NAPA

George Yount, in 1837, and Dr. Bale, in 1846, built gristmills for grinding grain into flour, as well as lumber mills. The Bale gristmill still exists in Bale Grist Mill Historical Park on Highway 29. Yount's blockhouse, adobe house, and mills are no more, but they are commemorated by a stone monument just north of Yountville on Yount Mill Road.

Nathan Coombs

The principal commercial activities in the Valley before 1850 consisted of cattle raising (hides for leather always made for good business), grain (wheat, barley, beans, and corn), a few orchards, the beginning of a lumber industry, and some quarrying. A primitive embarcadero was built on the Napa River from which Nicolas Higuerra shipped lime on a small sail-powered freight boat as early as 1844.

Nathan Coombs was a young man from Massachusetts who came to the Sacramento Valley in 1843, worked on a ranch, married the boss's daughter, and in 1845 moved to the Napa Valley. Coombs and John Grigsby were hired by pioneer Higuerra in 1847 to build his adobe residence to replace the thatch-and-mud cabin he had built himself. In payment, Higuerra gave them a large plot of land on the Napa River. Coombs soon bought out Grigsby's interest.

Just twenty-one, Coombs laid out the proposed town of Napa on his newly acquired property, using James Hudspeth as surveyor. Then Coombs began to sell lots. The first building erected was Harrison Pierce's Empire Saloon (first things first!), on Third Street near the Napa River. The streets were not marked clearly, and the saloon was framed out in the middle of Main Street and had to be rolled to its proper location. In 1848 J. T. Thompson opened the first store at the foot of Main Street, followed by a store built for Vallejo and Frisbie (the general and his son-in-law), and a spate of others in 1849. The spelling of *Napa* with a single *p* was settled, and the use of *Nappa* was abandoned by 1851.

After the discovery of easy gold in 1848 at Sutter's Mill near Coloma, Napa was virtually deserted by those who rushed to locate a claim and a fortune. Most would be disappointed, but Napa eventually benefited by the influx of immigrants pouring into northern California through San Francisco.

The Napa Valley's first school was established in 1847 by a survivor of the snow-trapped Donner Party, Sarah Graves Fosdick, the first American schoolteacher in California, who taught outdoors under the trees on the Bale property until a school was built for her in 1849. The first public elementary school opened in Napa in 1855.

In 1848 a ferry service across the Napa River was instituted. The first steamboat from San Francisco arrived at the Napa embarcadero at Soscol in 1850, and two years later it blossomed into regular commercial runs three times a week. From there stages and wagons transported passengers and goods northward. Soscol was a natural port, since the Napa River was still navigable there at low tide. Roads from Napa to Sonoma and Vallejo were improved in the early 1850s.

Napa County was one of the original twenty-seven California counties created in September 1850. It originally included present-day Lake County, which was split off in 1861. The first official census in 1850 numbered Napa County's population at 405, with 159 in the town of Napa. In two years it would multiply five times.

With increased population came crime. The most spectacular case stemmed from a minor lawsuit in 1850 between pioneers George Yount and Isaac Howell, which Justice of the Peace S. H. Sellers had decided in Howell's favor. A few days later a relative of Yount's, Hugh McCaully, encountered Judge Sellers at a store and began giving him an earful about the decision. The judge, who was sitting on a barrel, in effect told McCaully to "get lost." In response, McCaully pulled a large knife and stabbed Sellers in the back. The judge died instantly, and McCaully was tried, convicted, and sentenced to hang.

The killer's friends went to the state capital, which was in nearby Benicia (named for General Vallejo's wife) for that year, and convinced the governor to issue a reprieve. Friends of the slain judge were in Benicia and heard about the reprieve, so they chartered a little steamer to race to Napa, while the officer coming with the governor's order headed overland. To delay the officer, they stopped long enough to disable the ferry so that it could not cross the Napa River, thus forcing the officer to ride upstream to the Trancas area before crossing. In the meantime, the judge's friends invaded the temporary jail, located above a general store at Main and Second, threw a rope over a rafter, and lynched McCaully. No witnesses could be found.

Coombs built the American Hotel in 1850, the first hostelry in the Valley, which was followed by the Napa Hotel and inns connected with new saloons. Some of the enterprises were run in structures that were half wood and half tent but were soon replaced by something more substantial. Restaurants, a blacksmith shop, a butcher shop, and houses—a couple built of brick—made their appearance in the early 1850s.

Unfortunately, the quality of so-called streets did not match the development of businesses and homes, for they were unimproved mudholes part of the year and rough trails in summer. Vehicles were constantly getting stuck or tipping over. Inadequate bridges were built across neighboring creeks and the Napa River. Most of them collapsed or were swept away in heavy rains.

Coombs started a freight shipping line and from his ranch, The Willows, became the state's leading breeder of thoroughbred racehorses. He served two terms in the State Assembly. When he died at age fifty-one in 1877, his funeral cortege included 150 carriages and a procession of fifty Napa County pioneers.

THE BIRTH OF ST. HELENA

In 1849 Dr. Bale died, at just forty-one years of age, leading to the sell-off of portions of his property in the 1850s. One of the early buyers was Henry Still. In 1853 Still built a home and a general store in the middle of the upper portion of the Napa Valley. Trouble was, the population was so sparse that he could look miles in each direction and seldom spot a customer. So Still devised a remarkable strategy: He would give away—free, gratis—a lot of land to anyone willing to start a business on the property. Shortly there were takers—a shoe shop, a blacksmith, a wagon-building and -repair business, a hotel, and then two saloons. Houses soon followed, and the Baptists and the Cumberland Presbyterians built churches. The town of St. Helena had been born.

The county rejoiced when the rough trail up the center of the Valley was designated a county road, and development work began in 1852. Five years later a stagecoach service operating throughout the county and over the hills to Clear Lake was founded by William F. Fisher, who had been a station agent for Coombs. However, the main county road was not fully improved with gravel and oil until 1860. A telegraph line was strung between Vallejo and Napa in 1858, seven years before the telegraph reached the west coast from the east in 1865.

THE FIRST TRICKLE OF WINE

Still no wine? Well, barely. George Yount brought a few cuttings from the Sonoma mission vineyard when he first received his land grant in 1836, and he planted and nurtured these vines into a small vineyard, primarily for table grapes. He made a little bit of wine for serving to guests, with the grapes in leather bags stomped by foot.

John M. Patchett was fifty-three years old when he arrived at Napa in 1850, after gradually making his way west. He purchased a hundred-acre tract in 1852. It became known as "Patchett's Addition" to Napa between First Street and Laurel west of Jefferson. On it he planted a vineyard of Mission grapes and an orchard. In 1857 he crushed enough Mission grapes to produce six barrels and 600 bottles of wine, charging $2.00 a gallon. He built the Valley's first winery in 1859, a 50-by-33-foot stone structure in the city of Napa.

Napa Valley's first nurseryman was Simpson Thompson, a Pennsylvanian who arrived in 1852 and, with his brother, William, purchased a hundred acres of the Soscol Rancho south of the town. With a system of ditches and dikes, he established orchards and a great variety of fruit-bearing trees and plants, including forty-five varieties of grapevines by 1856. Just north of Napa at Oak Knoll, another orchardist, Joseph Warren Osborne, was also experimenting, in his case with 3,000 vines of European varietals, including Zinfandel, by the late 1850s.

Hungarian Augoston Haraszthy had fled his home country after an abortive attempt by army officers to liberalize the autocratic rule of the Hapsburgs. In Wisconsin, Illinois, and California, he had unsuccessfully searched for the ideal location for growing wine grapes equal to those of Europe. He wangled a job as the director of the U.S. mint in San Francisco but was sacked when accused of keeping the gold-dust sweepings.

Haraszthy visited the old Mission vineyard and Vallejo's little home vineyard at Sonoma in 1856. He believed that he had found the soil and climate he had been seeking. He purchased land and planted a vineyard, which he named Buena Vista, and crushed some purchased grapes in 1858. Ironically, he had to look to Napa Valley for cuttings of European varietals (vinefera) to plant his vineyard in Sonoma. He purchased cuttings of a relatively unknown varietal, Zinfandel—from either or both Simpson Thompson and Joseph Osborne—and planted them at Buena Vista.

In 1863 Osborne was shot and killed in his orchard by a disgruntled laborer in a dispute over a bounced paycheck. The murderer was convicted in a jury trial and became the first person legally hanged in Napa County.

Haraszthy inveigled the governor of California to appoint him official emissary to vineyardists in Europe so that he could explore the potential of bringing varietals to supplant the second-rate-tasting Mission grapes. He returned in 1861 with 100,000 seedlings for Sonoma and for distribution throughout California. Haraszthy's pioneering efforts launched California's commercial wine business big time and gave Sonoma Valley a running head start.

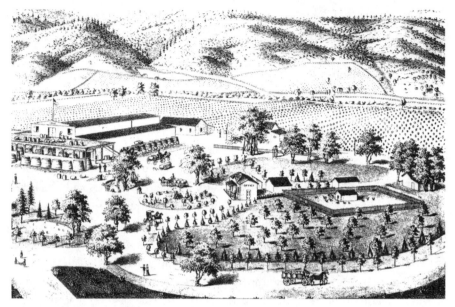

Charles Krug Winery—1870s

However, Napa Valley was already getting on the wine-grape bandwagon, without Haraszthy's help. Patchett, Thompson, and Osborne may have been first, but others were soon also busy. The number of vines climbed from 22,000 in 1856 to 90,000 in 1858, when there were thirteen grape growers in the Valley, including the Valley's first woman vintner, Lolita Bruck, in the St. Helena area.

Charles Krug had emigrated from Germany, winding up in California in 1852. He planted a small vineyard in San Mateo County, south of San Francisco, as had Haraszthy, and then became an assistant to the Hungarian at the U.S. Mint. Krug followed Haraszthy to Sonoma and planted 16,000 vines on land he had purchased next to Haraszthy's Buena Vista.

Using an apple press at Patchett's place, Krug crushed some grapes for wine in 1858. The next year he made a little wine for Dr. Bale's widow, and in 1860 he became winemaker for George Yount's small vineyard. Then, in rapid succession, Krug put his Sonoma vineyard up for sale in August 1860, became engaged to Caroline Bale—heiress to a substantial portion of the unsold lands of the late doctor—and married her the day after Christmas.

The newly wed Krug found himself master of a tract of 800 acres, and he planted 15,000 vines there in 1861. Within a few years he extended the planting to 60,000 vines, two-thirds in European varietals. Starting with a crude

14-by-20-foot wine cellar, each year Krug expanded, until he eventually built a new, concrete two-story winery.

Parallel to Krug's vineyard development was the operation of Dr. George Belden Crane, a physician '49er from New York, who had been director of the City and County Hospital in San Jose before moving to Napa Valley in 1858. Crane planted vines in St. Helena—the first in that township—and produced 300 gallons of varietal wines in 1864, a year before Krug's first vintage. Crane hired Swiss-born Henri Alphonse Pellet away from Patchett to manage his vineyard, where he planted sixty varieties.

Highly respected for his viticulture knowledge, Pellet eventually created Pellet & Carver Winery, with financing from partner D. B. Carver. Pellet also built the first steam-powered mill in the Valley. He later was elected city trustee of St. Helena and to two terms as a county supervisor.

Various pioneers had begun planting small vineyards along with orchards and grain, including John York, David Hudson, and George Tucker. Cattle raising suffered a blow in the late 1860s from legislation that permitted fencing of open spaces. The number of cattle in Napa County dropped from more than 10,000 to 5,000 by the end of the decade. However, well into the 1870s dairies were still the leading agricultural occupation in the Napa Valley.

George Yount died in 1865, leaving a will that provided that several thousand of his acres be divided into fifty-acre parcels and sold at public auction. The sun had set on the day of the giant land-grant ranchos. Two years after his death, the community that had grown up around his home, which he had named Sebastopol, officially changed its name to Yountville.

SAM BRANNAN'S CALISTOGA, SARAFORNIA

In 1848 John York had discovered natural hot springs on the Bale property. This was later named White Sulphur Springs, and a hotel catering to the wealthy of San Francisco was erected in 1855. When it burned down in 1859, it was rebuilt, and the grounds were developed by one Swen Alstrom, who built cottages and other amenities, including a private telegraph line to the financial district of San Francisco.

Sam Brannan was something of a rogue. He arrived in 1846 at the village of Yerba Buena, in charge of a shipload of Mormons and money to purchase land for Mormon colonies in California. He used some of those funds to acquire property for his own account. He opened a general store in the future San Francisco but needed more population to make it the success he envisioned.

While visiting Sutter's Fort, Brannan heard the details of James Marshall's gold discovery at Sutter's Mill. John Sutter was desperate to keep it quiet, fearing that an influx of settlers would overrun his inland empire. Brannan, with his eye on the gold ring, did not care what Sutter wanted to hide, for the Mormon colonist wanted California—just acquired by the United States—to be flooded with immigrants, who would be his customers. So he took a small bag of gold dust back to San Francisco and dramatically rode through the center of the little village shouting, "Gold! Gold at the American River!" The secret was out, the gold rush began, and Brannan emerged a rich man.

Learning of the hot waters that bubbled to the surface in the northern part of the Napa Valley (actually then called The Springs Township), in 1859 Brannan paid top dollar for a large parcel of property. He immediately began development of a resort for the recreation of the people of the San Francisco Bay Area—particularly the wealthy. He spent money on bathhouses, into which was pumped sulfurous hot water from the ground, twenty-five cabins, and a lavish community plan. After several drinks one night, he described his scheme to create a West Coast resort in the mode of the upscale Saratoga in New York: "It'll be the Calistoga of Sarafornia," he slurred. And the name stuck.

Brannan's Calistoga resort opened with a huge splash in 1862, when a chartered ship full of guests from San Francisco was met by coaches and carriages that carried them from the dock in Vallejo to a huge feast. There was champagne for the rich and influential—and free kegs of beer and barbecue for the multitudes. They found a racetrack, swimming pool, skating rink, exotic landscaping tended by Japanese gardeners, and an observatory from which to view the entire utopia. There was a private water reservoir, a distillery for making brandy, a winery, and 100,000 newly planted vines.

Almost immediately businesses to support this operation were attracted to Calistoga. But the road north of St. Helena was still too bumpy for the tender backsides of the ladies whom Brannan hoped to attract. What he and the Valley needed was a railroad. The legal means were in place.

THE NAPA VALLEY RAILROAD

Ex-judge Chancellor Hartson from Napa was elected to the State Assembly for the 1864 session. Shortly before taking office Hartson organized the Napa Valley

Railroad Company. Assemblyman Hartson's number-one priority was to shepherd a bill chartering the company with the right to receive subsidies of between $5,000 and $10,000 per mile, to be guaranteed by a bond issue submitted to the voters of Napa County. What the proposed railroad needed was a promoter, and Brannan was that man.

The bond issue was adopted easily, $60,000 was subscribed to meet additional costs (including $30,000 advanced for railroad cars by the corporation's directors), and farmers along the proposed route gladly donated the right-of-way.

The inaugural train ran from Soscol to Napa in June 1865. With the help of another Hartson bill, the Napa Valley Railroad was extended to Calistoga by August 1868. Winery owners were ecstatic, since they and other agriculturists could ship cheaply and travel from doorstep to San Francisco via rail and ferry in just six hours. In 1869 the Napa Valley line was connected to a railway running from Vallejo to Sacramento, and shortly thereafter with the transcontinental railroad.

But life was going downhill for the enthusiastic Brannan. In April 1868, when he personally tried to foreclose on a neighboring mill, the owner shot Brannan, hitting him eight times from neck to hip. Brannan almost died. Still, as the first train arrived in Calistoga in August, Brannan had recovered sufficiently to throw a party at his resort for 3,000 celebrants. It was to be his last hurrah.

To finance the elegance of his Calistoga Hot Springs resort and extravagant living, Brannan had borrowed heavily, with the resort put up as security. The Sacramento Savings Bank finally foreclosed in the early 1870s. In 1879 the bank began selling off twenty-five- to 200-acre parcels. His wife divorced him, he drank more heavily, and he died impoverished in Southern California.

Calistoga (population 1,259 in 1880) and the railroad were his heritage to the Napa Valley.

The Napa Valley Railroad also went into foreclosure and was purchased by the California Pacific, and through a series of mergers it eventually became part of the Southern Pacific.

PIONEER DAYS IN THE 1860S AND 1870S

Crimes in Napa Valley during the 1860s and 1870s were often exotic. There was the case of the adventurer Gilbert Jenkins, for instance, who killed the father of a seventeen-year-old woman of both beauty and wealth whom he hoped to seduce with her dad out of the way. Not only was he caught, but he also owned up to eight murders across the country before he was hanged.

Winery owner John Patchett was slipped knockout drops in his drink so that he would be unconscious; then two masked men terrified his housekeeper, ransacked his home, and burglarized the houses of the public administrator and a former judge. Hunters spotted two suspicious men by a cave in the hills. A notorious ex-con named "Black Jack" Bowen and his partner were soon surprised by a posse and packed off to San Quentin Prison.

When the manager of a bar with a bordello upstairs fired at some unruly customers outside and killed one, he was soon taken from jail by a small mob. They hanged him from a tree, apparently to prevent a trial in which testimony of witnesses would have revealed the names of the customers of the bawdy house. A conspiracy of silence protected the lynchers.

With a population in which men outnumbered women ten to one, in the 1860s Napa County held the distinction of having the most prostitutes per capita of any county in California.

To illuminate Napa city, a gas company was founded in 1867, with sixty-five customers. Lamps on principal streets were lit by a lamplighter who rode around town at dusk. The first public library opened in 1870. An imposing stone library (The Goodman Library) erected in 1902 is now the home of the Napa County Historical Society.

Adding to the tourist attraction of the Valley was the discovery in 1870 of the petrified forest—ancient trees turned to stone—by "Petrified Charlie" Evans, northwest of Calistoga.

NAPA WINES GROW AND GO NATIONAL

On the heels of Krug and Crane came Jacob Schram, an unlikely vintner in an unlikely place, who purchased his first land in Napa Valley in 1862. A barber by trade, Schram landed in New York from Germany in the mid-1850s and headed to San Francisco. Upon visiting Napa Valley Schram became convinced that he could succeed at making wine. The only land he could afford was a chaparral- and tree-studded slope of the Mayacamas north of St. Helena. He cleared a patch of land himself, cut hair at White Sulphur Springs resort on weekends to put food on the table, and in 1863 planted his first vineyard. By 1867 he had 14,000 vines.

Schram's first vintage encouraged another German, San Francisco wine merchant Gottlieb Groezinger, to buy vineyard land, plant vines, and produce wines. Groezinger was particularly interested in improving the quality of California wine to provide real competition for European wines being sold on the East Coast market. A San Francisco outfit, Kohler & Frohling, had begun shipping some California wines and brandy around the Horn to New York as early as 1857, but the price received (75 cents a gallon on average) was well below that of French and German products, and the reputation for quality was shaky at best.

Schram and Groezinger were the harbingers of a new wave of winemakers in the Napa Valley, including brothers John and Theodore Sigrist in Brown's Valley, west of Napa, who built a winery with a capacity of 100,000 gallons. John Lewelling was a noted nurseryman, whose brothers had brought west the seedlings that launched Oregon's agriculture. He had planted orchards in what he called Fruitvale (now a neighborhood in Oakland) and gave up his post as a county supervisor in Alameda County to move to Napa Valley, where he planted orchards and 35,000 vinifera grape vines in St. Helena.

By 1866 there were 700,000 grapevines in Napa County. However, wheat, particularly in Berryessa Valley, was still the leading farm product, ground into flour by local mills.

Alexander J. Cox, a printer who came west as a soldier with the regiment that took over Sonoma during the Mexican War, had started a newspaper there called *The Sonoma Bulletin*, which he shut down in 1855. He carted his old press to Napa and, on July 4, 1856, began publishing the four-page *Napa County Reporter*, which was erratically issued until 1858, when Cox moved on to Healdsburg. New ownership, led by the hard-drinking but popular writer R. T. Montgomery, took over and acquired a new press. For several years it was an influential newspaper. It went out of business in 1888.

The Napa Register came out as a weekly in August 1863 and went through a series of ownership changes. Popular from the outset, in December 1872, under new publisher G. W. Henning, the *Register* became a daily. It is still Napa's principal newspaper. Other journalistic attempts failed after short runs, including *The Pacific Echo*, a rabidly anti–President Lincoln paper—which died the day of Lincoln's death.

The *St. Helena Star* was founded in 1874 as a weekly newspaper. It has been in continuous publication ever since—one of the oldest weeklies in the state. Another survivor of the numerous pioneering publication efforts in the county is *The Weekly Calistogan*, which first came off the press in 1877.

Cinnabar, the ore that contains quicksilver, was discovered in Pope Valley in 1861 and later near Oakville. Various attempts were made to mine and process the ore, but the work stumbled along for a decade under various companies until the major mining efforts were consolidated under the Napa Mining Company in 1873. For more than sixty years thereafter, quicksilver was profitably mined in substantial amounts.

Silver mining in Napa County was a flash in the pan. In 1872 a vein of silver was discovered north of Calistoga, on the southeast slope of Mount St. Helena, near the toll road to Lake County. Alexander Badlam, a nephew of Sam Brannan, staked a claim, laid out a small town called Silverado City, dug a mine, and built a mill to process the ore. This activity triggered a silver rush, which drew 1,500 people, a host of mining claims in the hills, the Silverado Hotel, a stage station, several businesses, and the inevitable saloons. The silver was played out by the autumn of 1875 (the total was a puny $92,000 worth), and the population disappeared.

Chinese laborers had first arrived in the Valley after they had been drawn to the gold diggings in the mountains as early as 1849. By the time they had helped substantially to build the transcontinental railroad, completed in 1869, at least 400 had settled in the Valley. Grouped in "Chinatowns" on the outskirts of Napa, St. Helena, and Calistoga, they provided the brawn for building stone fences (which still exist), planting vineyards, digging mines, and harvesting crops. Some worked as cooks, gardeners, and household servants, while a few operated their own laundries. When the Chinese Exclusion Act was enacted in 1882, barring further immigration, Terrell Grigsby, owner of the Occidental Winery, personally fought off a mob intent on chasing out his Chinese workers. The wine industry needed their loyal, inexpensive labor. Eventually most Chinese migrated to the cities.

THE BUILDING BOOM

The Uncle Sam Wine Cellar was founded in 1870, in a large building at the corner of Main and Fourth Streets in Napa, with a storage capacity of 500,000 gallons for the bulk wine it made from the grapes of several growers. The structure still stands, albeit substantially altered.

Napa was chosen by a state commission as the site of the State Hospital for the Insane (now called Napa State Hospital). A five-story Gothic institution with seven towers was subsequently erected on spacious grounds southeast of

Palace Hotel in the 1870s

Napa city, where Father Altimira had first camped. Despite its rococo facade, it was extremely modern in amenities for the time (fire hydrants on every floor, lots of toilets, central steam heating, and gas lighting). In 1875 it opened to handle more than 600 patients.

A courthouse of classic design was dedicated in February 1879, built for a cost of $51,000 in downtown Napa. Amazingly, it still functions as Napa County's courthouse, almost without change from the day it opened, except that a nonfunctional tower was added and then later removed.

In Napa city the luxurious Palace Hotel, with seventy rooms, all with baths and fireplaces, opened in 1875 at the corner of Third and Soscol. When the old Napa Hotel, dating from 1851, burned down in 1884, it was immediately replaced by a brick structure just south of the Opera House. There was also the wooden Revere House, which was the largest building in Napa to collapse during the 1906 San Francisco earthquake.

Napa Valley was fortunate that Mark Strong, a photographer with an artistic eye and feel for history, came to town in 1886. From then on, almost to the day of his death in 1946, Strong recorded on film the changes in the city and Valley.

With the transcontinental railroad's completion in 1869, it became easy to ship goods to the east and practical to travel to New York and other business centers. Dr. Crane visited his native New York to promote Napa Valley wines, met with skepticism, and was discouraged. Charles Krug followed, and his enthusiasm carried the day. Krug's greatest contribution was to convince the eastern wine distributors that the best wines in the Western Hemisphere came from the Napa Valley.

Krug, Jacob Beringer (Krug's former winemaker who launched his own winery, Beringer Brothers, in 1875), and M. G. Ritchie established the Napa Valley Wine Company to combine forces to distribute wines. John Lewelling and H. W. Crabb, who had followed Lewelling from Alameda County to found his Hermosa Vineyards in Oakville, emulated the Krug/Beringer/Ritchie example by contracting with eastern distributors. Lewelling and Crabb pioneered the shipment of grapes packed in freight cars filled with ice.

The results are in the statistics. By 1873 Napa Valley wines were being shipped to the East Coast by the carload. The gallonage of wines vinted reached almost 500,000 that year, a far cry from the piddling 8,745 in 1860. Still, Napa County continued to trail Sonoma County in production. In 1877 Napa produced 640,000 gallons and Sonoma, 2,500,000. But that was soon to change. Total shipments of California wine to the Midwest and East Coast climbed to 1,243,000 gallons in 1878. In 1880 Crabb produced 300,000 gallons and Krug, 280,000. While Krug was the chief publicist for Napa's wines, Crabb became the Valley's most innovative experimenter. He later gave twenty acres to the University of California for enological testing.

STEVENSON AND OTHER CHARACTERS

An itinerant Scottish travel writer, Robert Louis Stevenson, showed up in Calistoga in the summer of 1880, on a honeymoon with his wife, Fanny, a divorcee he had just married. The Stevensons lived for most of the time at the old hotel in the ghost town of Silverado. The writer and winemaker Schram became friends who talked for hours. Three years later Stevenson burst on the literary world with his novel *Treasure Island,* in which the physical description of the island's interior was based on Mount St. Helena. In November and December 1883, Stevenson had two articles published in the magazine *Century Illustrated* about the Stevensons' stay, which were later issued in a small volume entitled *Silverado Squatters.*

The tubercular Stevenson died in 1894, before anyone in the Valley paid any attention to this book. His death was reported in just half a dozen lines in the *St. Helena Star,* with no mention at all in the *Register* or *Calistogan.*

Several prominent characters moved to the Valley during this period, including S. Clinton Hastings, chief justice of the California Supreme Court and founder of the state's first law school, Hastings College of the Law in San Francisco (now part of the University of California system); and Lilburn W. Boggs, former governor of Missouri, who had come west expecting to be appointed first governor of California. The highest West Coast office that Boggs achieved was alcalde (mayor/judge) of Sonoma. Former speaker of the Assembly and losing candidate for governor and U.S. Senate, Morris M. Estee built a winery on Atlas Peak in 1885 (it is still used for wine storage).

Former Union general and U.S. Senator John F. Miller purchased a large parcel east of Napa, upon which he built a fourteen-room mansion, which today is the Silverado Country Club.

Concerned with the condition of disabled veterans of the Civil War, the San Francisco chapter of the Grand Army of the Republic (GAR), with the assistance of a Mexican War veterans group, bought 910 acres just west of Yountville for $17,500 in 1881. With donated funds, the Veterans' Home Association opened its first building in 1884, to house forty-two veterans. Soon the legislature approved expense payments of $150 a year for each resident. The Veterans' Home expanded rapidly but was always short of funds. Finally, in 1897 the state took over the Home's operation, when it was the residence for 800 veterans.

OF BERINGER, NIEBAUM, AND BANDITS

Over the hills to the west, disaster struck the vineyards of Sonoma Valley, where phylloxera, plant lice that attacks vine roots, caused most vineyards to wither and die between 1876 and 1879. For the first time Napa County surpassed Sonoma County in wine production. Napa vineyardists breathed a collective sigh of relief that they had been spared. Their elation would prove to be premature.

New and larger wineries were constructed in the late 1870s and early 1880s. Jacob Beringer, with financing from brother Frederick in New York, built a three-story winery with a deep, cool cave in St. Helena. Nearby, John C. Weinberger erected a winery in 1876, which he soon enlarged to hold 180,000 gallons—it is now the location of the Markham Winery. In 1874 Napa grocer Giuseppe Migliavacca became the first Napa resident of Italian heritage to develop a major winery, and he was followed by Vittorio Sattui in 1885 and Anton Nichelini shortly thereafter. As early as 1882 some Valley growers began using smudge pots to ward off extreme frosts—now often replaced by more environmentally acceptable wind machines. In 1888 Greystone Winery in St. Helena became the first run by electricity from a gasoline-powered generator.

Gustave Niebaum, a Finnish sea captain, had made a fortune in the northern Pacific fur trade. When he became interested in winemaking, he had the time, money, and inclination to be a perfectionist. West of the hamlet of Rutherford, Niebaum found a poorly maintained attempt at a winery, which he bought. Its name: Inglenook (Scottish for "a seat by the fire").

During the early 1880s Niebaum expanded and cleared his acreage, went to Europe and brought back cuttings, read every book he could get in any language about winemaking, ordered the best equipment, and created cellars to maintain constant temperatures. And, to house it all, he had constructed an imposing stone mansion that overlooked the plain. Seven years after Inglenook's first wine release, Niebaum's winery was given the award for "excellence and purity" at the Paris Exposition in 1889. Other Napa Valley wineries brought home twenty medals—including a gold for Migliavacca—more than any American wine region. Napa Valley had secured its place on the international wine map.

Stagecoaches and delivery wagons that climbed the hills from Napa Valley to Lake County were occasionally robbed in the 1880s. In the '90s the highwaymen became a plague, time and again forcing drivers to "throw down the box" and passengers to empty their pocketbooks. In May 1895 one of a pair of robbers beat up a Chinese passenger, immediately casting suspicion on one Buck English, known to be a foul-mouthed Sinophobe. Sheriff George McKenzie put together a four-man posse, which included twenty-three-year-old District Attorney Ted Bell. They trailed English to the village of Monticello in Berryessa Valley. A Wild West–style chase followed, in which English was punctured by fifty-two shotgun pellets before being captured more dead than alive.

A couple of years later, David Dunlap, the leader of the local Democratic Party, was elected sheriff. With prior experience as a sheriff in Nevada, Dunlap looked like a Central Casting version of the Western lawman: tall, erect, with a drooping mustache and steel-blue eyes. A new gang of stage robbers went into business, and the frustrated sheriff kept losing their tracks in the hills. One newspaper began referring to Dunlap as "no catch-'em Dave." Finally, he and his deputies chased down and arrested the county's last highwayman. (The newspaper was unimpressed, calling the sheriff "no catch-'em Dave, except once.") At the turn of the twentieth century Napa was the scene of California's last public hanging, with tickets issued to spectators.

Frank Coombs, son of Nathan Coombs, was the county's most successful political figure. He was elected district attorney in 1880 at age twenty-seven as a Republican. His next successes were his election to the state assembly on seven occasions between 1887 and 1927. Coombs was twice chosen speaker of the assembly; was appointed U.S. minister to Japan in 1892; served a term in Congress; and for several years was U.S. attorney for Northern California.

His son, another Nathan Coombs, was elected state senator as a Republican in the 1950s. The sister of Senator Coombs married the son of Sheriff David Dunlap. Their union produced four sons: a farmer and three lawyers. One of them, Frank Dunlap, was Napa city attorney for many years. Another, Democrat John F. Dunlap, was elected to four terms as state assemblyman and served four years as state senator in the 1970s. He and his wife, Janet, still reside on a portion of founder Nathan Coombs's ranch.

KRUG'S DEATH AND THE
BATTLE AGAINST PHYLLOXERA

A slump in wine prices drove Charles Krug into bankruptcy in 1885—he had gotten easy credit based on his reputation—and forced the sale of his winery to a San Francisco banker. His wife, Caroline, went from eccentricity—like her father, Dr. Bale—into outright insanity before she died in December 1885. Krug, the man who loved to talk to reporters, lost the power of speech. The "Father of Napa Valley Wines" died on November 1, 1892.

The insidious phylloxera had made their migration gradually from Sonoma Valley into vineyards in the Carneros region, shared by Sonoma and Napa Valleys, by 1890. In 1893 a report commissioned by the state Board of Viticultural Commissioners revealed that 244 out of 577 Napa County vineyards showed signs of the voracious louse.

Napa's wine producers benefited from Sonoma's experience with the bug, since Sonoma grape growers had found some rootstock resistant to phylloxera. There was also the expertise available from the University of California's new enological study department. The state board pointed out that Judge John Stanly's vineyards in Carneros had not been harmed by the louse since they were planted in *Riparia* roots, proving they were resistant.

University of California professor Arthur Hayne argued that the rootstock *Rupestris* was superior to *Riparia* in California soil. Although most growers were slow to accept Hayne's view, George Schonewald met with remarkable success with grafting to *Rupestris*. A new face on the scene, French immigrant Georges de Latour, in 1900—the depth of the phylloxera calamity—ordered millions of *Rupestris* rootstock from France, which he sold throughout Northern California.

While Napa wines continued to win medals through the 1890s at various state and national expositions, by the turn of the century, there remained fewer than 5,000 acres in vines. Although some growers switched to fruit growing—French prunes were a new favorite—others began pulling vines in favor of replanting first with *Riparia* and then *Rupestris* root stock.

There were other industries in the Valley besides winemaking, however. There were fruit orchards, olive groves, dairying, the resort business, the bottling of mineral waters, and the processing of leather, which dated back to the 1860s. In fact, "Napa Leather" became a dictionary definition for soft leather.

Newcomer de Latour, barely speaking English and previously perpetually near-broke, became the leader of Napa Valley's winery resurgence. With the profits from his chancy purchase of rootstock—primarily on credit—he finally had some funds to purchase property and build a winery, which he opened in Rutherford in 1907 and named Beaulieu Vineyards, meaning "beautiful place."

De Latour planted extensively, obtained the endorsement of the San Francisco Catholic Archdiocese for use of his wine by churches, bottled bulk wine under his label while waiting for vines to mature, and soon was vinting large amounts of Bordeaux-type wines. By 1910 Beaulieu was Napa Valley's most famous winery—a far cry from the days when de Latour, a chemist trained in France, scraped out a living by making cream of tartar from wine-barrel leavings.

Victory over phylloxera encouraged new investors who built large wineries. The Salmina family built Larkmead, and Antonio Forni leased and rejuvenated Josephine Tychson's winery and vineyards.

The 1903 invention of a machine that would mass-produce glass bottles made bottles cheap and plentiful. This allowed each winery to identify its product with labels on the bottles and increased the Napa Valley wine exposure. Annual wine production in Napa County was reaching 4 million gallons.

It appeared that there were clear skies ahead for the Napa Valley wine industry. But there was one cloud on the horizon. It was called Prohibition.

PROHIBITION SHUTS DOWN THE WINERIES

By the second decade of the century, what started as a movement to close down saloons had become a crusade, with accelerating political momentum, to put an end to all alcohol manufacture and sale, but the margin was increasingly close. Many winemakers, as producers of the drink of moderation, hoped that if alcohol were prohibited, wine would be exempt as "food."

Congress passed the Eighteenth Amendment on December 18, 1917, and submitted it to the state legislatures. The California Assembly and Senate approved it on January 11, 1919, and five days later the last necessary state legislature ratified Prohibition, to take effect in 1920. There were exceptions: Wine for sacramental and medicinal purposes could be made and sold (on the technicality that it was not used for "beverage purposes"), and limited production of wine—200 gallons a year—for personal use was permitted.

The sacramental-wine exemption became a saving grace for de Latour and his Beaulieu, since he had one of ten California permits to provide wine for church altars.

More than 120 wineries in Napa County officially shut down. Grape growers could still ship grape juice or grapes—sometimes with the warning not to add yeast, which might cause "illegal fermentation." Many tore out their vines and substituted prunes, cherries, or walnuts.

Of course, like many Americans, there were winemakers who sneered at Prohibition as a joke, and they continued to make wine far in excess of personal needs. Although local law enforcement and federal officials were primarily concerned about halting the bootlegging of hard liquor, wine occasionally became the target. One day the revenuers raided large storage tanks on Dunaweal Lane and delighted in smashing them with axes. The resulting wine flood turned the road into what old-timers still call "the river of red."

The Sawyer Tanning Company, which had been in business since 1872, expanded with new products such as patent-leather shoes and softball covers. In 1915 Napans Peter Jensen and Edwin Pridham invented the loudspeaker, which they named Magnavox. As the company grew it moved to Indiana.

Napa County was essentially on hold: Between 1910 and 1930 the population increased slightly, from 19,800 to 22,879. In the 1920s the number of residents of the city of Napa actually dropped, from 6,757 in 1920 to 6,437 in 1930.

The Napa Valley Railroad eliminated passenger service in 1929, and the electric line from Vallejo to Calistoga shut down in 1939, giving way to the bus and automobile.

REPEAL AND RECOVERY

Like the rest of the nation, the Napa Valley was stagnant after the onset of the Great Depression in 1929. The resort business was hurt by the lack of personal income available for entertainment, and agriculture suffered from low prices.

One hope would be the repeal of Prohibition, which finally occurred on December 7, 1933.

Beaulieu Vineyards was first out of the gate, since it had been making sacramental wine during the twelve years of Prohibition and because shrewd de Latour built up a large pre-repeal inventory of wine, which he could ship immediately. Close on his heels was forty-three-year-old Louis M. Martini, a tall, blonde native of Italy, who since 1922 had run a company at Kingsburg in the San Joaquin Valley that made grape concentrate for sale to amateur winemakers. Martini built a winery in St. Helena, planted vineyards of Cabernet Sauvignon and Zinfandel in both Napa and Sonoma Counties, and began producing full-bodied wines at modest prices. They were an instant success. He was a founder of the California Wine Institute and the prime mover in creating a gathering of winery owners, the Napa Valley Vintners Association.

The leadership of Inglenook devolved on the grand-nephew of founder Captain Niebaum, young John Daniel. The handsome 1933 Stanford engineering graduate felt obligated to restore the old winery's preeminence and honor the legacy of Captain Niebaum. He studied viticulture with Sonoma wine sage Carl Bundschu. When John's aunt died in 1937, he took full command of the winery (owned jointly with his sister, who was not interested in its operation). Daniel hired an expert winemaster, George Deuer, diversified wine vintages, joined the Wine Institute Board in 1941, and put "Napa Valley" on Inglenook labels, which were vintage-dated.

Charles de Latour got another step on the competition in 1938, when he induced Andre Tchelistcheff to leave Paris and work for Beaulieu as a winemaster. Tchelistcheff was a dapper Russian refugee from the Communist regime who had studied agronomy in France and was an expert on grapes. Despite doubts about coming to America, Andre and his wife and child came to Napa.

He cleaned up Beaulieu Winery, had tanks scrubbed, set up a laboratory, and insisted on new equipment, including a corking device. The sensitivity of his taste buds for wines was remarkable, and Beaulieu's quality rose. For the next forty years he would be the United States' ruling authority on wines and winemaking. His influence on disciples like Joe Heitz, Mike Grgich, and Warren Winiarski raised the standard that winemasters expected. Tchelistcheff ushered in the era of the professional winemakers, who were often graduates of the University of California at Davis.

Beringer was back in business with absentee ownership. On land owned by the Catholic order for three-quarters of a century, the Christian Brothers were making wine and brandy. They would gain fame under the legendary winemaker Brother Timothy. But it was still the Depression, and the wine industry was only a shadow of what it would become.

Cesare Mondavi was an Italian immigrant who had settled in Lodi, California, where he shipped grapes to home winemakers around the country during Prohibition. Shortly after repeal he bought a small, vacant stone winery in St. Helena. Cesare sent his older son, Robert, fresh out of Stanford, to build up a bulk wine business there. Robert soon was crushing enough grapes to yield a million gallons a year. At the urging of his sons, Robert and Peter, Cesare bought the dilapidated Krug winery and property for $87,000 (mostly borrowed) in 1943, on the condition that Robert, as general manager, and Peter, as winemaker, would run the winery.

THE 1940S AND BEYOND

A military airport south of Napa city was built during the war and became Napa County Airport in 1946.

Famous people living in the valley included Jessamyn West, wife of Superintendent of Schools Harry McPherson, who wrote *Friendly Persuasion* in 1940. Her book became a best-seller and a popular movie. West (the outspoken Democratic cousin of Republican Richard Nixon) also authored another best-seller, *The Witch Diggers*. M. F. K. (Mary Frances Kennedy) Fisher was already famous for her classics on food appreciation and travel, like *How to Cook a Wolf*, when she moved to St. Helena in the early 1960s. During the time she lived there, she wrote regularly for *The New Yorker* magazine. The late Canadian writer Arthur Hailey lived in a large house overlooking St. Helena while writing several of his very popular novels like *Airport, Hotel,* and *The Bankers* in the 1970s and 1980s, before leaving for a home in the Bahamas.

Scarcely noticed in 1947 was the purchase of the old Sutter Home Winery by Mario Trinchero and his family from New York. Mario and his brother were so strapped for cash that they could not pay the $12,000 for the century-old Victorian next to the vineyards on Highway 29 in St. Helena.

In the meantime, John Daniel came to love Inglenook, but his beautiful wife, Betty, came to hate it. Isolated from the city society she enjoyed, she suffered depression, began drinking too much, and became involved in notorious affairs, which eventually led to their divorce. In 1964 John finally sold Inglenook to United Vintners, whose management promised to maintain Inglenook's integrity. With the winery out of his system, John and Betty reconciled and remarried. But United Vintners turned the main building into a storage house and began producing jug wine under the venerable Inglenook name. Soon thereafter John Daniel died of a heart attack, induced by an overdose of barbiturates. The cause was considered suicide, but some said that it was really a broken heart.

BIG BUSINESS AND BIG WINNERS

The sale of Inglenook was an omen. Big corporations were attracted to the existing wineries and had the bucks to make tempting offers. Soon Heublein, Coca-Cola, Seagram's, Nestlé, R. J. Reynolds, and Grand Metropolitan of London (which had bought Reynolds, which had bought Heublein) became owners. There would be others. Some cared about excellent wines; others were primarily interested in profits.

Tensions existed between brothers Robert and Peter Mondavi at Charles Krug Winery even before their father, Cesare, died. It was almost inevitable that Robert, as "Mr. Outside," and Peter, as "Mr. Inside," would not agree. Robert was outgoing and willing to spend money for promotion, while Peter was cautious and introverted.

The brothers argued over the future participation of their sons in the business. In 1965, when Robert set up a corporation to establish a small winery for his sons, which he called Robert Mondavi, Peter and mother Rosa—who owned the majority of the stock in Krug—pulled the plug. Robert was put on involuntary "leave," which really meant that he was out.

Robert Mondavi lined up financing, bought property in Oakville on Highway 29, and built a winery. The family split had a much greater impact on Napa Valley than the addition of another winery. It meant that Robert Mondavi was turned loose to promote himself, his winery, his wines, and Napa Valley.

The elegant mansion and grounds created by General Miller in the last century was purchased in 1967 by Amfak Corporation. Amfak spent $100 million to turn the estate into the private Silverado Country Club, with two golf courses designed by Robert Trent Jones, 400 condos, a spacious clubhouse, tennis courts, and a renovated mansion.

May 24, 1976, was a landmark date for Napa Valley wines. At a prestigious blind tasting in Paris that day, the Cabernet Sauvignon of Stag's Leap Cellars (Warren Winiarski, owner and winemaker) was rated the "Best Red," and the Chardonnay of Chateau Montelena (James Barrett, owner and winemaker) was named best of the white Burgundies. Their competition were the elite wineries from Bordeaux and Burgundy. These tasting triumphs proved that Napa Valley wines belonged among the best international wines and signaled that Napa Valley wineries should shift toward varietals rather than "jug" wines. Within the next twenty years, sales from Napa varietals leapt from $150 million to $2.5 billion.

THE POLITICS OF PRESERVATION

Political controversies over the future of Napa County broke out in the late 1960s and continued for the next thirty years. The first scrimmage came in 1968, when the Board of Supervisors had to decide whether to authorize "agricultural preserves" pursuant to the recently adopted state Williamson Act. Under that act, an owner of agricultural land could contract with the county to keep the property in agriculture (and not a subdivision) perpetually until ten years after the owner filed a notice of intent to cancel the contract. In return, the county would give the owner a property-tax reduction.

The Board of Supervisors had to pass an ordinance agreeing to county participation. "Ag preserves" are common today but were novel in the 1960s. Those Napans concerned with overdevelopment were in favor of permitting such preserves in Napa County, as were some vintners, including Louis Peter Martini, of the new generation of Martinis, and Jack Davies, who had just purchased the old Schramsberg winery, which he and his wife, Jamie, were restoring. At the crucial meeting of the board, one winery owner was so abusive to the supervisor from St. Helena, fence-sitter Julius Caiocco, that Julius voted to make it unanimous to approve agricultural preserves, saying, "Nobody's gonna shake a finger at me."

In 1972, supported by a coalition of environmentalists and neighborhood organizations, Virginia (Ginny) Simms, John Tuteur, and Henry Wigger were elected to the Board of Supervisors. They had pledged to enact zoning that would limit home sites on rural hillsides to forty acres per home. That limitation was adopted in 1973. For the next two decades, bitter supervisorial elections— unlimited development versus limited growth—were held every two years, with the board split one way or the other each term. The hillside limitation bounced down to twenty acres and then back up to forty. In 1989 a pro-development board majority abruptly dismissed the entire Planning Commission and fired the county's longtime planning director.

Another area of conflict needed to be resolved. Volker Eisele, with a Ph.D. from UC Berkeley, and his landscape architect wife, Liesel, had bought an old vineyard and rusty winery. He soon organized the Napa Valley Grape Growers Association to represent the position of independent growers not employed by major wineries. The local growers were concerned with the use of the Napa Valley address on bottles of wine made from so-called foreign grapes shipped in from outside the county. This was particularly true of wineries that had a second label with wine of lower quality. The growers' proposal: In order to use a Napa address or Napa appellation, or to become a new or expanded winery in Napa County, 75 percent of the wine had to be vinted from grapes grown in the county.

The 240 members of the growers' association were unanimous in favor, but the wineries were divided. It took almost three years of discussions, a moratorium on new winery permits, and two supervisorial elections before a compromise—first proposed by the growers—was adopted by the Board of Supervisors in the county's "definition" of wineries for permits. The ordinance allowed already existing wineries to continue any practices they were employing (including use of "foreign" grapes), but new wineries had to use 75 percent Napa grapes and could not have public tours and tastings. It did allow food to be served for promotional services. Any expansion of an existing winery had to meet the 75 percent requirement. In part, this explains the reason why many wineries today—even elegant facilities like Joseph Phelps—require visitors to call ahead for an appointment for tasting, to avoid the "open to the public" tasting-room prohibition.

As the 1990s opened, there was an important shift of sentiment: More and more vineyardists and winemakers became convinced that subdivisions and vineyards did not mix. Since Napa Valley wineries were a crucial business as well as a great tourist draw, maintaining the beauty of the hills and restricting the areas available for malls, outlet centers, and subdivisions made economic as well as aesthetic sense.

THE NEW WAVE

Napa Valley saw many changes in the 1980s and 1990s. Robert Mondavi won a large judgment against his brother Peter and the Krug winery. A lawsuit that began over the use of the Mondavi name on a company Peter set up climaxed in a ruling that Robert was owed millions for being forced out of Charles Krug. In 1980 he married Margrit Biever, who worked closely with him in developing his Robert Mondavi Winery. With his financial and personal conflicts in the past, Robert Mondavi had more time to spend as spokesman of Napa Valley wines to the world. He was not the only one, but certainly was the most ubiquitous.

Robert Trinchero, the son of Mario, who had bought little Sutter Home, experimented with making a white wine from Zinfandel grapes, after trying dozens of different varieties. He came out with 350 cases of his "invented" White Zinfandel in 1974. He caught the popular trend toward whites and surpassed the 4-million-cases mark early in the 1990s to become Napa Valley's largest producer. The headquarters is in the lovely Victorian house that his father and uncle could not afford to buy for $12,000.

Motion picture director Francis Ford Coppola *(The Godfather, Peggy Sue Got Married, Apocalypse Now)* purchased—some say "rescued"—Inglenook from Heublein, changed the name to Niebaum-Coppola Estate, and created a museum of cinematic history. Art and wine were linked with architectural innovation, exhibits, and museums, including avant-garde Clos Pegase and the winery/art museum called The Hess Collection.

More and more people from other disciplines and professions—doctors, lawyers, Silicon Valley pioneers, businesspeople, a rocket scientist—planted grapes and opened wineries, all dedicated to a search for quality. There were several new owners and winemakers who had grown up with European wine traditions. The number of wineries rose at a dizzying pace, as did the ratings by such magazines as *Wine Spectator* and *Wine Enthusiast.*

Resort business was also making a comeback. In the 1980s Auberge du Soleil and Meadowood, both rated among the best resorts in the world, became instant tourist magnets. Old mansions were being converted to bed-and-breakfasts every year. Upscale restaurants were drawing crowds. The Culinary Institute of America, the nationally known school for high-caliber chefs, purchased the old Greystone Cellars, restored the facility exquisitely, and opened its western campus in 1995.

Finally, in 1998 the voters passed a bond issue to pay for rerouting the Napa River to prevent the periodic flooding that has swept the city of Napa regularly since the days of Nathan Coombs.

The population of Napa Valley now exceeds 150,000—compared to the 5,000 Native Americans living there when Father Altimira surveyed the Valley from a hill in the Soscol, or when George Yount built his blockhouse. The glory is that the natural beauty remains.

8

The Napa Valley List of Lists

In this chapter we give you lots of handy information that we like to have ourselves when traveling, and we hope that it comes in handy for you, too. In each case, we list the best available.

WINERIES REQUIRING APPOINTMENTS FOR TASTING

Under Napa County regulations many wineries require that visitors make appointments to taste wines. Here are wineries that require appointments:

Anderson's Conn Valley Vineyards, 680 Rossi Road, St. Helena; (707) 963–8600.

Bouchaine Vineyards, 1075 Buchli Station Road, Napa; (707) 252–9065. Open 10:00 A.M. to 4:00 P.M. daily.

Calafia Cellars, 629 Fulton Lane, St. Helena; (707) 963–0114.

Caymus Vineyards, 8700 Conn Creek Road, Rutherford; (707) 967–3010. Open 10:00 A.M. to 4:00 P.M. daily.

Chappellet Winery, 1581 Sage Canyon Road, St. Helena; (707) 963–7136.

Chateau Woltner, 3500 Silverado Trail, St. Helena; (707) 963–1744.

Chrichton Hall, 1150 Darms Lane, Napa; (707) 224–4200.

Cosentino Winery, 7415 St. Helena Highway, Yountville; (707) 944–1220. Open 10:00 A.M. to 5:30 P.M. daily.

David Arthur Vineyards, 1521 Sage Canyon Road, St. Helena; (707) 963–5190.

Deer Park Winery, 1000 Deer Park Road, Deer Park; (707) 963–5411. Open 10:00 A.M. to 4:00 P.M. daily.

Domaine Charbay Winery & Distillery, 4001 Spring Mountain Road, St. Helena; (707) 963–9327. Open 10:00 A.M. to 4:00 P.M. daily.

Domaine Montreaux, 4242 Big Ranch Road, Napa; (707) 253–2802.

Duckhorn Vineyards, 1000 Lodi Lane, St. Helena; (707) 963–7108. Open 10:00 A.M. to 4:00 P.M. daily; no tasting.

Dunn Vineyards, 805 White Cottage Road North, Angwin; (707) 965–3642.

Frog's Leap Winery, 8815 Conn Creek Road, Rutherford; (707) 963–4704. Open 10:00 A.M. to 4:00 P.M. Monday–Saturday.

Graeser Winery, 255 Petrified Forest Road, Calistoga; (707) 942–4437.

Guilliams Vineyards, 3851 Spring Mountain Road, St. Helena; (707) 963–9059. Open 10:00 A.M. to 5:00 P.M. daily.

Gustavo Thrace Winery, 880 Vallejo Street, Napa; (707) 257–6796. Open 10:00 A.M. to 2:00 P.M. Monday–Friday.

Hansfahden Wineries, 5300 Mountain Home Ranch Road, Calistoga; (707) 942–6760.

Havens Wine Cellars, 2055 Hoffman Lane, Yountville, (707) 945–0921.

Helena View Johnson, 3500 Highway 128, Calistoga; (707) 942–4956. Open 10:00 A.M. to 5:00 P.M. Saturday–Sunday.

Joseph Phelps Vineyards, 200 Taplin Road (east off Silverado Trail), St. Helena; (707) 963–2745. Open 9:00 A.M. to 5:00 P.M. Monday–Saturday, 10:00 A.M. to 4:00 P.M. Sunday.

Kent Rasmussen Winery, 1001 Silverado Trail, St. Helena; (707) 963–5667.

Laird Family Estate, 5055 Solano, Napa; (707) 257–0360. Open 10:00 A.M. to 5:00 P.M. daily.

Mayacamas Vineyards, 1155 Lokoya Road, Yountville; (707) 224–4030. Open 8:00 A.M. to 4:30 P.M. Monday–Friday.

Moss Creek Winery, 6015 Steele Canyon Road, Yountville; (707) 252–1295.

Newton Vineyard, 2555 Madrona Avenue, St. Helena; (707) 963–9000.

Nichelini Winery, 2590 Sage Canyon Road, St. Helena; (707) 963–0717. Open 10:00 A.M. to 6:00 P.M. Sunday and holidays; by appointment rest of week.

Opus One Winery, 7900 St. Helena Highway, Oakville; (707) 944–9442. Open 10:30 A.M. to 3:30 P.M. daily.

Plam Vineyards, 6200 Washington Street, Yountville; (707) 944–1102. Open 9:00 A.M. to 5:00 P.M. daily, 9:00 A.M. to 3:00 P.M. Sunday.

Robert Keenan Winery, 3660 Spring Mountain Road, St. Helena; (707) 963–9177.

Robert Pecota Winery, 3299 Bennett Lane, Calistoga; (707) 942–6625.

Roundhill Family of Wines, 1680 Silverado Trail, St. Helena; (707) 963–9503. Open 10:00 A.M. to 4:30 P.M. daily; sales, no tasting.

Saintsbury, 1500 Los Carneros Avenue, Napa; (707) 252–0592. Open 9:00 A.M. to 5:00 P.M. Monday–Friday.

Schramsberg Vineyards, 1400 Schramsberg Road, Calistoga; (707) 942–4558. Open 10:00 A.M. to 4:00 P.M. daily.

Schweiger Vineyards, 4015 Spring Mountain Road, St. Helena; (707) 963–4882.

Shafer Vineyards, 6154 Silverado Trail, Napa; (707) 944–2877. Open 9:00 A.M. to 4:00 P.M. Monday–Friday.

Smith–Madrone Vineyards, 4022 Spring Mountain Road, St. Helena; (707) 963–2283. Open 10:00 A.M. to 4:00 P.M. Monday–Saturday.

Spottswoode Vineyard and Winery, 1902 Madrona Avenue, St. Helena; (707) 963–0134.

Stony Hill Vineyard, 3331 St. Helena Highway North, St. Helena; (707) 963–2636.

Storybook Mountain Vineyards, 3835 Highway 128, Calistoga; (707) 942–5310.

Summit Lake Vineyards, 2000 Summit Lake Drive, Angwin; (707) 965–2488.

Swanson Vineyards, 1271 Manley Lane, Rutherford; (707) 944–0905.

Truchard Vineyards, 3234 Old Sonoma Road, Napa; (707) 253–7153.

Tudal Winery, 1015 Big Tree Road, St. Helena; (707) 963–3947. Open 10:00 A.M. to 4:00 P.M. daily.

Van Asperen Vineyards, 1680 Silverado Trail, St. Helena; (707) 963–5251.

Viader Vineyards, 1120 Deer Park Road, Deer Park; (707) 963–3816.

Vine Cliff Winery, 7400 Silverado Trail, Napa; (707) 944–2388. Open 10:00 A.M. to 5:00 P.M. daily.

W Winery, 1001 Silverado Trail, St. Helena; (707) 259–2800.

SOME FINE WINERIES GENERALLY NOT OPEN TO THE PUBLIC

Many Napa Valley wineries do not have tasting or sales facilities but produce some of the best wines in the world. You can purchase their wines at fine wine shops, try them in restaurants, or get on winery mailing lists for newsletters and other special mailings.

Altamura Winery, 1700 Wooden Valley Road, Napa; (707) 253–2000.

Araujo Estate Wines/Eisele Vineyard, 2155 Pickett Road, St. Helena; (707) 942–6061.

Atlas Peak Vineyards, 3700 Soda Canyon Road, Napa; (707) 252–7971.

Azalea Springs Vineyards, 4301 Azalea Springs Way, Calistoga; (707) 942–4811.

Barnett Vineyards, 4070 Spring Mountain Road, St. Helena; (707) 963–7075.

Bacio Divino Cellars, 2610 Pinot Way, St. Helena; (707) 942–8101.

Benessere Vineyards, 1010 Big Tree Road, St. Helena; (707) 963–5853.

Buehler Vineyards, 820 Greenfield Road, St. Helena; (707) 963–2155.

Burgess Cellars, 1108 Deer Park Road, St. Helena; (707) 963–4766.

Cain Vineyard & Winery, 3800 Langtry Road, St. Helena; (707) 963–1616.

Colgin Cellars, 7830 St. Helena Highway, St. Helena; (707) 963–0999.

Conn Creek Winery, 8711 Silverado Trail, St. Helena; (707) 963–9100.

Dalla Valle Vineyards, 7776 Silverado Trail, Oakville; (707) 944–2676.

Diamond Creek Vineyards, 1500 Diamond Mountain Road, Calistoga; (707) 942–6926.

Diamond Mountain Vineyard, 2121 Diamond Mountain Road, Calistoga; (707) 942–0707.

Dominus Estate, 2570 Napanook Road, Yountville; (707) 944–8954.

Farella–Park Vineyards, 2222 North Third Avenue, Napa; (415) 954–4411.

Far Niente, 1 Acacia Drive, Oakville; (707) 944–2861.

Frazier, 40 Lupine Hill Road, Napa; (707) 255–3444.

Grace Family Vineyards, 1210 Rockland Road, St. Helena; (707) 963–0808.

Grandview Cellars, 1328 Main Street, St. Helena; (707) 967–9480.

Harlan Estate, 1551 Oakville Grade, Oakville; (707) 944–1441.

Harrison Vineyards, 1527 Sage Canyon Road, St. Helena; (707) 963–8271.

Honig Cellars, 850 Rutherford Road, Rutherford; (707) 963–5618.

Jaeger Family Wine Co., 4324 Big Ranch Road, Napa; (707) 255–4456.

Jarvis Vineyards, 2970 Monticello Road, Yountville; (707) 255–5280.

Lang & Reed Wine Company, 1961 Vineyard Avenue, St. Helena; (707) 963–3758.

Larkmead Vineyards, 1145 Larkmead Lane, St. Helena; (707) 942–6605.

Livingston Wines, 1895 Cabernet Lane, St. Helena; (707) 963–2120.

Lokoya Wines, 7585 St. Helena Highway, Oakville; (707) 944–2807.

Long Meadow Ranch Winery, 1775 Whitehall Lane, St. Helena; (707) 963–4555.

Louis Corthay Winery, 996 Galleron Road, Rutherford; (707) 963–2384.

Mount Veeder Winery, 1999 Mount Veeder Road, Yountville; (707) 963–7111.

Newton Vineyard, 2555 Madrona Avenue, St. Helena; (707) 963–9000.

Oakford Vineyards, 1575 Oakville Grade, Oakville; (707) 945–0445.

Oliver Caldwell Cellars, 3480 St. Helena Highway, St. Helena; (707) 963–2037.

Pahlmeyer Winery, 101 South Coombs Street, Napa; (707) 255–2321.

Paoletti, 4501 Silverado Trail, Calistoga; (707) 942–0689.

Paradigm, 683 Dwyer Road, Oakville; (707) 944–1683.

Quintessa, 1178 Galleron Road, Rutherford; (707) 963–7111.

Reverie on Diamond Mountain, 1520 Diamond Mountain Road, Calistoga; (707) 942–6800.

Screaming Eagle, P. O. Box 134, Oakville, CA 94562; (707) 944–0749.

Seavey Vineyards, 1310 Conn Valley Road, St. Helena; (707) 963–8339 or 788–0800.

Silverado Hill Cellars, 3105 Silverado Trail, Napa; (707) 253–9306 or 253–9307.

Spring Mountain Vineyard, 2805 Spring Mountain Road, St. Helena; (707) 967–4188 or 967–4190.

Stag's Leap Winery, 6150 Silverado Trail, Napa; (707) 944–1303 or 944–4493.

Star Hill Winery, 1075 Shadybrook Lane, Napa; (707) 255–1957.

Tulocay Winery, 1426 Coombsville Road, Napa; (707) 255–4064.

Turley Wine Cellars, 3358 St. Helena Highway, St. Helena; (707) 963–0940.

Villa Encinal Winery, 620 Oakville Crossroad, Oakville; (707) 944–1465.

Vineyard 29, 2929 Highway 29 North, St. Helena; (707) 963–9292.

Volker Eisele Family Estate, 3080 Lower Chiles Valley Road, St. Helena; (707) 965–2260.

Von Strasser Winery, 1510 Diamond Mountain Road, Calistoga; (707) 942–0930.

EVENTS AND FESTIVALS

The dates and times of regular events and festivals change from year to year. We encourage you to call the phone numbers listed for information.

February–March

Napa Valley Mustard Festival celebrates mustard in the vineyards at various locations, including the Culinary Institute of America, the Niebaum-Coppola Vineyards, and the Napa Fairgrounds in downtown Napa. The World Wide Mustard Competition is a big deal, with results announced with great fanfare at the opening party. It's all kicked off by the **Blessing of the Balloons** at Domaine Chandon Winery, 1 California Drive, Yountville 94599; phone (707) 259–9020, 944–8793, or 938–1133.

Taste of Yountville, along Washington Street in Yountville; phone (707) 944–0904. This event celebrates Yountville's claim that it has more world-class restaurants per square foot than any other town in the United States. And we are the beneficiaries, because they all cook and serve their delicacies at tables along the street. Lots of music and fun if it isn't raining.

April

Calistoga Maifest, Calistoga Fairgrounds; phone (707) 942–6524. This event takes place the first weekend in April (of course) and benefits the Rotary High School Scholarship Fund. Entertainment includes the Al Gruber band and mariachis. German and American food is available as well as German and local beers. Open from noon to 9:00 P.M.

April in Carneros, at all Carneros District wineries along the Sonoma–Napa border, promotes and celebrates the Carneros appellation with new wine releases, food, cigars, music, and general gustatory bliss; phone (800) 825–9475.

June

Beringer Celebrity Golf Classic, Chardonnay Golf Club, 2555 Jamieson Canyon Road east of Highway 12, Napa 94558; phone (707) 255–0950. This event benefits Justin–Siena Catholic High School in Napa, with big-name athletes mixing with lesser-known golfers. The fee is $375 to play with a celebrity of some sort.

Napa Valley Wine Auction, Meadowood Resort, 900 Meadowood Lane, St. Helena 94574; phone (707) 942–9783. This is the ultimate wine auction in the United States. The auction raises funds for local hospitals. The long weekend event includes barrel tastings, dinners with winemakers and owners, a Napa Valley collaborative chefs' dinner at Meadowood, and the auction itself. Most guests think the nearly $1,500 ticket price is well worth it.

Silverado Concours D'Elegance, Silverado Country Club, 1600 Atlas Peak Road, Napa 94558; phone (707) 428–3355; $10 in advance, $12 at the gate. This benefits the Children's Hospital of Oakland. Nearly 300 classic cars and their owners assemble to strut, wine, and dine. A fun event for all who enjoy a little elegance, old and new.

Yountville Italian Heritage Festival, at Vintage 1870 and other venues; phone (707) 968–2338. Friday evening–Sunday, third full weekend; golf, bocce ball, winemaker dinners at ten top restaurants.

Calistoga Art in the Park, one Saturday, Pioneer Park, on Cedar, 1 block north of Lincoln.

Vintage 1870 Father's Day Invitational Auto Show, at Vintage 1870 in Yountville; phone (707) 944–2451; free. The name pretty much says it all. Sunday, 11:00 A.M. to 4:00 P.M..

Zarzuela Festival, Friday 8:00 P.M., Saturday–Sunday 2:00 P.M., Jarvis Conservatory, 1711 Main Street, Napa; phone (707) 255–5445. Spanish music.

July

Summer Concert Series, July weekends to mid-August, Robert Mondavi Winery, 7801 St. Helena Highway, Oakville; phone (707) 963–9611.

Meadowood Croquet Classic, Meadowood Resort, 900 Meadowood Lane, St. Helena 94574; phone (707) 963–3646. Meadowood is the only winery with croquet courts and a full-time croquet pro. The U.S. Croquet Association holds this annual event of events, dressed all in white, of course. Inquire about new events and admission.

Napa Valley Shakespeare Festival, Rutherford Grove Winery, 1673 St. Helena Highway, St. Helena 94574; phone (707) 251–9455, Web site www .napashakespeare.org. Each weekend during the month. The festival recently moved to this lovely site, with Shakespeare being performed on the lawn under huge shade trees.

July 4 Parade in Calistoga, 11:00 A.M. Fireworks at Domaine Chandon, Yountville; Louis M. Martini, St. Helena; Veterans House, Yountville; Napa County Fairgrounds, Calistoga.

Wine Country Film Festival, last ten days of July through mid-August, at Sequoia Grove Vineyards, Rutherford, and COPIA, Napa.

August

Music in the Vineyards, phone (707) 578–5656, Web site www.napavalley music.org. Wednesday, Saturday, and Sunday, during first three weeks, classic music at several wineries. $25 per performance.

Napa Town and Country Fair, Napa Exposition Grounds, 575 Third Street, Napa 94558; phone (707) 253–4900. Second weekend. This is a truly local fair, more homey than a county fair for the southern end of the Napa Valley, featuring everything you would expect from 4–H projects living and cooked, carnivals, kids' games, wine tasting, cotton candy, and even a rodeo and—gads—a demolition derby.

September

Napa Symphony on the River, Third Street at the bridge, Napa; phone (707) 258–8762. Come here to celebrate life and music, with music from 7:00 to 9:00 P.M., food and fireworks in Veterans Park—it's a general down-home great time, held the Sunday of Labor Day weekend.

Napa Valley Open Studios Tours, second and third weekends, 10:00 A.M. to 5:00 P.M.; phone (707) 257–2117.

October

Calistoga Beer & Sausage Fest, Napa County Fairgrounds, 1435 North Oak Street, Calistoga 94515; phone (707) 942–0795. On the second weekend in October, twenty-four microbreweries from around Northern California show and pour, along with sausage- and mustard-making companies, local restaurants, and chili cook-off; $20 for everything, in toto. A wild-and-woolly time.

Jazz and Blues in Napa Valley, second weekend, Saturday, 11:00 A.M. to 9:30 P.M., Sunday 10:00 A.M. to 4:00 P.M.; $40 for one day, $65 for two; phone (707) 942–6333.

Harvest Festival, Hometown Style, Oak Avenue, St. Helena; phone (707) 963–5706. This is a resurrected and underpublicized local celebration of the grape harvest, held the last Saturday in October, with arts and crafts, run, carnival, and a pet parade (our favorite).

Old Mill Days, Bale Grist Mill State Historic Park, 3369 St. Helena Highway, St. Helena 94574; phone (707) 942–4575. Coopers, storytellers, millers, fiddlers, weavers, kids, and grown-ups all pretend it's 130 years ago. Why not. Great mill tours, grinding of flours of several kinds. A good healthy day.

November

Festival of Lights, Vintage 1870, Yountville; phone (707) 944–1171. This festival is held the Friday after Thanksgiving all over town, with Christmas carols, roasted chestnuts, Santa, street musicians and actors, and of course wine and food. Lots of fun for visitors and locals alike. The next day, Saturday, Santa moves on to Napa's Christmas Parade, beginning by the Cinedome multiplex theater at Pearl and Soscol. The parade and Santa, and a few throngs of locals, end up at the Napa Town Center to make the shopping season official and have a wee bit of sustenance.

Napa Valley Wine Festival, Napa Valley Country Club, 3385 Hagen Road, Napa 94558; phone (707) 253–3511. This event, held the first weekend in November, benefits the Napa Valley Unified School District. There are golf and tennis, fifty Napa Valley wineries, huge pasta dinner, and student music. A fun, charitable event. Tickets cost $30 in advance, $35 at the door.

Series

Jarvis Conservatory Opera, and other musical events, May–September, 1711 Main Street, Napa; phone (707) 255–5445.

New Orleans/Dixieland Jazz, second Sunday of each month, The Lodge, 2840 Soscol, Napa, 1:00 to 5:00 P.M., $10.00, $3.00 for teenagers.

ANTIQUES

Antique Fair, 6512 Washington Street, Yountville; phone (707) 844–8440.

Elrod Antiques, 3000 St. Helena Highway; phone (707) 963–1901.

European Country Antiques, 1148 Main Street, St. Helena; phone (707) 963–4666.

Hacienda Hardware, 1989 St. Helena Highway, Rutherford; phone (707) 963–8850.

The Irish Pedlar, 1988 Wise Drive, Napa; phone (707) 253–9091.

Jack Cole Antiques and Curios, 805 Washington Street, Calistoga; phone (707) 942–6712.

Mandrake's Antiques, 6525 Washington Street in Vintage 1870, Yountville; phone (707) 944–9479.

Neighborhood Antique Collective, 1400 First Street, Napa; phone (707) 259–1900.

Red Hen Antiques, 5091 St. Helena Highway, Napa; phone (707) 257–0822.

St. Helena Antiques, 1231 Main Street, St. Helena; phone (707) 963–5878.

Tin Barn Collective, 1510 Lincoln Avenue, Calistoga; phone (707) 942–0618.

BOOKSTORES

Bookends Book Store, 1014 Coombs Street, Napa; phone (707) 224–1077.

Calistoga Book Store, 1343 Lincoln Avenue, Calistoga; phone (707) 942–4123.

Copperfield's, 1303 First Street, Napa; phone (707) 252–8002.

Main Street Books, 1315 Main Street, St. Helena; phone (707) 963–1338.

Napa Children's Book Company, 1239 First Street, Napa; phone (707) 224–3893.

Waldenbooks, 1370 Napa Town Center, Napa; phone (707) 252–7326.

CAMPGROUNDS

Bothe–Napa Valley State Park, Highway 29 south of Calistoga and adjoining Bale Mill State Park; phone (707) 942–4575 or (800) 444–7275 for state park reservations. Forty-nine tent and RV sites, nine tent-only sites; picnic tables, fire pits, and barbecues; restrooms; showers; wheelchair accessible; $1.00 fee for pets; $3.00 fee for swimming pool.

Calistoga Ranch Club Resort & Campground, 580 Lommel Road south of Calistoga; phone (707) 942–6565. Sixty tent-only spaces, 84 RV sites, and some cabins. Enjoy 167 acres of trails, forest, fishing, swimming pool, and games. Facilities include barbecues, restrooms, and showers.

Napa County Fairgrounds, 1435 North Oak Street, Calistoga; phone (707) 942–5111. Tents and RVs. Walk to downtown Calistoga. Pets OK on leash.

Napa Fairgrounds, 575 Third Street, Napa; phone (707) 253–4905. Spaces for motor homes and 500 campers with cars. Facilities include restrooms and showers; grocery store and Laundromat nearby.

NIGHTCLUBS (SORT OF)

These are microbreweries, restaurants, and bars that occasionally have music.

Ana's Cantina, 1205 Main Street, St. Helena; phone (707) 963–4921. A local hangout featuring Mexican and El Salvadoran food and real drinks; rock, reggae, and country, 9:00 P.M. to 1:30 A.M. Thursday–Saturday; Sunday afternoon.

Calistoga Inn & Restaurant and Napa Valley Brewing Company, 1250 Lincoln Avenue, Calistoga; phone (707) 942–4101. Music in the bar Tuesday, Friday, and Saturday nights; on the patio occasionally in summer.

Club Bacchus, 1853 Trancas, Napa; phone (707) 258–1145. Disc jockey '50s funk Thursday–Saturday.

Cole's Chop House, 1122 Main Street, Napa; phone (707) 224–6328. Jazz, swing, Latin, 6:30 to 10:30 P.M. Saturday, 5:30 to 9:00 P.M. Sunday.

Downtown Joe's, 902 Main Street, Napa; phone (707) 258–2337. Microbrewery/restaurant with a lively rock, pop, and blues scene Thursday–Saturday. A $3.00 cover on weekends.

Hydro Bar & Grill, 1403 Lincoln Avenue, Calistoga; phone (707) 942–9777. Stays open late for great food, romantic bar-style jazz; Dixieland jam on Thursday.

Lord Derby Arms, Highway 29 (Lincoln Avenue) and Silverado Trail, Calistoga; phone (707) 942–9155. A distinctly British pub and hangout where local Irish singer John Kelley performs weekends.

Moore's Landing, 6 Cutting's Wharf Road, Napa; phone (707) 253–2439, Saturday evenings Cajun music on riverfront in summer.

Pacific Blues Cafe, 6525 Washington Street, Yountville; phone (707) 944–4455. Blues 6:00 to 9:00 P.M. Saturday, weather permitting.

Planet Rock, 3392 Solano Avenue, Napa; phone (707) 252–8200. Disc jockey, dancing with music style changing nightly. A $5.00 cover some nights. Call ahead for current details.

1351 Lounge, 1351 Main Street, St. Helena; phone (707) 963–1969. Jazz some evenings.

PICNIC SUPPLIES

Cantinetta Tra Vigne, 1050 Charter Oak Avenue, St. Helena; phone (707) 963–8888.

Genova Delicatessen & Ravioli Factory, 1550 Trancas, Napa; phone (707) 253–8686.

Giugni Grocery Company, 1227 Main Street, St. Helena; phone (707) 963–3421.

Oakville Grocery, 7856 St. Helena Highway, Oakville; phone (707) 944–8802.

Pometta's, 7787 Highway 29, Oakville; phone (707) 944–2365.

Sattui Winery, South St. Helena Highway, St. Helena; phone (707) 963–7774.

Soda Canyon Store, 4006 Silverado Trail, Napa; phone (707) 252–0285.

Index

About the Authors

Kathleen and Gerald Hill are coauthors of twenty-five books, including *Sonoma Valley: The Secret Wine Country, Monterey and Carmel: Eden by the Sea, Santa Barbara and the Central Coast: California's Riviera, Victoria and Vancouver Island: The Almost Perfect Eden, Northwest Wine Country: Wine's New Frontier, The Facts on File Dictionary of American Politics, The People's Law Dictionary*, and the *Encyclopedia of Federal Agencies and Commissions*.

The Hills are native Californians who live in Sonoma, just over the hill from Napa Valley. They have co-taught American government and politics at the University of British Columbia, University of Victoria, and Sonoma State University. They co-host two radio shows, one of which, "Traveling with the Hills," airs on California station WKSVY. Listen at www.ksvy.org and visit the Hill's Web site at www.hillguidebooks.com.

THE INSIDER'S SOURCE

With more than 540 West-related titles, we have the area covered. Whether you're looking for the path less traveled, a favorite place to eat, family-friendly fun, a breathtaking hike, or enchanting local attractions, our pages are filled with ideas to get you from one state to the next.

For a complete listing of all our titles, please visit our Web site at www.GlobePequot.com. The Globe Pequot Press is the largest publisher of local travel books in the United States and is a leading source for outdoor recreation guides.

FOR BOOKS TO THE WEST

INSIDERS' GUIDE®

FALCON GUIDE®

Available wherever books are sold.
Orders can also be placed on the Web at www.GlobePequot.com,
by phone from 8:00 A.M. to 5:00 P.M. at 1-800-243-0495,
or by fax at 1-800-820-2329.